FAQs

QUESTIONS	RELATED ENTRIES
THE WRITING PROCESS	
How do I determine my purpose and audience?	preparation, 38; purpose/objective, 41; audience/readers, 3
What is the best way to organize my paper?	organization, 27; outlining, 29
What should I check for when revising?	revision, 44
What sources should I use in my paper?	research, 42; library research, 20; Internet research, 10
BUSINESS WRITING FORMS AND DOCUMENTATION	
What kinds of reports can I expect to write in the workplace?	reports, 85; feasibility reports, 66; formal reports, 96; investigative reports, 69; progress and activity reports, 75; trip reports, 87; trouble reports, 88
How do I write a proposal?	proposals, 78; persuasion, 35
How do I plan a brochure or newsletter?	brochures, 51; newsletters, 71; promotional writing, 39; persuasion, 35
How do I cite and document electronic sources?	documenting sources, 54
FORMAL REPORTS	
What are the parts of a formal report?	formal reports (see sample formal report), 102; tables of contents, 101
How can my report meet the needs of many different readers?	formal reports, 96; abstracts, 93; executive summaries, 95; appendixes, 95
CORRESPONDENCE	
What is the standard format for a business letter?	correspondence, 128
How do I write an effective memo?	memos, 143
What makes a sales letter successful?	sales letters, 149; correspondence, 128; persuasion, 35; promotional writing, 39
What is the best way to handle a complaint? give bad news? collect on an account?	correspondence, 128; adjustment letters, 121; "you" viewpoint, 281; refusal letters, 147; collection letters, 124

CORRESPONDENCE (CONTINUED)

JOB APPLICATION

FORMAT AND VISUALS

ORAL COMMUNICATION

WORKPLACE TECHNOLOGY

STYLE AND CLARITY

USAGE

GRAMMAR

PUNCTUATION AND MECHANICS

The Business Writer's Companion

THIRD EDITION

THE BUSINESS WRITER'S COMPANION

Gerald J. Alred
University of Wisconsin–Milwaukee

Charles T. Brusaw
NCR Corporation (retired)

Walter E. Oliu
U.S. Nuclear Regulatory Commission

BEDFORD / ST. MARTIN'S   Boston ◆ New York

For Bedford / St. Martin's

Developmental Editor: Ellen Thibault
Editorial Assistant: Christine Turnier-Vallecillo
Senior Editor, Publishing Services: Douglas Bell
Production Supervisor: Tina Cameron
Project Management: Books By Design, Inc.
Marketing Manager: Richard Cadman
Text Design: Claire Seng-Niemoeller
Cover Design: Diana C. Coe/ko Design Studio
Cover Photo: Stock Exchange. Palmisano/Perfect © 2001.
Composition: Pine Tree Composition, Inc.
Printing and Binding: R. R. Donnelley & Sons Company

President: Charles H. Christensen
Editorial Director: Joan E. Feinberg
Editor in Chief: Karen S. Henry
Director of Marketing: Karen R. Melton
Director of Editing, Design, and Production: Marcia Cohen
Manager, Publishing Services: Emily Berleth

Library of Congress Control Number: 2001095263

Manufactured in the United States of America.

7 6 5 4 3 2
f e d c b a

For information, write: Bedford / St. Martin's, 75 Arlington Street,
Boston, MA 02116 (617-399-4000)

ISBN: 0-312-25977-8

Acknowledgments

Figures 1.1–1.3: Reprinted with the permission of Google, Inc.
Figure 1.4: Reprinted with the permission of Columbia University Libraries.
Figure 1.5: Reprinted with the permission of the Boston Public Library.
Figure, pages 102ff.: "CGF Aircraft Corporation Memo." Reprinted with the permission of Susan Litzinger.
Figure 4.2: Reprinted with the permission of the American Airlines, AMR Corporations, Inc. All rights reserved.
Figure 6.2: "Cutaway Drawing of a Hard Disk Drive" from P. D. Moulton and Timothy S. Stanley, *Hard Disk Quick Reference.* Reprinted with the permission of Macmillan Computer Publications, Indianapolis, Indiana.
Figure 6.15: Courtesy of Ken Cook Company.
Figure 8.3: Courtesy of the Nuclear Regulatory Commission.

Brief Contents

Preface

The Business Writer's Companion, a brief version of the popular *Business Writer's Handbook*, also published by Bedford/St. Martin's, is a concise, easy-to-use guide to the most common types of business writing and communication. The entries in each of its twelve thematic sections are alphabetized for quick access and provide practical guidance on the business writing process, coverage of the many types of business writing with real-world examples such as reports, proposals, and correspondence, and thorough coverage of grammar and usage. Spiral bound and tabbed for easy reference, streamlined and completely up to date, this edition of the *Companion* is a handy supplement in the classroom or a quick reference on the job.

Our focus in this edition has been threefold: to make the book even easier to use, to enrich our advice for writing and communicating at work, and to provide thoroughly updated information for using technology.

New to This Edition

A More Concise Book That Is Even Easier to Use

- **Streamlined text.** Each entry addresses concisely the basics that business writers need. Briefer section introductions offer concise previews of the entries in each tab.
- **More visual elements and improved reference features.** In addition to more Writer's Checklists, new Web Link boxes and ESL Tips boxes present information in an at-a-glance format. More prominent headings make entries more visible on the page. A more thorough table of contents, a revised FAQ page, and new "How to Use This Book" guidelines make it even easier for readers to find what they need.

Improved Advice for Writing and Communicating at Work

- **Improved writing process help throughout the text.** A revised introductory essay, "Five Steps to Successful Writing," provides general guidelines for successful writing. There is also a greater emphasis in this edition on the importance of writing persuasively.
- **Improved coverage of formal reports.** The new edition highlights the formal report in a separate section that includes a complete example of a formal report.

- **New and revised entries for promotional writing, brochures, newsletters, proposals, and writing for the Web.** These entries include examples and advice for writing brochures and newsletters, a revised proposals entry that emphasizes persuasion and includes a sales proposal, and a new writing for the Web entry that focuses on considerations of purpose and audience.
- **Improved job application coverage.** The job application section offers new entries for interviewing for a job, negotiating salary requirements, and writing thank-you letters, with updated information on creating electronic résumés and using Web resources.

Updated Information for Using Technology

- **Thoroughly revised coverage of research.** A new research entry, a new Internet entry, and a revised library research entry offer practical advice for using popular online research tools such as databases and directories, and provide guidelines for evaluating sources. The documenting sources entry provides the latest American Psychological Association (APA) and Modern Language Association (MLA) documentation models for print, online, and multimedia sources.
- **Updated coverage of presentations.** The presentations entry includes more examples and information on using presentation software. A new visuals entry provides guidelines for how to create effective graphics and integrate them within a document or presentation.
- **Revised Web design coverage.** This coverage includes a new entry on Web forms design, providing guidelines and examples, and a revised Web page design entry.
- **An updated email entry.** The email entry provides information on the appropriate use of email—tips on when and how to use it—with examples, guidelines on format, etiquette, and management.
- **New Web links boxes.** Annotated Web links throughout the text connect writers to select online resources relevant to the discussion of a given entry.

Acknowledgments

We are deeply grateful to the many instructors, students, professional writers, and others who have helped shape *The Business Writer's Companion,* Third Edition. For their sound advice on this revision, we wish to express our thanks to the following reviewers: Anne Bliss, University of Colorado at Boulder; Lauryn De George, University of Central Florida; Diann D. Dillingham, Texas A&M University; Terry A. Hinch, Johns Hopkins University; Laurence A. Jarvik, Johns Hopkins University; Nancy D. Kersell, Northern Kentucky University; Cynthia Kuhn, University of Denver; Judy A. Lange, Chapman University; N. L. Reinsch, Georgetown University; Elizabeth Robinson, Texas A&M University; Christopher Sawyer-Lancanno, Massachusetts Institute of Technology; Jeffrey L. Walls, Indiana Institute of Technology; and Deanna F. Wilson, Collin County Community College.

We are also indebted to many who made important contributions to the first two editions of *The Business Writer's Companion*. In particular, we appreciate the valuable feedback on the first edition provided by Chris Benson, Clemson University; Alma G. Bryant, University of South Florida; Kenneth W. Davis, Indiana University–Purdue University, Indianapolis; and Philip Vassallo. For the second edition, we wish to express our thanks to E. Wallace Coyle, Boston College; Zita Ingham, Southwestern Oregon Community College; James S. O'Rourke IV, University of Notre Dame College of Business Administration; and Robert P. Rimes, University of California, San Diego.

We are especially grateful to Rachel Spilka of the University of Wisconsin–Milwaukee for her thorough review and important contributions to this edition. For past contributions, we wish to thank Lisa Rivero, Milwaukee School of Engineering, and Peter Sands, University of Wisconsin–Milwaukee.

We most gratefully acknowledge the leadership of Bedford/St. Martin's, beginning with Charles Christensen, President; Joan Feinberg, Editorial Director; and Karen Henry, Editor in Chief, for their support of this book. We would also like to acknowledge the contributions of others at Bedford/St. Martin's over the years—Nancy Lyman, who conceived the first edition of this book; Carla Samodulski, for her expert editorial guidance; Mimi Melek, for her editorial development of the second edition; and Emily Berleth, for managing the quality production of this book.

For this edition, we would like to thank Doug Bell of Bedford/St. Martin's and Herb Nolan of Books By Design for their energy, care, and professionalism in turning manuscript into bound book. We are also pleased to acknowledge the unfailing support of Christine Turnier-Vallecillo, Editorial Assistant at Bedford/St. Martin's. Finally, we would like to thank Ellen Thibault, our Developmental Editor at Bedford/St. Martin's, for her outstanding editorial skills and her patience throughout the project.

We also thank those who assisted in the production and improvement of the book in many ways: Rosemary Lesnik, Nikki Brazy, Renee Tegge, Elizabeth Ignatowski, Andrea Deacon, and Margaret Artman. Special thanks go to Janice Alred for her many hours of substantive assistance and for holding everything together.

Gerald J. Alred
Charles T. Brusaw
Walter E. Oliu

Five Steps to Successful Writing

Successful writing on the job is not the product of inspiration, nor is it merely the spoken word converted to print; it is the result of knowing how to structure information using both words and design to achieve an intended purpose for a clearly defined audience. The best way to ensure that your writing will succeed—whether it is in the form of a memo, a résumé, a proposal, or a Web page—is to approach writing using the following steps:

1. Preparation
2. Research
3. Organization
4. Writing
5. Revision

You will very likely need to follow those steps consciously—even self-consciously—at first. The same is true the first time you use new software, interview a candidate for a job, or chair a committee meeting. With practice, the steps become nearly automatic. That is not to suggest that writing becomes easy. It does not. However, the easiest and most efficient way to write effectively is to do it systematically.

As you master the five steps, keep in mind that they are interrelated and often overlap. For example, your readers' needs and your purpose, which you initially determine in step one, should affect decisions you make in subsequent steps. You may also need to retrace steps. When you conduct research, for example, you may realize that you need to revise your initial impression of the document's purpose and audience. Similarly, when you begin to organize, you may discover the need to return to the research step to gather more information.

The time required for each step varies with different writing tasks. When writing an informal memo, for example, you might follow the first three steps (preparation, research, and organization) by simply listing the points in the order you want to cover them. In such situations, you gather and organize information mentally as you consider your purpose and audience. For a formal report, the first three steps require well-organized research, careful note-taking, and detailed outlining. For a routine email message to a coworker, the first four steps merge as you type the information on the screen. In short, the five steps expand, contract, and at times must be repeated to fit the complexity or context of the writing task.

Dividing the writing process into steps is especially useful for collaborative writing, in which you typically divide work among team members, keep track of a project, and save time by not duplicating effort. When you collaborate, you can use email to share text and other files, suggest improvements to each other's work, and generally keep everyone informed of your progress as you follow the steps in the writing process. See also **collaborative writing** (page 4).

Preparation

Writing, like most professional tasks, requires solid preparation. In fact, adequate preparation is as important as writing the draft. In preparation for writing, your goal is to accomplish the following four major tasks:

- Establish your primary purpose.
- Assess your audience (or readers).
- Determine the scope of your coverage.
- Select the appropriate medium.

Establishing Your Purpose. To establish your primary purpose simply ask yourself what you want your readers to know, believe, or be able to do after they have finished reading what you have written. Be precise. Often a writer states a purpose so broadly that it is almost useless. A purpose such as "to report on possible locations for a new facility" is too general. However, "to compare the relative advantages of Paris, Singapore, and San Francisco as possible locations for a new engineering facility so top management can choose the best location" is a purpose statement that can guide you throughout the writing process. In addition to your primary purpose, consider possible secondary purposes for your document. For example, a secondary purpose of the engineering facilities' report might be to make corporate executive readers aware of the staffing needs of the new facility so they can ensure its smooth operation in whatever location is selected. See also **purpose/objective** (page 41).

Assessing Your Audience. The next task is to assess your audience. Again, be precise and ask key questions. Who exactly is your reader? Do you have multiple readers? Who needs to see or use the document? What are your readers' needs in relation to your subject? What are your readers' attitudes about the subject? (Skeptical? Supportive? Anxious? Bored?) What do your readers already know about the subject? Should you define basic terminology or will such definitions merely bore, or even impede, your readers? Are you communicating with international readers and therefore dealing with issues inherent in writing international correspondence? See also **international correspondence** (page 141).

For the engineering facilities' report, the readers are described as "top management." *Who* is included in that category? Will one of the people evaluating the report be the Human Resources Manager? If so, that person likely would be interested in the availability of qualified professionals as well as in the presence of training, housing, and perhaps even recreational facilities available to potential employees in each city. The Purchasing Manager would be concerned about available sources for materials needed by the facility. The Marketing Manager would give priority to the facility's proximity to the primary markets for its products and services and the transportation options that are available. The Chief Financial Officer would want to know about land and building costs and about each country's tax structure. The Chief Executive Officer would be interested in all this information and perhaps more.

In addition to knowing the needs and interests of your readers, learn as much as you can about their background knowledge. Have they visited all three cities? Have they already seen other reports on the three cities? Is this the company's first new facility, or has the company chosen locations for new facilities before? As with this example, many workplace documents have audiences composed of multiple readers. You can accommodate their needs through one of a number of approaches described in the entry **audience/readers** (page 3).

Determining the Scope. Determining your purpose and assessing your readers will help you decide what to include and what not to include in your writing. Those decisions establish the scope of your

TIPS FOR CONSIDERING AUDIENCES

In North American English, *conciseness, coherence,* and *clarity* are what characterize good writing. In other words, be brief, make sure your writing holds together, be clear, and say only what is necessary to communicate your message. Of course, no writing style is inherently better than another, but to be a successful writer in any language, you must understand the cultural values that underlie the language in which you are writing. Throughout this book we have highlighted with an icon ESL entries that may be particularly helpful to nonnative speakers of English. See **awkwardness, biased language, coherence, conciseness/wordiness, copyright, documenting sources, plagiarism,** and **English as a second language.**

writing project. If you do not clearly define the scope, you will spend needless hours on research because you will not be sure what kind of information you need or even how much. Given the purpose and readers established for the report on facility locations, the scope would include such information as land and building costs, available labor force, cultural issues, transportation facilities, and proximity to suppliers. However, it probably would not include the early history of the cities being considered or their climate and geological features, unless those aspects were directly related to your particular business. See also **scope** (page 45).

Selecting the Medium. Finally, you need to determine the most appropriate medium for communicating your message. Professionals on the job face a wide array of options—from email, fax, voice mail, videoconferencing, and Web sites to more traditional means like letters and memos, telephone calls, and face-to-face meetings.

The most important considerations in selecting the appropriate medium are the audience and the purpose of the communication. For example, if you need to collaborate with someone to solve a problem or if you need to establish rapport with someone, written exchanges, even by email, could be far less efficient than a phone call or a face-to-face meeting. However, if you need precise wording or you need to provide a record of a complex message, communicate in writing. If you need to make information that is frequently revised accessible to employees at a large company, the best choice might be to place the information on the company's Web page. (See **Web page design,** page 239.) If reviewers need to make handwritten comments on a proposal, you may need to provide paper copies that can be faxed. The comparative advantages and primary characteristics of the most typical means of communication are discussed in **selecting the medium** (page 45).

Research

The only way to be sure that you can write about a complex subject is to thoroughly understand it. To do that, you must conduct adequate research, whether that means conducting an extensive investigation for a major proposal—through interviewing, library and Internet research, and careful note-taking—or simply checking a company Web page and jotting down points before you send an email to a colleague.

Methods of Research. Researchers frequently distinguish between primary and secondary research, depending on the types of sources consulted and the method of gathering information. *Primary research* refers to the gathering of raw data compiled from interviews, direct observation, surveys, experiments, questionnaires, and audio and video recordings, for example. In fact, direct observation and hands-on experience are the only ways to obtain certain kinds of information, such as the behavior of people and animals, certain natural phenomena, mechanical processes, and the operation of systems and equipment. *Secondary research* refers to gathering information that has been analyzed, assessed, evaluated, compiled, or otherwise organized into accessible form. Such forms or sources include books, articles, reports, Web documents, email, business letters, minutes of meetings, operating manuals, and brochures. Use the methods most appropriate to your research needs, recognizing that some projects will require several types.

Sources of Information. As you conduct research, numerous sources of information are available to you.

- Your own knowledge and that of your colleagues
- The knowledge of people outside of your workplace, gathered through **interviewing for information** (page 15)
- Internet sources, as discussed in **Internet research** (page 10)
- Library resources, including databases, as described in **library research** (page 20)
- Printed and electronic sources in the workplace, such as brochures, memos, email, and Web documents, as discussed in **note-taking** (page 26)

Consider all sources of information when you begin your research and use those that fit your needs. The amount of research you will need to do depends on the scope of your project. See also **research** (page 42).

Organization

Without organization, the material gathered during your research will be incoherent to your readers. To organize information effectively, you need to determine the best way to structure your ideas; that is, you must choose a primary method of development.

Methods of Development. An appropriate method of development is the writer's tool for keeping information under control and the readers' means of following the writer's presentation. As you analyze the information you have gathered, choose the method that best suits your subject, your readers' needs, and your purpose. For example, if you were writing instructions for assembling office equipment, you would naturally present the steps of the process in the order readers should perform them: the *sequential* method of development. If your subject naturally lends itself to a certain method of development, use it—do not attempt to impose another method on it. For example, if you were writing about the history of an organization, your account would most naturally go from the beginning to the present: the *chronological* method of development.

Sometimes you may need to use combinations of methods of development. For example, a persuasive brochure for a charitable organization might combine a *specific-to-general* with a *cause-and-effect* method of development. That is, you could begin with persuasive case histories of individual people in need and then move to general information about the positive effects of donations on recipients. The entry **organization** (page 27) describes the most typical methods of development used in on-the-job writing.

Outlining. Once you have chosen a method of development, you are ready to prepare an outline. Outlining breaks large or complex subjects into manageable parts. It also enables you to emphasize key points by placing them in the positions of greatest importance. Finally, by structuring your thinking at an early stage, a well-developed outline ensures that your document will be complete and logically organized, allowing you to focus exclusively on writing when you begin the rough draft. Even a short letter or memo needs the logic and structure that an outline provides, whether the outline exists in your mind or on screen or paper. See also **outlining** (page 29).

At this point, you must begin to consider layout and design elements that will be helpful to your readers and appropriate to your subject and purpose. For example, if illustrations, photographs, or tables will be useful, this is a good time to think about where they may be deployed and what kinds of visual elements will be effective, especially if they need to be prepared by someone else while you are writing and revising the draft. The outline can also suggest where headings, lists, and other special design features may be useful. See Tab 6, "Format and Visuals."

Writing

When you have established your purpose, your readers' needs, and your scope, and have completed your research and your outline, you will be well prepared to write a first draft. Expand your outline into paragraphs, without worrying about grammar, refinements of language, or punctuation. Writing and revising are different activities; refinements come with revision.

Write the rough draft quickly, concentrating entirely on converting your outline into sentences and paragraphs. You might try writing as though you were explaining your subject to a reader sitting across from you. Do not worry about a good opening. Just start. There is no need in the rough draft to be concerned about exact word choice unless it comes quickly and easily—concentrate instead on ideas.

Even with good preparation, writing the draft remains a chore for many writers. The most effective way to get started and keep going is to use your outline as a map for your first draft. Do not wait for inspiration; treat writing a draft as you would any on-the-job task. The entry **writing a draft** (page 47) describes tactics used by experienced writers; discover which ones are best suited to you and your task.

Consider writing an opening or introduction last because then you will know more precisely what is in the body. Your opening should announce the subject and give readers essential background information, such as the document's primary purpose. For longer documents, an introduction should serve as a frame into which readers can fit the detailed information that follows.

Finally, you will need to write a closing or a conclusion that ties the main ideas together and emphatically makes a final significant point. The final point may be to recommend a course of action, make a prediction or a judgment, or merely summarize your main points—the way you conclude depends on the purpose of your writing and your readers' needs. For help and examples, see **introductions** (page 16) and **conclusions** (page 6).

Revision

The clearer a finished piece of writing seems to the reader, the more effort the writer has likely put into its revision. If you have followed the steps of the writing process to this point, you will have a rough draft that needs to be revised. Revising, however, requires a different frame of mind than does writing the draft. During revision, be eager to find and correct faults and be honest. Be hard on yourself for the benefit of your readers. Read and evaluate the draft as if you were a reader seeing it for the first time.

Check your draft for accuracy, completeness, and effectiveness in achieving your purpose and meeting your readers' needs and expectations. Trim extraneous information: Your writing should give readers exactly what they need, but it should not burden them with unnecessary information or sidetrack them into loosely related subjects.

Do not try to revise for everything at once. Read your rough draft several times, each time looking for and correcting a different set of problems or errors. Concentrate first on larger issues, such as unity and coherence; save mechanical corrections, like spelling and punctuation, for later reviews. See also **ethics in writing** (page 261).

Finally, for important documents, consider having others review your writing and make suggestions for improvement. For further advice and a useful checklist, see the entry **revision** (page 44).

1

The Writing Process

Preview

The "Five Steps to Successful Writing" essay (page xiii) describes not only a systematic approach to writing, but also a diagnostic tool for assessing problems. That is, when you find that a document is not achieving its primary purpose, the five steps can help you pinpoint where a problem occurred. Was the audience not fully assessed? Is further research needed? Does the document only need further revision? Many of the entries in this section expand on the topics introduced in the "Five Steps," such as **audience/readers, collaborative writing, selecting the medium, writing a draft,** and others. This section also covers the crucial function of **research** and includes specific advice on **Internet research, library research,** and **interviewing for information.** Other entries related to the research process are **bibliographies** (page 51), **copyright** (page 53), **documenting sources** (page 54), **plagiarism** (page 73), and **quotations** (page 83), and are included in Tab 2, "Business Writing: Forms and Documentation."

audience / readers

The first rule of effective writing is to *help your readers*. If you overlook this commitment, your writing will not achieve its purpose, either for you or for your business or organization. See also **purpose/objective** (page 41).

To be able to help your readers, you should ask some key questions. Who specifically is your reader? Do you have multiple readers? Who needs to see or use the document? What are your readers' needs in relation to your subject? What are your readers' attitudes about the subject? (Skeptical? Supportive? Anxious? Bored?) What do your readers already know about your subject?

In the workplace, your readers are usually less familiar with the subject than you are. You have to be careful, therefore, when writing on a topic that is unique to your area of specialization to be sensitive to the needs of those whose training or experience lies in other areas; you need to provide definitions of nonstandard terms and explanations of principles that you, as a specialist, take for granted. Note that even if you write a journal article for others in your field, you should explain new or special uses of standard terms and principles.

Many workplace documents have audiences composed of multiple readers; you can accommodate their needs through one of a number of approaches.

For documents with groups of readers who have different needs, you might design parts of a document to reach different groups of readers: an executive summary for top managers, an appendix with detailed data for technical specialists, and the body of a report or proposal for those readers who need to make decisions based on the details. See also **formal reports** (page 96).

When you have multiple readers with various needs but cannot segment your document, you might prioritize audience segments and fulfill the needs of the most important readers first, such as those who will make decisions based on the document. Then you can fulfill the needs of others who might be affected by the document or those who need only know some of its contents. Meet the needs of those secondary audiences to the best of your ability, as long as you do not sacrifice the needs of your primary audience.

If your audience is relatively homogeneous, you might combine all your readers into one composite reader and write for *that* reader. You might also make a list of that reader's characteristics (experience, training, attitudes, and work habits, for example) to help you write at the appropriate level. This technique enables you to decide what should or should not be explained for the typical reader.

When you write to an individual reader in a letter, email, or memo, you may find it useful to visualize that person sitting across from you as you write. Doing so can help you to empathize with the reader and write in an appropriate style and tone. When you write to an individual reader, keep in mind that both electronic and paper correspondence might be read by others. Always maintain a style and tone that are appropriate to a wide professional audience.

Writer's Checklist: Meeting Your Reader's Needs

☑ Accept your responsibility to help the reader.

☑ Determine, specifically, the readers in your audience.

- Who exactly is your reader? Do you have multiple readers? Who are they?
- Who needs to see or use the document based on your purpose or goals?

☑ Consider your readers' needs relative to your purpose or goals.

- What are your readers' needs in relation to your subject? What do they already know about your subject? Do they need definitions of basic terminology?
- What are your readers' attitudes about the subject?
- Do you need to adapt your message for international readers? If so, see **global communication** (page 211) and **international correspondence** (page 141).

☑ Determine which method best accommodates multiple readers.

- Segment the document for different reader groups.
- Fulfill the needs of the most important readers first.
- Develop a composite reader for homogeneous reader groups.

See also Tab 6, "Format and Visuals," as well as **correspondence** (page 128), **email** (page 233), "Five Steps to Successful Writing" (page xiii), **persuasion** (page 35), and **"you" viewpoint** (page 281).

collaborative writing

Collaborative writing occurs when two or more writers work together to produce a single document for which they share responsibility and decision-making authority. Collaborative writing teams are formed when (1) the size of a project or the time constraints imposed on it require collaboration, (2) the project involves multiple areas of expertise, or (3) the project requires the melding of divergent views into a single perspective that is acceptable to the whole team or to another group.

The collaborating writers strive to achieve a compatible working relationship by dividing the work in a way that uses each member's expertise and experience to their collective advantage. To do so, the team should designate one person as its coordinator. This person does not normally have decision-making authority—he or she merely coordinates the team members' activities and organizes the final project. If the team often works together, the coordinator's duties can be determined by mutual agreement or assigned on a rotating basis.

Tasks of the Collaborative Writing Team

The collaborative writing team normally performs four tasks. The team plans the document, researches and writes the draft, reviews the drafts of other team members, and revises drafts on the basis of these reviews.

Planning. The team collectively identifies the audience, purpose, and scope of the project. The team conceptualizes the document to be produced, creates a broad outline of the document, divides it into segments, and assigns each segment to individual team members, often on the basis of expertise. See also "Five Steps to Successful Writing" (page xiii).

In the planning stage, the team projects a schedule and sets any writing style standards that the team is expected to follow. The schedule includes due dates for drafts, reviews of the drafts, revisions, and the final document. It is important that milestone deadlines be met, even if the drafts are not as polished as the individual writers would like: One missed deadline can delay the entire project.

Research and Writing. Planning is followed by research and writing, a period of intense independent activity by members of the team. Each member researches his or her assigned segment of the document, fleshes out the broad outline in greater detail, and produces a draft from the detailed outline. Then, by the deadline established for the drafts, writers submit copies of the drafts to their teammates for review. See also **research** (page 42).

Reviewing. During the review stage, team members assume the role of the reader to address any potential problems. Each member critically yet diplomatically reviews the work of the other team members. Reviewers evaluate colleagues' drafts, from the organization to the clarity of each paragraph and sentence. They offer advice to help the writer improve his or her segment of the document. Team members can easily solicit feedback by sharing files on a network system, by emailing documents back and forth, or by exchanging disks. Redlining or highlighting allows the reviewer to show the suggested changes without deleting the original text. The author can then easily accept or reject the proposed changes. See also **proofreader's marks** (facing inside back cover).

Revising. In this stage, individual writers evaluate their colleagues' reviews and accept or reject their suggestions. Once each member revises his or her draft, all drafts can be consolidated into a final master copy maintained by the team leader. Integral to this process is that team members evaluate their colleagues' suggestions objectively and accept criticism constructively. See also **revision** (page 44).

Conflict

Team members may not agree on every subject, and differing perspectives can easily lead to conflict, ranging from mild differences over minor points to major showdowns. However, creative differences resolved respectfully can energize the team and, in fact, strengthen a finished document by compelling writers to reexamine assumptions and issues in unanticipated ways.

Writer's Checklist: Writing Collaboratively

- ☑ Designate one person as the team coordinator.
- ☑ Collectively identify the audience, purpose, and scope of the project.
- ☑ Create a working outline of the document.
- ☑ Assign segments or tasks to each team member.
- ☑ Establish a schedule: due dates for drafts, revisions, and final documents.
- ☑ Agree on a standard reference guide for style and format.
- ☑ Research and write drafts of document segments.
- ☑ Exchange segments for team member reviews. See **revision** (page 44) and **proofreading** (page 40).
- ☑ Revise segments as needed.
- ☑ Meet your established deadlines.

As you collaborate, be ready to tolerate some disharmony, but temper it with mutual respect.

conclusions

The conclusion of a document ties the main ideas together and can do so emphatically and persuasively by making a final significant point. This final point may, for example, recommend a course of action, make a prediction or a judgment, or merely summarize main points.

The way you conclude depends on both the purpose of your writing and your readers' needs. For example, a committee report about possible locations for a new production facility might end with a recommendation. The following examples are typical concluding strategies:

RECOMMENDATION

These results indicate that you need to alter your testing procedure to eliminate the impurities we found in specimens A through E.

PREDICTION

Although I have exceeded my original estimate for equipment, I have reduced my original labor estimate; therefore, I will easily stay within the original bid.

JUDGMENT

Although our estimate calls for a substantially higher budget than in the three previous years, we believe that it is reasonable given our planned expansion.

SUMMARY

As this letter indicates, we would attract more recent graduates with the following strategies:

1. Establishing a Web site where students can register and submit online résumés
2. Increasing our advertising in local student newspapers and our attendance at college career fairs
3. Expanding our local co-op program

The concluding statement may merely present ideas for consideration, call for action, or deliberately provoke thought.

IDEAS FOR CONSIDERATION

The new prices become effective the first of the year. Price adjustments are routine for the company, but some of your customers will not consider them acceptable. Please bear in mind the needs of both your customers and the company as you implement these new prices.

CALL FOR ACTION

Send us a check for $250 now if you wish to keep your account active. If you have not responded to our previous letters because of some special hardship, I will be glad to work out a solution with you personally.

THOUGHT-PROVOKING STATEMENT

Can we continue to accept the losses incurred by inefficiency? Or should we consider steps to control it now?

Be especially careful not to introduce a new topic when you conclude. A conclusion should always relate to and reinforce the ideas presented earlier in your writing. Moreover, the conclusions must be consistent with what the introduction promised the report would examine (its purpose) and how it would do so (its method). Figure 1–1 is a conclusion from a proposal to reduce health-care costs by increasing employee fitness through health-club subsidies. It makes recommendations that pull the various parts of the proposal together.

FIGURE 1–1. Sample Conclusion

CONCLUSION AND RECOMMENDATION

As shown earlier, building and equipping fitness centers at all five company locations would require an initial investment of nearly $2 million. Such facilities would also occupy valuable office space. Therefore, this option would be costly.

Enrolling employees in the corporate program at AeroFitness would allow them to attend on a trial basis. Those interested in continuing could join the club and pay half of the $400 annual membership cost, less a 30-percent discount. The other half of the membership ($140) would be paid for by First Investment. Employees who leave the company would be given the option to purchase First Investment's share of the membership.

I recommend that First Investment, Inc., participate in the corporate membership program at AeroFitness Clubs by subsidizing employee memberships. First Investment benefits from such a program in several ways: We demonstrate our commitment to a fit workforce, we augment our already generous package, and we boost employee morale. Most importantly, implementing this program will help First Investment, Inc., reduce its health-care costs both by building a healthier workforce and by qualifying for insurance premium discounts.

For guidance about the location of the conclusion section in a report, see **formal reports** (page 96). For letter and other short closings, see **correspondence** (page 128) and entries on specific types of documents throughout this book. See also **introductions** (page 16).

defining terms

Good writing ensures that readers understand key terms and concepts used. Terms can be defined either formally or informally, depending on your purpose and your readers.

A *formal definition* is a form of classification. You define a term by placing it in a category and then identifying the features that distinguish it from other members of the same category.

TERM	CATEGORY	DISTINGUISHING FEATURES
An *auction* is	a public sale	in which property passes to the highest bidder through successively increased offers.

An *informal definition* explains a term by giving a more familiar word or phrase as a synonym.

- Plants have a *symbiotic,* or *mutually beneficial,* relationship with certain kinds of bacteria.

State definitions positively; focus on what the term *is* rather than on what it is not.

NEGATIVE	In a legal transaction, *real property* is not personal property.
POSITIVE	*Real property* is legal terminology for the right or interest a person has in land and the permanent structures on that land.

For a discussion of when negative definitions are appropriate, see **organization** (page 27).

Avoid circular definitions, which merely restate the term to be defined and therefore fail to clarify it. A circular statement such as "*Spontaneous combustion* is fire that begins spontaneously," can be improved as follows:

- *Spontaneous combustion* is the self-ignition of a flammable material through a chemical reaction.

In addition, avoid "is when" and "is where" definitions. Such definitions fail to include the category and are too indirect.

- A *contract* is ~~when two or more people agree to something.~~ ^ *a binding agreement between two or more people.*

description

The key to effective description is the accurate presentation of details, whether for simple or complex descriptions. Notice that in Figure 1–2, the description contained in the purchase order includes five specific details in addition to the part number.

PURCHASE ORDER

PART NO.	DESCRIPTION	QUANTITY
IW 8421	Infectious-waste bags, 12″ × 14″, heavy-gauge polyethylene, red double closures with self-sealing adhesive strips	5 boxes containing 200 bags per box

FIGURE 1–2. Sample Description

Complex descriptions, of course, involve more details. In describing a mechanical device, for example, describe the whole device and its function before giving a detailed description of how each part works. The description should conclude with an explanation of how each part contributes to the functioning of the whole.

In descriptions intended for readers who are unfamiliar with the topic, details are crucial. For these readers, show or demonstrate (as opposed to "tell") primarily through the use of images and details.

- Their corporate headquarters, which reminded me of a rural college campus, are located north of the city in a 90-acre wooded area. The complex consists of five three-story buildings of colonial design. The buildings are spaced about 50 feet apart and are built in a U shape . . .

You can also use analogy to explain unfamiliar concepts in terms of familiar ones. See also **figures of speech** (page 263).

Illustrations can be powerful aids in descriptive writing. For a discussion of how to incorporate visual material into text, see Tab 6, "Format and Visuals."

Internet research

The Internet provides access to a staggering amount of information, including access to many public and university library catalogs and databases. You can also conduct primary research by participating in discussion groups and news groups, and by using email to request information from specific audiences. See also **research** (page 42) and the Internet Glossary included in **Internet** (page 237).

Using Search Engines and Subject Directories

Search Engines. Search engines enable you to find what you need at your library and on the Internet. Some search engines, such as Northern Light, search not only the Web but also their own database of articles—content that is edited and compiled by staff librarians and not available elsewhere on the Web.

Many search engines offer the option of conducting an advanced search, which provides you with a number of ways to control and restrict your search and allows you to obtain more selective results. Figure 1–3 shows an advanced search conducted on Google for business writing programs—a search limited to results in English and to sites within the ".edu" domain. This particular advanced search resulted in ten selective hits. Although search engines vary in what and how they search, you can use some basic strategies (see Writer's Checklist: Using Search Engines).

FIGURE 1–3. Advanced Google Search

Writer's Checklist: Using Search Engines

☑ Enter words and phrases that are as specific to your topic as possible. For example, if you are looking for information about *nuclear power* and enter only the term *nuclear,* the search will also yield listings for *nuclear family*, *nuclear medicine*, and *nuclear winter.*

☑ Consider using a subject directory (see Figure 1–4).

☑ Consider conducting an advanced search (see Figure 1–3).

☑ Check any search tips available at the engine you use. For example, some engines allow you to narrow your search by enclosing phrases in double quotation marks: "usability testing." Others have different options for narrowing your search.

☑ Use a variety of search engines.

☑ If you are interested in obtaining as many hits as possible, consider using a metasearch engine.

The following search engines are used widely on the Web:

AltaVista	(www.altavista.com)
Excite	(www.excite.com)
Google	(www.google.com)
Hotbot	(www.hotbot.lycos.com)
Infoseek	(www.infoseek.go.com)
Lycos	(www.lycos.com)
Northern Light	(www.northernlight.com)
WebCrawler	(www.webcrawler.com)
Yahoo!	(www.yahoo.com)

The Writer's Checklist suggests using a metasearch engine, which searches the Web using multiple search engines at the same time. For example, a metasearch could allow you to search AltaVista, Google, and public and university libraries. Keep in mind, however, that metasearches result in numerous hits, so be prepared to refine and narrow your results. Two useful metasearch engines are Dogpile (www.dogpile.com) and Metacrawler (www.metacrawler.com).

WEB LINK ▶ EVALUATING SEARCH ENGINES

SEARCH ENGINE WATCH
www.searchenginewatch.com

This site provides up-to-date information about search engines — classifying, evaluating, and summarizing the current features of each.

Subject Directories. A *subject directory* organizes information on the Web by broad subject categories and related subtopics. A search conducted through a subject directory produces a more streamlined results list than a search conducted broadly on the Web. Figure 1–4 shows Google's Web Directory.

In addition to the subject directories offered by many search engines, the following directories will help you to conduct selective, scholarly research on the Web:

Argus Clearinghouse	(www.clearinghouse.net)
Infomine	(infomine.ucr.edu)
World Wide Web Virtual Library	(www.vlib.org)

Locating Business and Government Sites

The Web includes numerous sites devoted to specific subject areas. Some suggested resources for researching a business topic follow.

Web Directory

Arts Movies, Music, Television, ...	**Home** Consumers, Homeowners, Family, ...	**Regional** Asia, Europe, North America, ...
Business Industries, Finance, Jobs, ...	**Kids and Teens** Computers, Entertainment, School, ...	**Science** Biology, Psychology, Physics, ...
Computers Internet, Hardware, Software, ...	**News** Media, Newspapers, Current Events, ...	**Shopping** Autos, Clothing, Gifts, ...
Games Board, Roleplaying, Video, ...	**Recreation** Food, Outdoors, Travel, ...	**Society** Issues, People, Religion, ...
Health Alternative, Fitness, Medicine, ...	**Reference** Education, Libraries, Maps, ...	**Sports** Basketball, Football, Soccer, ...

World
Deutsch, Español, Français, Italiano, Japanese, Korean, Nederlands, Polska, Svenska ...

FIGURE 1–4. Google's Main Subject Directory

Business Resources

Business Resources on the Web (webbusiness.cio.com/)

Business Internet Resources (www.pace.edu/library/links/links.html)

Inc. Business Resources on the Web (www.inc.com/ibr)

Yahoo!'s Business Resources (dir.yahoo.com/Business_and_Economy)

Government Resources

Federal Government Agencies Directory (www.lib.lsu.edu/gov/fedgov.html)

FedStats (www.fedstats.gov)

Evaluating Internet Sources

Evaluate the usefulness and reliability of information on the Internet by the same standards that you use to evaluate information from other sources. For Internet sources, be especially concerned about the validity of the information provided.

To ensure that information is valid, obtain it from a reputable source. For example, American businesses rely on and widely use the compilations of data from the Bureau of Labor Statistics, the Securities and Exchange Commission, and the Bureau of the Census. Likewise, the online versions of established, reputable journals in medicine, management, engineering, computer software, and the like, merit the same level of trust as the printed versions. However, as you move away from established, reputable sites such as those provided by higher education sites, exercise more caution. Be especially wary of unmoderated discussion groups on Usenet and other public Web forums. Use the following cues for determining the sponsor of an Internet site:

ADDRESS	TYPE OF SOURCE
.com	a company or personal site
.edu	higher education site
.gov	federal government site
.net	a network
.org	an organization's site

Keep aware of emerging domain addresses, such as .biz and .info, as they evolve. For information about citing Internet sources, see **documenting sources** (page 54).

Writer's Checklist: Evaluating Internet Sources

- ☑ Who is the author of the site? Does the site include information about the author, such as an academic affiliation? Does the author seem credible?
- ☑ What group or organization sponsors or maintains the site? A commercial entity (.com)? A university (.edu)? A government agency (.gov)? A network (.net)? An organization (.org)? (Also check the "About Us" page.)
- ☑ Are the purpose and scope of the site clearly stated? (Check the "Mission Statement" or "About Us" pages. Are there any disclaimers?)
- ☑ What audience(s) does the site seem to target?
- ☑ Is the information at the site accurate and current? Is the documentation authoritative and credible? (Check the links that take the place of traditional documentation at Web sites and also check facts against those at other reputable Web sites, such as academic ones.)
- ☑ Is the information presented in an objective, nonbiased way? Are any biases made clear? Are opinion pieces clearly labeled?
- ☑ What do you think of the presentation of the site? Is it well designed? Is it easily navigated? Are links functional and up to date? Is the material well written and error-free?

See also Writer's Checklist: Evaluating Library Resources (page 26).

WEB LINK ▶ EVALUATING ONLINE SOURCES

Some resources for evaluating content on the Web are provided at the following sites:

PURDUE UNIVERSITY
thorplus.lib.purdue.edu/~techman/eval.html

UC BERKELEY
www.lib.berkeley.edu/TeachingLib/Guides/Internet/EvalQuestions.html

WIDENER UNIVERSITY
muse.widener.edu/Wolfgram-Memorial-Library/webevaluation/webeval.htm

interviewing for information

The process of interviewing can be divided into four parts: (1) determining the proper person to interview, (2) preparing for the interview, (3) conducting the interview, and (4) expanding your notes immediately after the interview.

Determining Who to Interview

Many times your subject or purpose logically points to the proper person to interview for information. If you were writing about using the Web to market a software-development business, you would want to interview someone with extensive experience in Web marketing as well as someone who has built a successful business developing software. The following sources can help you determine the appropriate person to interview: (1) workplace colleagues or faculty in appropriate academic departments, (2) a search on the Internet, (3) local chapters of professional societies, and (4) the yellow pages of the local telephone directory. See also **Internet research** (page 10).

Preparing for the Interview

Before the interview, learn as much as possible about the person you are going to interview and the organization for which he or she works. When you contact the prospective interviewee, explain who you are, why you would like to interview him or her, the subject and purpose of the interview, and how much time it will take. Let your interviewee know that you will allow him or her to review your draft.

After you have made the appointment, prepare a list of questions to ask your interviewee. Avoid vague, general questions. A question such as "What do you think of the Internet?" is too general to elicit useful information. It is more helpful to ask specific but open-ended questions that prompt interviewees to respond: "Some local companies in your business are making extensive use of the Internet for marketing. How do you use the Internet?"

Writer's Checklist: Interviewing for Information

- ☑ Arrive promptly for the interview and set the interviewee at ease.
- ☑ Be pleasant but purposeful. Do not be timid about asking leading questions on the subject. Use your prepared list of questions as your guide: Begin with the least complex aspects of the topic, then move to the more complex aspects.
- ☑ Don't get sidetracked. If the interviewee strays too far from the subject, ask a specific question to direct the conversation back on track.
- ☑ Avoid being rigid; if a prepared question is no longer suitable, move to the next question.
- ☑ Some answers prompt additional questions; ask them as they arise.
- ☑ Let your interviewee do most of the talking. Remember that the interviewee is the expert.
- ☑ Take only memory-jogging notes that will help you recall the conversation later. Concentrate on key facts and figures. Use a tape recorder if both you and your interviewee are comfortable with it.
- ☑ As the interview is reaching a close, take a few minutes to skim your notes. If time allows, ask the interviewee to clarify anything that is ambiguous.
- ☑ After thanking the interviewee, ask permission to telephone to clarify a point or two as you complete your interview notes.
- ☑ Immediately after leaving the interview, expand your memory-jogging notes to help you mentally review the interview. Do not postpone this step.
- ☑ A day or two following the interview, send the interviewee a note of thanks in a brief letter or email.

introductions

This entry discusses full-scale introductions to large writing projects, such as formal reports and major proposals, as well as opening strategies for short and routine types of **correspondence** (page 128), such as letters and **email** (page 233). See also **conclusions** (page 6).

The purpose of a full-scale introduction is to give readers enough general information about the subject to enable them to understand the details in the body of the document. An introduction should accomplish the following:

- *State the Subject:* Provide background information, such as definition, history, or theory to provide context for the reader.
- *State the Purpose:* Make your readers aware of why the document exists and whether the material provides a new perspective or clarifies an existing perspective.
- *State the Scope:* Tell readers the amount of detail you plan to cover.
- *Preview the Development of the Subject:* Especially in a longer document, outline how you plan to develop the subject. Providing such information allows readers to anticipate how the subject will be presented and helps them evaluate your conclusions or recommendations.

Consider writing the introduction last. Many writers find that it is only when they have drafted the body of the document that they have a full enough perspective on the subject to introduce it adequately.

Opening Strategies

For use with full-scale introductions as well as with shorter documents, the following section provides strategies for focusing the readers' attention and motivating them to read the document.

Objective. In reporting on a project, you might open with a statement of the project's objective to give the reader a basis for judging the results.

- The primary goal of this project was to develop new techniques to solve the problem of waste disposal. Our first step was to investigate . . .

Problem Statement. One way to give readers the perspective of your report is to present a brief account of the problem that led to the study or project being reported.

- Several weeks ago a manager noticed a recurring problem in the software developed by Datacom Systems. Specifically, error messages repeatedly appeared when, in fact, no specific trouble . . . After an extensive investigation, we found that Datacom Systems . . .

Scope. You may want to present the scope of your document in your opening. By providing the parameters of your material, the limitations of the subject, or the amount of detail to be presented, you enable your readers to determine whether they need to read your document.

- This pamphlet provides a review of the requirements for obtaining an FAA pilot's license. It is not intended as a textbook to prepare you for the examination itself; rather, it outlines the steps you need to take and the costs involved.

Background. The background or history of a subject may be interesting and lend perspective and insight to a subject. Consider the following example from a newsletter describing the process of oil drilling.

- From the bamboo poles the Chinese used when the pyramids were young to today's giant rigs drilling in a hundred feet of water, there has been considerable progress in the search for oil. But whether in ancient China or a modern city, under water or on a mountaintop, the object of drilling has always been the same—to manufacture a hole in the ground, inch by inch.

Summary. You can provide a summary opening by briefly describing the results, conclusions, or recommendations of your article or report. Be concise. Do not begin a summary by writing "This report summarizes . . .".

CHANGE	This report summarizes the advantages offered by the photon as a means of examining the structural features of the atom.
TO	As a means of examining the structure of the atom, the photon offers several advantages.

Interesting Detail. Often an interesting detail will gain the readers' attention and arouse their interest. Readers of an annual report for a manufacturer of telescopes and scientific instruments, for example, may be persuaded to invest if they believe that the company is developing innovative, cutting-edge products.

- The rings of Saturn have puzzled astronomers ever since they were discovered by Galileo in 1610, using the first telescope. Recently, even more rings have been discovered.

  Our company designs and manufactures research-quality, computer-controlled telescopes that promise to solve the puzzles of Saturn's rings by enabling scientists to use multicolor differential photometry to determine the rings' origins and compositions.

Definition. Although a definition can be useful as an opening, do not define something with which the reader is familiar or provide a definition that is obviously a contrived opening (such as "Webster defines *technology* as . . ."). A definition should be used as an opening only if it offers insight into what follows.

- *Risk* is a loosely defined term. For the purposes of this report, risk refers to a qualitative combination of the probability of an event and the severity of the consequences of that event.

Anecdote. An anecdote can also be used to attract and build interest in a subject that may otherwise be mundane; however, this strategy is best suited to longer documents and presentations.

- In his poem "The Calf Path," Sam Walter Foss tells of a wandering, wobbly calf trying to find its way home at night through the lonesome woods. It made a crooked path, which was taken up the next day by a lone dog. Then "a bellwether sheep pursued the trail over vale and steep, drawing behind him the flock, too, as all good bellwethers do." The path became a country road, and at last the main street of a flourishing city. The poet ends by saying, "A hundred thousand men were led by a calf, three centuries dead." Many companies today follow a "calf path" because they react to events rather than planning. . . .

Quotation. Occasionally, you can use a quotation to stimulate interest in your subject. However, the quotation must be pertinent—not some loosely related remark selected from a book of quotations.

- Richard Smith, president of P. R. Smith Corporation, recently said, "I believe that managers need to be more 'people smart' than ever before. Management style now involves much more than just managing the operations of a department—it requires understanding the personalities within a corporation." His statement represents a growing feeling among corporate leaders that . . .

Forecast. Sometimes you can use a forecast of a new development or trend to arouse the readers' interest.

- In the not-too-distant future, we may be able to use a hand-held medical diagnostic device similar to those in science fiction to assess the complete physical condition of accident victims. This project and others are now being developed at The Seldi Group, Inc.

Persuasive Hook. While all opening strategies contain persuasive elements, the hook is the most overtly persuasive. A brochure touting the newest innovation in tax-preparation software might address readers as follows.

- Welcome to the newest way to do your taxes! TaxPro EZ ends the headache of last-minute tax preparation with its unique WebLink feature.

Routine Openings

Not every document needs a fully developed introduction or opening. When your readers are already familiar with your subject, or if what you are writing is short, a brief or routine opening, as shown in the following examples, is adequate.

CORRESPONDENCE

Dear Mr. Ignatowski:
You will be happy to know that we have corrected the error in your bank balance. The new balance shows . . .

PROGRESS REPORT LETTER

Dear Dr. Chang:
To date, 18 of the 20 specimens you submitted for analysis have been examined. Our preliminary analysis indicates . . .

LONGER PROGRESS REPORT

Progress Report on Rewiring the Sports Arena

The rewiring program at the Sports Arena is proceeding ahead of schedule. Although the costs of certain equipment are higher than our original bid, we expect to complete the project without exceeding our budget because the speedy completion will save labor costs.

Work Completed

As of August 15, we have . . .

EMAIL

Jane,
As I promised in my earlier email, I've attached the personnel budget estimates for fiscal year 20--.

library research

This entry, along with the **Internet research** entry (page 10), is intended to provide you with a starting point for conducting research; the Web link boxes and references throughout provide resources for more detailed information. See **research** (page 42) for other methods of gathering information and **note-taking** (page 26) for advice about recording notes during research.

The first step for conducting library research is to develop a search strategy appropriate to the information needed for your topic. You may want to begin by meeting with a research librarian. Research librarians are information specialists who can help you quickly find the best print or online resources for your topic—a brief conversation can focus your research and save you time. In addition, use your library's homepage for access to its catalogs, databases of articles, subject directories to the Web, and more. A sample of a library's homepage is shown in Figure 1–5.

FIGURE 1–5. Sample of a Library Homepage

Your search strategy depends on the kind of information you are seeking. For example, if you need the latest data offered by government research, check the Web. Likewise, if you need a current article on a topic, search an online database—such as InfoTrac—subscribed to by your library. For an overview of a subject, you might turn to an encyclopedia; for historical background, your best resources are books, journals, and primary documents.

Online Catalogs (Locating Books)

An online catalog—accessed through a library terminal and through the Internet—allows you to search a library's holdings, indicates an item's location and availability, and may allow you to arrange an interlibrary loan.

You can search a library's online catalog by author, title, or subject. The most typical way of searching the catalog is to search by subject. Most catalogs allow you to search by subject in two ways: by keyword or by subject. If your search turns up too many results, you can usually narrow your search by using the "limit search" or "advanced search" option offered by many catalogs. An example of an advanced search by keyword is shown in Figure 1–6.

1. Select database(s) to search:

Metro Boston Library Network
BPL Research Lib, 1974-Present
Minuteman
CLAMS
Fenway Libraries Online

2. Enter a word or phrase to search:

(Searching by ***"Keyword"*** *permits the use of operators and qualifiers.)*

Business AND environmental protection

Pressing ***<Enter>*** *without selecting a searchtype searches by the* ***highlighted*** *search button.*

3. Search records by:

Author | Title | Subject | Keyword

Press Button to Submit Search

4. Limit the search (optional):

By language: English | **By material type:** All Materials | **By date:** All Dates

FIGURE 1–6. Advanced Search of a Catalog

WEB LINK ▶ ACCESSING LIBRARY CATALOGS

THE LIBDEX LIBRARY INDEX
www.libdex.com

LibDex is a worldwide directory of library homepages, Web-based Online Public Access Catalogs (OPACs).

THE LIBRARY OF CONGRESS
lcweb.loc.gov

This site offers access to the online catalog holdings and special collections of the Library of Congress, including the Thomas Legislative Information site and the American Memory project.

THE GOOGLE DIRECTORY OF LIBRARIES
directory/google.com/Top/Reference/Libraries

This directory provides access to online archives, college and university libraries, and government documents.

Databases and Indexes (Locating Articles)

Most college, university, and public libraries subscribe to online databases—such as collections of online articles—many of which are available through a library's Web site. Examples of databases include the following:

- *InfoTrac* is a collection of databases of articles, with many available in full text. InfoTrac access can also provide specialized databases in business, health, and other fields.
- *ProQuest* is a database of articles, with many available in full text. ProQuest access can also provide specialized databases for nursing, biology, and psychology.
- *EBSCOhost* is a database of articles, with many available in full text. EBSCOhost access can also provide specialized databases in a range of subjects.
- *FirstSearch* is a collection of specialized databases such as WorldCat (library collections) and ArticleFirst (articles; some in full text).
- *Lexis/Nexis Universe* is a collection of databases containing news, business, legal, and congressional information, with most available in full text.

These databases, sometimes called *periodical indexes,* are excellent resources for articles published within the last ten to twenty years. Some include descriptive abstracts and full texts of articles. To find older articles, you may need to consult a print index, such as the *Readers' Guide to Periodical Research* and the *New York Times Index,* or a reference librarian. (For more information on print indexes, see Reference Works, page 24.)

To locate articles in a database, conduct a keyword search, as shown in Figure 1–7. If your search turns up too many results, narrow your search by connecting two search terms with *AND*—"business

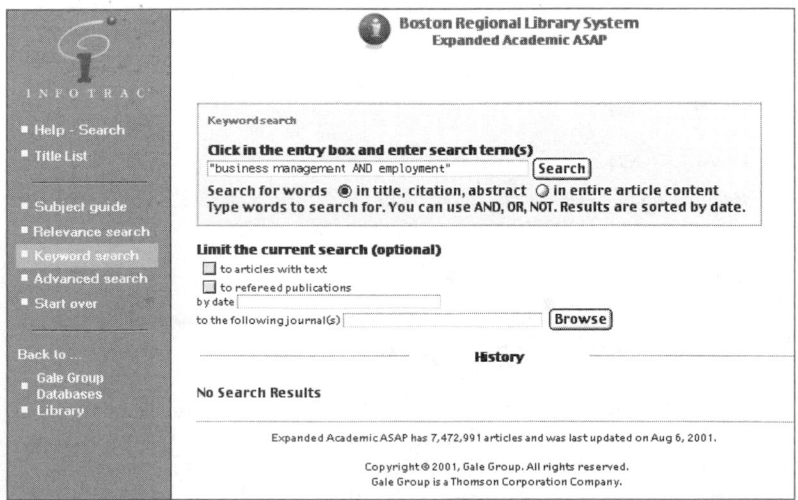

FIGURE 1–7. InfoTrac Search Page

management AND employment"—or use other options offered by the database, such as a limited, modified, or advanced search.

Reference Works

In addition to articles, books, and Web sources (see **Internet research,** page 10), you may want to consult reference works such as encyclopedias, dictionaries, and atlases for a brief overview of your subject. Bibliographies, which are lists of works written about a topic, can direct you to more specialized sources. Ask your reference librarian to recommend reference works and bibliographies that are most relevant to your topic.

Encyclopedias. Encyclopedias are comprehensive, multivolume collections of articles arranged alphabetically. Some, such as the *Encarta Encyclopedia* (www.encarta.msn.com), cover a wide range of subjects, while others, such as *The Encyclopedia of Careers and Vocational Guidance* (11th ed.), edited by William Hopke (Chicago: Ferguson, 1999), and *Encyclopedia of Banking and Finance* (10th ed.), edited by Charles J. Woelfel (New York: McGraw-Hill, 1996), focus on specific areas.

Dictionaries. General and specialized dictionaries are available in print, on CD-ROM, and on the Web. General dictionaries can be compact or comprehensive, unabridged publications. Specialized dictionaries define terms used in a particular field, such as business, computers, architecture, or consumer affairs, and offer detailed definitions of field-specific terms, usually written in straightforward language. Examples of dictionaries include the following:

GENERAL

Microsoft® Encarta® World English Dictionary. CD-ROM. Microsoft Corporation, 1999.

UNABRIDGED

Random House Unabridged Dictionary. Ed. Random House Staff and Leonore Crary Hauck. New York: Random House, 1998.

SUBJECT

The IEBM Dictionary of Business and Management. London; Boston: International Thomson Publishing Services Ltd., 1998.

Handbooks and Manuals. Handbooks and manuals are typically one-volume compilations of frequently used information in a particular field. They offer brief definitions of terms or concepts, standards for presenting information, procedures for documenting sources, and visuals such as graphs and tables. For examples of handbooks and manuals for citing sources, see **documenting sources** (page 54).

Bibliographies. Bibliographies list books, periodicals, and other research materials published in areas such as business, engineering, medicine, the humanities, and the social sciences. One example is *The St. Martin's Bibliography of Business and Technical Communication* by Gerald J. Alred (New York: St. Martin's, 1997).

General Guides. The annotated *Guide to Reference Books,* 11th ed., by Robert Balay (Chicago: American Library Association, 1996) can help you locate reference books, indexes, and other research materials. The following are specialized indexes. (Check your library's homepage or with your reference librarian to find out if your library subscribes to a particular index, and whether it is available online.)

Business Periodicals Index, 1958—. Alphabetical subject listing; issued monthly.

Government Reports Announcements and Index, 1965—. Semimonthly index of reports, arranged by subject, author, and report number.

Index to the Times (London), 1790—. Monthly.

Monthly Catalog of U.S. Government Publications, 1895—. Unclassified publications of all federal agencies, listed by subject, author, and report number; issued monthly.

New York Times Index, 1851—. Alphabetical list of subjects covered in *New York Times* articles; issued bimonthly.

Readers' Guide to Periodical Literature, 1900—. Monthly index of about 200 general U.S. periodicals, arranged alphabetically by subject.

Wall Street Journal Index, 1958—. Monthly index of business and financial news covered in the *Journal.*

Atlases and Statistical Sources. Atlases provide representations of the physical and political boundaries of countries, climate, population, or natural resources. Statistical sources, collections of numerical data, provide such information as the U.S. gross domestic product, consumer price index, or the demographic breakdown of the general population. Following are examples of atlases and statistical sources:

ATLASES

Microsoft® Encarta® World Atlas 2000. CD-ROM for Windows®. Microsoft Corporation, 2000.

STATISTICAL SOURCES

American Statistics Index. Washington: Congressional Information Service, 1978—. Monthly, quarterly, and annual supplements.

United States Bureau of the Census. *Statistical Abstract of the United States.* Washington: Government Printing Office, 1879—. Annual. (www.census.gov)

Writer's Checklist: Evaluating Library Resources

For a book:

- ☑ Is the text recent enough and relevant to your topic? Is it readily available?
- ☑ Who is the author? Does the preface or introduction indicate the author's purpose?
- ☑ What is the book's scope? (How broad or specific is its coverage?)
- ☑ Does the table of contents relate to your topic? Does the index contain terms related to your topic? Does the text contain a bibliography, reference list, and footnotes?
- ☑ Are the chapters useful? (Skim through one that seems related to your topic—notice especially the introduction, headings, and closing.)
- ☑ Does the author present information in an unbiased way? Are the language, tone, and style inviting?

For an article:

- ☑ Is the article recent enough and relevant to your topic? Is it readily available?
- ☑ Is the publisher of the magazine or other periodical well known? Who is the publication's main audience? (The mainstream public? A small group of professionals?) Does the publication target or show bias toward a particular audience?
- ☑ What is the article's purpose? (For a journal article, read the abstract; for a newspaper article, read the headline and lead sentences.)
- ☑ Does the article contain informative diagrams or other visuals that indicate its scope?

For evaluating Web sources, see the Writer's Checklist: Evaluating Internet Sources (page 14).

note-taking

The purpose of note-taking is to summarize and record information you extract during **research** (page 42). The great challenge in taking notes is to condense another writer's thoughts into your own words without distorting the original thinking or plagiarizing. As you extract information, let your knowledge of the audience and the purpose of your writing guide you. Resist the temptation to copy your source word for word as you take notes; instead, paraphrase the author's idea or concept. You must do more than just change a few words in the original passage; otherwise, you will be guilty of **plagiarism** (page 73). See also **paraphrasing** (page 34).

On occasion, when your source concisely sums up a great deal of information or points to a trend important to your subject, you are justified in directly quoting the source and incorporating it into your document. As a general rule, you will rarely need to quote anything longer than a paragraph. If you decide to use a direct quote, enclose the material in quotation marks in your notes. In your finished writing, provide the source of your quotation. See also **documenting sources** (page 54) and **quotations** (page 83).

Writer's Checklist: Taking Notes

- ☑ What information do you need to fulfill your purpose? How much do your readers know about your subject? What are their needs?
- ☑ Write down only the most important ideas and concepts. Be sure to record all vital names, dates, and definitions.
- ☑ When in doubt about whether to take a note, consider the difficulty of finding the source again should you want it later.
- ☑ To give proper credit, record the author, title, publisher, place and date of publication, and page number.
- ☑ Use your own shorthand and record notes in a way that you find efficient, whether in an electronic document or on notecards.
- ☑ Photocopy and highlight passages that you intend to quote.
- ☑ Print out key sections from online sources or download the information to a notes file: Be sure to copy the full URL and date for Web sites.
- ☑ Check your notes for accuracy against the original material before moving on to another source.

organization

Organization is essential to the success of any writing project. An organized document is based on an effective outline produced from a method of development that suits your subject, fulfills your purpose, and satisfies your readers' need for shape and structure. Following are the most common methods of developing any document—from an email to a formal report to a Web page. See also **outlining** (page 29).

- *Sequential development* emphasizes the order of elements and is particularly useful when writing instructions.

- *Chronological development* emphasizes the time element of a sequence. For example, a Federal Aviation Administration (FAA) report on an airplane crash might begin with takeoff and proceed sequentially to the crash.
- *Comparison* is useful when writing about a new topic that is in many ways similar to another, more familiar topic. For example, an online tutorial for a new operating system might compare that system to one that is familiar to the readers.
- *Division and classification* is useful for describing physical objects or structures with component parts. Use division and classification to explain each part's function and how all the parts work together. *Division* could be used to describe a physical object, such as the parts of a fax machine; *classification* could be used to organize individual components, such as a grouped listing of Web sites.
- *Spatial development* describes the physical appearance of an object from top to bottom, inside to outside, front to back, and so on. A crime scene report might start at the site of the crime and proceed in concentric areas from that point.
- *Cause-and-effect development* begins with either the cause or the effect of an event. For example, if you were reporting on an airplane disaster, you might start your report with the causes and lead up to the crash itself. Conversely, you might start with the crash and trace the events back to the cause. This approach can also be used to develop a report that offers a solution to a problem, beginning with the problem and moving on to the solution, or vice versa.
- *General-to-specific development* proceeds from general information to specific details. If you are writing about a new software product, for example, you might begin with a general statement of the function of the total software package, then explain the functions of the major routines in the package, and finally describe the functions of the various subroutines.
- *Specific-to-general development* begins with specific information and builds to a general conclusion. For example, you might describe a software problem in a minor application, leading to a larger, more global problem with the software.
- *Order-of-importance development* presents a sequence that reflects the relative importance of each detail. The information can be presented in either decreasing or increasing order of importance. For example, you might explain the decision-making responsibilities in a company by discussing the executive staff first and the temporary support staff last, with all other personnel categories arranged in decreasing order of importance within that company.

Methods of development often overlap—rarely does a writer rely on only one method. Nevertheless, you should select one primary method of development and base your outline on it, and then subordinate any other methods to it. For example, in describing the organization of a company, you could use elements from three methods of development. You could divide the larger topic (the company) into departments, arrange the departments by their order of importance within the company, and present their operations sequentially.

During organization, you must consider a design and layout that will be helpful to your reader and a format appropriate to your subject and purpose. If you intend to include visuals, plan them as you complete your outline, especially if they need to be prepared by someone else while you are writing and revising the draft. See also Tab 2, "Business Writing Forms and Documentation" (page 49) and Tab 6, "Format and Visuals" (page 183).

outlining

An outline—the skeleton of the document you are going to write—provides structure to your writing by ensuring that it has a beginning (introduction), a middle (main body), and an end (conclusion). An outline gives your writing coherence so that one part flows smoothly to the next. See also **coherence** (page 256) and **transition** (page 277).

Types of Outlines

Two types of outlines are most common: short topic outlines and lengthy sentence outlines. A *topic outline* consists of short phrases arranged in your primary method of development. (See also **organization,** page 27.) A topic outline is especially useful for short documents such as letters, emails, or memos. See also **correspondence** (page 128).

On a large writing project, create a topic outline first and then use it as a basis for creating a sentence outline. A *sentence outline* summarizes each idea in a complete sentence that may become the topic sentence for a paragraph in the rough draft. If most of your notes can be shaped into topic sentences for paragraphs in your rough draft, you can be relatively sure that your document will be well organized.

Creating an Outline

When you are outlining large and complex subjects with many pieces of information, the first step is to group related notes into categories. Sort the notes by major and minor division headings. (See also **note-taking,** page 26). Use an appropriate method of development to arrange items and label them with Roman numerals. For example, the major divisions for this discussion of outlining could be as follows:

I. Advantages of outlining
II. Types of outlines
III. Creating an outline

The second step is to establish your minor points by deciding on the minor divisions within each major division. Arrange them using a method of development under their major division and label them with capital letters.

II. Types of outlines
  A. Topic outlines
  B. Sentence outlines

Division and Classification

III. Creating an outline
  A. Establish major and minor divisions.
  B. Sort notes by major and minor divisions.
  C. Complete the sentence outline.

Sequential

You will often need more than two levels of headings. If your subject is complicated, you may need three or four levels of headings to better organize all of your ideas in proper relationship to one another. In that event, use the following numbering scheme:

I. First-level heading
  A. Second-level heading
    1. Third-level heading
      a. Fourth-level heading

The third step is to mark each of your notes with the appropriate Roman numeral and capital letter. Organize the notes logically within each minor heading, and mark each with the appropriate sequential Arabic number. As you do, make sure your organization is logical and your headings have parallel structure. For example, all the second-level headings under "III. Creating an outline" are complete sentences in the active voice. See **voice** (page 236).

Treat illustrations as an integral part of your outline, and plan approximately where each should appear. At each place, either include a rough sketch of the visual or write "illustration of . . ." As with other information in an outline, feel free to move or delete illustrations. See also Tab 6, "Format and Visuals."

The outline samples shown earlier use a combination of numbers and letters to differentiate the various levels of information. You could also use a decimal numbering system, such as the following, for your outline.

1. FIRST-LEVEL HEADING
    1.1 Second-level heading
    1.2 Second-level heading
        1.2.1 Third-level heading
        1.2.2 Third-level heading
            1.2.2.1 Fourth-level heading
            1.2.2.2 Fourth-level heading
        1.3 Second-level heading
2. FIRST-LEVEL HEADING

This system should not go beyond the fourth level because the numbers get too cumbersome beyond that point. In many documents, the decimal numbering system is carried over from the outline to the final version of the document for ease of cross-referencing sections.

Create your draft by converting your notes into complete sentences and paragraphs. If you have a complete sentence outline, the most difficult part of the writing job is over. However, whether you have a topic or a sentence outline, remember that an outline is not set in stone; it may need to change as you write the draft, but it should always be your point of departure and return.

paragraphs 

A paragraph performs three functions: (1) it develops the unit of thought stated in the topic sentence; (2) it provides a logical break in the material; and (3) it creates a visual break on the page, which signals a new topic.

Topic Sentence

A topic sentence states the paragraph's main idea; the rest of the paragraph supports and develops that statement with carefully related details. The topic sentence is often the first sentence because it tells the reader what the paragraph is about.

- *The cost of training new employees is high.* In addition to the cost of classroom facilities and instructors, an organization must pay employees a salary to sit in the classroom while they are learning. We have determined that for the company to break even on professional employees, they must stay in the job for which they have been trained for at least one year.

On rare occasions, the topic sentence logically falls in the middle of a paragraph.

- . . . [It] is time to insist that science does not progress by carefully designed steps called "experiments," each of which has a well-defined beginning and end. *Science is a continuous and often a disorderly and accidental process.* We shall not do the young psychologist any favor if we agree to reconstruct our practices to fit the pattern demanded by current scientific methodology.

  —B. F. Skinner, "A Case History in Scientific Method"

The topic sentence is usually most effective early in the paragraph, but a paragraph can lead up to the topic sentence, which is sometimes done to achieve **emphasis** (page 259).

- Energy does far more than simply make our daily lives more comfortable and convenient. Suppose you wanted to stop—and reverse—the economic progress of this nation. What would be the surest and quickest way to do it? Find a way to cut off the nation's oil resources! . . . The economy would plummet into the abyss of national economic ruin. *Our economy, in short, is energy-based.*

  —*The Baker World* (Los Angeles: Baker Oil Tools)

Paragraph Length

Paragraph length should aid the reader's understanding of ideas. A series of short, undeveloped paragraphs can indicate poor organization and sacrifice unity by breaking a single idea into several pieces. A series of long paragraphs, however, can fail to provide the reader with manageable subdivisions of thought. A paragraph should be just long enough to deal adequately with the subject of its topic sentence. A new paragraph should begin whenever the subject changes significantly. Occasionally, a one-sentence paragraph is acceptable if it is used as a transition between larger paragraphs or in letters and memos, in which one-sentence openings and closings are appropriate. See also **introductions** (page 16) and **conclusions** (page 6).

Writing Paragraphs

Careful paragraphing reflects the writer's logical organization and helps the reader follow the writer's thoughts. A good working outline makes it easy to group ideas into appropriate paragraphs. (See also **outlining,** page 29.) Notice how the following partial topic outline plots the course of the subsequent paragraphs:

TOPIC OUTLINE (PARTIAL)

I. Advantages of Chicago as location for new facility
   A. Transport infrastructure
      1. Rail
      2. Air

    3. Truck
    4. Sea (except in winter)
  B. Labor supply
    1. Engineering and scientific personnel
      a. Many similar companies in the area
      b. Several major universities
    2. Technical and manufacturing personnel
      a. Existing programs in community colleges
      b. Possible special programs designed for us

RESULTING PARAGRAPHS

- Probably the greatest advantage of Chicago as a location for our new facility is its excellent transport facilities. The city is served by three major railroads. Both domestic and international air cargo service is available at O'Hare International Airport; Midway Airport's convenient location adds flexibility for domestic air cargo service. Chicago is a major hub of the trucking industry, and most of the nation's large freight carriers have terminals there. Finally, except in the winter months when the Great Lakes are frozen, Chicago is a seaport, accessible through the St. Lawrence Seaway.

  Chicago's second advantage is its abundant labor force. An ample supply of engineering and scientific staff is assured not only by the presence of many companies engaged in activities similar to ours but also by the presence of several major universities in the metropolitan area. Similarly, technicians and manufacturing personnel are in abundant supply. The colleges in the Chicago City College system, as well as half a dozen other two-year colleges in the outlying areas, produce graduates with associate degrees in a wide variety of technical specialties appropriate to our needs. Moreover, three of the outlying colleges have expressed an interest in developing off-campus courses attuned specifically to our requirements.

Paragraph Unity and Coherence

A good paragraph has unity and coherence, as well as adequate development. *Unity* is singleness of purpose, based on a topic sentence that states the core idea of the paragraph. When every sentence in the paragraph develops the core idea, the paragraph has unity. See also **unity** (page 279).

Coherence is holding to one point of view, one attitude, one tense; it is the joining of sentences into a logical pattern. (See also **coherence,** page 256.) A careful choice of transitional words ties ideas together and thus contributes to coherence in a paragraph as shown here. Notice how the underlined words tie together the ideas in the following paragraph:

TOPIC SENTENCE *Over the past several months, I have heard complaints about the Merit Award Program. Specifically,* many employees feel that this program should be linked to annual *salary increases.* They believe that *salary increases* would provide a much better incentive than the current $500 to $700 cash awards for exceptional service. *In addition,* these *employees believe* that their supervisors consider the cash awards a satisfactory alternative to salary increases. Although I don't think this practice is widespread, the fact that the *employees believe* that it is justifies a reevaluation of the Merit Award Program.

Simple enumeration (*first, second, then, next,* and so on) also provides effective transition within paragraphs. Notice how the underlined words and phrases give coherence to the following paragraph. See also **transition** (page 277).

- Most adjustable office chairs have nylon tubes that hold metal spindle rods. To keep the chair operational, lubricate the spindle rods occasionally. *First,* loosen the set screw in the adjustable bell. *Then* lift the chair from the base. *Next,* apply the lubricant to the spindle rod and the nylon washer. *When you have finished,* replace the chair and tighten the set screw.

paraphrasing

Paraphrasing is restating or rewriting in your own words the essential ideas of another writer. Because the paraphrase does not quote the source word for word, quotation marks are not necessary. However, paraphrased material should be credited because the *ideas* are taken from someone else. The following example is an original passage explaining the concept of object blur. The paraphrased version restates the essential information of the passage in a form appropriate for a report.

ORIGINAL One of the major visual cues used by pilots in maintaining precision ground reference during low-level flight is that of object blur. We are acquainted with the object-blur phenomenon experienced when driving an automobile. Objects in the foreground appear to be rushing toward us, while objects in the background appear to recede slightly.

PARAPHRASED Object blur refers to the phenomenon by which observers in a moving vehicle report that foreground objects appear to rush at them, while background objects appear to recede slightly.

See also **ethics in writing** (page 261), **note-taking** (page 26), **plagiarism** (page 73), and **quotations** (page 83).

persuasion

Persuasive writing attempts to convince the reader to adopt the writer's point of view or take a particular action. Much workplace writing uses persuasion to reinforce ideas that readers already have, to convince readers to change their current ideas, or to lobby for a particular suggestion or policy. You may find yourself pleading for safer working conditions, justifying the expense of a new program, or writing a proposal for a large purchase. See also **audience/readers** (page 3), **proposals** (page 78), and **purpose/objective** (page 41).

In persuasive writing, the way you present your ideas is as important as the ideas themselves. You must support your appeal with logic and a sound presentation of facts, statistics, and examples. Avoid ambiguity: Do not wander from your main point, and above all never make false claims. You should also acknowledge any real or potentially conflicting opinions; doing so allows you to anticipate and overcome objections and builds your credibility. See also **ethics in writing** (page 261).

The memo shown in Figure 1–8 was written by an MIS administrator to persuade a staff to accept and participate in a change to a new computer system. Notice that not everything in this memo is presented in a positive light. Change brings disruption, and the writer acknowledges that fact.

A writer also gains credibility, and thus persuasiveness, through the readers' impressions of the document's appearance. For this reason, consideration of a document's **layout and design** (page 196) is important. See also **résumés** (page 166) and **promotional writing** (page 39).

Memo

TO: Engineering Sales Staff
FROM: Bernadine Kovak, MIS Administrator BK
DATE: April 8, 20--
SUBJECT: Plans for Changeover to NRT/R4 System

As you all know, our workload has jumped by 30 percent in the past month. It has increased because our customer base and resulting technical support services have grown dramatically. This growth is a result, in part, of our recent merger with Datacom.

This growth has meant that we have all experienced the difficulty of providing our customers with up-to-date technical information when they need it. In the next few months, we anticipate that the workload will increase another 20 percent. Even a staff as experienced as ours cannot handle such a workload without help.

To cope with this expansion, we will install in the next month the NRT/R4 mainframe and QCS enterprise software with Web-based applications and global sales and service network. This system will speed processing dramatically and give us access to all relevant company-wide databases. It should enable us to access the information both we and our customers need.

The new system, unfortunately, will cause some disruption at first. We will need to transfer many of our existing programs and software applications to the new format. And all of us need to learn to navigate in the R4 and QCS environments. However, once we have made these adjustments, I believe we will welcome the changes.

I would like to put your knowledge and experience to work in getting the new system into operation. Let's meet in my office to discuss the improvements on Friday, April 12, at 1:00 P.M. I will have details of the plan to discuss with you. I'm also eager to get your comments, suggestions, and—most of all—your cooperation.

FIGURE 1–8. Persuasive Memo

point of view

Point of view is the writer's relation to the information presented, as reflected in the use of grammatical person. The writer usually expresses point of view in first-, second-, or third-person personal pronouns. (See also **person,** page 331.) Use of the first person indicates that the writer is a participant or observer. Use of second or third person indicates that the writer is giving directions, instructions, or advice, or writing about other people or something impersonal.

FIRST PERSON	*I* scrolled down to find the settings option.
SECOND PERSON	Scroll down to find the settings option and double-click. [*You* is understood.]
THIRD PERSON	*He* scrolled down to the settings option.

Consider the following sentence, revised from an impersonal to a more personal point of view. Although the meaning of the sentence does not change, the revision indicates that people are involved in the communication.

- *I regret* ~~It is regrettable~~ that *we cannot accept* the equipment shipped on the 12th ~~is unacceptable~~.

Many people think they should avoid the pronoun *I* in their on-the-job writing. Such practice, however, leads to awkward sentences with people referring to themselves in the third person as *one* or as *the writer* instead of as *I*.

- *I believe* ~~The writer believes~~ that this project will be completed by the end of June.

However, do not use the personal point of view when an impersonal point of view would be more appropriate or more effective. This technique emphasizes the subject matter over the writer or the reader.

PERSONAL	I received objections to my proposal from several of your managers.
IMPERSONAL	Several managers have raised objections to the proposal.

In the example, it does not help to personalize the situation; in fact, the impersonal version may be more tactful.

TIPS: STATING AN OPINION

In some cultures, stating an opinion in writing is considered impolite or unnecessary, but in North American writing, readers expect to see a writer's opinion stated clearly and explicitly. The opinion should be followed by specific examples to help the reader understand the writer's point of view.

Whether you adopt a personal or an impersonal point of view depends on the purpose and the readers of the document. For example, in an informal email to an associate, you would most likely adopt a personal point of view. However, in a report to a large group, you would probably emphasize the subject by using an impersonal point of view.

- The evidence suggests that the absorption rate is too fast.

In letters on company stationery, use of the pronoun *we* may be interpreted as reflecting company policy, whereas *I* clearly reflects personal opinion. Which pronoun to use should be decided according to whether the matter discussed in the letter is a corporate or an individual concern.

- *I* understand your frustration with the price increase, but *we* must now include the import tax.

preparation

The preparation stage of the writing process is essential. By determining your readers' needs, your primary purpose, and your scope of coverage, you understand the information you will need to gather during research. During preparation, you also need to consider the appropriate medium.

Writer's Checklist: Preparing to Write

☑ Determine who your readers are and learn certain key facts about them — their knowledge, attitudes, and needs relative to your subject.

☑ Determine the document's primary purpose: What exactly do you want your readers to know, believe, or be able to do when they have finished reading your document?

☑ Establish the scope of your document — the type and amount of detail you must include — by considering any external constraints, such as word limits for trade journal articles or the space limitations of Web page design, and by understanding your purpose and readers' needs. See also **Web page design** (page 238).

☑ Consider the appropriate medium for your message.

See also **selecting the medium** (page 45) and "Five Steps to Successful Writing" (page xiii).

process explanation

Many kinds of workplace writing explain a process, an operation, or a procedure. A process explanation describes the steps that a mechanism or system uses to accomplish a certain result, such as the steps necessary to form a corporation. In your opening, present a brief overview of the process or let readers know why it is important for them to become familiar with the process you are explaining. Be sure to define terms that readers might not understand and provide illustrations to clarify the process. See also **visuals** (page 205).

In describing a process, transitional words and phrases create unity within paragraphs, and headings often mark the transition from one process to the next. Notice in the following example how obtaining a company tuition refund is described as a step-by-step process.

Tuition Refund Process

1. PROCEDURES
   - 1.1 Degree Approval
     - 1.1.1 An employee who meets school requirements and is interested in receiving tuition refunds should gain the approval of his or her manager and submit the request to the Human Resources Department. Human Resources may ask the manager to justify, in writing, the benefits of approving the degree request if the reason is not obvious.
     - 1.1.2 After agreement has been reached, the employee should complete Sections I and II of Form F-6970. After Human Resources has obtained two levels of management approval, it approves the employee's enrollment in the degree program.
     - 1.1.3 The employee who has been granted approval must complete Sections I and II of Form F-6970 when registering for each course required for the degree.

See also **transition** (page 277).

promotional writing

Promotional writing is vital to the success of any company or organization; high-quality, state-of-the-art products or services are of little value if customers and clients do not know they exist. The specific types of promotional writing discussed in this book include **brochures** (page 51),

newsletters (page 71), **proposals** (page 78), **sales letters** (page 149), and Web pages. See **Web page design,** page 238, and **writing for the Web,** page 246.

Although you may not work in marketing or public relations departments, you may be called on to prepare promotional (or marketing) materials, especially if you work for a small organization or are self-employed. Even at a large company, you may be asked to help prepare a brochure, a Web page, or a department newsletter.

Several elements are central to promotional writing. First, like most documents, understanding your audience is central (see **audience/readers,** page 3). For promotional writing, analyzing the needs, interests, concerns, and makeup of your audience is crucial.

Second, you must understand the principles of **persuasion** (page 35) because good promotional writing must gain attention, build interest, reduce resistance, and motivate readers to act. Because readers are persuaded only if they believe the source is credible, you need to be aware of **ethics in writing** (page 261) and possible **logic errors** (page 266) in your document.

Third, promotional writing needs to make information both easy to find and visually appealing. That means you need to make the most effective use of **organization** (page 27) as well as **layout and design** (page 196). You need to select the most appropriate **visuals** (page 205) and integrate them with the text.

Fourth, you need to make sure your writing has **coherence** (page 256) and **conciseness** (page 257). No matter how attractive the design, if readers don't understand the message, you will not achieve your **purpose/objective** (page 41). To make information accessible, of course, you must thoroughly understand the product or service you are promoting—to do so may require **research** (page 42).

Keep in mind that many other documents described in this book often include the additional or secondary purpose of promoting an organization. For example, **adjustment letters** (page 121), which are usually concerned with resolving a specific problem, offer opportunities to promote your organization. Likewise, **progress and activity reports** (page 75) provide an opportunity to promote the value of your work in an organization.

proofreading

Computer grammar checkers and spellcheckers, while a boon to proofreading, can make writers overconfident. If a typographical error results in a legitimate English word (for example, *coarse* instead of *course*), the spellchecker will not flag the misspelling. Therefore, you still must proofread your work carefully—both on your monitor and on paper. See also **spelling** (page 348).

Proofread your work in several stages. Read through the material four times: three times to check specific items each time and a final time to check for accuracy. See also **revision** (page 44).

Writer's Checklist: Proofreading

During the first reading, ask yourself, "Does it look right?" Look for the following:

☑ Aesthetic placement of material on the page; see **layout and design** (page 196)

☑ Acceptable format, as for a letter or memo; see also **correspondence** (page 128)

☑ Correct spelling of names and places

☑ Accuracy of **numbers** (page 384)

☑ Correct usage; see Tab 10, "Usage" (page 284)

During the second reading, ask, "Am I following the rules?" Check for these items:

☑ Typographical errors

☑ Capitalization; see **capital letters** (page 348)

☑ Accurate **abbreviations** (page 363)

☑ Punctuation; see Tab 12, "Punctuation and Mechanics" (page 362)

☑ General **spelling** (page 348)

☑ Correct grammar; see Tab 11, "Grammar" (page 306)

During the third reading, ask, "Is the text complete?" Look for the following:

☑ Omitted or deleted words, letters, or numbers

☑ Incomplete Web or email addresses and the like

When you read the document the final time, check to make certain that everything is there, that it is correct, and that it is in the right place. See the chart of proofreader's marks (facing inside back cover).

purpose / objective

What do you want your readers to know, believe, or do when they have read your document? When you answer that question, you have determined the primary purpose, or objective, of your document. Too often, beginning writers state their purposes too broadly. A purpose such as "to explain a fax machine" is too general to be helpful to you as you write. In contrast, "to instruct the reader how to use a fax machine to send and retrieve faxes" is a specific purpose that will help you focus on what you need your document to accomplish.

However, a writer's primary purpose is often more complex than simply to explain something. To fully understand this complexity, ask yourself not only *why* you are writing the document but *what* you want to influence your reader to believe or do after reading it. Suppose a writer for a newsletter has been assigned to write an article about cardiopulmonary resuscitation (CPR). In answer to the question *what,* the writer could state the purpose as "to show the importance of CPR." To the question *why,* the writer might respond, "to encourage employees to sign up for evening classes." Putting the answers to the two questions together, the writer's purpose might be stated as, "To write a document that will show the importance of CPR and encourage employees to sign up for evening classes." Note that the purpose of the document on CPR was not only to persuade the readers of the importance of CPR but also to motivate them to sign up for the classes. Secondary goals often involve such abstract notions as motivating, persuading, reassuring, or inspiring your reader. See also **persuasion** (page 35).

If you answer the questions *what* and *why* and put the answers into writing as a stated purpose that includes both primary and any secondary goals, you will simplify your writing task and achieve your purpose. Remember that even a specific purpose is of no value unless you keep it in mind as you work. Be careful not to lose sight of your purpose as you become engrossed in the other steps of the writing process. See also "Five Steps to Successful Writing" (page xiii).

research

Research is the process of investigation—the discovery of facts. To be focused, research must be preceded by preparation, especially consideration of your readers, purpose, and scope. See "Five Steps to Successful Writing" (page xiii).

In an academic setting, your preparatory resources include conversations with your peers, instructors, and especially your research librarian. On the job, your main resources are your own knowledge and experience and that of your colleagues. In this setting, begin by brainstorming with colleagues about what sources will be most useful to your topic and how you can track them down.

Primary Research

Primary research is the gathering of raw data compiled from interviews, direct observation, surveys and questionnaires, experiments, recordings, and the like. In fact, direct observation and interaction are the only ways to obtain certain kinds of information, such as behavior, certain natural phenomena, and the operation of systems and equipment.

If you are planning research that involves observation, choose your sites and times carefully, and be sure to obtain permission in advance. During your observations, remain as unobtrusive as possible, and keep accurate, complete records that indicate date, time of day, duration of the observation, and so on. Save interpretations of your observations for future analysis. Be aware that observation can be valuable research, but it may also be time-consuming, complicated, and expensive, and you may inadvertently influence the subjects you are observing.

You may want to conduct primary research to test the usability of written instructions that you have created. First, using the instructions, try to perform the task yourself and create a rough outline of your experience. After you write a draft, have someone unfamiliar with the task test your instructions by using them to operate the equipment or perform the procedure. If the tester has a problem, rewrite the passage until it is clear and easy to follow.

Secondary Research

Secondary research is the gathering of information that has been analyzed, assessed, evaluated, compiled, or otherwise organized into accessible form. Sources include books, articles, reports, Web documents, email discussions, business letters, minutes of meetings, operating manuals, brochures, and so forth. The entries **Internet research** (page 10) and **library research** (page 20) provide strategies for finding and evaluating these sources.

Research Strategies

As you seek information, keep in mind that the more recent the information, the better. Articles in periodicals and newspapers are very current sources because they are published frequently. Academic, organizational, and governmental Web sites can be good sources of current information about recent research or works in progress and can include interviews, articles, papers, and conference proceedings. Be sure to consider authorship and other aspects of a text or document as outlined in the Writer's Checklists: Evaluating Library Resources (page 26) and Evaluating Internet Resources (page 14). See also **documenting sources** (page 54), **paraphrasing** (page 34), and **plagiarism** (page 73).

When a resource seems useful, read it carefully, and take notes that include any additional questions about your topic. Some of your questions may eventually be answered in other sources; those that remain unanswered can guide you to further research. For example, you may discover that you need to talk with an expert. See **interviewing for information** (page 15), **listening** (page 212), and **note-taking** (page 26).

revision

The more natural a piece of writing seems to the reader, the more effort the writer has probably put into its revision. If possible, put your draft away for a day or two before you begin to revise it. If that is not possible, take a break from your writing and try to do something else before you revise. Without such a cooling period, you are too close to the draft to evaluate it objectively.

When you return to revise your draft, read and evaluate it primarily from the point of view of your readers. Be determined to find and correct faults—be objective.

Do not try to revise everything at once. Read through your draft several times, each time searching for and correcting a different set of problems.

Writer's Checklist: Revising Your Draft

- ☑ *Completeness.* Does the document achieve its primary purpose? Will it fulfill the readers' needs? Your writing should give readers exactly what they need but not overwhelm them.
- ☑ *Appropriate introduction.* Check to see that your introduction frames the rest of the document and accounts for any other revisions. See **introductions** (page 16).
- ☑ *Accuracy.* No matter how careful you may have been in conducting your research, compiling your notes, and creating your outline, you could easily have made errors when transferring your thoughts from the outline to the draft. Look for any inaccuracies that may have crept into your draft.
- ☑ *Unity and coherence.* Check to see that sentences and ideas are closely tied together and contribute directly to the main idea expressed in the topic sentence of the paragraph. Provide transitions where they are missing and strengthen those that are weak. See also **coherence** (page 256), **paragraphs** (page 31), and **unity** (page 279).
- ☑ *Consistency.* Make sure that both your visual elements and use of language are consistent. (See also **layout and design,** page 196.) Do not call the same item by one term on one page and an alternative term on another page.
- ☑ *Conciseness.* Tighten your writing so that it says exactly what you mean. Prune unnecessary words, phrases, sentences, and even paragraphs. See **conciseness/wordiness** (page 257).
- ☑ *Awkwardness.* Look for awkward passive-voice constructions; the active voice makes your writing more direct. See also **awkwardness** (page 252) and **voice** (page 356).

Writer's Checklist: Revising Your Draft (continued)

- ☑ *Word choice.* Delete or replace vague or pretentious words and unnecessary intensifiers. Check for **affectation** (page 251) and unclear pronoun references. See also **word choice** (page 280).
- ☑ *Ethical language.* Check for **ethics in writing** (page 261), including language that might be interpreted as implying bias against a particular group. See also **biased language** (page 252).
- ☑ *Jargon.* If you have any doubt that *all* your readers will understand any jargon you have used, eliminate it.
- ☑ *Clichés.* Replace clichés with fresh figures of speech or direct statements.
- ☑ *Grammar.* Check your draft for possible grammatical errors. See Tab 11, "Grammar."
- ☑ *Typographical errors.* Check your final draft for typographical errors with your spellchecker, then proofread your draft. See also **spelling** (page 348) and **proofreading** (page 40).

scope

Scope is the depth and breadth of detail needed to cover a subject. Determine the scope during the preparation stage of the writing process; even though you may refine it later. Your readers' needs and your primary purpose determine the kind of information and the amount of detail you will need to include. Defining your scope will expedite your research.

Your scope will also be affected by the type of document you are writing as well as the medium you select for your message. For example, government agencies often prescribe the general content and length for proposals and some organizations set limits for the length of memos and email. See **selecting the medium** (below) and "Five Steps to Successful Writing" (page xiii).

selecting the medium

Early in your preparation, you must select the most appropriate medium for communicating your message. You can choose from such recent technologies as email, fax, voice mail, and videoconferencing to more traditional means such as letters and memos, telephone calls, and face-to-face meetings.

The most important considerations in selecting the medium are audience expectations and the purpose of the communication. For example, if you need to collaborate with someone to solve a problem or need to establish rapport, written exchanges (even by email) may be far less efficient than a phone call or a face-to-face meeting. However, if you need precise wording or a record of a complex message, communicate in writing. Following are descriptions of typical means of communicating on the job. Understanding their primary characteristics will help you select the most appropriate medium.

Letters on Organizational Stationery

Letters are often the most appropriate choice for initial contacts with new business associates or customers and for other formal communications. Letters written on your organization's letterhead communicate formality, respect, and authority. See also **correspondence** (page 128).

Memos

Memos on printed company stationery are appropriate for internal communication among members of the same organization, even when offices are geographically separated. They have many of the same characteristics as letters, such as formality and authority, but they are used for a wider variety of functions—from reminders to short reports. The use of memos must follow an organization's protocol. See **memos** (page 143).

Email

Email can replace letters and memos or deliver them as attachments. It can be a less formal medium to send information, elicit discussions, collect opinions, and transmit many other kinds of messages quickly. Because email recipients can print copies of messages and attachments they receive and easily forward them to others, always write your email with care, and reread the message carefully before you send it. See **email** (page 233).

Faxes

A fax is most useful when speed is essential and when the information—a drawing or contract, for example—must be viewed in its original form. Faxes are also useful when the recipient does not have email or when the material is not available in electronic form. See **fax** (page 236).

Telephone Calls

The information exchanged through telephone calls can range from a brief call to answer a question to a lengthy call to negotiate or clarify the conditions of a contract. Because phone calls enable participants to interpret tone of voice, they can make it easier to resolve misunderstandings, although they do not provide the visual cues possible during face-to-face meetings.

A conference call among three or more participants is less expensive than a face-to-face meeting requiring travel. For efficiency, the person coordinating the call works from an agenda shared by all the participants and directs the discussion as though he or she were leading a meeting.

Voice Mail

Voice mail allows callers to leave a brief message ("Call me about the deadline for the new project," or "I got the package, so you don't need to call the distributor."). If the message is complicated or contains numerous details, use another medium, such as an email message or a letter. If you want to discuss a subject, let the recipient know the subject so he or she can prepare a response before returning your call. When you leave a message, give your name, phone number, the date, and time of the call.

Face-to-Face Meetings

Face-to-face meetings are most appropriate for initial contacts with associates and clients with whom you intend to develop an important, long-term relationship. Meetings may also be best for brainstorming, negotiating, solving a technical problem, or handling a controversial issue. For instructions on how to conduct meetings and record discussions and decisions, see **meetings** (page 214) and **minutes of meetings** (page 218).

Videoconferencing

Videoconferencing is particularly useful for meetings when travel is impractical. Unlike telephone conference calls, video conferences have the advantage of allowing participants to see as well as to hear one another. Video conferences work best with participants who are at ease in front of the camera.

writing a draft

You are well prepared to write a rough draft when you have established your purpose and readers' needs, defined your scope, completed adequate research, and prepared an outline (whether formal or informal). Writing a draft is simply transcribing and expanding the notes from your outline into paragraphs, without worrying about grammar, refinements of language, or spelling. Refinement will come with revision and proofreading. See "Five Steps to Successful Writing" (page xiii).

Writing and revising are different activities. Write a rough draft as though you were casually explaining your subject to someone. Do not let worrying about a good opening or transitions slow you down. Instead, concentrate on getting your ideas on paper. Do not try to polish or revise.

Even with good preparation, writing a draft can be a chore for many writers. Do not wait for inspiration to strike you—treat writing a rough draft as you would any other on-the-job task.

Writer's Checklist: Writing a Rough Draft

☑ Set up your writing area with the writing tools (paper, pens, computer, dictionary, sourcebooks, etc.) you will need to keep going once you get started. Then hang out the "Do Not Disturb" sign.

☑ The most effective way to start and keep going is to use a good outline as a springboard for your writing. See also **outlining** (page 29).

☑ As you write your draft, keep your readers' needs, expectations, and knowledge of the subject in mind. This will help you write directly to your reader and suggest which ideas need further development.

☑ When you are trying to write quickly and you come to something difficult to explain, try to relate the new concept to something with which the reader is already familiar, as discussed in **figures of speech** (page 263).

☑ Start with the section that seems easiest. Your reader will never know that the middle section of the document was the first section you wrote.

☑ Give yourself a set time (ten or fifteen minutes, for example) in which you write continuously, regardless of how good or bad your writing seems to be. The point is to keep writing.

☑ Don't let anything stop you when you are rolling along easily—if you stop and come back, you may lose momentum.

☑ Give yourself a small reward—a short walk, a soft drink, a brief chat with a friend, an easy task—after you have finished a section.

☑ Reread what you have written when you return to your writing. Seeing what you have written can return you to a productive frame of mind.

2

Business Writing Forms and Documentation

Preview

This section contains entries on various forms of business documents, including **proposals** and a number of typical **reports (investigative reports, progress and activity reports, trip reports,** and **trouble reports).** Because of their size and complexity, **formal reports** are covered in a separate section, beginning on page 96, which includes a SAMPLE FORMAL REPORT (page 102).

Also included in this section are **brochures** and **newsletters** – types of promotional writing that you may encounter on the job.

A number of entries will help you prepare business documents. Because business documents may require research that, in turn, must be cited, this section includes an entry on **documenting sources,** which serves as an important resource for citing sources by providing an explanation and numerous examples of both Modern Language Association (MLA) and American Psychological Association (APA) documentation styles. It also contains entries on **copyright, plagiarism,** and using **quotations.** In addition to a general entry on reports and entries on various types of reports, this section includes entries on **titles** and **bibliographies** – important individual parts of these documents.

bibliographies

A bibliography is an alphabetical list of books, articles, Web sources, and other materials that is often used to record the works consulted in preparing a document. This standardized list helps readers interested in getting further information on the topic or in assessing the scope of the research.

While a *works-cited list* (MLA) and a *list of references* (APA) refer to works actually cited in the text, a bibliography includes works consulted for general background information. For information on using both MLA and APA styles, see **documenting sources** (page 54).

Entries in a bibliography are listed alphabetically by the author's last name. If an author is unknown, the entry is alphabetized by the first word in the title (following *a, an,* or *the*). Entries also can be arranged by subject and then ordered alphabetically within those categories. An annotated bibliography includes complete bibliographic information about a work (author, title, publisher) followed by a brief description or evaluation of what the work contains.

See **formal reports** (page 96) for guidance on the placement of a bibliography in a report and **documenting sources** (page 54) for information on the style of bibliographic entries.

brochures

Brochures are printed publications that promote the products and services offered by a business or that promote the image of a business or organization by providing information important to the target audience. The goal of any brochure is to persuade. See **persuasion** (page 35).

There are two major types of brochures: *sales brochures* and *informational brochures.* Sales brochures are created specifically to sell a company's products and services. For example, a brochure for a cell phone company might describe the various phones and calling services available; a brochure for a consulting company would detail its seminars or specific services. Informational brochures are created to inform and educate the reader as well as to promote goodwill and raise the profile of the organization. For example, a health food company might create an informational brochure that shows the reader how to clean fruits and vegetables before they are eaten and offers healthful recipes; a psychiatric hospital might create a brochure describing how to recognize depression in teenagers.

Before you begin to write, you must decide on the specific purpose of your brochure—to sell a product? to provide information about a product? to describe a process? You must also identify your target audience—general reader? expert? potential client? Understanding your purpose and audience is crucial to creating content and design that will be both rhetorically appropriate and persuasive to your target audience.

The main goal of the cover panel of a sales brochure is to gain the attention of your target audience. The cover panel, which should clearly identify the company being promoted, usually features a carefully selected visual image geared toward the interests of your audience. Accompanying the image, there may be a minimal amount of text—for example, a statement about the company's mission and success, or a brief promotional quotation from a satisfied customer.

The first inside panel of the sales brochure should again identify the company and attract the reader with headlines and brief, readable content, such as that used in advertising. Figure 2–1 shows the first inside panel of a sales brochure for a real estate firm. Notice that the introductory text positions CREC as a well-established, experienced company with a solid client base. The text that follows the introduction poses a question from the reader's point of view—Why CREC?—and answers that question with brief text that is laid out effectively, using headings and white space.

In subsequent panels of your brochure, describe your product or service with your readers' needs in mind, clearly stating the benefits and solutions to problems that your product offers. Include relevant and accurate supporting facts and visuals, and you might further establish credibility with a company history, board members' credentials, a list of clients, and brief quotations or testimonials. Use subheadings and bullet points to break up the text and make the brochure easy to read. In the final panel, be clear about the action you want the reader to take, such as calling for an appointment or sending in the enclosed reply card.

When finalizing the design for your brochure, refer to your rough planning sketch. To find the best way to present your content, experiment with margins, spacing, and the arrangement and amount of text on each panel (you may want to make changes to content or length, based on concerns of layout). Be sure there is adequate white space for readability. Experiment with various fonts and formatting of fonts, such as enlarging the first letter of the first word in a paragraph, but do not overdo the use of unusual fonts or alternative styles (running type vertically, for example). Choose a style that unifies your brochure, and use it consistently throughout. Be judicious about color choices. For some brochures, black and white is cheaper and more effective; in other circumstances (such as brochures for travel) color, though more expensive, is a must. Depending on your budget and the scale of your project, consider using a professional printer.

CREC . . .
The **C**orporate **R**eal **E**state **C**onnection

CREC, established in 1962, has a long tradition of serving corporate America. Well known for our relationship-based services, over eighty percent of our business is derived from repeat customers. Our brokers have an average of more than 18 years of experience in the corporate real estate business and are capable of managing local and national office and industrial projects. Current clients include Bell Computers, American Rent-A-Car, and RayTrust National Bank.

Why CREC?

CREC understands that you need an agent who is looking out for you and your business. One who understands the need for honesty, experience and professionalism. Our brokers meet these standards.

✔ HONESTY
Our agents will act above board and keep you out of potential legal entanglements.

✔ EXPERIENCE
Our agents are familiar with the CBD and suburban markets in their respective areas and will be able to show you those properties most suited to your needs.

✔ PROFESSIONALISM
Our agents are members of NAR (National Association of Realtors) and continuously keep themselves updated with additional courses and training.

FIGURE 2-1. Sales Brochure (First Inside Panel)

copyright

The Copyright Act protects all original works from the moment of their creation, regardless of whether they are published or even contain a notice of copyright (©). However, all works created by U.S. government agencies are in the public domain—that is, they are not copyrighted—and can be used without prior approval. For information on the Copyright Act, visit the Library of Congress copyright Web site (lcweb.loc.gov/copyright/).

Writer's Checklist: Using Copyrighted Materials

- ☑ In general, give credit to any source from which material is taken, unless it is boilerplate or common knowledge, as described in **plagiarism** (page 73). See also **documenting sources** (page 54).
- ☑ A small amount of material from a copyrighted source may be used without permission or payment as long as the use satisfies the fair-use criteria, as described at the Library of Congress Web site (lcweb.loc.gov/copyright/).
- ☑ Copyright law applies to electronic works just as it does to their print counterparts. Web pages that are copyrighted include the symbol © and provide information on terms of use.
- ☑ If you plan to reproduce or further distribute copyrighted works posted on the Internet, you must obtain permission from the copyright holder, unless the fair-use provision of copyright law applies to your intended use. To obtain permission, read the site's terms-of-use information and email your request to the appropriate party. As with printed works, document the source of all materials (text, graphics, tables) obtained.
- ☑ Any work first published after March 1, 1989, receives copyright protection regardless of whether it bears a notice of copyright. Works published before March 1, 1989, without a notice of copyright are in the public domain.

documenting sources

Documenting sources achieves three important purposes. First, it allows readers to locate and consult the sources used and to find further information on the subject. Second, documentation enables writers to support their assertions and arguments in such documents as proposals, reports, and trade-journal articles. Finally, by identifying where they obtained facts, ideas, **quotations** (page 83), and paraphrases and by giving proper credit to others, writers avoid **plagiarism** (page 73). See also **bibliographies** (page 51) and **copyright** (page 53).

This entry describes two principal systems for documenting sources, one developed by the Modern Language Association (MLA) and the other by the American Psychological Association (APA). Samples of formats appear at the end of each discussion.

MLA-Style Parenthetical Documentation

MLA style includes two main components: parenthetical documentation within the text of a paper and a works-cited list at the end of a paper. The MLA method is detailed in the *MLA Handbook for Writers of*

Research Papers (fifth edition) and the *MLA Style Manual and Guide to Scholarly Publishing* (second edition). MLA parenthetical documentation gives a brief citation of the author and relevant page numbers (in parentheses within the text). The following examples show parenthetical citations using MLA style.

- As Peterson writes, preparing a videotape of measurement methods is cost effective and can expedite training (151).
- The results of these studies have led even the most conservative managers to adopt technologies that will "catapult the industry forward" (Peterson, 183–91).

If the parenthetical citation refers to an indented quotation, place it outside the last sentence of the quotation, as shown.

- . . . a close collaboration with the physics and technology staff is essential. (Minsky 42)

If you are using more than one work by the same author, give the title of the work (or a shortened version if the title is long) in the parenthetical citation, unless you mention it in a signal phrase in the text. If, for example, you use more than one work by Thomas J. Peters, a proper parenthetical citation for his book *The Pursuit of Wow: Every Person's Guide to Topsy-Turvy Times* would appear as (Peters, *Pursuit* 93). Use only one space between the title and the page number.

Citation Format for Works Cited. The MLA works-cited list—a separate alphabetical section placed at the end of the paper and organized by authors' last names—includes full information about the sources cited within the text of the paper. The list should begin on the first new page following the end of the text. Each new entry should begin at the left margin, with the second and subsequent lines within an entry indented five spaces. Double-space within and between entries.

AUTHOR. List entries in alphabetical order by the author's last name (for multiple authors, begin with the last name of the first listed author). For multiple works by the same author, alphabetize the entries by the first major word of the title (following *a, an,* or *the*) and put three hyphens and a period in place of the author's name for the second and subsequent entries.

If the author is a corporation, alphabetize the entry by the name of the corporation. If the author is a government agency, alphabetize the entry by the government entity, followed by the individual agency. If no author is given, begin the entry with the title, alphabetized by the first significant word. If an editor and no author is given, alphabetize by the editor's name.

TITLE. The second element of the entry is the title of the work. Capitalize the first word of the title and each significant word thereafter. Underline the title of a book or pamphlet. Place quotation marks around the title of an article, an essay, or a published paper. The title should be followed by a period.

PERIODICALS. For an article in a journal, list the volume number, the date, and the page numbers immediately after the title of the periodical. For an article in a magazine or newspaper, omit the volume number.

SERIES OR MULTIVOLUME WORKS. For works in a series, give the name of the series and the series or volume number of the work after the title. If the edition used is not the first, specify the edition.

PUBLICATION INFORMATION. The final elements of the entry for a book, a pamphlet, or conference proceedings are the place of publication (city only, if well known), publisher, and date of publication. Use a shortened form of the publisher's name (for example, *Random* for Random House and *Oxford UP* for Oxford University Press). If publication information cannot be found in the work, use the abbreviations *n.p.* (no publication place), *n.p.* (no publisher), and *n.d.* (no date).

ONLINE SOURCES. Citations for online sources are similar to citations for printed sources. To cite an online source, begin with the author; title; date the source was posted (if available); and, if the information is also included in a printed version, publication information. Indicate the date the information was retrieved. Include in angle brackets the Web address (URL) or enough address information to allow the reader to retrieve the source. If you access an article from a database such as InfoTrac, for example, include that information in your citation (see the example on page 58). Personal communications, such as email messages, follow the format for letters and interviews, with URL information provided.

Standards continue to evolve for citations of online and electronic sources. When citing online information, keep in mind that the two primary goals are to give credit to the author and, whenever possible, to enable readers to retrieve the source. See MLA's Web site for up-to-date information on citing online sources (www.mla.org).

Sample Entries (MLA Style)

BOOKS

Single Author

Hassab, Joseph C. <u>Systems Management: People, Computers, Machines, Materials</u>. New York: CRC, 1997.

Multiple Authors

Testerman, Joshua O., Thomas J. Kuegler, Jr., and Paul J. Dowling, Jr. Web Advertising and Marketing. 2nd ed. Roseville, CA: Prima, 1998.

Corporate Author

Ernst and Young. Ernst and Young's Retirement Planning Guide. New York: Wiley, 1999.

Edition Other Than First

Estes, Jack C., and Dennis R. Kelley. McGraw-Hill's Interest Amortization Tables. 3rd ed. New York: McGraw, 1998.

Multivolume Work

Standard and Poor. Standard and Poor's Register of Corporations, Directors and Executives. 3 vols. New York: McGraw, 1998.

Work in an Edited Collection

Gueron, Judith M. "Welfare and Poverty: Strategies to Increase Work." Reducing Poverty in America: Views and Approaches. Ed. Michael R. Darby. Thousand Oaks: Sage, 1996. 237-55.

Encyclopedia or Dictionary Entry

Gibbard, Bruce G. "Particle Detector." World Book Encyclopedia. 1999 ed.

ARTICLES IN PERIODICALS (*See also* Electronic Sources that follows)

Magazine Article

Coley, Don. "Compliance for the Right Reasons." Business Geographics June 1997: 30-32.

Journal Article

Rossouw, G. J. "Business Ethics in South Africa." Journal of Business Ethics 16 (1997): 1539-47.

Newspaper Article

Mathews, Anna Wilde. "The Internet Generation Taps into Morse Code." Wall Street Journal 1 Oct. 1997, natl. ed.: B1+.

Article with Unknown Author

"American City Adds Nashville, Memphis." Business Journal 26 Sept. 1997: 16.

ELECTRONIC SOURCES

An Entire Web Site

Association for Business Communication. Association for Business Communication. Aug. 1999. 20 Apr. 2001 <http://www.theabc.org/>.

A Short Work from a Web Site, with an Author

Locker, Kitty O. "The History of the Association for Business Communication." Association for Business Communication. 25 Oct. 1995. 20 Apr. 2001 <http://www.theabc.org/history.htm>.

A Short Work from a Web Site, with a Corporate Author

General Motors. "Company Profile." General Motors. 2001. 19 Apr. 2001 <http://www.gm.com/company/corp_info/profiles/>.

A Short Work from a Web Site, with an Unknown Author

"Forgotten Inventors." Forgotten Inventors. 2001. PBS Online. 19 Apr. 2001 <http://www.pbs.org/wgbh/amex/telephone/sfeature/index.htm>.

Article from a Database

Goldbort, Robert C. "Scientific Writing as an Art and as a Science." Journal of Environmental Health, 63.7 (2001). Expanded Academic ASAP. InfoTrac. Salem State Coll. Lib., Salem, MA. 19 Apr. 2001.

Article in an Online Periodical

Ray, Tiernan. "Waiting for Wireless." SmartMoney.com 18 Apr. 2001. 19 Apr. 2001 <http://www.smartmoney.com/techmarket/index.cfm?story=20010418>.

Publication on CD-ROM

Money 99. CD-ROM. Redmond: Microsoft, 1998.

Email Message

Kahl, Jonathan D. "Re: Web page." E-mail to the author. 2 Oct. 2001.

MULTIMEDIA SOURCES (Print and Electronic)

Map or Chart

Wisconsin. Map. Chicago: Rand, 2000.

"Asia." Map. Maps.com. 2000. 20 Apr. 2001 <http://www.maps.com/explore/atlas/political/asia.html>.

Film or Video

Massingham, Gordon, dir., and Jane Christopher, ed. Introduction to Hazardous Chemicals. Video cassette. Edgartown: Emergency Film Group, 1998.

Lawrence, Detrick, dir. Emergency Film Group: Homepage Web Video. 2001. 20 Apr. 2001 <http://www.efilmgroup.com/video1.rm>.

Radio or Television Program

"Do Americans Really Want a Tax Cut?" CNN: Crossfire. Host Robert Novak. CNN. 16 Apr. 2001.

"Energy Supplies." All Things Considered. Host Emily Harris. Natl. Public Radio. WGBH, Boston. 3 Apr. 2001. 20 Apr. 2001 <http://www.npr.org/programs/atc/>.

OTHER SOURCES

Published Inteview

Gates, Bill. "The View from the Very Top." Interview. Newsweek 17 Apr. 2000: 36–39.

Personal Interview

Sariolgholam, Mahmood. Personal Interview. 29 Nov. 2000.

Personal Letter

Viets, Hermann. Letter to all students, fac., and staff. University of Wisconsin, Milwaukee. 1 Sept. 1998.

Brochure or Pamphlet

Library of Congress. U.S. Copyright Office. Copyright Registration for Online Works. Washington: GPO, 1999.

Government Document

United States Dept. of Energy. The Energy Situation in the Next Decade. Technical Pub. 11346–53. Washington: GPO, 1998.

Report

Bertot, John Carlo, Charles R. McClure, and Douglas L. Zweizig. The 1996 National Survey of Public Libraries and the Internet: Progress and Issues: Final Report. Washington: GPO, 1996.

APA-Style Parenthetical Documentation

APA style includes two main components: parenthetical documentation within the text of a paper and a reference list at the end of a paper. The APA method is described in the *Publication Manual of the American Psychological Association* (fifth edition) and is augmented at the APA Web site (www.apa.org/journals/webref.html). APA parenthetical documentation gives a brief citation—in parentheses—of the author, year of publication, and relevant page numbers. The following passages contain sample APA parenthetical citations.

- World War II was the occasion of radar's first application in warfare, and Great Britain led the way in radar research (Butrica, 2000).

- According to Butrica (2000), the use of radar as an offensive and defensive warfare agent made World War II "the first electronic war" (p. 2).
- The so-called first electronic war (Butrica, 2000, p. 2) was fought as much in the research laboratory as on the battlefield.

When APA parenthetical citations are added in midsentence, place them after the closing quotation marks and continue with the rest of the sentence. If the APA parenthetical citation follows a block quotation, place it after the final punctuation mark.

If you are using more than one work by the same author published in the same year, add the lowercase letters a, b, c, and so forth, to the year in both the reference-list entries and the text citations: (Ostro, 1993b, p. 347). When a work has two authors, cite both names joined by an ampersand: (Hey & Walters, 1997). For the first citation of a work with up to five authors, include all names. For subsequent citations, include only the name of the first author followed by *et al.* When two or more works by different authors are cited in the same parentheses, list the citations alphabetically and use semicolons to separate the citations: (Hey & Walters, 1997; Ostro, 1993a). The references cited in the examples are listed alphabetically, as follows, in a reference list.

> Hey, T., & Walters, P. (1997). *Einstein's mirror.* Cambridge, England: Cambridge University Press.
>
> Ostro, S. J. (1993a). Planetary radar astronomy. *Reviews of Modern Physics, 65,* 1235–1279.
>
> Ostro, S. J. (1993b). Radar astronomy. In S. P. Parker & J. M. Pasachoff (Eds.), *McGraw-Hill encyclopedia of astronomy* (pp. 347–348). New York: McGraw-Hill.

Citation Format for Reference List. The APA reference list—a separate alphabetical section placed at the end of the paper—includes full information about the sources cited within the text of the paper. The reference list should begin on the first new page following the end of the text. Each new entry should begin at the left margin, with the second and subsequent lines indenting five spaces from the left margin. (Your instructor may require you to use a paragraph indent instead. If so, begin at a paragraph indent, with subsequent lines continuing at the left margin.)* Double-space within and between entries.

---

*The APA now uses a hanging indent as shown above and in the examples shown on pages 62–65.

AUTHOR. List entries in alphabetical order by the author's last name (for multiple authors, alphabetize beginning with the name of the first author listed). Give the author's surname followed by a comma and initials only. Works by the same author should be listed chronologically according to the year of publication, from earlier to later dates. If the author is a corporation, alphabetize the entry by the name of the corporation; if the author is a government agency, alphabetize the entry by the government entity that published the work. If no author is given, begin the entry with the title, alphabetized by the first significant word. If an editor but no author is given, alphabetize by the editor's name, followed by *Ed.* (or *Eds.*) in parentheses.

PUBLICATION DATE. The second element of the entry is the work's date of publication. Place the copyright date or the date of publication in parentheses. For periodicals other than journals, include the year, a comma, and the month, week, or day. Place a period after the parentheses. For journals and books, give only the year.

TITLE. Give the title of the work after the date of publication. For titles of articles, chapters, or books, capitalize only the first word of the title and the subtitle and any proper names. Italicize titles of books, but do not italicize or use quotation marks for titles of articles or chapters. Follow the title with a period.

PERIODICALS. For an article in a periodical (journal, magazine, or newspaper), give the title of the periodical in upper- and lowercase letters. The volume number and the page numbers should immediately follow the periodical title. Separate the elements by commas and end with a period. Italicize the periodical title, the volume number, and the comma that follows the volume number.

SERIES OR MULTIVOLUME WORKS. For works in a series, the series number of the work follows the title. For multivolume works, the number of volumes follows the title. If the edition is not the first, specify the edition.

PUBLISHING INFORMATION. The final elements of the entry for any print work are the place of publication (city only, if well known) and the publisher. Use a shortened form of the publisher's name when possible and abbreviate names of associations, corporations, and university presses. Omit terms such as *Publisher, Co.,* and *Inc.,* but do not omit or abbreviate the words *Books* and *Press.*

ONLINE SOURCES. When citing online sources, begin with the author, the date of publication if available, and the title, just as for printed sources. At the end of the reference, indicate the retrieval date and the complete URL or the name of the online database so that interested readers can find the source.

APA style calls for you to cite personal communications, such as email messages and bulletin-board postings, in the text only—not in the reference list. Include the communicator's initials and surname and the date: (J. D. Kahl, personal communication, October 2, 20--).

Standards continue to evolve for citations of online and electronic sources. When citing online information, keep in mind that the two primary goals are to give credit to the author and to allow the reader to find the source. For updates on APA style, visit the APA Web site (http://www.apa.org/journals/webref.htm).

Sample Entries (APA Style)

BOOKS

Single Author

Hassab, J. C. (1997). *Systems management: People, computers, machines, materials.* New York: CRC Press.

Multiple Authors

Testerman, J. O., Kuegler, T. J., Jr., & Dowling, P. J., Jr. (1998). *Web advertising and marketing* (2nd ed.). Rocklin, CA: Prima.

Corporate Author

Ernst and Young. (1999). *Ernst and Young's retirement planning guide.* New York: Wiley.

Edition Other Than First

Estes, J. C., & Kelley, D. R. (1998). *McGraw-Hill's interest amortization tables* (3rd ed.). New York: McGraw-Hill.

Multivolume Work

Standard and Poor. (1998). *Standard and Poor's register of corporations, directors and executives* (Vols. 1-3). New York: McGraw-Hill.

Work in an Edited Collection

Thorne, K. S. (1997). Do the laws of physics permit wormholes for interstellar travel and machines for time travel? In Y. Terzian & E. Bilson (Eds.), *Carl Sagan's universe* (pp. 121-134). Cambridge, England: Cambridge University Press.

Encyclopedia or Dictionary Entry

Gibbard, B. G. (1997). Particle detector. In *World Book encyclopedia* (Vol. 15, pp. 186-187). Chicago: World Book.

ARTICLES IN PERIODICALS (*See also* Electronic Sources that follows)

Magazine Article

Coley, D. (1997, June). Compliance for the right reasons. *Business Geographics, 12,* 30-32.

Journal Article

Rossouw, G. J. (1997). Business ethics in South Africa. *Journal of Business Ethics, 16,* 1539-1547.

Newspaper Article

Mathews, A. W. (1997, October 1). The Internet generation taps into Morse code. *Wall Street Journal,* pp. B1, B7.

Article with Unknown Author

American City adds Nashville, Memphis. (1997, September 26). *The Business Journal,* p. 16.

ELECTRONIC SOURCES

An Entire Web Site

The APA recommends that at minimum, a reference to a Web source should provide a document title or description, a date (of the publication or retrieval of the document), an address (URL) that links directly to the document or section, and an author, whenever possible. On the rare occasion that you need to cite multiple pages of a Web site (or the entire site), provide a URL that links to the site's home page.

Association for Business Communication. (2001). Retrieved April 20, 2001, from http://www.theabc.org

A Document on a Web Site, with an Author

Locker, K. O. (1995). *The history of the association for business communication.* Retrieved April 20, 2001, from the Association for Business Communication Web site: http://www.theabc.org/history.html

A Document from a Web Site, with a Corporate Author

General Motors. (2001). *Company profile.* Retrieved April 20, 2001, from http://www.gm.com/company/corp_info/profiles/

A Document from a Web Site, with an Unknown Author

Forgotten inventors. (2001). PBS Online. Retrieved April 19, 2001, from http://www.pbs.org/wgbh/amex/telephone/sfeature/index.html

Article or Other Work from a Database

Goldbort, R. C. (2001, March). Scientific writing as an art and as a science. *Journal of Environmental Health, 63*(7). Retrieved April 19, 2001, from Expanded Academic ASAP database.

Article in an Online Periodical

Tiernen, R. (2001, April 18). Waiting for wireless. *SmartMoney.com.* Retrieved April 19, 2001, from http://www.smartmoney.com/techmarket/index.cfm?story=20010418

Email

Personal communications (including email, discussion groups, and messages from electronic bulletin boards) are not cited in an APA reference list. They can be cited in the text as follows: "According to J. D. Kahl (personal communication, October 2, 2001), Web pages need to reflect. . . ."

Publication on CD-ROM

Money 99. (1997). [CD]. Redmond: Microsoft.

MULTIMEDIA SOURCES (Print and Electronic)

Map or Chart

Asia. (2001). Maps.com [Map]. Retrieved April 20, 2001, from http://www.maps.com/explore/atlas/political/asia.html

Wisconsin. (2000). [Map]. Chicago: Rand.

Film or Video

Lawrence, D. (Director), & Christopher, J. (Editor). (2001). *Emergency film group video.* [Video cassette]. Retrieved April 20, 2001, from http://www.efilmgroup.com/video1.rm

Massingham, G. (Director), & Christopher, J. (Editor). (1998). *Introduction to hazardous chemicals.* [Motion picture]. Edgartown, MA: Emergency Film Group.

Radio or Television Program

Norris, R. (Host). (2001, April 3). Energy supplies. [Radio broadcast]. *All things considered.* Boston: WGBH, National Public Radio. Retrieved April 20, 2001, from http://www.npr.org/programs/atc

Novack, R. (Host). (2001, April 16). Do Americans really want a tax cut? [Television broadcast]. *CNN: Crossfire.* Washington, DC: CNN.

OTHER SOURCES

Published Inteview

Gates, B. (2000, April 17). The view from the very top. [Interview]. *Newsweek, 135,* 36–39.

Personal Interview and Letters

Personal communications (including telephone conversations) are not cited in a reference list. They can be cited in the text as follows: "According to J. D. Kahl (personal interview, October 2, 2001), Web pages need to reflect. . . ."

Brochure or Pamphlet

Library of Congress. U.S. Copyright Office. (1999). *Copyright registration for online works* [Brochure]. Washington, DC: U.S. Government Printing Office.

Government Document

U.S. Department of Energy. (1998). *The energy situation in the next decade* (Technical Publication No. 11346-53). Washington, DC: U.S. Government Printing Office.

Report

Bertot, J. C., McClure, C. R., & Zweizig, D. L. (1996). *The 1996 national survey of public libraries and the Internet: Progress and issues: Final report.* Washington, DC: U.S. Government Printing Office.

Style Manuals

Many professional societies, publishing companies, and other organizations publish manuals that prescribe bibliographic reference formats for their publications or publications in their fields. In addition, several general style manuals are well known and widely used.

Specific Areas

American Chemical Society. *ACS Style Guide: A Manual for Authors and Editors.* 2nd ed. Washington, D.C.: American Chemical Society, 1998. See also www.oup-usa.org/j778/isbn/0841234620.html.

American Medical Association. *American Medical Association Manual of Style.* 9th ed. Baltimore: Williams, 1998.

American Psychological Association. *Publication Manual of the American Psychological Association.* 5th ed. Washington, D.C.: American Psychological Association, 2001. See also (www.apa.org/journals/webref.html).

Council of Science Editors. *Scientific Style and Format: The CBE Manual for Authors, Editors, and Publishers*. 6th ed. New York: Cambridge University Press, 1994. See also (www.councilscienceeditors.org).

General

The Chicago Manual of Style. 14th ed. Chicago: University of Chicago Press, 1993. See also (www.press.uchicago.edu/Misc/Chicago/cmosfaq.html).

Gibaldi, J. *MLA Handbook for Writers of Research Papers*. 5th ed. New York: Modern Language Association of America, 1999.

Gibaldi, J. *MLA Style Manual and Guide to Scholarly Publishing.* 2nd ed. New York: Modern Language Association of America, 1998. See also (www.mla.org).

National Information Standards Organization. *Scientific and Technical Reports—Elements, Organization, and Design*. Bethesda, Md.: National Information Standards Organization, 1995. ANSI Z39.18-1995. See also (www.niso.org).

Skillin, M. E., and R. M. Gay. *Words into Type*. 3rd ed. Englewood Cliffs, N.J.: Prentice, 1974.

feasibility reports

When organizations plan to undertake a new project—develop a new product or service, expand a customer base, purchase new equipment, or consider a move—they first try to determine the project's chances for success. A feasibility report presents evidence about the practicality of a proposed project based on specific criteria. For example: Is new construction or development necessary? Is sufficient staff available? What are the costs involved? What are the legal or other special requirements? Based on the findings of this analysis, the writer recommends whether the project should be carried out.

Before beginning to write a feasibility report, state clearly and concisely the primary purpose of the study: "The purpose of this study is to determine the best ways to expand our Pacific Rim operations."

Report Sections

Every feasibility report should contain an introduction, a body, a conclusion, and a recommendation. See also **proposals** (page 78) and **formal reports** (page 96).

Introduction. The introduction states the purpose of the report, describes the circumstances that led to the report, and includes any pertinent background information. It may also discuss the scope of the report and any procedures or methods used in the analysis of alternatives, and it notes any limitations of the study. See also **introductions** (page 16).

Body. The body of the report presents a detailed evaluation of all the alternatives under consideration. Evaluate each alternative according to specific criteria, such as cost, availability of staff and financing, and other relevant requirements, separating the subsections with headings, if needed.

Conclusion. The conclusion summarizes the evaluation of alternatives and usually points to one alternative as the best or most feasible. See also **conclusions** (page 6).

Recommendation. This section clearly presents the writer's opinion on which alternative best meets the criteria as summarized in the conclusion.

Typical Feasibility Report

Consider a scenario in which an engineering consulting firm needs to upgrade its computer system and Internet capability. The staff might conduct a feasibility study to determine the hardware and software that would best meet their requirements. The staff will evaluate the alternatives according to the organization's established requirements. Figure 2–2 shows how a feasibility report might be organized.

Introduction
The purpose of this report is to determine which of two proposed options would best enable ACM Technology Consulting to upgrade its mainframe computer system and its Internet capacity to meet its increasing data and communication requirements.

Background. In October 20--, the Information Development and Technical Support Group at ACM put the MISSION System into operation. Since then, the volume of processing transactions has increased fivefold (from 1,000 to 5,000 updates per day). This increase has severely impaired system response time; in fact, average response time has increased from less than 10 seconds to 120 seconds. Further, our new Web-based client services system has increased exponentially the demand for processing speed and access capacity.

Scope. Two alternative solutions to provide increased processing capacity have been investigated: (1) purchase of a new ARC 98 processor to supplement the first, and (2) purchase of an HRS 60/EP with PRS enterprise software and expandable peripherals to replace the current ARC 98. The two alternatives are evaluated here according to cost and, to a lesser extent, according to expanded capacity for future operations.

Purchasing a Second ARC 98 Processor
This alternative would require additional annual maintenance costs, salary for an additional computer specialist, increased energy costs, and a one-time construction cost for necessary remodeling as well as installing Internet and other connections.

Annual maintenance costs	$35,000
Annual costs for computer specialist	75,000
Annual increased energy costs	7,500
Annual operating costs	$117,500
Construction cost (one-time)	50,000
Total first-year cost	$167,500

The costs for the installation and operation of another ARC 98 processor are expected to produce savings in system reliability and readiness.

System Reliability. A second ARC 98 would reduce current downtime periods from four to two per week. Downtime recovery averages 30 minutes and affects 40 users. Assuming that 50 percent of users require the system at a given time, we determined that the following reliability savings would result:

2 downtimes × 0.5 hours × 40 users × 50%
× $12.00/hour overtime × 52 weeks = $12,480 (annual savings)

FIGURE 2–2. Feasibility Report

Conclusion
A comparison of costs for both systems indicates that the HRS 60/EP would cost $2,200 more in first-year costs.

ARC 98 Costs	
Net additional operating	$56,300
One-time (construction)	50,000
First-year total	$106,300
HRS 60/EP Costs	
Net additional operating	$84,000
One-time (facility)	24,500
First-year total	$108,500

Installation of a second ARC 98 processor would permit the present information-processing systems to operate relatively smoothly and efficiently. It would not, however, provide the expanded processing capacity that the HRS 60/EP processor would for implementing new subsystems required to increase processing speed and Internet access.

Recommendation
The HRS 60/EP processor should be purchased because of the long-term savings and because its additional capacity and flexibility will allow for greater expansion in the future.

FIGURE 2–2. Feasibility Report *(continued)*

2. Business Writing Forms and Documentation

investigative reports

Investigative reports may be written for a variety of reasons—most often in response to a request for information. You might be asked, for instance, to research the Web sites of competing companies in your industry or to conduct an opinion survey among your customers. An investigative report gives a precise analysis of a topic and offers conclusions and recommendations.

Open the report with a statement of its primary and (if any) secondary purposes, then define the scope of your investigation. (See also **purpose/objective,** page 41, and **scope,** page 45.) If the report is on a survey of opinions, indicate the number of people surveyed, income categories, occupations, and other identifying information. Include any information that is pertinent in defining the extent of the investigation. Then report your findings and, if necessary, discuss their significance. End the report with your conclusions and any recommendations. An example of an investigative report is shown in Figure 2–3.

Memo

To: Noreen Rinaldo, Training Manager
From: Charles Lapinski, Senior Instructor *CL*
Date: February 14, 20--
Subject: Adler's Basic English Program

As requested, I have investigated Adler Medical Instruments' (AMI's) Basic English Program to determine whether we might adopt a similar program.

The purpose of AMI's program is to teach medical technologists outside the United States who do not speak or read English to understand procedures written in a special 800-word vocabulary called *Basic English.* This program eliminates the need for AMI to translate its documentation into a number of different languages. The Basic English Program does not attempt to teach the medical technologists to be fluent in English but, rather, to recognize the 800 basic words that appear in Adler's documentation.

Course Requirements

The course does not train technologists. Students must know, in their own language, what a word like *hemostat* means; the course simply teaches them the English term for it. As prerequisites, students must have basic knowledge of their specialty, must be able to identify a part in an illustrated parts book, must have used AMI products for at least one year, and must be able to read and write in their own language.

Students are given an instruction manual, an illustrated book of equipment with parts and their English names, and pocket references containing the 800 words of the Basic English vocabulary plus the English names of parts. Students can write the corresponding word in their language beside the English word and then use the pocket reference as a bilingual dictionary. The course consists of 30 two-hour lessons, each lesson introducing approximately 27 words. No effort is made to teach pronunciation; the course teaches only recognition of the 800 words, which include 450 nouns, 70 verbs, 180 adjectives and adverbs, and 100 articles, prepositions, conjunctions, and pronouns.

Course Outcomes

The 800-word vocabulary enables the writers of documentation to provide medical technologists with any information that might be required because the subject areas are strictly limited to usage, troubleshooting, safety, and operation of AMI medical equipment. All nonessential words (such as *apple, father, mountain,* and so on) have been eliminated, as have most synonyms (for example, *under* appears, but *beneath* does not).

Conclusions

I see two possible ways in which we could use some or all of the elements of AMI's Program: (1) in the preparation of our student manuals or (2) as AMI uses the program.

I think it would be unnecessary to use the Basic English methods in the preparation of manuals for *all* of our students. Most of our students are English speakers to whom an unrestricted vocabulary presents no problem.

As for our initiating a program similar to AMI's, we could create our own version of the Basic English vocabulary and write our instructional materials in it. Because our product lines are much broader than Adler's, however, we would need to create illustrated parts books for each of the different product lines.

FIGURE 2–3. Investigative Report

newsletters

Newsletters are publications that are designed to inform and to create and sustain interest and membership in an organization. They can also be used to sell products and services.

There are two main types of newsletters: *organizational newsletters* and *subscription newsletters*. Organizational newsletters are sent to employees or members of an association to keep them informed about issues regarding their company or group, such as the development of new products or new policies, or the accomplishments of individuals or teams. Stories included in organizational newsletters can also be created to call members to take a specific action. For example, a health club's newsletter could detail new equipment to be installed and explain how to use it. See also **persuasion** (page 35) and **promotional writing** (page 39).

Subscription newsletters are designed to attract and build a readership interested in buying specific products or services or in learning more about investing or financial matters. Here subscribers are buying information and they expect a certain level of value for their money. For example, a person with experience in the stock market could create a financial newsletter and charge subscribers a monthly fee for the investing advice in that newsletter; a person who collects movie memorabilia could create an online newsletter that includes stories about ways to find and sell rare movie posters.

When planning a newsletter, first decide on its specific purpose and the specific audience you will be targeting; then make sure that your plan for the newsletter's appearance and your editorial choices create a sense of identification among the readership.

You will need to acquire a mailing list (names and addresses of your readers), and you will need to decide on the most strategic way to get the newsletter to the readers, whether through interoffice mail, the post office, or online. Because it can be time consuming and technically problematic to send out hundreds or thousands of online newsletters by yourself, you may also need to subscribe to a list hosting service.

Before you begin to write, you need to research the topic and interview relevant sources. As you research in trade journals, business magazines, newspapers, or the Internet, find a specific angle for the article that will appeal to your select audience. Attempt to provide content that they won't read elsewhere. Other strategies include interviewing and profiling customers or your employees. Be aware that your fact-checking needs to be meticulous. Unlike the general readership of a newspaper, newsletter readers are often specialists in their fields.

As shown in Figure 2–4, a newsletter's format should be simple and consistent, yet visually appealing to your readership. Use the active voice and a conversational tone. Boldface names of customers or association members included in your articles to identify them and bring attention to their contributions. Use subheadings and bullet points to break up the text and make the newsletter easy to read. Keep your sentences simple and paragraphs short. See **conciseness/wordiness** (page 257), **tone** (page 276), and **voice** (page 356).

Using word-processing or desktop publishing software, create newspaper columns and one or two visuals per page that complement the text. On the front page, identify the organization, include the date and volume and issue numbers, and include a contents box. Depending upon the length and quantity of the text and photos or other visuals to be included, newsletters are usually 8½″ by 11″ or 17″ by 22″ pages folded in half. If your budget is generous and the scale of your project is substantial, you may want to work with a professional printer to produce your newsletter.

Independent Boutique Assoc. Newsletter *Vol. 2 No. 3 Spring 200X p. 2*

Forecasting This Fall's Fashions

By Sarah Nesmith

More than 75 members of the Independent Boutique Association attended the one-day workshop on future trends in independent retailing on February 23rd at the Grand Moret Hotel. Besides discussing new retailing software and hiring strategies, participants offered their forecasts for this fall's fashions. According to members, the focus this fall is on color, comfort, and classic tailoring.

Expect rich earth tones like camel, chocolate, and charcoal gray, as well as burgundy reds and mossy greens. "The bright colors of last fall have taken on deeper tones this year," says **Jessie Sary,** owner of Kouture.

Comfortable knit suits and longer, a-line skirts will also be popular, according to Sary. Based on what she saw in Milan, she also predicts that tailored, hip- and calf-length jackets will gain in popularity, and will be accessorized with simple jewelry and leather and fabric handbags.

Sary suggests that independent retailers be on the lookout for women's shoes that are narrower than last year's styles and classic in design. However, shoes and boots with chunky, platform heels continue to be the trend for teens and women in their early twenties.

Rebecca Dona, owner of Paragon, looks forward to offering comfortable stretch Capri pantsuits, fitted ribbed tops, and sleeveless cashmere sweaters for women.

"The emphasis is on tailoring," says Dona. "Women's clothing this fall should accent the silhouette and offer a mix and match versatility through the simplicity of their designs."

"Corporate casual is still in for men but expect a softer look under suits and solid colors," says **Mike Van Dermer,** associate manager of Blyers. An updated look in sports coats with four buttons, in the English style, will also be in this fall, worn with cashmere mock turtlenecks.

"There is a return to some very classic designs but with an updated look, subtle patterning, and softness of fabric, especially knits," adds **James Trady,** owner of Assent, Inc.

"The emphasis for children's clothes for the fall will also be on knits with an added focus on durable fabrics, such as denim and canvas," says **Terry Williams,** assistant manager of Hambshey's. Also, there is a general trend away from prominent logos on clothing.

Williams suggests stocking up on cotton and knit tees and more fitted canvas pants and jackets for kids. "And even though logos are out," adds Williams, "t-shirts and sweatshirts that tie in with movie products like *Galactica* and *Lizard Land* will, inevitably, be popular."

Kudos to **Brian Halifax,** owner of Hally's Hats, for organizing the workshop.

FIGURE 2–4. Newsletter Format

plagiarism

Plagiarism is the use of someone else's unique ideas without acknowledgment, or the use of someone else's exact words without quotation marks and appropriate credit. Plagiarism is considered to be the theft of someone else's creative and intellectual property and is not accepted in business, science, journalism, academia, and other fields. For detailed guidance on quoting correctly, see **quotations** (page 83).

In addition to quoting, you may paraphrase the words and ideas of another if you document your source. (See also **paraphrasing,** page 34, and **documenting sources,** page 54.) Although you do not enclose paraphrased ideas or materials in quotation marks, you must provide citations that indicate their sources. Paraphrasing a passage without citing the source is permissible only when the information paraphrased is common knowledge in a field. *Common knowledge* refers to information on a topic widely known and readily available in handbooks, manuals, atlases, and other references. If you intend to publish, reproduce, or distribute material that includes quotations from published works, you may need to obtain written permission from the copyright holder to do so.

In the workplace, employees often borrow from in-house manuals, reports, and other company documents. Using such "boilerplate" information is neither plagiarism nor a violation of copyright. See also **copyright** (page 53) and **ethics in writing** (page 261).

policies and procedures

A *policy* states an organization's position on a subject; a *procedure* provides instructions for carrying out the policy. They are often written at the same time, usually by top or middle managers. Policies and procedures are subjected to a careful review process (often by legal staff), mainly because they are considered to be a "bible" for management. Writing these documents requires careful thought and planning as well as precise language and word choice so that the policies and procedures are clear and understandable.

Policies

A statement of policy is often preceded by an explanation of the policy's purpose or rationale, as in the following policy regarding tuition refunds.

2. POLICY
   2.1 The Tuition Refund Plan is intended for all full-time staff.
   2.2 To receive a refund, an individual must be employed by the company at the time of enrollment and at the completion of the course. Should an individual's employment be terminated because of a reduction of staff, fees will be refunded for approved courses upon their satisfactory completion.
   2.3 Satisfactory completion means that the employee has completed the course work and has achieved a grade at least one level above passing. If a course is not satisfactorily completed, reimbursement may be deferred if the employee, upon completion of the degree, attains a cumulative grade average of at least C (B for most graduate-degree programs).

Procedures

Procedures provide a step-by-step explanation of how to carry out a policy. They provide instructions not only for employees but also for managers who must ensure that the company's policy is properly implemented.

To prepare for writing procedures, keep track of who must do what. An easy and effective way is to draw a vertical line down a notepad page. Label the left column "Actor" and the right "Directions." Under "Actor," list who must perform the action in each step; under "Directions," describe each step of the procedure. Describe each step fully and in the correct sequence. In effect, the list—which you may create as a chart, as shown below—serves as an outline for the procedure you will write.

ACTOR	DIRECTION
Employee	Determines his or her eligibility for degree program, gains approval of manager, and submits request to Human Resources Department.
Human Resources Department	Reviews request and, if reason is not obvious, asks manager to justify, in writing, the benefits of approving the degree program.
Employee	Completes Sections I and II of Form F-6970.
Human Resources Department	Sends form to the employee's supervisor and the head of the department for approval.

progress and activity reports

Progress and activity reports document ongoing activities. Progress reports are often used to report on major projects, whereas activity reports focus on the work of individual employees.

Progress Reports

A progress report provides information about a project—its status, whether it is on schedule and within budget, and so on. Progress reports are often submitted by a contracting company to a client company. They are used mainly for projects that involve many steps over a period of time and are issued at regular intervals to state what has been done and what remains to be done. Progress reports help keep projects running smoothly by helping managers assign work, adjust schedules, allocate budgets, and schedule supplies and equipment. All progress reports dealing with a particular project should have the same format.

The introduction to the first progress report should identify the project, any materials needed, and the project's completion date. Subsequent reports summarize the progress to date, include the status of schedules and costs, list the steps that remain to be taken, and conclude with recommendations about changes in the schedule, materials, and so on. Figure 2–5 shows the initial progress report submitted by a construction company to a client.

Activity Reports

Within an organization, employees often submit activity reports on the progress of ongoing projects. Managers may combine the activity reports (also called *status reports*) of several individuals or teams into larger activity reports and, in turn, submit those larger reports to their own managers.

Because the activity report is issued periodically (usually monthly) and contains material familiar to its readers, it normally needs no introduction or conclusion, although it may need a brief opening to provide context. (See also **introductions,** page 16.) Although format varies from company to company, the following sections are typical: *Current projects, Current problems, Plans for the next period,* and *Current staffing level* (for managers).

The activity report shown in Figure 2–6 was submitted by a manager of applications programs (Wayne Tribinski) who supervises 11 employees. The reader of the report (Kathryn Hunter) is Tribinski's manager and the Director of Engineering.

Hobard Construction Company
9032 Salem Avenue
Lubbock, TX 79409

www.hobardcc.com
(808) 769-0832
Fax: (808) 769-5327

August 17, 20--

Walter M. Wazuski
County Administrator
109 Grand Avenue
Manchester, NH 03103

Dear Mr. Wazuski:

The renovation of the County Courthouse is progressing on schedule and within budget. Although the cost of certain materials is higher than our original bid indicated, we expect to complete the project without exceeding the estimated costs because the speed with which the project is being completed will reduce overall labor expenses.

Costs
Materials used to date have cost $78,600, and labor costs have been $193,000 (including some subcontracted plumbing). Our estimate for the remainder of the materials is $59,000; remaining labor costs should not exceed $64,000.

Work Completed
As of August 15, we had finished the installation of the circuit-breaker panels and meters, of level-one service outlets, and of all subfloor wiring. The upgrading of the courtroom, the upgrading of the records-storage room, and the replacement of the air-conditioning units are in the preliminary stages.

Work Schedule
We have scheduled the upgrading of the courtroom to take place from August 25 to October 5, the upgrading of the record-storage room from October 6 to November 12, and the replacement of the air-conditioning units from November 15 to December 17. We see no difficulty in having the job finished by the scheduled date of December 23.

Sincerely yours,

Tran Nuguélen

Tran Nuguélen
ntran@hobardcc.com

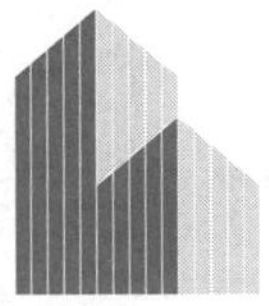

FIGURE 2–5. Progress Report

INTEROFFICE MEMO

Date: June 5, 20--
To: Kathryn Hunter, Director of Engineering
From: Wayne Tribinski, Manager, Applications Programs *WT*
Subject: Activity Report for May 20--

We are dealing with the following projects and problems, as of May 31.

Projects

1. For the *Software Training Mailing Campaign,* we anticipate producing a set of labels for mailing software training information to customers by June 10.
2. The *Search Project* is on hold until the PL/I training has been completed, probably by the end of June.
3. The project to provide a database for the *Information Management System* has been expanded in scope to provide a database for all training activities. We are rescheduling the project to take the new scope into account.

Problems

The *Information Management System* has been delayed. The original schedule was based on the assumption that a systems analyst who was familiar with the system would work on this project. Instead, the project was assigned to a newly hired systems analyst who was inexperienced and required much more learning time than expected.

Bill Michaels, whose activity report is attached, is correcting a problem in the *CNG Software.* This correction may take a week.

Plans for Next Month

- Complete the *Software Training Mailing Campaign.*
- Resume the *Search Project.*
- Restart the project to provide a database on information management with a schedule that reflects its new scope.
- Write a report to justify the addition of two software engineers to my department.
- Congratulate publicly the recipients of Meritorious Achievement Awards: Bill Thomasson and Nancy O'Rourke.

Current Staffing Level

Current staff: 11
Open requisitions: 0

FIGURE 2–6. Activity Report

proposals

A proposal is a document written to persuade someone to follow a plan or course of action. (See also **persuasion,** page 35.) You may need to send a proposal to those within your organization or to potential clients outside the organization.

Because a proposal offers a plan to fill a need, readers will evaluate your plan based on how well you answer their questions about what you are proposing to do, how and when you plan to do it, and how much it will cost. See also **audience/readers** (page 3).

To answer those questions satisfactorily, write a proposal aimed at your readers' level of knowledge. Because proposals often require more than one level of approval, take all of your readers into account. For example, if your primary reader is an expert on your subject, but his or her supervisor, who must also approve the proposal, is not, provide an executive summary written in nontechnical language. You might also include a glossary of terms used in the body of the proposal or an appendix that explains highly technical information in nontechnical language. If your primary reader is not an expert, but his or her supervisor is, write the proposal with the nonexpert in mind and include an appendix that contains the technical details. See also **appendixes** (page 95), **executive summaries** (page 95), and **glossaries** (page 101).

This entry discusses two typical types of proposals: internal and external (sales). See also **promotional writing** (page 39).

Internal Proposals

An internal proposal suggests a change or an improvement within an organization. For example, an internal proposal may recommend a change in the way something is being done, that something new be done, or that funding be authorized for a large purchase. An internal proposal, often in memo format, is sent to a superior in the organization who has the authority to accept or reject it.

In the opening of a proposal, establish that a problem exists that needs a solution or a benefit to be gained from a change—otherwise, your proposal will be unsuccessful. Notice how the proposal opening in Figure 2–7 states the benefit directly. See also **introductions** (page 16).

The body of a proposal should offer a specific and practical solution to the problem. When appropriate, include the following typical sections:

- Schedule (steps for completing the task)
- Resources (equipment, material, and staff requirements)
- Budget (breakdown of costs)

Consider the body of the proposal introduced in Figure 2–7.

HVS Accounting Services Memo

Date: May 13, 20--
To: Harriet V. Sullivan, President
From: Christine Thomas, Systems Administrator *CT*
Subject: The Advantages of Telecommuting to HVS Accounting Services

This memo presents the results of my research on telecommuting practices in our industry. Based on my findings and on the success of such programs elsewhere, I propose that HVS set up a work-at-home program on a three-month trial basis.

What Are the Advantages?
The greatest advantage to HVS is that overall employee productivity would very likely increase. I have reviewed a dozen trade-journal articles in our field and several Web sites that show average productivity gains of from 15 to 30 percent. In conversations with managers at competing companies, they mention gains in the 20 to 30 percent range.

Another important advantage is that telecommuting would help us to recruit and retain qualified employees. Companies report that telecommuting can save employees time and money; it can also reduce their stress levels, allowing them to better focus on their jobs. Our competitors also note that they have an easier time recruiting and retaining valuable employees when they offer telecommuting as an option. This is an important benefit that we can offer to our employees, especially in the current competitive job market.

How Will Telecommuting Work at HVS?
Any new program of this kind raises questions about how well it will work in practice. One key issue is keeping track of employees working away from the office. HVS is in an ideal position to benefit from telecommuting. Each member of the professional staff has well-defined tasks. As you know from our monthly reports, we currently maintain detailed information that quantifies staff productivity by billable hours. This system would apply equally to work-at-home employees. Additionally, we could set up and maintain measurable goals for those in the program. We would then review these goals in the middle and at the end of the three-month trial period with you.

As for cost, because all participating employees have home computers and Internet access, there are essentially no startup expenses for HVS for this trial program. Employees can keep bills and receipts for long-distance calls and other expenses and submit them for reimbursement.

Can We Protect Customer Information?
Customer confidentiality would also be protected. HVS has secure electronic information exchange software that allows us to send and receive confidential client information electronically. Those in the program can be given password access to confidential and other client information at home using pcEverywhere, their current remote-access software.

Can We Make It Happen?
Our staff has a proven record of getting the job done regardless of where they are working, which I believe makes them well suited to a work-at-home program. I look forward to discussing this option with you at your convenience.

FIGURE 2–7. Internal Proposal

The function of the conclusion in an internal proposal is to tie everything together, restate your recommendation, and close in a spirit of cooperation (offering to set up a meeting, supply additional information, or provide any other assistance that might be needed). Your conclusion should be brief, as in Figure 2–7.

External Proposals

The external (or sales) proposal, one of the major marketing tools in business and industry, is a company's offer to provide specific goods or services to a potential buyer. Your primary purpose as a proposal writer is to persuade a prospective customer that your products or services will solve a problem, improve operations, or offer other benefits.

External proposals vary greatly in size and formality. A short proposal of a page or two might bid for the construction of a single home; a proposal of moderate length might bid for the installation of a network of computer systems; and a very long proposal—written by a team of writers and hundreds of pages long—might be used to bid for the construction of a multimillion-dollar water-purification system.

Your first task as a writer is to find out exactly what your prospective customer needs and whether your organization can satisfy these needs. You must also be aware of what your competitors offer. Before preparing your proposal, compare your company's strengths with those of competing firms.

Unsolicited and Solicited Proposals. External proposals may be either unsolicited or solicited. Unsolicited proposals are not unusual. Companies and organizations often operate for years with a problem they have never recognized (poor inventory-control methods, for example) until an unsolicited proposal points it out.

Many unsolicited proposals are preceded by an inquiry to determine potential interest. Once you receive a positive response, you would conduct a detailed study of the prospective customer's needs to determine whether and how you can help. You would then prepare your proposal on the basis of your study—one that clearly identifies a problem, offers a potential solution, and emphasizes the potential benefits to the customer.

Solicited proposals are responses to requests for goods or services. Procuring organizations that would like competing companies to bid for a job commonly issue a request for proposals (RFP). An RFP is a tool that many companies and government agencies use to find the best method of doing a job and the most qualified company to do it. Normally, the RFP simply defines the basic work that the firm needs. It may also specify how the proposal should be submitted.

The procuring organization generally publishes its RFP in journals or on the Web; it also sends an RFP to select companies. Managers of companies interested in responding to a specific RFP present the data to their executive committee. If agreeable to the committee, the technical staff develops an approach to the work described in the RFP—a concept that is both feasible and profitable. The staff's concept is presented to the executive committee, which decides whether the company will present a proposal. If the decision is to proceed, the company prepares the proposal.

Short Sales Proposals. Even a short and uncomplicated sales proposal should be carefully planned and organized; it should include an introduction, a body, and a conclusion. The introduction should state the purpose and scope of the proposal. It should indicate the start and completion dates, the benefits of your approach, and the total cost of the project. The introduction could also refer to any previous positive association your company may have had with the potential customer.

The body should itemize the products and services you are offering, discuss the procedures and materials to be used, present a specific schedule for each stage of the project, and provide a breakdown of the costs of the project.

The conclusion should express your appreciation for the opportunity to submit the proposal and your confidence in your company's ability to do the job. It should review any advantages your company has over its competitors. It should also specify the time period during which your proposal can be considered a valid offer. If any supplemental materials, such as blueprints or price sheets, accompany the proposal, include a list of them at the end of the proposal. Figure 2–8 shows a typical short sales proposal.

Long Sales Proposals. While the short sales proposal is typically divided into the introduction, body, and conclusion, the long sales proposal contains more parts to accommodate the increased variety of information it represents. The long sales proposal may include some or all of the following sections:

- Transmittal (or cover letter)
- Title page
- Executive summary
- Product description
- Rationale
- Cost analysis
- Delivery schedule
- Site preparation
- Training requirements
- Statement of responsibilities
- Description of vendor
- Institutional sales pitch
- Conclusion
- Appendixes

The cover letter should express your appreciation for the opportunity to submit your proposal and acknowledge any previous positive

PROPOSAL
TO LANDSCAPE THE NEW CORPORATE HEADQUARTERS
OF THE
WATFORD VALVE CORPORATION

Submitted to: Ms. Tricia Olivera, Vice-President
Submitted by: Jerwalted Nursery, Inc.
Date Submitted: February 1, 20--

Introduction

Jerwalted Nursery, Inc., proposes to landscape the new corporate headquarters of the Watford Valve Corporation, on 1600 Swanson Avenue, at a total cost of $14,871. The lot to be landscaped is approximately 600 feet wide and 700 feet deep. Landscaping will begin no later than April 30, 20--, and will be completed by May 31.

The following trees and plants will be planted, in the quantities and sizes given and at the prices specified.

Body

4 maple trees (not less than 7 ft.) @ $110 each—$440
41 birch trees (not less than 7 ft.) @ $135 each—$5,535
2 spruce trees (not less than 7 ft.) @ $175 each—$350
20 juniper plants (not less than 18 in.) @ $15 each—$300
60 hedges (not less than 18 in.) @ $12 each—$720
200 potted plants (various kinds) @ $12 each—$2,400

Total Cost of Plants = $ 9,745
Labor = $ 5,126
Total Cost = $14,871

Conclusion

All trees and plants will be guaranteed against defect or disease for a period of 90 days, the warranty period to begin June 1, 20--.

The prices quoted in this proposal will be valid until June 30, 20--.

Thank you for the opportunity to submit this proposal. Jerwalted Nursery has been in the landscaping and nursery business in the St. Louis area for 30 years, and our landscaping has won several awards and commendations, including a citation from the National Association of Architects. We are eager to put our skills and knowledge to work for you, and we are confident that you will be pleased with our work. If we can provide any additional information or assistance, please call.

FIGURE 2–8. Short Sales Proposal

association with the customer. Then it should summarize the recommendations offered in the proposal and express your confidence that they will satisfy the customer's needs. Some long sales proposals include a conclusion that summarizes the proposal's salient points and stresses your company's main strengths. Appendixes can be used to include statistical analyses, maps, charts, tables, and personal biographies of key staff.

quotations 

Using direct and indirect quotations is an effective way to make or support a point. However, avoid the temptation to overquote during the note-taking phase of your research; concentrate on summarizing what you read. When you do use a quotation (or an idea of another writer), cite your source properly. If you do not, you will be guilty of **plagiarism** (page 73). For specific details on MLA and APA citation styles, see **documenting sources** (page 54).

Direct Quotations

A direct quotation is a word-for-word copy of the text of an original source. Choose direct quotations (which can be of a word, a phrase, a sentence, or, occasionally, a paragraph) carefully and use them sparingly. Direct quotations are enclosed in quotation marks and separated from the rest of the sentence by a comma or colon.

- The economist stated, "Regulation cannot supply the dynamic stimulus that in other industries is supplied by competition."

When a quotation is divided, the material that interrupts the quotation is set off, before and after, by commas, and quotation marks are used around each part of the quotation.

- "Regulation," he said in a recent interview, "cannot supply the dynamic stimulus that in other industries is supplied by competition."

Indirect Quotations

An indirect quotation is a paraphrased version of an original text. It is usually introduced by the word *that* and is not set off from the rest of the sentence by punctuation marks. (See also **paraphrasing,** page 34.)

- In a recent interview he said that regulation does not stimulate the industry as well as competition does.

Deletions or Omissions

Deletions or omissions from quoted material are indicated by three ellipsis dots (. . .) within a sentence and a period plus three ellipsis dots (. . . .) at the end of a sentence.

- "If monopolies could be made to respond . . . we would be able to enjoy the benefits of . . . large-scale efficiency. . . ."

If you are following the MLA guidelines, enclose the ellipses in brackets. When a quoted passage begins in the middle of a sentence rather than at the beginning, ellipsis dots are not necessary; the fact that the first letter of the quoted material is not capitalized tells the reader that the quotation begins in midsentence.

- Rivero goes on to conclude that "coordination may lessen competition within a region."

Inserting Material into Quotations

When it is necessary to insert a clarifying comment within quoted material, use brackets.

- "The industry is organized as a large system serving an extensive [geographic] area, with smaller systems existing as islands within the larger system's sphere of influence."

When quoted material contains an obvious error or might be questioned in some other way, the expression *sic* (Latin for "thus"), in italic type and enclosed in brackets, follows the questionable material to indicate that the writer has quoted the material exactly as it appeared in the original.

- The company considers the Baker Foundation to be a "guilt-edged [*sic*] investment."

Incorporating Quotations into Text

Quote word for word only when your source concisely sums up a great deal of information or reinforces a point you are making. Quotations must also relate logically, grammatically, and syntactically to the rest of the sentence and surrounding text.

Depending on the length, there are two mechanical methods of handling quotations in your text. For MLA style, a quotation of three or fewer lines is incorporated into the text and enclosed in quotation marks. For APA style, a quotation of fewer than 40 words is incorporated into the text and enclosed in quotation marks.

Material that runs four lines or longer (MLA) or at least 40 words (APA) is usually inset; that is, set off from the body of the text by being indented from the left margin ten spaces (MLA) or five to seven spaces (APA). The quoted passage is spaced the same as the surrounding text and is not enclosed in quotation marks, as shown in Figure 2–9, which uses MLA style. If you are not following a specific style manual, you may block indent ten spaces from both the left and right margins for reports and other documents.

Notice in Figure 2–9 that the quotation blends with the content of the surrounding text, which uses transitions to introduce and comment

After reviewing a larger number of works in business and technical communication, Alred sees an inevitable connection between theory, practice, and pedagogy:

> Therefore, theory is necessary to prevent us from being overwhelmed by what is local, particular, and temporal. In turn, pedagogy both mediates practice and transforms our theory. Indeed, one reason I find this work rewarding is that I sense it puts me at the intersection of theory, practice, and pedagogy as they are involved with writing in the workplace. (ix–x)

The use of the Web today has reinforced this connection because it calls on the Web page designer to engage in a teaching function as well as reflect on the practice of Web design. For example, the widespread use of . . .

FIGURE 2–9. Long Quotation (MLA Style)

on the quotation. At the end of the document, the following entry appears in the MLA-style list of works cited as the source of the quotation in Figure 2–9.

- Alred, Gerald J. The St. Martin's Bibliography of Business and Technical Communication. New York: St. Martin's, 1997.

Do not rely too heavily on the use of quotations in the final version of your document. Generally, avoid including a quotation that is more than one paragraph.

reports

This book includes many typical reports, which may be formal or informal and vary in length and complexity. Following is a list of relevant entries:

feasibility reports 66
formal reports 96
investigative reports 69
progress and activity reports 75
trip reports 87
trouble reports 88
See also **proposals** (page 78).

A report is an organized presentation of factual information, often aimed at multiple audiences, that may present the results of an investigation, a trip, or a research project. For any report—whether formal or informal—assessing the readers' needs is important. See **audience/readers** (page 3).

Formal reports present the results of long-term projects that may involve large sums of money. Such projects may be done either for your own organization or as a contractual requirement for another organization. Formal reports generally follow a precise format and include some or all of the report elements discussed in **formal reports** (page 96). See also **abstracts** (page 93) and **executive summaries** (page 95).

Informal and short reports normally run from a few paragraphs to a few pages and include only the essential elements of a report: introduction, body, conclusions, and recommendations. Because of their brevity, informal reports are customarily written as letters (if sent outside your organization) or memos (if internal). See also **correspondence** (page 128) and **memos** (page 143).

The introduction announces the subject of the report, states the purpose, and gives any essential background information. It may also summarize the conclusions, findings, or recommendations made in the report. The body presents a clearly organized account of the report's subject—the results of a test carried out, the status of a project, and so on. The amount of detail to include depends on the complexity of the subject and on your readers' familiarity with it.

The conclusion summarizes your findings and tells readers what you think their significance may be. In some reports, a final, separate section gives recommendations; in others, the conclusions and the recommendations sections are combined into one section. This final section makes suggestions for a course of action based on the data you have presented.

titles

The title of a report or other document should both state its topic and indicate its **scope** (page 45) and **purpose/objective** (page 41), such as "Using Chaos Theory to Explain Small Business Growth Management." A title should be concise but not so short that it is not specific. For example, the title "Management Theory and Small Businesses" announces the topic of a report, but it does not answer important questions, such as "What is the relationship between management theory and small businesses?" and "What kind of management theory does it discuss?" Titles are important because many readers decide to read a document, such as a trade-journal article, based on the title.

For guidelines on how to capitalize titles and when to use **italics** (page 383) and **quotation marks** (page 390), see those entries and **capital letters** (page 368).

trip reports

Many companies require or encourage employees to prepare reports of the business trips they take. A trip report provides both a permanent record of a business trip and its accomplishments and enables many employees to benefit from the information that one employee has gained.

A trip report—typically an internal document—is normally written in memo format and addressed to an immediate superior. The

Subject: **Trip to Smith Electric Co., Huntington, West Virginia, January 20--**
To: Roberto Camacho <rcamacho@smithelec.com>
From: James D. Kerson <jdkerson@smithelec.com>
Date: Tues, 13 Jan 20-- 12:16:30

I visited the Smith Electric Company in Huntington, West Virginia, to determine the cause of a recurring failure in a Model 247 printer and to fix it.

Problem
The printer stopped printing periodically for no apparent reason. Repeated efforts to bring it back online eventually succeeded, but the problem recurred at irregular intervals. Neither customer personnel operating the printer nor the local maintenance specialist was able to solve the problem.

Action
On January 3, I met with Ms. Ruth Bernardi, the Office Manager, who explained the problem. My troubleshooting did not reveal the cause of the problem then or on January 4.

Only when I tested the logic cable did I find that it contained a broken wire. I replaced the logic cable and then ran all the normal printer test patterns to make sure no other problems existed. All patterns were positive, so I turned the printer over to the customer.

Conclusion
There are over 12,000 of these printers in the field and to my knowledge this is the first occurrence of a bad cable. Therefore, I do not believe the logic cable problem found at Smith Electric Company warrants further investigation.

=================================
James D. Kerson, Maintenance Specialist
Smith Electric Company
1366 Federal St., Allentown PA 18101
(610) 747-9955 Fax: (610) 747-9956
jdkerson@smithelec.com
www.smithelec.com
=================================

Figure 2–10. Trip Report (Email)

subject line gives the destination and dates of the trip. The body of the report explains why you made the trip, whom you visited, and what you accomplished. The report should devote a brief section to each major event and may include a heading for each section (you need not give equal space to each event—instead, elaborate on the more important events). Follow the body of the report with the appropriate conclusions and recommendations. A typical trip report is shown in Figure 2–10.

trouble reports

The trouble report is used to report such events as accidents, equipment failures, or health emergencies. The report assesses the causes of the problem and suggests changes necessary to prevent its recurrence. Because it is an internal document, the trouble report normally follows a simple memo format. Usually, trouble reports are not large enough in either size or scope to require the format of a formal report.

In the subject line of the memo, state the precise problem you are reporting. Then, in the body of the report, provide a detailed, precise description of the problem. What happened? Where and when did it occur? Was anybody hurt? Was there any property damage? Was there a work stoppage? Because insurance claims, worker's compensation awards, and even lawsuits may hinge on the information contained in a trouble report, be sure to include precise times, dates, locations, treatment of injuries, names of any witnesses, and any other crucial information. Be thorough and accurate in your analysis of the problem and support any judgments or conclusions with facts. Be objective; always use a neutral tone and avoid assigning blame. (See **tone,** page 276.) If you speculate in your report about the cause of the problem, make it clear to your reader that you are speculating. See also **ethics in writing** (page 261).

In your conclusion, state what has or will be done to correct the conditions that led to the problem. That may include training in safety practices, improved equipment, protective clothing (for example, shoes or goggles), and so on.

The report shown in Figure 2–11 describes an accident involving personal injury. Notice the careful use of language and factual detail.

Consolidated Energy, Inc.

To: Marvin Lundquist, Vice-President
Administrative Services
From: Kalo Katarlan, Safety Officer *KK*
Field Service Operations
Date: August 19, 20--
Subject: Field Service Employee Accident on August 7, 20--

The following is an initial report of an accident on Wednesday, August 7, 20--, involving John Markley that resulted in two days of lost time.

Accident Summary
John Markley stopped by a rewiring job on German Road. Chico Ruiz was working there, stringing new wire, and John was checking with Chico about the materials he wanted for framing a pole. Some tree trimming had been done in the area, and John offered to help remove some of the debris by loading it into the pickup truck he was driving. While John was loading branches into the bed of the truck, a piece broke off in his right hand and struck his right eye.

Accident Details

1. John's right eye was struck by a piece of tree branch. John had just undergone laser surgery on his right eye on Monday, August 5, to reattach his cornea.
2. John immediately covered his right eye with his hand, and Chico Ruiz gave him a paper towel with ice to cover his eye and help ease the pain.

7. On Monday, August 12, John returned to his eye surgeon. Although bruised, his eye was not damaged, and the surgically implanted lens was still in place.

To prevent a recurrence of such an accident, the Safety Department will require the following actions in the future:

- When working around and moving debris, such as tree limbs or branches, all service-crew employees must wear safety eyewear with side shields.
- All service-crew employees must always consider the possibility of shock for an injured employee. If crew members cannot leave the job site to care for the injured employee, someone on the crew must call for assistance from the Service Center. The Service Center phone number is printed in each service-crew member's Handbook.

FIGURE 2–11. Trouble Report

3

Formal Reports

Preview

This section includes entries about the formal report and its components. Although the number and arrangement of elements in formal reports vary, often depending on an organization's preferred style, the guidelines given in the **formal reports** entry follow the most common pattern. This section also includes entries that provide more detailed guidance for preparing key sections often included in formal reports. A sample formal report appears on pages 102–18. For specific types of reports and other documents that may be presented in formal-report form, see Tab 2, "Business Writing Forms and Documentation."

abstracts

An *abstract* summarizes and highlights the major points of a formal report, trade journal article, dissertation, or other work. Its primary purpose is to enable readers to decide whether to read the work in full. For a discussion of how summaries differ from abstracts, see **executive summaries** (page 95).

Although abstracts, typically 200 to 250 words long, are published with the longer works they condense, they can also be published separately in periodical indexes (see **library research,** page 20). For this reason, an abstract must be able to stand on its own.

Depending on the kind of information they contain, abstracts are often classified as *descriptive* or *informative.* A *descriptive abstract* includes information about the purpose, scope, and methods used to arrive at the reported findings. It is a slightly expanded table of contents in sentence and paragraph form. A descriptive abstract need not be longer than several sentences. An *informative abstract* is an expanded version of the descriptive abstract. In addition to information about the purpose, scope, and research methods used, the informative abstract includes the results, **conclusions** (page 6), and any recommendations. The informative abstract retains the **tone** (page 276) and essential scope of the report, omitting its details. The first two paragraphs of the abstract shown in Figure 3–1 alone would be descriptive; with the addition of the paragraphs that detail the conclusions of the report, the abstract becomes informative.

The organization or publication that you are writing for determines your audience and the type of abstract you should write. Informative abstracts work best for wide audiences that need to know conclusions and recommendations; descriptive abstracts work best for compilations, such as proceedings and progress reports, that do not contain conclusions or recommendations.

Writing Style

Write the abstract *after* finishing the report or document. Otherwise, the abstract may not accurately reflect the longer work. Begin with a topic sentence that announces the subject and scope of your report or document. Then, using the major and minor headings of your outline or table of contents to distinguish primary ideas from secondary ones, decide what material is relevant to your abstract. Write with clarity (see Tab 9, "Style and Clarity," pages 249–82) and conciseness (see **conciseness/wordiness,** page 257), eliminating unnecessary words and ideas. Do not, however, become so terse that you omit articles (*a, an, the*) and important transitional words and phrases (*however,*

Purpose

Methods and scope

Findings and conclusions

Recommendations

ABSTRACT

This report investigates the long-term effects of long-distance running on the bones, joints, and general health of runners aged 50 to 72. The Sports Medicine Institute of Columbia Hospital sponsored this investigation, first to decide whether to add a geriatric unit to the Institute, and second to determine whether physicians should recommend long-distance running for their older patients.

The investigation is based on recent studies conducted at Stanford University and the University of Florida. The Stanford study tested and compared male and female long-distance runners between 50 and 72 years of age with a control group of runners and nonrunners. The groups were also matched by sex, race, education, and occupation. The Florida study used only male runners who had run at least 20 miles a week for five years and compared them with a group of runners and nonrunners. Both studies based findings on medical histories and on physical and x-ray examinations.

Both studies conclude that long-distance running is not associated with increased degenerative joint disease. Control groups were more prone to spur formation, sclerosis, and joint-space narrowing and showed more joint degeneration than runners. Female long-distance runners exhibited somewhat more sclerosis in knee joints and the lumbar spine area than matched control subjects. Both studies support the role of exercise in retarding bone loss with aging. The investigation concludes that the health risk factors are fewer for long-distance runners than for those less active between the ages of 50 and 72.

The investigation recommends that the Sports Medicine Institute of Columbia Hospital consider the development of a geriatric unit a priority and that it inform physicians that an exercise program that includes long-distance running can be beneficial to their patients' health.

iii

FIGURE 3–1. Abstract

therefore, but, in summary). Write complete sentences, but avoid stringing a group of short sentences end to end; instead, combine ideas by using **subordination** (page 274) and **parallel structure** (page 269). Spell out most acronyms and all but the most common **abbreviations** (page 363). Typically, an abstract follows the title page and is numbered page iii. See also **formal reports** (page 96).

appendixes

An appendix, located at the end of a formal report, a proposal, or other major document, supplements or clarifies the information in the body of the document. Appendixes (or appendices) can provide information that is too detailed or lengthy for the primary audience of the text. For example, an appendix could contain complex graphs and tables, profiles of key personnel involved in a proposed project, or documentation of interest only to secondary readers. See **audience/readers** (page 3).

A document may have more than one appendix, with each offering only one type of information. When the document contains more than one appendix, arrange them in the order they are mentioned in the text. Begin each appendix on a new page, and identify each with a letter, starting with the letter *A;* for example, "Appendix A: Sample Questionnaire." (If you have only one appendix, title it simply "Appendix.") List the titles and beginning page numbers of the appendixes in the **table of contents** (page 101).

executive summaries

An executive summary consolidates the principal points of a report or proposal. Executive summaries differ from abstracts in that readers use abstracts to decide whether to read the work in full. However, an executive summary may be the only section of a longer work read by many readers, so it must accurately and concisely reflect the original document. Executive summaries tend to be about 10 percent the length of the documents they summarize and generally follow the same sequence. See also **abstracts** (page 93).

Write the executive summary so that it can be read independently of the report or proposal. Do not refer by number to figures, tables, or references contained elsewhere in the document. Executive summaries may occasionally include a figure, table, or footnote if that information is integral to the summary. For an example, see the executive summary in the **SAMPLE FORMAL REPORT** on page 106.

Writer's Checklist: Writing Executive Summaries

- ☑ Write the executive summary after you have completed the orig document.
- ☑ Avoid using terminology that may not be familiar to your re

Writer's Checklist: Writing Executive Summaries (continued)

- ☑ Spell out all uncommon symbols and **abbreviations** (page 363) because executive summaries frequently are read in place of the full document.
- ☑ Make the summary concise, but do not omit transitional words and phrases (*however, moreover, therefore, for example, in summary*).
- ☑ Include only information discussed in the original document.
- ☑ Place the executive summary at the very beginning of the body of the report, as described in **formal reports** (page 96).

forewords / prefaces

The terms *foreword* and *preface* usually refer to different parts of a publication. A *foreword* is an optional introductory statement about a formal report or a book, which is written by someone other than the author. The foreword author is usually an authority in the field or an executive of the company. The foreword author's name and affiliation appear at the end of the foreword, along with the date it was written. The foreword generally provides background information about the publication's significance and places it in the context of other works in the field. The foreword precedes the preface when a work has both.

The *preface,* another type of optional introductory statement, is written by the author of the book or formal report. The preface may announce the work's purpose, scope, and background (including any special circumstances leading to the work). A preface may also specify the audience for a work, it may contain acknowledgments of those who helped in its preparation, and it may cite permission obtained for the use of copyrighted works. See also **copyright** (page 53).

formal reports

Formal reports are written accounts of major projects. Most are di-ided into three primary parts—front matter, body, and back matter—h of which contains a number of elements. See the **SAMPLE FORMAL** **ORT** on page 102.

ote that the number and arrangement of the elements may vary, ng on the subject, the length of the report, and the kinds of maered. Further, many organizations have a preferred style for orts and furnish guidelines for report writers to follow. If you ired to follow a specific style, use the format recommended in this entry. The following list includes most of the elements a formal report might contain, in the order of their appearance in the report. Often, a cover letter or memo precedes the front matter and identifies the report by title, the person or persons to whom it is being sent, and the reason for its being sent.

FRONT MATTER
Title page
Abstract
Table of contents
List of figures
List of tables
Foreword
Preface
List of abbreviations and symbols

BODY
Executive summary
Introduction
Text (including headings)
Conclusions
Recommendations
Explanatory notes
References (or "Works Cited")

BACK MATTER
Appendixes
Bibliography
Glossary
Index

Front Matter

The front matter serves several purposes: It gives the reader a general idea of the author's purpose; it gives an overview of the type of information in the report; and it lists where specific information is covered in the report. Not all formal reports include every element of front matter described here. A title page and table of contents are usually mandatory, but the scope of the report and its intended audience determine whether the other elements are included.

Title Page. Although the formats of title pages for formal reports may vary, the example in the **SAMPLE FORMAL REPORT** (page 103) is typical. Title pages include the following information:

- *The full title of the report.* Reflect the topic, scope, and purpose of the report as shown in the entry **titles** (page 86).

- *The name of the writer, principal investigator, or compiler.* Sometimes contributors identify themselves by their job title in the organization or by their tasks in contributing to the report (such as Gina Hobbs, Principal Investigator).
- *The date or dates of the report.* For one-time reports, list the date when the report is to be distributed. For periodic reports (monthly, quarterly, or yearly), list in a subtitle the period that the report covers. Elsewhere on the title page, list the date when the report is to be distributed, as shown on page 103.
- *The name of the organization for which the writer works.*
- *The name of the organization to which the report is being submitted.* This information is included if the report is written for a customer or client.

The title page, although unnumbered, is considered page i. The back of the title page, which is blank and unnumbered, is considered page ii, and the abstract falls on page iii. The body of the report begins with Arabic number 1, and a new chapter or large section typically begins on a new right-hand (odd-numbered) page. Reports with printing on only one side of each sheet can be numbered consecutively regardless of where new sections begin. Center page numbers at the bottom of the page throughout the report.

Abstract. An abstract, which normally follows the title page, highlights the major points of the report, enabling readers to decide whether to read the entire report. See the **SAMPLE FORMAL REPORT** (page 104) and **abstracts** (page 93).

Table of Contents. A **table of contents** (page 101) lists all the major sections or **headings** (page 194) of the report in their order of appearance, along with their page numbers, as shown in the **SAMPLE FORMAL REPORT** (page 105).

List of Figures. When a report contains more than five figures, list them, along with their page numbers, in a separate section beginning on a new page immediately following the table of contents. Number figures consecutively with Arabic numbers. Figures include all illustrations—drawings, photographs, maps, charts, and graphs—contained in the report. See Tab 6, "Format and Visuals" (page 183).

List of Tables. When a report contains more than five **tables** (page 203), list them, along with their titles and page numbers, in a separate section immediately following the list of figures (if there is one). Number tables consecutively with Arabic numbers.

reword. A foreword is an optional introductory statement written omeone other than the author. See **forewords/prefaces** (page 96).

Preface. The preface is an optional introductory statement written by the author of the report. It announces the purpose, background, and scope of the report. See **forewords/prefaces** (page 96).

List of Abbreviations and Symbols. When the report uses numerous abbreviations and symbols and there is a chance that readers will not be able to interpret them, the front matter should include a list of all symbols and abbreviations (including acronyms) and what they stand for.

Body

The body is the section of the report in which the author describes in detail the methods and procedures used to generate the report, demonstrates how results were obtained, describes the results, and draws conclusions and, if appropriate, makes recommendations.

Executive Summary. The body of the report begins with the executive summary, which provides a more complete overview of the report than an abstract does. See the **SAMPLE FORMAL REPORT** (page 106) and **executive summaries** (page 95).

Introduction. The introduction gives readers any general information, such as the report's purpose and scope, necessary to understand the detailed information in the rest of the report. See **introductions** (page 16).

Text. The text of the body presents, as appropriate, the details of how the topic was investigated, how a problem was solved, what alternatives were explored, and how the best choice among them was selected. This information is often persuasively developed by the use of illustrations and tables and supported by references to other publications.

Conclusions. The conclusions section pulls together the results of the research and offers conclusions based on the analysis. See **conclusions** (page 6) and **research** (page 42).

Recommendations. Recommendations, which are sometimes co bined with the conclusions, state what course of action should be t based on the earlier arguments and results of the study. The re mendations section may state, for example, "I think we should new markets in . . ." or "I recommend we expand our marketir on the Internet."

Explanatory Notes. Occasionally, reports contain notes that amplify terms or points for some readers. If such notes are not included as footnotes on the page where the term or point appears, they may appear in a final section, often referred to simply as "Notes."

References (or "Works Cited"). A list of references or "works cited" appears in a separate section if the report refers to material in, or quotes directly from, a published work or other research sources, including online sources. If your employer has a preferred reference style, follow it; otherwise, use the guidelines provided in **documenting sources** (page 54) and see an example in the **SAMPLE FORMAL REPORT** (page 118). For a relatively short report, place the references at the end of the body of the report. For a report with a number of sections or chapters, place the reference section at the end of each major section or chapter. In either case, title the reference or works-cited section as such and begin it on a new page. If a particular reference appears in more than one section or chapter, repeat it in full in each appropriate reference section. See also **quotations** (page 83) and **plagiarism** (page 73).

Back Matter

The back matter of a formal report contains supplementary material, such as where to find additional information about the topic (bibliography), and expands on certain subjects (appendixes). Other back matter elements clarify the terms used (glossary) and provide information on how to easily locate information in the report (index).

Appendixes. An appendix contains information that clarifies or supplements the text. It provides information that is too detailed or lengthy for the primary audience but that is relevant to secondary audiences. See **appendixes** (page 95).

Bibliography. A bibliography is an alphabetical list of all sources that were consulted (not just those cited) in researching the report. A bibliography is not necessary if the reference listing contains a complete list of sources. See **bibliographies** (page 51).

Glossary. A glossary is an alphabetical list of selected terms used in ...e report and their definitions. See **glossaries** (page 101).

...ex. An index is an alphabetical list of all the major topics and ...ubtopics discussed in the report. It cites the page numbers where ...on of each topic can be found and allows readers to find infor... ...n topics quickly and easily. The index is always the final sec... ...port.

glossaries

A glossary is an alphabetical list of definitions of terms used in a formal report, a manual, or other long document. (See **formal reports,** page 96.)

If you are writing a report that will go to readers who are not familiar with many of the terms you use, you may want to include a glossary. If you do, keep the entries concise and be sure they are written in plain language that all readers can understand. Arrange the terms alphabetically, with each entry beginning on a new line. The definitions then follow the terms, dictionary style. In a formal report, the glossary appears after the appendix(es) and bibliography, and it begins on a new page.

Inclusion of a glossary does not relieve you of the responsibility of defining in the text any terms your reader will not know when those terms are first mentioned. See also **defining terms** (page 8).

tables of contents

A table of contents is a list of headings in a report or chapters in a book in their order of appearance and with their corresponding page numbers. A table of contents is typically included in a document longer than ten pages. Because it appears at the front of a work, a table of contents previews what is in the work and allows readers to assess the work's usefulness. It also helps those looking for specific information to locate sections quickly and easily.

When creating a table of contents, use the major headings and subheadings of your document exactly as they appear in the text, as shown in the SAMPLE FORMAL REPORT (page 105). Note that the table of contents is typically placed in the front matter so that it follows the title page and abstract, and precedes the list of tables or figures, the foreword, and the preface. See **formal reports** (page 96).

SAMPLE FORMAL REPORT

CGF Aircraft Corporation
Memo

To: Members of the Ethics and Business Conduct Committee
From: Susan Litzinger, Director of Ethics and Business Conduct SL
Date: March 1, 20--
Subject: Reported Ethics Cases 20--

Enclosed is the annual Ethics and Business Conduct Report, as required by CGF Policy CGF-EP-01, for your evaluation, covering the first year of our Ethics Program. This report contains a review of the ethics cases handled by CGF Ethics officers and managers during 20--.

The ethics cases reported are analyzed according to two categories: (1) major ethics cases, or those potentially involving serious violations of company policy or illegal conduct, and (2) minor ethics cases, or those that do not involve serious policy violations or illegal conduct. The report also examines the mode of contact in all of the reported cases and the disposition of the substantiated major ethics cases.

It is my hope that this report will provide the Committee with the information needed to assess the effectiveness of the first year of CGF's Ethics Program and to plan for the coming year. Please let me know if you have any questions about this report or if you need any further information. I may be reached at (555) 211-2121 and by email at <sl@cgf.com>.

Cover Memo Formal Report. Reprinted by permission of Susan Litzinger, a student at Pennsylvania State University, Altoona.

REPORTED ETHICS CASES
Annual Report 20--

Prepared by Susan Litzinger
Director of Ethics and Business Conduct

Report Distributed March 1, 20--

Prepared for
The Ethics and Business Conduct Committee
CGF Aircraft Corporation

Title Page

ABSTRACT

This report examines the nature and disposition of 3,458 ethics cases handled companywide by CGF Aircraft Corporation's ethics officers and managers during 20--. The purpose of this annual report is to provide the Ethics and Business Conduct Committee with the information necessary for assessing the effectiveness of the Ethics Program's first year of operation. Records maintained by ethics officers and managers of all contacts were compiled and categorized into two main types: (1) major ethics cases, or cases involving serious violations of company policies or illegal conduct, and (2) minor ethics cases, or cases not involving serious policy violations or illegal conduct. This report provides examples of the types of cases handled in each category and analyzes the disposition of 30 substantiated major ethics cases. Recommendations for planning for the second year of the Ethics Program are (1) continuing the channels of communication now available in the Ethics Program, (2) increasing financial and technical support for the Ethics Hotline, (3) disseminating the annual ethics report in some form to employees to ensure employees' awareness of the company's commitment to uphold its Ethics Policies and Procedures, and (4) implementing some measure of recognition for ethical behavior to promote and reward ethical conduct.

iii

Abstract

TABLE OF CONTENTS

iv

Table of Contents

EXECUTIVE SUMMARY

This report examines the nature and disposition of the 3,458 ethics cases handled by the CGF Aircraft Corporation's ethics officers and managers during 20--. The purpose of this report is to provide CGF's Ethics and Business Conduct Committee with the information necessary for assessing the effectiveness of the first year of the company's Ethics Program.

Effective January 1, 20--, the Ethics and Business Conduct Committee (the Committee) implemented a policy and procedures for the administration of CGF's new Ethics Program. The purpose of the Ethics Program, established by the Committee, is to "promote ethical business conduct through open communication and compliance with company ethics standards." The Office of Ethics and Business Conduct was created to administer the Ethics Program. The director of the Office of Ethics and Business Conduct, along with seven ethics officers throughout the corporation, was given the responsibility for the following objectives:

- Communicate the values and standards for CGF's Ethics Program to employees.
- Inform employees about company policies regarding ethical business conduct.
- Establish companywide channels for employees to obtain information and guidance in resolving ethics concerns.
- Implement companywide ethics-awareness and education programs.

Employee accessibility to ethics information and guidance was available through managers, ethics officers, and an ethics hotline.

Major ethics cases were defined as those situations potentially involving serious violations of company policies or illegal conduct. Examples of major ethics cases included cover-up of defective workmanship or use of defective parts in products; discrimination in hiring and promotion; involvement in monetary or other kickbacks; sexual harassment; disclosure of proprietary or company information; theft; and use of corporate Internet resources for inappropriate purposes, such as conducting personal business, gambling, or access to pornography.

1

Executive Summary

Minor ethics cases were defined as including all reported concerns not classified as major ethics cases. Minor ethics cases were classified as informational queries from employees, situations involving coworkers, and situations involving management.

The effectiveness of CGF's Ethics Program during the first year of implementation is most evidenced by (1) the active participation of employees in the program and the 3,458 contacts employees made regarding ethics concerns through the various channels available to them, and (2) the action taken in the cases reported by employees, particularly the disposition of the 30 substantiated major ethics cases. Disseminating information about the disposition of ethics cases, particularly information about the severe disciplinary actions taken in major ethics violations, sends a message to employees that unethical or illegal conduct will not be tolerated.

Based on these conclusions, recommendations for planning the second year of the Ethics Program are (1) continuing the channels of communication now available in the Ethics Program, (2) increasing financial and technical support for the Ethics Hotline, the most highly utilized mode of contact in the ethics cases reported in 20--, (3) disseminating this report in some form to employees to ensure their awareness of CGF's commitment to uphold its Ethics Policy and Procedures, and (4) implementing some measure of recognition for ethical behavior, such as an "Ethics Employee of the Month" award to promote and reward ethical conduct.

2

Executive Summary *(continued)*

INTRODUCTION

This report examines the nature and disposition of the 3,458 ethics cases handled companywide by CGF's ethics officers and managers during 20--. The purpose of this report is to provide the Ethics and Business Conduct Committee with the information necessary for assessing the effectiveness of the first year of CGF's Ethics Program. Recommendations are given for the Committee's consideration in planning for the second year of the Ethics Program.

Ethics and Business Conduct Policy and Procedures

Effective January 1, 20--, the Ethics and Business Conduct Committee (the Committee) implemented Policy CGF-EP-01 and Procedure CGF-EP-02 for the administration of CGF's new Ethics Program. The purpose of the Ethics Program, established by the Committee, is to "promote ethical business conduct through open communication and compliance with company ethics standards" (CGF's "Ethical Business Conduct").

The Office of Ethics and Business Conduct was created to administer the Ethics Program. The director of the Office of Ethics and Business Conduct, along with seven ethics officers throughout CGF, was given the responsibility for the following objectives:

- Communicate the values, standards, and goals of CGF's Ethics Program to employees.
- Inform employees about company ethics policies.
- Provide companywide channels for employee education and guidance in resolving ethics concerns.
- Implement companywide programs in ethics awareness, education, and recognition.
- Ensure confidentiality in all ethics matters.

Employee accessibility to ethics information and guidance became the immediate and key goal of the Office of Ethics and Business Conduct in its first year of operation. The following channels for contact were set in motion during 20--:

Introduction

- Managers throughout CGF received intensive ethics training; in all ethics situations, employees were encouraged to go to their managers as the first point of contact.
- Ethics officers were available directly to employees through face-to-face or telephone contact, to managers, to callers using the ethics hotline, and by email.
- The Ethics Hotline was available to all employees, 24 hours a day, 7 days a week, to anonymously report ethics concerns.

Confidentiality Issues

CGF's Ethics Policy ensures confidentiality and anonymity for employees who raise genuine ethics concerns. Procedure CGF-EP-02 guarantees appropriate discipline, up to and including dismissal, for retaliation or retribution against any employee who properly reports any genuine ethics concern.

Documentation of Ethics Cases

The following requirements were established by the director of the Office of Ethics and Business Conduct as uniform guidelines for the documentation by managers and ethics officers of all reported ethics cases:

- Name, position, and department of individual initiating contact, if available
- Date and time of contact
- Name, position, and department of contact person
- Category of ethics case
- Mode of contact
- Resolution

Managers and ethics officers entered the required information in each reported ethics case into an ACCESS database file, enabling efficient retrieval and analysis of the data.

Introduction *(continued)*

Major/Minor Category Definition and Examples

Major ethics cases were defined as those situations potentially involving serious violations of company policies or illegal conduct. Procedure CGF-EP-02 requires notification of the Internal Audit and the Law Departments in serious ethics cases. The staffs of the Internal Audit and the Law Departments assume primary responsibility for managing major ethics cases and for working with the employees, ethics officers, and managers involved in each case.

Examples of situations categorized as major ethics cases:

- Cover-up of defective workmanship or use of defective parts in products
- Discrimination in hiring and promotion
- Involvement in monetary or other kickbacks from customers for preferred orders
- Sexual harassment
- Disclosure of proprietary customer or company information
- Theft
- Use of corporate Internet resources for inappropriate purposes, such as conducting private business, gambling, or access to pornography

Minor ethics cases were defined as including all reported concerns not classified as major ethics cases. Minor ethics cases were classified as follows:

- Informational queries from employees
- Situations involving coworkers
- Situations involving management

Introduction *(continued)*

ANALYSIS OF REPORTED ETHICS CASES

Reported Ethics Cases by Major/Minor Category

CGF ethics officers and managers companywide handled a total of 3,458 ethics situations during 20--. Of these cases, only 172, or 5 percent, involved reported concerns of a serious enough nature to be classified as major ethics cases (see Figure 1). Major ethics cases were defined as those situations potentially involving serious violations of company policy or illegal conduct.

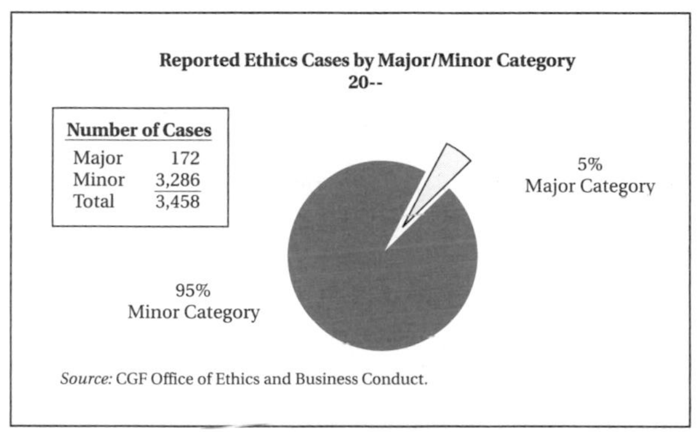

Figure 1. Reported ethics cases by major/minor category in 20--.

Major Ethics Cases

Of the 172 major ethics cases reported during 20--, 57 percent, upon investigation, were found to involve unsubstantiated concerns. Incomplete information or misinformation most frequently was discovered to be the cause of the unfounded concerns of misconduct in 98 cases. Forty-four cases, or 26 percent of the total cases reported, involved incidents partly substantiated by ethics officers as serious misconduct; however, these cases were discovered to also involve inaccurate information or unfounded issues of misconduct.

6

Body

Only 17 percent of the total number of major ethics cases, or 30 cases, were substantiated as major ethics situations involving serious ethical misconduct or illegal conduct (CGF, "20-- Ethics Hotline Results") (see Figure 2).

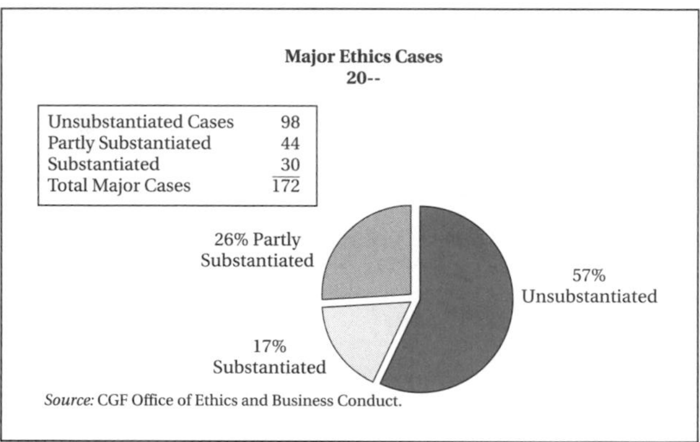

Figure 2. Major ethics cases in 20--.

Of the 30 substantiated major ethics cases, seven remain under investigation at this time, and two cases are currently in litigation. Disposition of the remainder of the 30 substantiated reported ethics cases included severe disciplinary action in five cases: the dismissal of two employees and the demotion of three employees. Seven employees were given written warnings, and nine employees received verbal warnings (see Figure 3).

7

Body *(continued)*

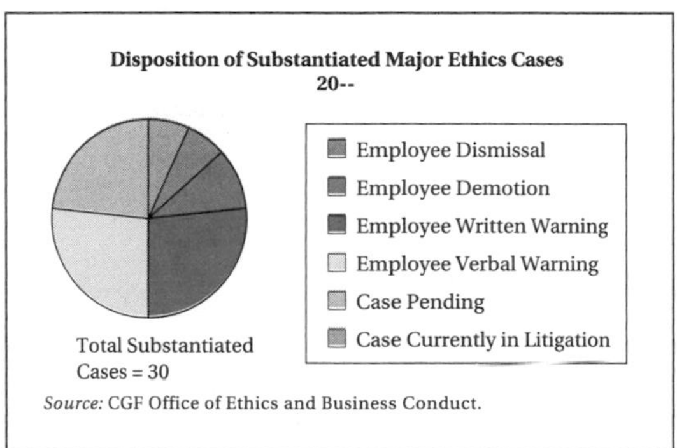

Figure 3. Disposition of substantiated major ethics cases in 20--.

Minor Ethics Cases

Minor ethics cases included those that did not involve serious violations of company policy or illegal conduct. During 20--, ethics officers and company managers handled 3,268 such cases. Minor ethics cases were further classified as follows:

- Informational queries from employees
- Situations involving coworkers
- Situations involving management

As might be expected during the initial year of the Ethics Program implementation, the majority of contacts made by employees were informational, involving questions about the new policies and procedures. These informational contacts comprised 55 percent of all contacts of a minor nature and numbered 2,148. Employees made 989 contacts regarding ethics concerns involving coworkers and 149 contacts regarding ethics concerns involving management (see Figure 4).

8

Body ***(continued)***

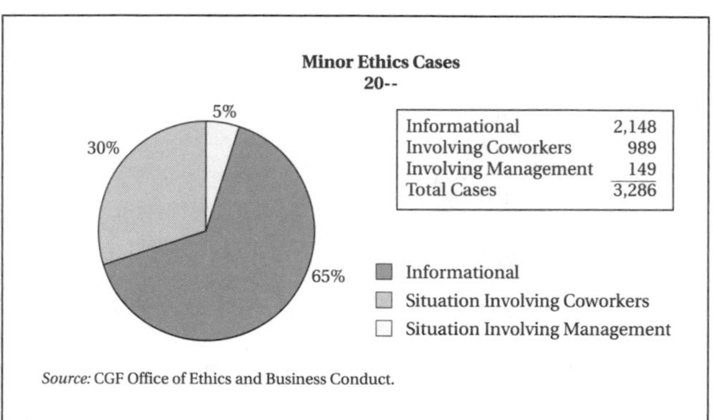

Figure 4. Minor ethics cases in 20--.

Mode of Contact

The effectiveness of the Ethics Program rested on the dissemination of information to employees and the provision of accessible channels through which employees could gain information, report concerns, and obtain guidance. Employees were encouraged to first go to their managers with any ethical concerns, because those managers would have the most direct knowledge of the immediate circumstances and individuals involved.

Other channels were put into operation, however, for any instance in which an employee did not feel able to go to his or her manager. The ethics officers companywide were available to employees through telephone conversations, face-to-face meetings, and email contact. Ethics officers also served as contact points for managers in need of support and assistance in handling the ethics concerns reported to them by their subordinates.

The Ethics Hotline became operational in mid-January 20-- and offered employees assurance of anonymity and confidentiality. The Ethics Hotline was accessible to all employees on a 24-hour, 7-day basis. Ethics officers companywide took responsibility on a rotational basis for handling calls reported through the hotline.

9

Body *(continued)*

In summary, ethics information and guidance was available to all employees during 20-- through the following channels:

- Employee to manager
- Employee telephone, face-to-face, and email contact with ethics officer
- Manager to ethics officer
- Employee Hotline

The mode of contact in the 3,458 reported ethics cases was as follows (see Figure 5):

- In 19 percent of the reported cases, or 657, employees went to managers with concerns.
- In 9 percent of the reported cases, or 311, employees contacted an ethics officer.
- In 5 percent of the reported cases, or 173, managers sought assistance from ethics officers.
- In 67 percent of the reported cases, or 2,317, contacts were made through the Ethics Hotline.

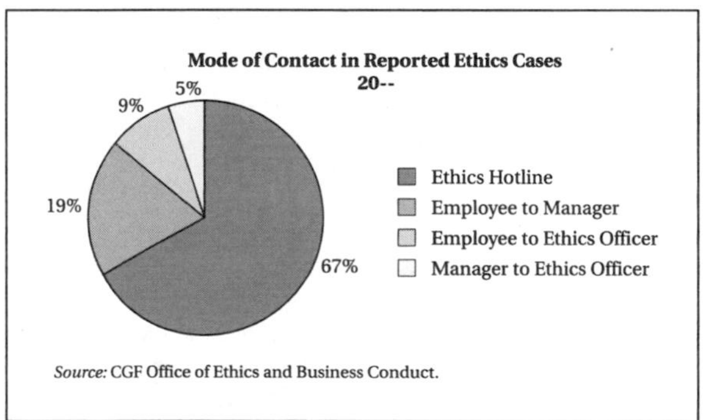

Figure 5. Mode of contact in reported ethics cases in 20--.

Body *(continued)*

CONCLUSIONS AND RECOMMENDATIONS

The effectiveness of CGF's Ethics Program during the first year of implementation is most evidenced by (1) the active participation of employees in the program and the 3,458 contacts employees made regarding ethics concerns through the various channels available to them, and (2) the action taken in the cases reported by employees, particularly the disposition of the 30 substantiated major ethics cases.

One of the 12 steps to building a successful Ethics Program identified by Frank Navran in *Workforce* magazine is an ethics communication strategy. Navran explains that such a strategy is crucial in ensuring

> that employees have the information they need in a timely and usable fashion and that the organization is encouraging employee communication regarding the values, standards and the conduct of the organization and its members (Navran 119).

The 3,458 contacts by employees during 20-- attest to the accessibility and effectiveness of the communication channels that exist in CGF's Ethics Program.

An equally important step in building a successful ethics program is listed by Navran as "Measurements and Rewards," which he explains as follows:

> In most organizations, employees know what's important by virtue of what the organization measures and rewards. If ethical conduct is assessed and rewarded, and if unethical conduct is identified and dissuaded, employees will believe that the organization's principals mean it when they say the values and code of ethics are important (Navran 121).

Disseminating information about the disposition of ethics cases, particularly information about the severe disciplinary actions taken in major ethics violations, sends a message to employees that unethical or illegal conduct will not be tolerated. Making public the tough-minded actions taken in cases of ethical misconduct provides "a golden opportunity to make other employees aware that the behavior is unacceptable and why" (Ferrell and Gardiner 129).

11

Conclusions and Recommendations

With these two points in mind, I offer the following recommendations for consideration for plans for the Ethics Program's second year:

- Continuation of the channels of communication now available in the Ethics Program
- Increased financial and technical support for the Ethics Hotline, the most highly utilized mode of contact in the reported ethics cases in 20--
- Dissemination of this report in some form to employees to ensure employees' awareness of CGF's commitment to uphold its Ethics Policy and Procedures
- Implementation of some measure of recognition for ethical behavior, such as an "Ethics Employee of the Month," to promote and reward ethical conduct

To ensure that employees see the value of their continued participation in the Ethics Program, feedback is essential. The information in this annual review, in some form, should be provided to employees. Knowing that the concerns they reported were taken seriously and resulted in appropriate action by Ethics Program administrators would reinforce employee involvement in the program. While the negative consequences of ethical misconduct contained in this report send a powerful message, a means of communicating the *positive* rewards of ethical conduct at CGF should be implemented. Various options for recognition of employees exemplifying ethical conduct should be considered and approved.

Continuation of the Ethics Program's successful 20-- operations, with the implementation of the above recommendations, should ensure the continued pursuit of the Ethics Program's purpose: "to promote a positive work environment that encourages open communication regarding ethics and compliance issues and concerns."

12

Conclusions and Recommendations *(continued)*

WORKS CITED

CGF. "Ethics and Conduct at CGF Airlines." 5 April 1998. <www.cgfac.com/aboutus/ethics.html>.

CGF. "1995 Ethics Hotline Investigation Results." 5 April 1998. <www.cgfac.com/html/ethics.html>.

Ferrell, O. C., and Gareth Gardiner. In Pursuit of Ethics: Tough Choices in the World of Work. Springfield: Smith Collins, 1991.

Kelley, Tina. "Corporate Prophets, Charting a Course to Ethical Profits." The New York Times 8 Feb. 1998: BU12.

Navran, Frank. "12 Steps to Building a Best-Practices Ethics Program." Workforce Sept. 1997: 117–122.

13

Works Cited

4

Correspondence

Preview

The entries **correspondence** and **memos** cover the general principles that will help you get the most out of the more specific entries in this section. You may also wish to review the entry **email** (page 233), especially the discussion of netiquette, for correspondence sent in email form. The other entries in this section cover specific situations, such as complaints and adjustments, and how to handle **international correspondence.** Finally, remember that the process of writing letters and memos involves many of the same steps that go into most other on-the-job writing tasks, as described in "Five Steps to Successful Writing" (page xiii).

acknowledgment letters

One way to build goodwill with colleagues and clients is to let them know that something they sent arrived and to express thanks. A letter that serves this function is called an *acknowledgment letter.* It is usually a short, polite note. If you have established a working relationship with someone, letting that person know by email is appropriate. The example shown in Figure 4–1 is typical and could be sent as a letter or an email. See also **email** (page 233).

FIGURE 4–1. Acknowledgment by Email

> Dear Mr. Evans:
>
> I received your report today; it appears to be complete and well done.
>
> When I finish studying it in detail, I'll send you our cost estimate for the installation of the Mark II Energy Saving System.
>
> Again, thanks for your effort.
>
> Regards,
>
> Roger Vonblatz

adjustment letters

An adjustment letter is written in response to a complaint letter and tells the customer what your company intends to do about the complaint (see **complaint letters,** page 126). You should settle such matters quickly and courteously, and always try to satisfy the customer at a reasonable cost to your company.

Although sent in response to a problem, an adjustment letter actually provides an excellent opportunity to build goodwill for your company. An effective adjustment letter both repairs the damage that has been done and restores the customer's confidence in your company.

Grant adjustments graciously; a settlement made grudgingly will do more harm than good. No matter how unreasonable the complaint, your response and tone should be positive and respectful. Avoid emphasizing the unfortunate situation, but do take responsibility for it and focus on what you are doing to correct it. Not only must you be gracious, but you must also acknowledge the error in such a way that the customer will not lose confidence in your company. (See also **tone,** page 276, and **correspondence,** page 128). The adjustment letter in Figure 4–2, for example, begins by accepting responsibility and offers an apology for the customer's inconvenience (note the use of the pronouns *we* and *us*). The second paragraph expresses a desire to restore goodwill and offers compensation. The third paragraph thanks the customer for her letter and assures her that her complaint has been taken seriously.

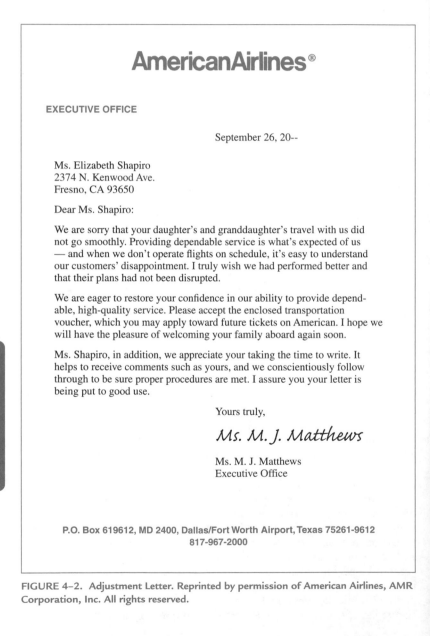

AmericanAirlines®

EXECUTIVE OFFICE

September 26, 20--

Ms. Elizabeth Shapiro
2374 N. Kenwood Ave.
Fresno, CA 93650

Dear Ms. Shapiro:

We are sorry that your daughter's and granddaughter's travel with us did not go smoothly. Providing dependable service is what's expected of us — and when we don't operate flights on schedule, it's easy to understand our customers' disappointment. I truly wish we had performed better and that their plans had not been disrupted.

We are eager to restore your confidence in our ability to provide dependable, high-quality service. Please accept the enclosed transportation voucher, which you may apply toward future tickets on American. I hope we will have the pleasure of welcoming your family aboard again soon.

Ms. Shapiro, in addition, we appreciate your taking the time to write. It helps to receive comments such as yours, and we conscientiously follow through to be sure proper procedures are met. I assure you your letter is being put to good use.

Yours truly,

Ms. M. J. Matthews

Ms. M. J. Matthews
Executive Office

P.O. Box 619612, MD 2400, Dallas/Fort Worth Airport, Texas 75261-9612
817-967-2000

FIGURE 4–2. Adjustment Letter. Reprinted by permission of American Airlines, AMR Corporation, Inc.

Writer's Checklist: Writing Adjustment Letters

☑ Open with what the reader will consider good news:

- Grant the adjustment, if appropriate, for uncomplicated situations ("Enclosed is a replacement for the damaged part.").
- Reveal that you intend to grant the adjustment by admitting that the customer was right ("Yes, you were incorrectly billed for the delivery."). Then explain the specific details of the adjustment. This method is good for adjustments that require detailed explanations.
- Apologize for the error ("Please accept our apologies for the error in your account."). This method is effective when the customer's inconvenience is as much an issue as money.
- Use a combination of these techniques. Often, situations that require an adjustment also require flexibility.

☑ If an explanation will help restore your reader's confidence or goodwill, explain what caused the problem.

☑ Explain specifically how you intend to make the adjustment, if it is not obvious in your opening.

☑ Express appreciation to the customer for calling your attention to the problem. Explain that customer feedback helps your firm keep the quality of its product or service high. Also, point out any steps you may be taking to prevent a recurrence of the problem.

☑ Close pleasantly, looking forward, not back. Avoid recalling the problem in your closing ("Again, we apologize . . .").

WEB LINK ▶ WRITING AND FORMATTING DOCUMENTS

MODEL DOCUMENTS GALLERY
www.bedfordstmartins.com/modeldocs/

This site provides annotated examples of correspondence, reports, and other types of business writing.

Before granting an adjustment to a claim for which your company is at fault, you must determine what happened and what you can do to satisfy the customer. Be certain that you are familiar with your company's adjustment policy. In addition, be careful about your wording; for example, "We have just received your letter of May 7 about our *defective product*" could be ruled in a court of law as an admission that the product is in fact defective. Treat every claim individually, and lean toward giving the customer the benefit of the doubt.

You may sometimes need to grant a partial adjustment—even if a claim is not really justified—to regain the lost goodwill of a customer.

In some cases, in which a problem resulted from a customer's incorrect use of a product, for example, you may need to educate your reader about the use of your product or service. When writing a letter of adjustment in this situation, remember that your customer believes that his or her claim is justified. Therefore, it is wise to give the explanation before granting the claim—otherwise, your reader may skip the explanation. If your explanation establishes customer responsibility, be sure to do so tactfully. Figure 4–3 is an example of an educational adjustment letter.

FIGURE 4–3. Educational Adjustment Letter (Accompanying a Product)

Dear Mr. Ortiz:

Enclosed is your SWELCO Coffeemaker, which you sent to us on August 17.

In various parts of the country, tap water may contain a high mineral content. If you fill your SWELCO Coffeemaker with water for breakfast coffee before going to bed, a mineral scale will build up on the inner wall of the water tube — as explained on page 2 of your SWELCO Instruction Booklet.

We have removed the mineral scale from the water tube of your coffeemaker and thoroughly cleaned the entire unit. To ensure the best service from your coffeemaker in the future, clean it once a month by operating it with four ounces of white vinegar and eight cups of water. To rinse out the vinegar taste, operate the unit twice with clear water.

With proper care, your SWELCO Coffeemaker will serve you well for many years to come.

Sincerely,

collection letters

Collection letters serve two purposes: (1) collecting the overdue bill and (2) preserving the customer relationship.

Most companies use a series of collection letters in which the letters become increasingly demanding and urgent. Even so, letters should be courteous and show a genuine interest in the customer as well as concern for whatever problems are preventing prompt payment. See also **"you" viewpoint** (page 281).

The first stage consists of reminders stamped on the invoice, form letters, or brief personal notes. These early reminders should maintain a friendly tone that emphasizes the customer's good credit record until now. As in the example of a first-stage collection letter in Figure 4–4, you might suggest that nonpayment may be a result of a simple oversight.

FIGURE 4–4. First-Stage Collection Letter

Dear Mr. Holland:

With the new school year about to begin, your shoe store must be busier than ever as students purchase their back-to-school footwear. Perhaps in the rush of business you've overlooked paying your account of $742.00, which is now 60 days overdue.

Enclosed is our fall sales list. When you send in your check for your outstanding account, why not send in your next order and take advantage of these special prices.

Sincerely,

In the second stage, you now assume that some circumstances are preventing payment. Ask directly for payment, and inquire about possible problems, perhaps suggesting an installment payment plan if you are able to offer one. Mention the importance of good credit and remind the customer that he or she has always received good value from you. Make it easy to respond by enclosing a return envelope or by offering a toll-free telephone or fax number or a Web address where the customer can pay with a credit card. At this stage, your tone should be firmer and more direct than in the early stage, but it should never be rude, sarcastic, or threatening. Notice how the second-stage letter in Figure 4–5 is more direct than the first letter, but it is no less polite.

The third stage of collection letters reflects a sense of urgency because the customer has not responded to your previous letters. Although your tone should remain courteous, make your demand for payment explicit. Point out how reasonable you have been and urge the customer to pay at once to avoid legal action. An example of a third-stage letter appears in Figure 4–6.

Dear Mr. Holland:

We are concerned that we have not heard from you about your overdue account of $742.00 even though we have written three times in the past 90 days. Because you have always been one of our best customers, we have to wonder if some special circumstances have caused the delay. If so, please feel free to discuss the matter with us.

By sending us a check today, you can preserve your excellent credit record. Because you have always paid your account promptly in the past, we are sure that you will want to settle this balance now. If your balance is more than you can pay at present, we will be happy to work out mutually satisfactory payment arrangements.

Please use the enclosed envelope to send in your check, or call (800) 526-1945, toll-free, to discuss your account.

Sincerely,

FIGURE 4–5. Second-Stage Collection Letter

Dear Mr. Holland:

Your account in the amount of $742.00 is now 180 days overdue. You have already received a generous extension of time and, in fairness to our other customers, we cannot permit a further delay in payment.

Because you have not responded to any of our letters, we will be forced to turn your account over to our attorney for collection if we do not receive payment immediately. Such action, of course, will damage your previously fine credit rating.

Why not avoid this unpleasant situation by sending your check in the enclosed return envelope within 10 days or by calling (800) 526-1945 to discuss payment.

Sincerely,

FIGURE 4–6. Third-Stage Collection Letter

complaint letters

Companies sometimes make mistakes when they provide goods and services, and customers write complaint letters asking that such situations be corrected. The tone of a complaint letter is important; the most effective ones do not sound complaining. If you write a letter that reflects only your annoyance and anger, you may not be taken seriously. Assume that the recipient will be conscientious in correcting the problem. However, anticipate reader reactions or rebuttals.

- I reviewed carefully the "safe operating guidelines" in the user manual before I installed the device.

Without such explanations, readers may be tempted to dismiss your complaint.

Although the circumstances and severity of the problem may vary, effective complaint letters generally follow this pattern:

1. Identify the problem or faulty item(s) and include relevant invoice numbers, part names, and dates. It is often a good idea to include a copy of the receipt, bill, or contract.
2. Explain logically, clearly, and specifically what went wrong, especially for a problem with a service. (Avoid guessing at why you *think* some problem occurred.)
3. State what you expect the reader to do to solve the problem.

If you are writing to a large organization, address your complaint to Customer Service. In smaller organizations, you might write to a vice-president in charge of sales or service, or directly to the owner. As a last resort, you may find that sending copies of a complaint letter to more than one person in the company will get faster results. Figure 4–7 shows a typical complaint letter. See also **adjustment letters** (page 121) and **refusal letters** (page 147).

Subject: HV3 Monitors

On July 9, I ordered nine HV3 monitors for your model MX-15 scanner. The monitors were ordered from your Web site.

On August 2, I received from your Newark, New Jersey, parts warehouse seven HL monitors. I immediately returned these monitors with a note indicating the mistake that had been made. However, not only have I failed to receive the HV3 monitors I ordered, but I have also been billed repeatedly.

Would you please either send me the monitors I ordered or cancel my order. I have enclosed a copy of my original order letter, the return shipping form, and the most recent bill.

Sincerely,

FIGURE 4–7. Complaint Letter

correspondence

The process of writing letters (or emails or memos that function as letters) involves many of the same steps that go into writing most other documents, as described in "Five Steps to Successful Writing" (page xiii). One important consideration in correspondence is the impression you convey to readers. To convey a professional image—of yourself and your company or organization—take particular care with the tone and style of your writing. See also **email** (page 233), **memos** (page 143), and **business writing style** (page 254).

Audience: Tone and Goodwill

To focus the relevance of any correspondence for the reader, identify your subject in the opening.

- Yesterday, I received your letter and the pager, number AJ 50172. I sent the pager to our quality control department for tests.
  Carol Moore, our lead technician, reports that preliminary tests indicate . . .

Your closing should let the reader know what he or she should do next and reinforce goodwill.

- Thanks again for the report, and let me know if you want me to send you a copy of the tests.

Because a closing is in a position of emphasis, be especially careful to avoid clichés. Of course, some very commonly used closings are so appropriate, even though they are routine, that they are hard to replace ("If you have further questions, please let me know.").

Do not use such a closing just because it is easy. Make your closing work for you. It may be helpful to provide prompts to which the reader can respond.

- If you would like further information, such as a copy of the questionnaire we used, please email me at delgado@prn.com.

Although correspondence must convey a professional image, it is always more personal than reports or other forms of business writing. To achieve a conversational style, imagine your reader sitting across the desk from you and write to the reader as if you were talking face to face. Take into account your readers' needs and feelings. Ask yourself, "How might I feel if I were the recipient of such a letter?" and then tailor your message accordingly. Remember, an impersonal and unfriendly letter to a customer can tarnish the image of you and your business, but a thoughtful and sincere letter can enhance it. Suppose, for example, you received a refund request from a customer who forgot to enclose the receipt with the request. In a response to that customer, you might write the following:

- We must receive the sales receipt with your letter before we can process a refund.

If you consider how you might keep the customer's goodwill, you might word the request this way:

- Please mail or fax the sales receipt with your letter so that we can process your refund.

You can put the reader's needs and interests foremost in the letter by writing from the reader's perspective. Often, doing so means using the words *you* and *your* rather than *we, our, I,* and *mine*—a technique called the **"you" viewpoint** (page 281). Consider the following revision, which is written with the "you" viewpoint:

- So you can receive your refund promptly, please mail or fax the sales receipt with your letter.

That version stresses the reader's benefit and interest. By emphasizing the reader's needs, the writer will be more likely to accomplish the objective: to get the reader to act. See also **purpose/objective** (page 41).

Writer's Checklist: Using Tone to Build Goodwill

☑ Be respectful, not demanding.

DEMANDING	Submit your answer in one week.
RESPECTFUL	I would appreciate your answer within one week.

☑ Be modest, not arrogant.

ARROGANT	My report is thorough, and I'm sure that you won't be able to continue without it.
MODEST	I have tried to be as thorough as possible in my report, and I hope you find it useful.

☑ Be polite, not sarcastic.

SARCASTIC	I just now received the shipment we ordered six months ago. I'm sending it back—we can't use it now. Thanks a lot!
POLITE	I am returning the shipment we ordered on March 12, 20--. Unfortunately, it arrived too late for us to be able to use it.

Writer's Checklist: Using Tone to Build Goodwill (continued)

☑ Be positive and tactful, not negative and condescending.

NEGATIVE Your complaint about our prices is way off target. Our prices are definitely not any higher than those of our competitors.

TACTFUL Thank you for your suggestion concerning our prices. We believe, however, that our prices are competitive with, and in some cases are below, those of our competitors.

Good-News and Bad-News Patterns

Although the relative directness of correspondence may vary, it is generally more effective to present good news directly and bad news indirectly, especially if the stakes are high.* This principle is based on the fact that (1) readers form their impressions and attitudes very early in letters and (2) you as a writer may want to subordinate the bad news to reasons that make the bad news understandable. Further, if you are writing international correspondence, be aware that far more cultures are generally indirect in business messages than are direct. See also **international correspondence** (page 141).

Consider the thoughtlessness and direct rejection in Figure 4–8. Although the letter is concise and uses the pronouns *you* and *your,* the writer does not consider how the recipient is likely to feel as she reads the letter. Its pattern is (1) bad news, (2) explanation, (3) close.

FIGURE 4–8. A Poor Bad-News Letter

> Ms. Barbara L. Mauer
> 157 Beach Drive
> San Diego, CA 92113
>
> Dear Ms. Mauer:
>
> Your application for the position of records administrator at Southtown Dental Center has been rejected. We have found someone more qualified than you.
>
> Sincerely,

4. Correspondence

*Gerald J. Alred, "'We Regret to Inform You': Toward a New Theory of Negative Messages," in *Studies in Technical Communication,* ed. Brenda R. Sims. (Denton: University of North Texas and NCTE, 1993), 17–36.

A better general pattern for bad-news letters is (1) an opening that provides context, (2) an explanation, (3) the bad news, and (4) goodwill. (See also **refusal letters,** page 147.) The opening introduces the subject and establishes a professional tone. The body provides an explanation by reviewing the facts that make the bad news understandable. Although bad news is never pleasant, information that either puts the bad news in perspective or makes it seem reasonable maintains goodwill between the writer and the reader. The closing should reinforce a positive relationship through goodwill or helpful information. Consider, for example, the rejection letter shown in Figure 4–9. It carries the same disappointing news as does the letter in Figure 4–8, but the writer is careful to thank the reader for her time and effort, explain why she was not accepted for the job, and offer her encouragement.

FIGURE 4–9. A Courteous Bad-News Letter

	Dear Ms. Mauer:
Context	Thank you for your time and effort in applying for the position of records administrator at Southtown Dental Center.
Explanation leading to bad news	Because we need someone who can assume the duties here with a minimum of training, we have selected an applicant with over ten years of experience.
Goodwill	I am sure that with your excellent college record you will find a position in another office.
	Sincerely,

Presenting good news is, of course, easier. Present good news at the beginning of the letter. By presenting the good news first, you increase the likelihood that the reader will pay careful attention to details, and you achieve goodwill from the start. The pattern for good-news letters should be (1) good news, (2) explanation of facts, and (3) goodwill. Figure 4–10 is a good example of a good-news letter.

Writing Style and Accuracy

Letter-writing style varies from informal, as in a letter to a close business associate, to formal (or restrained) as in a letter to someone you do not know.

INFORMAL It worked! The new process is better than we had dreamed.

	Dear Ms. Mauer:
Good news	Please accept our offer of the position of records administrator at Southtown Dental Center.
Explanation	If the terms we discussed in the interview are acceptable to you, please come in at 9:30 A.M. on November 15. At that time, we will ask you to complete our human resources form, in addition to . . .
Goodwill	I, as well as the others in the office, look forward to working with you. Everyone was favorably impressed with you during your interview.
	Sincerely,

FIGURE 4–10. A Good-News Letter

RESTRAINED You will be pleased to know that the new process is more effective than we had expected.

You will probably find yourself using the restrained style more frequently than the informal one. Remember that an overdone attempt to sound casual or friendly can sound insincere. However, do not adopt so formal a style that your letters read like legal contracts. (See **affectation,** page 251.)

AFFECTED In response to your query, we no longer possess an original copy of the brochure requested. Please be advised that a photographic copy is enclosed herewith. Address further correspondence to this office for assistance as required.

IMPROVED Because we are currently out of original copies of our brochure, I am sending you a photocopy. If I can help further, please let me know.

Check your letters for accuracy. Incorrect punctuation or grammar and unconventional usage can undermine your credibility. Likewise, facts, figures, and dates that are incorrect or misleading may cost time, money, and goodwill. Remember that when you sign a letter, you are accepting responsibility for it. Therefore, allow yourself time to review correspondence carefully before sending it.

Format and Design

Although word-processing software provides templates for correspondence, it may not provide specific dimensions and spacing. To achieve a professional appearance, center the letter on the page vertically and horizontally. Although one-inch margins are the default standard in many word-processing programs, it is more important to establish a picture frame of blank space surrounding the page of text. When you use organizational letterhead stationery, consider the bottom of the letterhead as the top edge of the paper. The right margin should be approximately as wide as the left margin. To give a fuller appearance to very short letters, increase both margins to about an inch and a half. Use your computer's full-page or print-preview feature to check for proportion.

The two most common formats for business letters are the *full-block* style shown in Figure 4–11 and the *modified-block* style shown in Figure 4–12. In the full-block style, which should be used only with letterhead, the entire letter is aligned at the left margin. In the modified-block style, the return address, date, and complimentary closing begin at the center of the page and the other elements are aligned at the left margin. All other letter styles are variations of the full-block and modified-block styles.

If your employer requires a particular format, use it. Otherwise, follow the guidelines provided here, and review the examples in Figures 4–11 and 4–12.

Heading. Place your full address and the date in the heading. Because your name appears at the end of the letter, it need not be included in the heading. Spell out words like *street, avenue, first,* and *west* rather than abbreviating them. You may either spell out the name of the state in full or use the standard Postal Service abbreviation. The date usually goes directly beneath the last line of the return address. Do not abbreviate the name of the month. If you are using company letterhead that gives the address, enter only the date, three lines below the last line of printed copy or two inches from the top of the letter.

Inside Address. Include the recipient's full name, title, and address in the inside address, two to six lines below the date, depending on the length of the letter. The inside address should be aligned with the left margin, and the left margin should be at least one inch wide.

The Salutation. Place the salutation, or greeting, two lines below the inside address and align it with the left margin. In most business letters, the salutation contains the recipient's personal title (*Mr., Ms., Dr.,* and so on) and last name, followed by a colon. If you are on a first-name basis with the recipient, use only the first name in the salutation.

Address women as *Ms.,* unless they have expressed a preference for *Miss* or *Mrs.* However, other titles (such as *Dr., Senator, Major*) take precedence over *Ms.* If you do not know whether the recipient is a man or a woman, use a title appropriate to the context of the letter. The following are examples of the kinds of titles you may find suitable: Dear Customer:, Dear Colleague:, Dear IT Professional:.

Letterhead	 520 Niagara Street Braintree, MA 02184 Phone: (781) 787-1175 Fax: (781) 787-1213 Email: 92000.121@CompuServe.com
Date	May 15, 20--
Inside address	Mr. George W. Nagel Director of Operations Boston Transit Authority 57 West City Avenue Boston, MA 02210
Salutation	Dear Mr. Nagel:
Body	Enclosed is our final report evaluating the safety measures for the Boston Intercity Transit System. We believe that the report covers the issues you raised and that it is self-explanatory. However, if you have any further questions, we would be happy to meet with you at your convenience. We would also like to express our appreciation to Mr. L. K. Sullivan of your committee for his generous help during our trips to Boston.
Compli-mentary close	Sincerely,
Signature	*Carolyn Brown*
Typed name Title	Carolyn Brown, Ph.D. Director of Research
Additional information	CB/ls bt515.doc Enclosure: Final Safety Report cc: ITS Safety Committee Members

FIGURE 4–11. Full-Block Style Letter (with Letterhead)

Center

Heading from center to right

3814 Oak Lane
Dedham, MA 02180
December 8, 20--

Inside address

Dr. Carolyn Brown
Director of Research
Evans & Associates
Transportation Engineers
520 Niagara Street
Braintree, MA 02184

Salutation

Dear Dr. Brown:

Body

Thank you very much for allowing me to tour your testing facilities. The information I gained from the tour will be of great help to me in preparing the report for my class at Marshall Institute. The tour has also given me some insight into the work I may eventually do as a laboratory technician.

I especially appreciated the time and effort Vikram Singh spent in showing me your facilities. His comments and advice were most helpful.

Again, thank you.

Complimentary close aligned with heading

Sincerely,

Signature

Leslie Warden

Typed name

Leslie Warden

Center

FIGURE 4–12. Modified-Block Style Letter (without Letterhead)

If you are writing to a large company and you do not know the name or title of the recipient, you may address the letter to an appropriate department or identify the subject in a subject line and use no salutation.

- National Business Systems
  501 West National Avenue
  Minneapolis, MN 55407

  Attention: Customer Relations Department

  I am returning three pagers that failed to operate. . . .

- National Business Systems
  501 West National Avenue
  Minneapolis, MN 55407

  Subject: Defective Parts for SL-100 Pagers

  I am returning three pagers that failed to operate. . . .

When a person's first name could be either feminine or masculine, one solution is to use both the first and the last names in the salutation.

- Dear Pat Smith:

Avoid "To Whom It May Concern" because it is impersonal and dated.

For multiple recipients, the following salutations are appropriate:

- Dear Professor Allen and Dr. Rivera: [two recipients]
- Dear Ms. Becham, Ms. Moore, and Mr. Stein: [three recipients]
- Dear Colleagues: [Members, or other suitable collective term]

The Body. The body of the letter should begin two lines below the salutation (or any element that precedes the body, such as a subject or attention line). Single-space within paragraphs, and double-space between paragraphs. To provide a fuller appearance to a very short letter, you can increase the side margins or increase the font size. You can also insert extra space above the inside address, the typed (signature) name, and the initials of the person keying the letter—but do not exceed twice the recommended space for each of these elements.

Complimentary Closing. Type the complimentary closing two spaces below the body. Use a standard expression like *Sincerely, Sincerely yours,* or *Yours truly.* (If the recipient is a friend as well as a business associate, you can use a less formal closing, such as *Best wishes* or *Best regards* or, simply, *Best.*) Capitalize only the initial letter of the first word, and follow the expression with a comma. Place your full name four lines below, aligned with the closing. On the next line include your business title, if it is appropriate to do so. Sign the letter in the space between the complimentary closing and your name.

Second Page. If a letter requires a second page, always carry at least two lines of the body text over to that page. Use plain (nonletterhead) paper of quality equivalent to that of the letterhead stationery for the second page. It should have a header with the recipient's name, the page number, and the date. The heading can go in the upper left-hand corner or across the page, as shown in Figure 4–13.

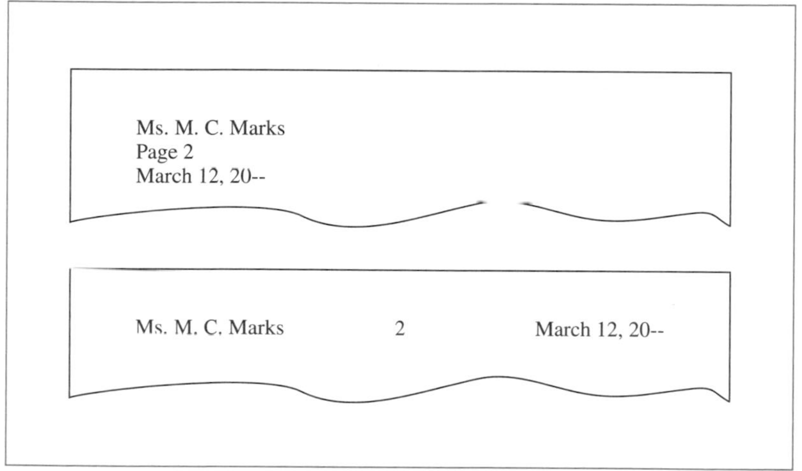

FIGURE 4–13. Headers for the Second Page of a Letter

Additional Information. Business letters sometimes require additional information that is placed at the left margin, two spaces below the typed name and title of the writer in a long letter, four spaces below in a short letter.

Reference initials identify the person keying the letter, if that person is not the writer. Show the letter writer's initials in capital letters, followed by a slash mark, and then the initials of the person keying the letter in lowercase letters, as shown in Figure 4–11. When the writer is also the person keying the letter, no initials are needed.

Filename notation is sometimes included to indicate where the document is stored electronically (for example, *bt515.doc*), as shown in Figure 4–11.

Enclosure notations indicate that the writer is sending material along with the letter (an invoice, an article, and so on). Enclosure notations may take several forms:

- Enclosure: Final Safety Report
- Enclosures (2)
- Enc. (or Encs.)

Note that you also must mention the enclosure in the body of the letter.

Copy notation (cc:) tells the reader that a copy of the letter is being sent to the named recipients (see Figure 4–11). Use a blind-copy notation (bcc:) when you do not want the addressee to know that a copy is being sent to someone else. A blind-copy notation appears only on the copy, not on the original.

- bcc: Dr. Brenda Shelton

For additional details on letter format and design, you may wish to consult a guide such as *The Gregg Reference Manual* (9th edition) by William A. Sabin.

Writer's Checklist: Writing Correspondence

- ☑ Establish your purpose, analyze your audience, and determine your scope.
- ☑ Prepare an outline, even if it is only a list of points to be covered in the order you want to cover them (see **outlining,** page 291).
- ☑ Write the first draft (see **writing a draft,** page 47).
- ☑ Allow for a cooling period prior to **revision** (page 44), especially for correspondence that addresses a problem.
- ☑ Revise the draft, checking for key problems in clarity and **coherence** (page 256).
- ☑ Use the appropriate format.
- ☑ Check for accuracy: make sure that all facts, figures, and dates are correct.
- ☑ Check for appropriate punctuation (pages 361–94) and use good **proofreading** (page 40) techniques.
- ☑ Review your letter before you send it. Remember that when you sign a letter, initial a memo, or send an email, you are accepting responsibility for it.

cover letters

A *cover letter* identifies an item that is being sent, the person to whom it is being sent, and the reason that it is being sent; it provides a permanent record for both the writer and the reader. See also **application letters** (page 154).

Keep your remarks brief in a cover letter. Your opening should explain what is being sent and why. Then, you might highlight or briefly summarize the information you are sending. A cover letter for a proposal, for example, might point out sections in the proposal of particular interest to the reader and go on to present a key point or two, explaining why the writer's firm is the best one to do the job. This paragraph could also mention the conditions under which the material was prepared, such as limitations of time or budget. The closing paragraph might contain acknowledgments, offer additional assistance, or express the hope that the material will fulfill its purpose.

The example in Figure 4–14 is concise, but it also includes details such as how the report's information was gathered.

FIGURE 4–14. Cover Letter (for a Report)

Mr. Roger Hammersmith
Ecology Systems, Inc.
1015 Clarke Street
Chicago, IL 60615

Dear Mr. Hammersmith:

Enclosed is the report estimating our power consumption for the year as requested by John Brenan, Vice-President, on September 4.

The report is a result of several meetings with the Manager of Plant Operations and her staff and an extensive survey of all our employees. The survey was delayed by the transfer of key staff in Building "A." We believe, however, that the report will provide the information you need in order to furnish us with a cost estimate for the installation of your Mark II Energy Saving System.

We would like to thank Diana Biel of ESI for her assistance in preparing the survey. If you need any more information, please let me know.

Sincerely,

inquiry letters and responses

Your purpose in writing an inquiry letter will probably be to obtain answers to specific questions, as shown in Figure 4–15. You will be more likely to receive a prompt, helpful reply if you follow these guidelines:

- Keep your questions specific and clear but concise.
- Phrase your questions so that the reader will immediately know the type of information you are seeking, why you need it, and how you will use it.

Jane E. Metcalf
Engineering Services
Miami Valley Power Company
P.O. Box 1444
Miamitown, OH 45733

Dear Ms. Metcalf:

Could you please send me some information on heating systems for a computerized, energy-efficient house that a team of engineering students at the University of Dayton is designing?

The house, which contains 2,000 square feet of living space (17,600 cubic feet), meets all the requirements stipulated in your brochure "Insulating for Efficiency." We need the following information:

1. The proper-size heat pump to use in this climate for such a home.
2. The wattage of the supplemental electrical heating units that would be required for this climate.
3. The estimated power consumption and current rates of those units for one year.

We will be happy to send you a copy of our preliminary design report and any further information about the project that may be of interest to you. If you have questions or suggestions, please contact me at kjp@fly.ud.edu or call 513-229-4598.

Thank you for your help.

FIGURE 4–15. Inquiry Letter

- If possible, present your questions in a numbered list to make it easy for your reader to respond to them.
- Keep the number of questions to a minimum.
- Offer some inducement for the reader to respond, such as promising to share the results of what you are doing.
- Promise to keep responses confidential, if appropriate.

At the end of the letter, thank the reader for taking the time to respond. In addition, make it convenient for the recipient to respond by providing contact information, such as a phone number or an email address, as shown in Figure 4–15.

Responding to Inquiries

When you receive an inquiry, determine whether you have both the information and authority to respond. If you are the right person in your organization to respond, answer as promptly as you can, and be sure to answer every question asked. How long and how detailed your response should be depends on the nature of the question and the information provided in the letter by the writer. If you have received a letter that you feel you cannot answer, find out who can and forward the letter to that person. Notify the letter writer that you have forwarded the letter.

When the person to whom the inquiry has been forwarded replies, he or she should state in the first paragraph of the response why someone else is answering the original inquiry, as shown in Figure 4–16.

FIGURE 4–16. Response to an Inquiry

Dear Ms. Parsons:

Jane Metcalf forwarded to me your inquiry of March 11 about the house that your engineering team is designing. I can estimate the insulation requirements of a typical home of 17,600 cubic feet as follows:

1. For such a home, we would generally recommend a heat pump capable of delivering 40,000 Btus. Our model AL-42 (17 kilowatts) meets that requirement.
2. With the AL-42's efficiency, you don't need supplemental heating units.
3. Depending on usage, the AL-42 unit averages between 1,000 and 1,500 kilowatt-hours from December through March. To determine the current rate for such usage, check with Dayton Power and Light Company.

I can give you an answer that would apply specifically to your house only with information about its particular design (such as number of stories, windows, and entrances). If you send me more details, I will be happy to provide more precise figures. Your project sounds interesting.

Sincerely,

Michael Wang

Michael Wang
Engineering Assistant
mwang@mvpc.org

4. Correspondence

international correspondence

Because business is conducted in an increasingly global marketplace, you need to be aware of how correspondence varies among cultures. For example, in the United States, direct, concise correspondence may demonstrate courtesy by not wasting another person's time; in other cultures (in countries such as Spain and India), such directness and brevity may suggest that the writer dislikes the reader so much that he or she wishes to make the communication as short as possible. As another example, where an American writer might consider one brief letter sufficient to communicate a request, a writer in another culture may expect an exchange of three or four longer letters to pave the way for action.

When you read correspondence from businesspeople in other cultures or countries, be alert to differences in such features as customary expressions, openings, and closings. Japanese business writers, for example, have traditionally used openings that reflect on the season, compliment the reader's success, and offer hopes for the reader's continued prosperity.

You should also be alert to how writers from other cultures express bad news. Japanese business writers, for example, traditionally express negative messages and **refusal letters** (page 147) indirectly to avoid embarrassing the recipient. (To learn more about this subject, see **global communication** (page 211) and **global graphics** (page 168). Use the term *intercultural communication* to search library and Internet sources.)

Writer's Checklist: Writing International Correspondence

☑ Avoid idioms ("it's a slam dunk," "give a heads up"), unusual figures of speech, and allusions to events or attitudes particular to American life. See also **figures of speech** (page 263) and **idioms** (page 265).

☑ Avoid humor, irony, and sarcasm; they are easily misunderstood outside their cultural context.

☑ Consider whether jargon or technical terminology can be found in abbreviated English-language dictionaries. See also **affectation** (page 251) and **word choice** (page 280).

☑ Write clear and complete sentences; unusual word order or rambling sentences will frustrate and confuse readers. See **sentence construction** (page 341), **sentence fragments** (page 347), and **garbled sentences** (page 264).

☑ Avoid using an overly simplified style that will potentially offend the reader.

☑ Read your writing aloud to identify misplaced **modifiers** (page 324) and **awkwardness** (page 252).

☑ Write out the date and name of the month to make the entire date immediately clear (January 11, 20-- *not* 1/11/--).

☑ Specify time zones or refer to international standards, such as Greenwich Mean Time (GMT) or Universal Time Coordinated (UTC).

Writer's Checklist: Writing International Correspondence (continued)

☑ Where possible, use international measurement standards, such as the metric system (18° C, 14 cm, 45 kg, and so on).

☑ Proofread your correspondence. See **proofreading** (page 40) and **English as a second language** (page 320).

WEB LINK ▶ USING A DIRECTORY

THE GOOGLE INTERNATIONAL BUSINESS AND TRADE DIRECTORY
directory.google.com/Top/Business/International_Business_and_Trade/

This directory provides an excellent starting point for information related to customs, communication, and international standards.

memos

Memos—paper and electronic—are used for many of the types of workplace writing described in entries throughout this book. Memos are internal documents that, for example, announce policies, disseminate information, delegate responsibilities, instruct employees, and report results. They provide a record of decisions made and actions taken. They also play a key role in the management of many organizations because managers use memos to inform and motivate employees.

Writing Memos

Keep in mind that many of the principles discussed in **correspondence** (page 128) and **email** (page 233) apply to writing memos. To produce an effective memo, outline it first, even if you simply jot down points to be covered and then order them logically. With careful preparation, your memos will be both concise and adequately developed. Adequate development of your thoughts is crucial to the memo's clarity, as the following example indicates.

ABRUPT	Be more careful on the loading dock.
DEVELOPED	To prevent accidents on the loading dock, follow these procedures: 1. Check . . . 2. Load only . . . 3. Replace . . .

Although the abrupt version is concise, it is not as clear and specific as the developed revision. Do not assume your reader will know what you mean. Readers who are pressed for time may misinterpret a vague memo.

Openings. Although methods of development vary, a memo normally begins with a statement of its main point. Consider the following example:

- Because of our inability to serve our clients efficiently, I recommend we hire an additional attorney.

When your reader is not familiar with the subject or with the background of a problem, provide an introductory paragraph before stating the main point of the memo. Doing so is especially important in memos that will serve as records of crucial information. Generally, longer or complex memos benefit most from more thorough introductions. However, even when you are writing a short memo about a familiar subject, remind readers of the context. In the following example, words that provide context are shown in italics.

- *As Maria recommended,* I reviewed the office reorganization plan. I like most of the features; however, . . .

Do not state the main point first when (1) the reader is likely to be highly skeptical or (2) you are disagreeing with persons in positions of higher authority. In such cases, a more persuasive tactic is to state the problem first, then present the specific points supporting your final recommendation. See also **persuasion** (page 35).

Writing Style and Tone. Whether your memo is formal or informal depends entirely on your readers and your purpose. A message to a coworker who is also a friend is likely to be informal, while an internal proposal to several readers or to someone two or three levels higher in your organization is likely to be more formal. Consider the following versions of a statement:

TO AN EQUAL	I can't go along with the plan because I think it poses serious logistical problems. First, . . .
TO A SUPERIOR	The logistics of moving the department may pose serious problems. First, . . .

A memo that gives instructions to a subordinate should also be relatively formal, impersonal, and direct, unless you are trying to reassure or praise. When writing to subordinates, remember that *managing* does not mean *dictating.* (See **affectation,** page 251.) In fact, it may both irritate and baffle readers, cause a loss of time, and produce costly errors. Consider the unintended secondary messages the following notice conveys:

- It has been decided that the office will be open the day after Thanksgiving.

"It has been decided" not only sounds impersonal but also communicates an authoritarian, management-versus-employee tone. The passive voice also suggests that the decision-maker does not want to say "I have decided" and thus be identified. (See **voice,** page 356.) One solution is to remove the first part of the sentence.

- The office will be open the day after Thanksgiving.

The best solution would be to suggest both that there is a good reason for the decision and that employees are privy to (if not a part of) the decision-making process.

- Because we must meet the December 15 deadline to be eligible for the government contract, the office will be open the day after Thanksgiving.

By subordinating the bad news (the need to work on that day), the writer focuses on the reasoning behind the decision to work. Employees may not necessarily like the message, but they will at least understand that the decision is not arbitrary and is tied to an important deadline.

Lists and Headings. Lists can give impact to important points by making it easier for your reader to quickly grasp information. Be careful, however, not to overuse lists. A memo that consists almost entirely of lists is difficult to understand because it forces the reader to connect the separate and disjointed items on the page. Further, lists lose their effectiveness when they are overused. See also **lists** (page 201).

Headings are another attention-getting device, particularly in long memos. They divide material into manageable segments, call attention to main topics, and signal a shift in topic. Readers can scan the headings and read only the section or sections appropriate to their needs. See also **headings** (page 194).

Closings. A memo closing can accomplish many important tasks, such as building positive relationships with readers, encouraging colleagues and employees, and letting recipients know what you will do or what you expect of them.

- I will discuss the problem with the marketing consultant and let you know by Monday what we are able to change.

Although routine statements are sometimes unavoidable ("Thanks again for your help"), make your closing work for you by providing specific prompts to which the reader can respond.

- If you would like further information, such as a copy of the questionnaire we used, please email me at delgado@prn.com.

Format and Design

Memos vary greatly in format and customs. Although there is no single standard, Figure 4–17 shows a typical 8½-by-11 inch format with a printed company name. Subject lines announce the topic; because they

PROFESSIONAL PUBLISHING SERVICES
MEMORANDUM

TO: Barbara Smith, Publications Manager
FROM: Hannah Kaufman, Vice-President HK
DATE: April 14, 20--
SUBJECT: Schedule for ACM Electronics Brochure

ACM Electronics has asked us to prepare a comprehensive brochure for its Milwaukee office by August 9, 20--. We have worked with electronics firms in the past, so this job should be relatively easy to prepare. My guess is that the job will take nearly two months. Ted Harris has requested time and cost estimates for the project. Fred Moore in production will prepare the cost estimates, and I would like you to prepare a tentative schedule for the project.

Additional Personnel

In preparing the schedule, check the availability of the following:

1. Production schedule for all staff writers
2. Available freelance writers
3. Dependable graphic designers

Ordinarily, we would not need to depend on outside personnel; however, because our bid for the *Wall Street Journal* special project is still under consideration, we could be short of staff in June and July. Further, we have to consider vacations that have already been approved.

Time Estimates

Please give me time estimates by April 19. A successful job done on time will give us a good chance to obtain the contract to do ACM Electronics' annual report for its stockholders' meeting this fall.

I know your staff can do the job.

cc: Ted Harris, President
Fred Moore, Production Editor

FIGURE 4–17. Typical Memo Format

4. Correspondence

also aid filing and later retrieval, they must be specific and accurate. For example, "Tuition Reimbursement for Time-Management Seminar" is a better, more specific subject line than "Tuition Reimbursement." Also, capitalize all major words in a subject line, except articles, prepositions, and conjunctions with fewer than four letters unless they are the first or last words. Remember that the subject line should not substitute for an opening that provides context for the message. The final step is signing or initialing a memo, a practice that lets readers know that you approve of its contents. Where you sign or initial the memo depends on the practice of your organization. Figure 4–17 shows a typical placement of initials.

refusal letters

When you must deliver a negative message (or bad news), you may need to write a refusal letter, which could also take the form of a **memo** (page 143) or an **email** message (page 233). See also **correspondence** (page 128) and **inquiry letters and responses** (page 139).

Your letter should lead logically to the refusal. Often, stating the bad news in your opening will affect your reader negatively. The ideal refusal letter says *no* in such a way that you not only avoid antagonizing your reader but also maintain goodwill. To do so, you must convince your reader that your reasons for refusing are logical or understandable *before* you present the bad news. The following pattern is an effective way to deal with this problem:

1. In the opening, provide context and establish a professional tone.
2. Review the facts leading to the bad news.
3. Give the bad news, based on the facts.
4. In the closing, establish or reestablish a positive relationship.

The purpose of the opening is to establish a professional tone and introduce the subject and its context. If your refusal is in response to a complaint letter, do not begin by recalling the reader's disappointment ("We regret your dissatisfaction . . ."). (See **complaint letters,** page 126.) You can express appreciation for your reader's time, effort, or interest, if appropriate, to soften the disappointment.

- The Screening Procedures Committee appreciates the time and effort you spent on your proposal for a new security-clearance procedure.

Next, analyze the circumstances of the situation sympathetically by placing yourself in the reader's position. Clearly establish the reasons you cannot do what the reader wants—even though you have not yet said you cannot do it. A good explanation should detail the reasons for your refusal so thoroughly that the reader will accept your refusal as a logical conclusion, as shown in the following example:

- We reviewed the potential effects of implementing your proposed security-clearance procedure companywide. We asked the Security Systems Department to review the data, surveyed industry practices, sought the views of senior management, and submitted the idea to our legal staff. As a result of this process, we have reached the following conclusions:
  - The cost savings you project are correct only if the procedure could be required universally.
  - The components of your procedure are legal, but most are not widely accepted by our industry.
  - Based on our survey, some components could alienate employees who would perceive them as violating an individual's rights.
  - Enforcing companywide use would prove costly and impractical.

Don't belabor the bad news—state your refusal quickly, clearly, and as positively as possible. The refusal letter in Figure 4–18 declines an invitation to speak.

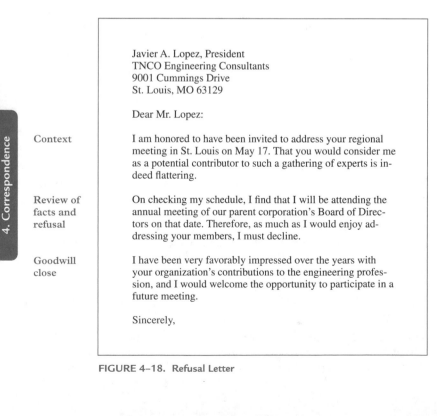

Javier A. Lopez, President
TNCO Engineering Consultants
9001 Cummings Drive
St. Louis, MO 63129

Dear Mr. Lopez:

Context

I am honored to have been invited to address your regional meeting in St. Louis on May 17. That you would consider me as a potential contributor to such a gathering of experts is indeed flattering.

Review of facts and refusal

On checking my schedule, I find that I will be attending the annual meeting of our parent corporation's Board of Directors on that date. Therefore, as much as I would enjoy addressing your members, I must decline.

Goodwill close

I have been very favorably impressed over the years with your organization's contributions to the engineering profession, and I would welcome the opportunity to participate in a future meeting.

Sincerely,

FIGURE 4–18. Refusal Letter

- For those reasons, the committee recommends that divisions continue their current security-screening procedures.

Close your letter or message in a way that reestablishes goodwill. You might provide an option, offer a friendly remark, assure the reader of your high opinion of his or her product or service, or merely wish the reader success.

- Because some components of your procedure may apply in certain circumstances, we would like to feature your ideas in the next issue of *The Guardian.* I have asked the editor to contact you next week. On behalf of the committee, thank you for the thoughtful proposal.

sales letters

A sales letter—a letter that promotes a product, service, or business—requires both a thorough knowledge of the product or service and an understanding of the potential customer's needs.

An effective sales letter (1) catches readers' attention, (2) arouses their interest, (3) convinces them that your product or service will fulfill a need or desire, and (4) confidently asks them to take the course of action you suggest. See also **persuasion** (page 35) and **promotional writing** (page 39).

Your first task is to determine to whom your letter should be sent. One good source of names is a list of your customers; people who have at some time purchased a product or service from you may do so again. Other sources are lists of people who may be interested in certain products or services. Companies that specialize in marketing techniques compile such lists from the membership rolls of professional associations, lists of trade-show attendees, and the like. Because outside lists tend to be expensive, select them with care.

Once you determine who is to receive your sales letter, learn as much as you can about your readers. Knowledge of their sex, age, vocation, geographical location, educational level, financial status, and interests will help determine your approach. You must be aware of your readers' needs so that you can effectively tell them how your product or service will satisfy them.

Analyze your product or service carefully to determine your strongest psychological sales points. Psychological selling involves stressing a product's benefits, which may be intangible, rather than its physical features. Select the most important psychological selling point about your product or service and build your sales letter around it. Show how your product or service will make your readers' jobs easier, increase their status, make their personal lives more pleasant, and so on.

In the body of your letter, show how your product or service can satisfy your readers' needs or desires, which you identified in your opening. Then describe the physical features of your product in terms of their benefit to your readers. Help your readers imagine themselves using your product or service—and enjoying the benefits of doing so. See also **"you" viewpoint** (page 281).

Writer's Checklist: Writing Sales Letters

☑ Attract your readers' attention and arouse their interest in the opening. Start out, for example, by describing a feature of the product or service that you believe would appeal strongly to their needs.

☑ Be certain that any claim you make in a sales letter is valid. Make no claims that are not true. Be careful of overstatement. If you say only that a product is safe, you are guaranteeing its absolute safety. Therefore, say that the product is safe provided that normal safety precautions are taken. (See also **ethics in writing,** page 261.)

☑ Present evidence to convince readers that your product or service is everything you claim it to be. You can offer a money-back guarantee, a free trial use of your product, testimonials, or case histories. Do not exaggerate; you will lose readers' confidence if your claims sound unreasonable. Do not speak negatively of a competitor.

☑ Minimize the negative effect price can have on readers. You can do this in one of several ways.

- Mention the price along with a reminder of the benefits of the product.
- State the price in terms of a unit rather than a set ($2 per item instead of $60 per set).
- Identify the daily, monthly, or even yearly cost based on the estimated life of the product.
- Suggest a series of payments rather than the total.
- Compare the cost of your product with that of something readers accept readily.

☑ Suggest ways readers can make immediate use of the product or service.

☑ Make it easy and worthwhile for customers to respond. You might include directions to your store, a discount coupon, instructions for phone-in orders and free delivery, or a Web address where customers can view special discounts and order online.

5

Job Application

Preview

This section includes entries related to a successful **job search** – from the crucial **application letters** and **résumés** to **follow-up letters** and **acceptance/refusal letters.** The section also offers strategies for **interviewing for a job** and advice on the often sensitive process of **salary negotiations.**

acceptance / refusal letters

When you decide to accept a job offer, you can notify your new employer in a phone conversation or a meeting—but to make your decision official, you need to send an acceptance letter to your new employer. For general advice on letter writing, see **correspondence** (page 128).

Figure 5–1 shows an example of an acceptance letter written by a college student. Of course, the details you include in your own letter will vary depending on your previous conversations with your new employer. Note that in the first paragraph of Figure 5–1, the student identifies the job he is accepting and the salary he has been offered—doing so can avoid any misunderstandings about the job or the salary. The second paragraph details his plans for moving and reporting for work. Even if the student discussed these arrangements during earlier conversations, he needs to confirm them, officially, in this letter. The student

Mr. F. F. Vallone
Manager of Human Resources
Calcutex Industries, Inc.
3275 Commercial Park Drive
Raleigh, NC 27609

Dear Mr. Vallone:

I am pleased to accept your offer of $30,500 per year as a junior ACR designer in the Calcutex Group.

After graduation, I plan to leave Charlotte on Tuesday, June 16. I should be able to find suitable living accommodations within a few days and be ready to report for work on the following Monday, June 22. Please let me know if this date is satisfactory to you.

I look forward to working with the design team at Calcutex.

Very truly yours,

Philip Ming

Philip Ming

FIGURE 5–1. Acceptance Letter

then concludes with a brief but enthusiastic statement that he looks forward to working for the new employer.

When you decide to reject a job offer, send a job refusal letter to make that decision official, even if you have already notified the employer during a meeting or on the phone. Writing a letter is a gesture that the employer will appreciate. Be especially tactful and courteous—the employer you are refusing has spent time and effort interviewing you and may have counted on your accepting the job. Remember, you may apply for another job at that company in the future. In Figure 5–2, an example of a job refusal letter, the applicant mentions something positive about his contact with the employer and refers to the specific job offered. He indicates his serious consideration of the offer, provides a logical reason for the refusal, and concludes on a pleasant note. For further strategy on handling refusals and negative messages generally, see **refusal letters** (page 147).

FIGURE 5–2. Letter of Refusal

Dear Mr. Vallone:

I enjoyed talking with you about your opening for a technical writer, and I was gratified to receive your offer. Although I have given the offer serious thought, I have decided to accept a position as a copywriter with an advertising agency. I feel that the job I have chosen is better suited to my skills and long-term goals.

I appreciate your consideration and the time you spent with me. I wish you the best of luck in filling the position.

Sincerely,

application letters

When applying for a job, you usually need to submit both a **résumé** (page 166) and an application letter (also referred to as a cover letter). Unless the prospective employer requests a résumé only, be sure to submit an application letter as well. See also **job search** (page 163).

The application letter is essentially a sales letter in which you market your skills, abilities, and knowledge (see also **sales letters,** page 149). Therefore, your application letter must be persuasive. The successful application letter accomplishes four tasks: (1) it catches the reader's attention favorably, (2) it explains which particular job interests you and why, (3) it convinces the reader that you are qualified for the job by drawing your reader's attention to particular elements in your résumé, and (4) it requests an interview. See also **audience/readers** (page 3) and **interviewing for a job** (page 160).

Opening Paragraph

In the opening paragraph, provide context and show your enthusiasm:

1. Indicate how you heard about the opening. If you have been referred to a company by an employee, a career counselor, a professor, or someone else, be sure to mention this even before you state your job objective, as illustrated in Figure 5–4 (page 158) ("I recently learned from Jodi Hammel").
2. State your job objective and mention the specific job title, as shown in Figure 5–5 (page 159) ("Karen Jarrett informed me of a possible opening for a district manager"). Those who make hiring decisions review many application letters. To save them time while also calling attention to your strengths as a candidate, state your job objective directly in your first paragraph.
3. Explain why you are interested in the job, as in Figure 5–3 (page 157)("Your firm's buyer training program is considered one of the most effective") and Figure 5–4 (page 158) ("Your position interests me . . . because . . . I can further develop my skills and talents").

Central Paragraphs

In the second and third paragraphs, show through examples that you are highly qualified for the job. Limit each of these paragraphs to just one basic point that is clearly stated in the topic sentence. (See also **paragraphs**, page 31.) For example, your second paragraph might focus on work experience and your third paragraph on educational achievements. Don't just *tell* readers that you're qualified—*show* them by including examples and details. Come across as proud of your achievements and refer to your enclosed résumé. Indicate how (with your talents) you can make valuable contributions to their company, such as "I am confident that my ability to take the initiative would be a valuable asset to your company."

Closing Paragraph

In the final paragraph, request an interview. Let the reader know when you are available for an interview, and include your phone number or email address. End with a statement of goodwill, even if only "thank you."

Proofread your letter very carefully. Research indicates that if employers notice even one spelling, grammatical, or mechanical error, they might eliminate you from consideration immediately. Such errors will give employers the impression that you lack writing skills or that you are generally sloppy and careless in the way you present yourself professionally. See also **proofreading** (page 40).

Sample Letters

The three sample application letters shown in Figures 5–3 through 5–5 (pages 157–159) follow the application-letter structure described in this tab. Each is adapted according to the emphasis, tone, and style that fits its particular audience.

- In Figure 5–3 a college student seeks an internship in a retailing business.
- In Figure 5–4 a college graduate applies for a job in an advertising company.
- In Figure 5–5 a person with many years of work experience applies for a job as a district manager.

follow-up letters

A day or two following a job interview, send the interviewer a note of thanks in a brief letter or email. The thank-you note is an easy and effective way to set yourself apart from other candidates. In fact, some employers expect a thank-you note. This note should include the following:

- Your thanks for the interview and to individuals or groups that gave you special help or attention during the interview
- The name of the specific job for which you interviewed
- Your impression that the job is attractive
- Your confidence that you can fill the job well
- An offer to provide further information or answer further questions

Figure 5–6 (page 160) shows a typical follow-up letter.

7188 Virginia Avenue
Pittsburgh, PA 15232
27 February 20--

Patrice C. Crandal
Executive Recruiter
Abel's Department Stores, Inc.
599 Seventh Avenue
Pittsburgh, PA 15219

Dear Ms. Crandal:

Recently, I learned that you may be hiring undergraduates for summer internships. Through personal research and sources in the retailing industry, I have discovered that your firm's buyer training program is considered one of the most effective. For this reason, I am interested in your company and I would like to be considered as a possible summer intern.

As indicated in my résumé, I have the professional and analytical qualities necessary to excel at an innovative company such as Abel's. My experiences with the Alumni Relations Program and the University Center Committee have enhanced my communication and persuasive abilities as well as my understanding of compromise and negotiation. For example, in the alumni program, my priority focused on convincing both hostile and friendly alumni to become more involved with the direction of the university. On the University Center Committee, my goal was to balance the students' demands with financial and structural constraints of the administration. In both cases, I succeeded in achieving these important goals through persuasion.

I'd also like to point out that throughout my work experiences and education I have been determined and innovative. My efforts to excel at Abel's will reflect my commitment to these qualities.

I would appreciate the opportunity to meet with you to discuss your summer internship further. If you have questions or would like to speak with me personally, please contact me at (412) 863-2289 any weekday after 3 P.M. Thank you for your time and consideration.

Sincerely,

Marsha S. Parker

Marsha S. Parker

FIGURE 5–3. Letter by a Student Applying for an Internship

449 Samson Street, Apt. 19
Providence, RI 02906
September 19, 20--

Alice Tobowski
Employee Relations Department
Advertising Media, Inc.
1007 Market Street
Providence, RI 02912

Dear Ms. Tobowski:

I recently learned from Jodi Hammel, a graphic designer at Advertising Media, Inc. and a former colleague, that you are looking for outstanding advertising assistants. Your position interests me greatly, not only because your firm is number one in the region but also because I feel that Advertising Media is, as Jodi and I have discussed, the kind of place where I can further develop my skills and talents.

I understand that you especially need bilingual assistants because of your zone's ethnic diversity. As noted in my enclosed résumé, I speak and write Spanish fluently. I would welcome the chance to apply my language skills at Advertising Media. Ms. Tobowski, I am aware that hundreds of applicants are applying for this position, but I have a combination of qualities probably few can match: in addition to my bilingual skills, I have a degree and experience in advertising, outstanding verbal and written communication skills, an innate ability to work well with colleagues, and the common sense to solve both simple and challenging problems. I have developed my skills by contributing to advertising for Quilted Bear in Providence, where we develop campaigns for diverse audiences. I have also been promoted to leadership positions in my jobs, schools, and community organizations, and I have worked well both individually and in team efforts in each environment.

I would enjoy meeting with you at your convenience to discuss this career opportunity further. Also, I have many references that I encourage you to contact. Feel free to call me any weekday morning or email me at <singh@pcexec.com> if you have any questions, need further information, or would like to set up an interview. Thank you for your consideration.

Sincerely,

Sarah Singh

Sarah Singh

FIGURE 5–4. Letter by a College Graduate Applying for a Job

522 Beethoven Drive
Roanoke, VA 24017
November 15, 20--

Ms. Cecilia Smathers
Vice-President, Dealer Sales
Hamilton Office Machines, Inc.
6194 Main Street
Hampton, VA 23661

Dear Ms. Smathers:

During the recent NOMAD convention in Washington, one of your sales representatives, Karen Jarrett, informed me of a possible opening for a district manager in your Dealer Sales Division. My extensive background in the office systems industry makes me highly qualified for the position.

I was with Technology, Inc., Dealer Division from its formation in 1990 until its closing last year. During that period, I was involved in all areas of dealer sales, both within Technology, Inc., and through personal contact with a number of independent dealers. From 19-- to 19--, I served as Assistant to the Dealer Sales Manager as a Special Representative. My education and work experience are indicated in the enclosed résumé.

I would like to discuss my qualifications in an interview at your convenience. Please write to me, telephone me at (804) 449-6743 any weekday, or email me at gm302.476@sys.com.

Sincerely,

Gregory Mindukakis

Gregory Mindukakis

Enclosure: Résumé

FIGURE 5–5. Letter by an Applicant with Years of Experience

Dear Mr. Vallone:

Thank you for the informative and pleasant interview we had last Wednesday. Please extend my thanks to Mr. Wilson of the Media Group as well.

I came away from our meeting most favorably impressed with Calcutex Industries. I find the position of junior ACR designer to be an attractive one and feel confident that my qualifications would enable me to perform the duties to everyone's advantage.

If I can answer any further questions, please let me know.

Sincerely yours,

FIGURE 5–6. Follow-up Letter

interviewing for a job

A job interview may last 30 minutes, an hour, several hours, or more. Sometimes, an initial job interview is followed by a series of interviews that can last a half or full day. Often, just one person or a few people conduct a job interview, but, at times, a group of four or more might do so. Job interviews can take place in person, by phone, or by teleconferencing. Because it is impossible to know exactly what to expect, it is important that you be well prepared.

Before the Interview

The interview is not a one-way communication. It presents you with an opportunity to ask questions of your potential employer. In preparation, learn everything you can about the company before the interview. Use the following questions as a guide.

- What kind of organization is it? nonprofit? government?
- How diversified is the organization?
- Is it locally owned?
- Does it provide a product or service? If so, what kind?
- How large is the business? How large are its assets?
- Is the owner self-employed? Is the company a subsidiary of a larger operation? Is it expanding?
- How long has it been in business?
- Where will you fit in?

You can obtain information from current employees, the Internet, company publications, and the business section of back issues of local newspapers (available in the library or online). You may be able to learn the company's size, sales volume, product line, credit rating, branch locations, subsidiary companies, new products and services, building programs, and other such information from its annual reports; publications such as *Moody's Industrials, Dun and Bradstreet, Standard and Poor's,* and *Thomas' Register;* and other business reference sources a librarian might suggest. Ask your interviewer about what you cannot find through your own research. Now is your chance to make certain that you are considering a healthy and growing company. It is also your chance to demonstrate your interest in the company.

Try to anticipate the questions your interviewer might ask, and prepare your answers in advance. Be sure you understand a question before answering it, and avoid responding too quickly with a canned answer—be prepared to answer in a natural and relaxed manner. Interviewers typically ask the following questions:

- What are your short-term and long-term occupational goals?
- Where do you see yourself five years from now?
- What are your major strengths and weaknesses?
- Do you work better with others or alone?
- Why do you want to work for this company?
- How do you spend your free time?
- What are your personal goals?
- Describe an accomplishment you are particularly proud of.
- Why are you leaving your current job?
- Why should I hire you?
- What salary and benefits do you expect?

Many employers use behavioral interviews. Rather than traditional, straightforward questions, the behavioral interview focuses on asking the candidate to provide examples or respond to hypothetical situations. Interviewers who use behavior-based questions are looking for specific examples from your experience. Prepare for the behavioral interview by recollecting challenging situations or problems that were successfully resolved. Examples of behavior-based questions include the following:

- Tell me about a time when you experienced conflict on a team.
- If I were your boss and you disagreed with a decision I made, what would you do?
- How have you used your leadership skills to bring about change?
- Tell me about a time when you failed.

Be sure that you arrive for your interview on time, or even 10 or 15 minutes early—you may be asked to fill out an application or other paperwork before you meet your interviewer. Always bring extra copies of your résumé and samples of your work (if applicable). If you are asked to complete an application form, read it carefully before you write and proofread it when you are finished. The form provides a written record for company files and indicates to the company how well you follow directions and complete a task.

During the Interview

The interview actually begins before you are seated: What you wear and how you act make a first impression. In general, dress simply and conservatively and avoid extremes in fragrance and cosmetics. Be well-groomed.

Behavior. First, thank the interviewer for his or her time, express your pleasure at meeting him or her, and remain standing until you are offered a seat. Then sit up straight (good posture suggests self-assurance), look directly at the interviewer, and try to appear relaxed and confident. During the interview, you may find yourself feeling a little nervous. Use that nervous energy to your advantage by channeling it into the alertness that you will need to listen and respond effectively. Do not attempt to take extensive notes during the interview, although it is acceptable to jot down a few facts and figures. See also **listening** (page 212).

Responses. When you answer questions, do not ramble or stray from the subject. Say only what you must to answer each question properly and then stop, but avoid giving just yes or no answers—they usually don't allow the interviewer to learn enough about you. Some interviewers allow a silence to fall just to see how you will react. The burden of conducting the interview is the interviewer's, not yours—and he or she may interpret your rush to fill a void in the conversation as a sign of insecurity. If such a silence makes you uncomfortable, be ready to ask an intelligent question about the company.

If the interviewer overlooks important points, bring them up. However, let the interviewer mention salary first, if possible. If you are forced to bring up the subject, put it into a straightforward question. Make sure that you are aware of prevailing salaries in your field, so you will be better prepared to discuss salary. See also **salary negotiations** (page 180).

Interviewers look for a degree of self-confidence and an applicant's understanding of the field, as well as genuine interest in the field, the company, and the job. Ask questions to communicate your interest in the job and company. Interviewers respond favorably to applicants who can communicate and present themselves well.

Conclusion. At the conclusion of the interview, thank the interviewer for his or her time. Indicate that you are interested in the job (if true) and try to get an idea of the company's hiring timeline. Reaffirm friendly contact with a firm handshake.

After the Interview

After you leave the interview, jot down the pertinent information you obtained, as it may be helpful in comparing job offers. As soon as possible, send the interviewer a note of thanks in a brief letter or email, as discussed in **follow-up letters** (page 156). If you are offered a job you want, accept the offer verbally and write a brief letter of acceptance as soon as possible—certainly within a week—or if you do not want the job, you will need to write a refusal letter, as described in **acceptance/refusal letters** (page 153).

job search

Whether you are trying to land your first job or you want to change careers entirely, begin by assessing your skills, interests, and abilities. Next, ask yourself what are your career goals and values. For instance, do you prefer working independently or collaboratively? Do you enjoy public settings? meeting people? How important are career stability and a certain standard of living? Finally, ask yourself what you would most like to be doing in the immediate future, two years, and five years from now. Your campus career services office has resources to help with this process.

Once you've reflected and brainstormed about the job that's right for you, a number of sources can help you locate the job you want. Of course you should not rely on any one of these sources exclusively:

- Networking
- Campus career services
- Internet resources
- Advertisements in newspapers
- Trade and professional journal listings
- Private (or temporary) employment agencies
- Letters of inquiry

Keep records during your job search of dated job ads, copies of letters of application and résumés, notes requesting interviews, and the names of important contacts. This collection can serve as a future resource and reminder. See also **interviewing for a job** (page 160).

Networking

Networking involves communicating with people who might provide useful advice or might be able to connect you with potential jobs in your interest areas. They may include people already working in your chosen field, contacts in professional organizations, professors, family members, or friends. Use your contacts to develop a network of even more contacts. Keep in mind that 80 percent of all positions are filled without employer advertising. They are filled through networking.[1]

Campus Career Services

A college career-development center is another good place to begin your job search. Government, business, and industry recruiters often visit campus career offices to interview prospective employees; recruiters also keep career counselors aware of their company's current employment needs and submit job descriptions. Not only can career counselors help you select a career, they can also put you in touch with the best, most current resources—identifying where to begin your search and saving you time. Career development centers often hold workshops on résumé preparation and other job-finding resources and skills. Although many career-development centers have their own Web sites, nothing replaces talking with a career counselor about your interests.

Internet Resources

Using the Web can enhance your job search in a number of ways. First, you can consult sites that give advice to college graduates about careers, job seeking, and résumé preparation. Second, you can learn about businesses and organizations that may hire employees in your area by visiting their Web sites. Such sites often list job openings and provide instructions for applicants and offer other information, such as employee benefits. Third, you can learn about jobs in your field and post your résumé for prospective employers at employment databases, such as Monster.com or America's Job Bank. (See the Web Link Box, "Finding a Job," page 165.) Fourth, you can post your résumé at your personal Web site. Although posting your résumé at an employment database will undoubtedly attract more potential employers, including your résumé at your own site has some benefits. For example, you might provide a link to your site in email correspondence or provide your Web site's URL in an inquiry letter to a prospective employer.

---

[1]From *JobStar Central,* an online job search guide hosted by *The Wall Street Journal* (jobstar.org).

WEB LINK ▶ FINDING A JOB

The Web offers sites that provide guidance for job seekers, listings of job openings, and useful links. Several current popular sites are the following:

COLLEGE GRAD JOB HUNTER
www.collegegrad.com

AMERICA'S JOB BANK
www.ajb.dni.us

MONSTER.COM
www.monster.com

CAREERTECH.COM
www.careertech.com/

Employment specialists suggest that you spend time on the Web in the evening or early morning so that you can use business hours to focus on in-person contacts. See also **Internet research** (page 10).

Advertisements in Newspapers

Many employers advertise in the classified sections of newspapers and on their own Web sites. For the widest selection of help-wanted listings, look in the Sunday editions or the help-wanted Web pages of local and big-city newspapers. An item-by-item check is necessary because many times a position can be listed under various classifications. A clinical medical technologist seeking a job, for example, might find the specialty listed under "Medical Technologist" or "Clinical Laboratory Technologist." Depending on a hospital's or a pathologist's needs, the listing could be even more specific, such as "Blood Bank Technologist" or "Hematology Technologist." As you read the ads, take notes on salary ranges, job locations, job duties and responsibilities, and even the terminology used in the ads to describe the work. A knowledge of keywords and expressions that are generally used to describe a particular type of work can be helpful when you prepare your résumé and letters of application.

Trade and Professional Journal Listings

In many industries, associations publish periodicals of interest to people working in the industry. Such periodicals (print and online) often contain job listings. To learn about the trade or professional associations for your occupation, consult resources on the Web, such as Google's Directory of Professional Organizations (directory.google.com/Top/Society/Organizations/Professional/) or online resources offered by your library or campus career office. You may also consult the following references at a library: *Encyclopedia of Associations, Encyclopedia of Business Information Sources,* and *National Directory of Employment Services.* See also **library research** (page 20).

Private (or Temporary) Employment Agencies

Private employment agencies are profit-making organizations that are in business to help people find jobs—for a fee. Reputable agencies provide you with job leads, help you organize your job search, and supply information on companies doing the hiring. A staffing agency, or temporary placement firm, could match you with an appropriate temporary or permanent job in your field. Temping at an organization for which you might want to work permanently is an excellent way to build your network while continuing your job search.

Choose an employment or temporary placement agency carefully. Some are well established and reputable; others are not. Check with your local Better Business Bureau (www.bbb.org/) and your college career office before you sign an agreement with a private employment agency. Also, be sure you understand who is paying the agency's fee. Often the employer pays the agency's fee; however, if you have to pay, make sure you know exactly how much. As with any written agreement, read the fine print carefully.

Letters of Inquiry

If you would like to work for a particular firm, write and ask whether it has any openings for people with your qualifications. Normally, you can send the letter to the department head, director of human resources, or both; for a small firm, however, write to the head of the firm. For more information and examples of inquiry letters, see **application letters** (page 154).

Other Sources

Local, state, and federal government agencies offer many employment services. Local government agencies are listed in telephone and Web directories under the name of your city, county, or state. For information about jobs with the federal government, contact the U.S. Office of Personnel Management (www.usajobs.opm.gov) or visit Fedquest.com (www.fedquest.com).

résumés

A résumé is the key tool of the job search; it itemizes the qualifications that you summarize in your **application letter** (page 154). A résumé should be limited to one page or two (only if you have substantial experience). On the basis of the information in the résumé and application letter, prospective employers decide whether to ask you to come in for an interview. If you are invited to an interview, the interviewer can base specific questions on the contents of your résumé. See also **interviewing for a job** (page 160) and **job search** (page 163).

Because résumés affect a potential employer's first impression, take the time to make sure that yours is well organized, well designed, easy to read, and free of errors. Proofread your résumé carefully, verify the accuracy of the information, and have someone else review it. Experiment with the design to determine a layout that is attractive and highlights your strengths. Use a quality printer and high-grade paper. See also **layout and design** (page 196) and **proofreading** (page 40).

Analyzing Your Background

In preparing to write your résumé, determine what kind of job you are seeking. Then ask yourself what information about you and your background would be most important to a prospective employer. Brainstorm by asking the following questions:

- What college(s) did you attend? What degree(s) do you hold? What was your major field of study? What academic honors were you awarded? What was your grade point average? What particular academic projects reflect your best work?
- What jobs have you held? What were your principal and secondary duties in each of them? When and how long did you hold each job? Were you promoted? What skills did you develop in your jobs that potential employers value and seek in ideal job candidates? What projects or accomplishments reflect your important contributions?
- What other experiences and skills have you developed that would be of value in the kind of job you are seeking? What extracurricular activities have contributed to your learning experience? What leadership, interpersonal, and communication skills have you developed? Do you have any collaborative experience? What computer skills do you have?

Use your answers as a starting point and let one question lead to another. Then, based on your answers, decide which details to include in your résumé and how you can most effectively present your qualifications.

Organizing Your Résumé

A number of different organizational patterns can be used effectively. A common one arranges information chronologically in the following typical categories:

- Heading (name and contact information)
- Job Objective (optional)

- Education
- Employment Experience
- Computer Skills (optional)
- Honors and Activities
- References

Whether you place education or employment experience first depends on the job you are seeking and on which credentials would strengthen your résumé the most. If you are a recent graduate without much work experience, you would probably list education first. If you have years of job experience, including jobs directly related to the kind of position you are seeking, you would probably list employment experience first because your interviewer will most likely be interested in the skills you gained in those jobs. In your education and employment sections, use a chronological sequence and list the most recent experience first, the next most recent experience second, and so on.

Heading. At the top of your résumé, include your name, address, telephone and fax numbers, and email address. Make sure that your name is large and stands out on the page. If you have just one address, center it at the top of the page, as shown in Figure 5–8. If you have both a school and a permanent home address, place your school address on the left side of the page and your permanent home address on the right side of the page, both underneath your name. Indicate the dates you can be reached at each address (but do not date the résumé itself).

Job Objective. Many potential employers prefer to see a clear employment objective in résumés. If you decide to include an objective, use a heading such as "Objective," "Employment Objective," "Career Objective," or "Job Objective." State not only your immediate job objective but also the direction you hope your career will take. A job objective introduces the material in a résumé and helps the reader quickly understand your goal. Try to write your objective in no more than three lines as illustrated in the following examples.

- A full-time computer-science position aimed at solving engineering problems. Special interest in the potential to gain valuable management experience.
- A position involving meeting the concerns of women, such as family planning, women's health services, or a shelter for women in distress.
- Full-time management of a high-quality, local restaurant.
- A summer research or programming position providing opportunities to further develop problem-solving skills.

Education. List the college(s) you have attended, the degrees you received and the dates you received them, your major field(s) of study, and any academic honors you have earned. A list of computer skills in this section or elsewhere in the résumé can be especially effective with prospective employers (as shown in Figure 5–7, page 173). Include your grade point average only if it is 3.0 or higher. List courses only if they are unusually impressive or if your résumé is otherwise sparse (as shown in Figure 5–8, page 174). Mention your high school only if you want to call attention to special high school achievements, awards, projects, programs, internships, or study abroad.

Employment Experience. You can organize your employment experience chronologically, starting with your most recent job and working backward under a single major heading called "Experience," "Employment," "Professional Experience," or the like (as shown in Figure 5–9, page 175). You could also organize your experience functionally by clustering similar types of jobs into one or several sections with specific headings such as "Major Accomplishments" or "Accounting Experience" (as shown in Figure 5–11, page 177).

In general, follow these conventions when working on the "Experience" section of your résumé.

- Include jobs or internships when they relate directly to the position you are seeking. Although some applicants choose to omit internships and temporary or part-time jobs, including such experiences can make a résumé more persuasive if they have helped the applicant develop specific related skills.
- Similarly, include extracurricular experiences, such as taking on a leadership position in a fraternity or sorority, or directing a community-service project, if they demonstrate that you have developed skills valued by potential employers.
- List military service as a job; give the dates served, the duty specialty, and the rank at discharge. Discuss military duties if they relate to the job you are seeking.
- For each job or experience, list both the job and company titles. Throughout each section, consistently begin with either the job or the company title, depending on which will likely be more impressive to potential employers.
- Under each job or experience, provide a concise description of your primary and secondary duties. If a job is not directly relevant, provide only a job title and a brief description of duties that helped you develop skills valued in the position you are seeking. For example, if you were a lifeguard and now seek a management position, focus on supervisory experience or even experience in averting disaster to highlight your management, decision-making, and crisis-control skills.

- Use action verbs (for example, "managed" rather than "was the manager") and state ideas succinctly (as shown in Figure 5–11, page 177). Even though the résumé is about you, do not use "I" (for example, instead of "I was promoted to Section Leader," use "Promoted to Section Leader").

Computer Skills. Employers are interested in hiring applicants with knowledge of a variety of computer skills or who can learn new ones fairly quickly. If you are applying for a job that will require computer knowledge, include a section on computer skills that includes specific languages, software, and hardware.

Honors and Activities. If you have room on your résumé, it can be persuasive to list any honors and unique activities near the end. Include items such as fluency in foreign languages; writing and editing abilities; specialized technical knowledge; student or community activities; professional or club memberships; and published works. Be selective: Do not duplicate information given in other categories, and include only information that supports your employment objective. Provide a heading for this section that fits its contents, such as "Activities," "Honors," "Professional Affiliations," or "Publications and Memberships."

References. The primary purpose of the résumé is to obtain a job interview. At the end of a successful interview, a potential employer is likely to ask for a list of your references. Unless your résumé is sparse, avoid listing references here. Instead, just write a phrase such as "References available upon request" at the bottom of your résumé, either centered or flush left, or write "Available upon request" after the heading "References." Have a printed list of references available for a prospective employer; your list should include the main heading "References for [your name]."

Special Advice for Résumés

Be truthful in your résumé. The consequences of giving false information are serious. In fact, the truthfulness of your résumé reflects not only your own ethical stance but also the integrity with which you would represent the organization. See also **ethics in writing** (page 261).

Salary. Avoid listing the salary you desire in the résumé. On the one hand, you may price yourself out of a job you want if the salary you list is higher than a potential employer is willing to pay. On the other hand, if you list a low salary, you may not get the best possible offer. See **salary negotiations** (page 180).

Returning Job Seekers. If you are returning to the workplace after an absence, most career experts say that it is important to acknowledge the gap in your career. That is particularly true if, for example, you are reentering the workforce because you have devoted a full-time period to care for children or dependent adults. Do not undervalue such work. Although unpaid, it often provides experience that develops important time-management, problem-solving, organizational, and interpersonal skills. The following examples illustrate how you might reflect such experiences in a résumé.

- **Primary Child-Care Provider, 20-- to 20--**
  Provided full-time care to three preschool children at home. Instructed in beginning scholastic skills, time management, basics of nutrition, arts, and swimming. Organized activities, managed household, and served as neighborhood-watch captain.
- **Home Caregiver, 20-- to 20--**
  Provided 60 hours per week in-home care to Alzheimer's patient. Coordinated medical care, developed exercise programs, completed and processed complex medical forms, administered medications, organized budget, and managed home environment.

If you have participated in volunteer work during such a period, list that experience. Volunteer work often results in the same experience as does full-time paid work, a fact that your résumé should reflect, as in the following example.

- **School Association Coordinator, 20-- to 20--**
  Managed special activities of the Briarwood High School Parent-Teacher Association. Planned and coordinated meetings, scheduled events, and supervised fund-drive operations. Raised $70,000 toward refurbishing the school auditorium.

Electronic Résumés

In addition to the traditional paper résumé, you can submit a résumé on disk or through email to a potential employer, you can submit an electronic version to an employment database (such as Monster.com), or you can post your electronic résumé at your own Web site for general inquiries. If you plan to post your résumé on the Web, keep the following points in mind.

- Follow the general advice for **Web page design** (page 239), such as viewing your résumé on several browsers to see how it looks.
- Do not list your home address or phone number; instead, include an email link ("mailto") at the top of the résumé.

- Format the résumé as an ASCII text file (as shown in Figure 5–12, page 179), so it will scroll correctly and be universally readable.
- Just below your name, you may wish to provide a series of hypertext links to such important categories as "experience" and "education."
- Use a counter to keep track of the number of times your résumé Web page has been visited.

Electronic résumés submitted to an organization are often posted in a searchable database on the company's Intranet so that those who are a part of the hiring process can access and screen the résumés of many applicants. Although an applicant's paper résumé can be scanned into computer files, employers appreciate receiving an electronic version that they can easily load into their résumé database.

An electronic résumé that will be included in a company's searchable database differs from the traditional résumé—not only in format (as explained below)—but also in the use of nouns rather than verbs to describe experience, skills, and other items in your résumé (*designer* and *management* rather than *designed* and *managed*). The nouns function as keywords, also called *descriptors,* which are terms that a potential employer might use to search the database for qualified candidates. Be sure to use keywords that are the same as those used in the employer's description of the jobs that best match your interests and qualifications.

The electronic résumé is formatted in ASCII text so that it can be read in any application. When preparing an ASCII document, do not use underlining, italics, or boldface type. Avoid uncommon typefaces; use simple font styles (sans serif, for example), and sizes between 10 and 14 points. Use white space between sections and keep your résumé as simple, clear, and concise as possible—and ideally limited to one page unless you have extensive experience or keywords. Include a section in your electronic résumé titled "Keywords." This section, which can include up to 50 terms, can be placed to follow the main heading of your résumé or near the end of your résumé (for example, before the "References" heading). Figure 5–12 (see page 179) is a sample of an electronic résumé that demonstrates ASCII text and the use of keywords.

Sample Résumés

This section includes sample résumés that are formatted for paper, email attachments, PDF documents, or ASCII-compatible versions. These samples are here to stimulate your thinking; your own résumé, tailored to your own job search, will look quite different. Before you design and write your résumé, look at as many samples as possible, and then organize and format your own to best suit your professional goals and to make the most persuasive case to your target employers.

Figures 5–7 and 5–8 both present typical student résumés, but notice how different they look. The résumé in Figure 5–7 is conventional

CAROL ANN WALKER
1436 W. Schantz Avenue
Laurel, Pennsylvania 17322
(717) 339-2712
caw@hbk.com

OBJECTIVE

Position in financial research, leading to management in corporate finance.

EDUCATION

Bachelor of Science in Business Administration, expected June 2001
Indiana University

Emphasis: Finance Minor: Technical Communication
Dean's List: 3.88 grade point average out of possible 4.0
Senior Honor Society

FINANCIAL EXPERIENCE

FIRST BANK, INC., of Bloomington, Indiana, 2000
Research Assistant, Summer and Fall Quarters
Assisted manager of corporate planning and developed long-range planning models.

MARTIN FINANCIAL RESEARCH SERVICES, Bloomington, Indiana, 1999
Financial Audit Intern
Developed a design concept for in-house financial audits and provided research assistance to staff.
Associate Editor, *Martin Client Newsletter,* 1999–present
Wrote articles on financial planning with computer models; surveyed business periodicals for potential articles; edited submissions.

COMPUTER SKILLS

Software: Microsoft Word, Excel, PowerPoint, Pagemaker, Quark XPress
Hardware: Macintosh, IBM-PC, scanners
Languages: FORTRAN, PASCAL

REFERENCES

Available upon request.

FIGURE 5–7. Student Résumé

because the student is seeking an entry-level business position. The format used in the Figure 5–8 résumé is appropriately a bit nonconventional because this student needs to demonstrate skills in graphic design for his potential audience.

JOSHUA S. GOODMAN
222 Morewood Avenue
Pittsburgh, PA 15212
Jgoodman@aol.com

OBJECTIVE:
A position as a graphic designer with responsibilities in information design, packaging, and media presentations.

EDUCATION:
Carnegie Mellon University, Pittsburgh, Pennsylvania
Candidate for BFA in Graphic Design—May 2001.

Graphic Design	Corporate Identity
Industrial Design	Graphic Imaging Processes
Color Theory	Computer Graphics
Typography	Serigraphy
Photography	Video Production

GRAPHIC DESIGN EXPERIENCE:

Assistant Designer

Dyer/Khan, Los Angeles, California, Summer 1999; Summer 2000
Assistant Designer in a versatile design studio.
Responsibilities: design, layout, comps, mechanicals, and project management.
Clients: Paramount Pictures, Mattel Electronics, and Motown Records.

Photo Editor

Paramount Pictures Corporation, Los Angeles, California, Summer 1988
Photo Editor for merchandising department.
Responsibilities: establish art files for movie and television properties, edit images used in merchandising, maintain archive and database.

Production Assistant

Grafis, Los Angeles, California, Summer 1977
Production assistant and miscellaneous studio work at fast-paced design firm.
Responsibilities: comps and mechanicals.
Clients: ABC Television, A&M Records, and Ortho Products Division.

COMPUTER SKILLS:
XML, HTML, JavaScript, Forms, Macromedia Dreamweaver 3, Macromedia Flash 4, Photoshop 5.5, Image Ready (Animated GIFs), CorelDRAW, DeepPaint, iGrafx Designer, MapEdit (Image Mapping), Scanning, Microsoft Access/Excel, Quark XPress.

ACTIVITIES:
Member, Pittsburgh Graphic Design Society; Member, The Design Group.

REFERENCES AND PORTFOLIO:
Available upon request.

FIGURE 5–8. Résumé for a Student Seeking a Graphic Design Job

Figures 5–9, 5–10, and 5–11 present typical résumés written by applicants with more advanced work records. The résumé in Figure 5–9 focuses on the applicant's management experience. The résumé in Figure 5–10 focuses on how the applicant advanced and was promoted

ROBERT MANDILLO
7761 Shalamar Drive
Dayton, Ohio 45424

Home: (513) 255-4137 Fax: (513) 255-3117
Business: (513) 543-3337 mand@juno.com

MANAGEMENT EXPERIENCE

MANAGER, ENGINEERING DRAFTING DEPARTMENT — 3/95–Present
Wright-Patterson Air Force Base, Dayton, Ohio

Supervise 17 Drafting Mechanics in support of the engineering design staff. Develop, evaluate, and improve materials and equipment for the design and construction of exhibits. Write specifications, negotiate with vendors, and initiate procurement activities for exhibit design support.

SUPERVISOR, GRAPHICS ILLUSTRATORS—5/83–2/95
Henderson Advertising Agency, Cincinnati, Ohio

Supervised five Illustrators and four Drafting Mechanics after promotion from Graphics Technician; analyzed and approved work-order requirements; selected appropriate media and techniques for orders; rendered illustrations in pencil and ink; converted department to CAD system.

EDUCATION

BACHELOR OF SCIENCE IN MECHANICAL ENGINEERING TECHNOLOGY, 1982
Edison State College, Wooster, Ohio

ASSOCIATE'S DEGREE IN MECHANICAL DRAFTING, 1980
Wooster Community College, Wooster, Ohio

PROFESSIONAL AFFILIATIONS

National Association of Mechanical Engineers and Drafting Mechanics

REFERENCES

References, letters of recommendation, and a portfolio of original designs and drawings available upon request.

FIGURE 5–9. Résumé by an Applicant with Extensive Experience

within a single company. Figure 5–11 illustrates how an applicant can organize a résumé according to skills or functions, instead of the more conventional chronological order.

Finally, Figure 5–12 (page 179) presents an ASCII résumé. Notice how this résumé emphasizes keywords so that potential employers searching online for applicants will be able to find it easily.

CAROL ANN WALKER
1436 W. Schantz Avenue
Dayton, Ohio 45401
(937) 555-1212
caw@hbk.com

FINANCIAL EXPERIENCE

KERFHEIMER CORPORATION, Dayton, Ohio

Senior Financial Analyst, June 2001–Present
Report to Senior Vice-President for Corporate Financial Planning. Develop manufacturing cost estimates totaling $30 million annually for mining and construction equipment with Department of Defense.

Financial Analyst, November 2000–June 2001
Developed $50-million funding estimates for major Department of Defense contracts for troop carriers and digging and earth-moving machines. Researched funding options, recommending those with most favorable rates and terms.

FIRST BANK, INC., Bloomington, Indiana

Planning Analyst, September 1999–November 2000
Developed successful computer models for short- and long-range planning.

EDUCATION

Ph.D. in Finance: expected, June 2001
The Wharton School of the University of Pennsylvania

M.S. in Business Administration, 1998
University of Wisconsin–Milwaukee
"Executive Curriculum" for employees identified as promising by their employers.

B.S. in Business Administration (*magna cum laude*), 1996
Indiana University
Emphasis: Finance Minor: Technical Communication

FIGURE 5–10. Advanced Résumé

Carol Ann Walker Page 2

PUBLISHING AND MEMBERSHIP

Published "Developing Computer Models for Financial Planning," *Midwest Finance Journal* (Vol. 34, No. 2, 2000), pp. 126–136.

Association for Corporate Financial Planning, Senior Member.

REFERENCES

References and a portfolio of financial plans are available upon request.

FIGURE 5-10. Advanced Résumé *(continued)*

CAROL ANN WALKER
1436 W. Schantz Avenue
Dayton, Ohio 45401
(937) 555-1212
caw@home.com

MAJOR ACCOMPLISHMENTS

Financial Planning

- Researched funding options to achieve a 23% return on investment.
- Developed long-range funding requirements for over $1 billion in government and military contracts.
- Developed a computer model for long- and short-range planning that saved 65% in proposal-preparation time.
- Received the Financial Planner of the Year Award from the Association of Financial Planners, a national organization composed of both practitioners and academics.

Capital Acquisition

- Developed strategies to acquire over $1 billion at 3% below market rate.
- Secured over $100 million through private and government research grants.
- Developed computer models for capital acquisition that enabled the company to decrease its long-term debt during several major building expansions.

Research and Analysis

- Researched and developed computer models applied to practical problems of corporate finance.
- Functioned primarily as a researcher at two different firms for over 11 years.
- Published research in financial journals while pursuing an advanced degree at the Wharton School.

FIGURE 5-11. Advanced Résumé (Organized by Function)

Carol Ann Walker Page 2

EDUCATION

Ph.D. in Finance: expected, June 2001
The Wharton School of the University of Pennsylvania

M.S. in Business Administration, 1995
University of Wisconsin–Milwaukee
"Executive Curriculum" for employees identified as promising by their employers.

B.S. in Business Administration (*magna cum laude*), 1996
Indiana University
Emphasis: Finance Minor: Technical Communication

EMPLOYMENT EXPERIENCE

KERFHEIMER CORPORATION, Dayton, Ohio
November 2000–Present
Senior Financial Analyst
Financial Analyst

FIRST BANK, INC., Bloomington, Indiana
September 1999–November 2000
Planning Analyst

PUBLICATIONS AND MEMBERSHIPS

Published "Developing Computer Models for Financial Planning," *Midwest Finance Journal* (Vol. 34, No. 2, 2000), pp. 126–136.

Association for Corporate Financial Planning, Senior Member.

REFERENCES

References and a portfolio of financial plans are available upon request.

FIGURE 5–11. Advanced Résumé (Organized by Function) *(continued)*

DAVID B. EDWARDS
6819 Locustview Drive
Topeka, Kansas 66614
(913) 233-1552
dedwards@cpu.fairview.edu

JOB OBJECTIVE
Work as a programmer with writing, editing, and training responsibilities, leading to a career in information design management.

KEYWORDS
Programmer, Operating Systems, Unipro, Newsletter, Graphics, Cybernetics, Listserv, Technical Writer, Editor, Trainer, Teacher, Instructor, Tutor, Designer, Manager, Information Design.

EDUCATION
** Fairview Community College, Topeka, Kansas
** Associate's Degree, Computer Science, June 1999
** Dean's Honor List Award (six quarters)

RELEVANT COURSE WORK
** Operating Systems Design
** Database Management
** Introduction to Cybernetics
** Computer Graphics
** Data Structures
** Technical Writing

EMPLOYMENT EXPERIENCE
** Computer Consultant: September 1999 to June 2001
Fairview Community College Computer Center: Advised and trained novice computer users; wrote and maintained Unipro operating system documentation.
** Tutor: January 1998 to June 2001
Fairview Community College: Assisted students in mathematics and computer programming.

SKILLS AND ACTIVITIES
** Unipro Operating System: Thorough knowledge of word-processing, text-editing, and file-formatting programs.
** Writing and Editing Skills: Experience in documenting computer programs for beginning programmers and users.
** Fairview Community Microcomputer Users Group: Cofounder and editor of monthly newsletter ("Compuclub"); listserv manager.

FURTHER INFORMATION
** References, college transcripts, a portfolio of computer programs, and writing samples available upon request.

FIGURE 5–12. Electronic Résumé in ASCII Format

salary negotiations

Salary negotiations usually take place either at the end of an interview when a potential employer says something like "We are ready to make an offer" or after a formal offer has been made. If possible, delay discussing salary until after you receive a formal written job offer because you will have more negotiating power at that point.

Before a job interview, prepare for possible salary negotiations by researching the following:

- The company's range of salaries for the position you are seeking. Call the company and ask to talk with the human resources manager. Explain that you will be interviewing for a particular position and ask about the salary range for that job.
- The current range of salaries for the work you hope to do at your level (beginner? intermediate? advanced?) in your region of the country. Check trade journals and organizations in your field, or ask a reference librarian for help in finding this information. Job listings that include salary can also be helpful.
- Salaries made by last year's graduates from your college or university at your level and in your line of work. Your campus career development office should have these figures.
- Salaries made by people you know at your level and in your line of work. Attend local organizational meetings in your field or contact officers of local organizations who might have this information or steer you to useful contacts.

If a potential employer requests your salary requirements with a résumé, consider your options carefully. If you provide a salary that is too high, the company might never interview you; if you provide a salary that is too low, you may have no opportunity later in the hiring process to negotiate for a higher salary. However, if you fail to follow the potential employer's directions and omit the requested information, an employer may disqualify you on principle. If you choose to provide salary requirements, always do so in a range (for example, $30,000 to $35,000).

If an interviewer asks your salary requirements toward the end of the job interview, you can try these strategies to delay salary negotiations.

- Say something like "I am sure that this company always pays a fair salary for a person with my level of experience and qualifications," "I am ready to consider your very best offer," or "I'll consider any reasonable offer."
- Indicate that you would like to find out more details about the position before discussing salary because your primary goal is to

work in an exciting environment with growth potential, not to earn a specific salary. Discuss specific considerations such as the opportunity to learn new skills and the chance to make valuable contributions to corporate goals.

- Express a strong interest in the position and the organization.
- Emphasize your unique qualifications (or combination of skills) for the job. Show what you can do for the company that other candidates cannot.

If the interviewer or company demands to know your salary requirements during a job interview, provide a wide salary range that you know would be reasonable for someone at your level in your line of work in that region of the country. For example, you could say, "I would hope for a salary somewhere between $28,000 and $38,000, although of course this is highly negotiable because I am greatly impressed by this job opportunity."

Once salary negotiations begin, resist the temptation to accept, immediately, the first salary offer you receive. If you have done thorough research, you'll know if the first salary offer is at the low, middle, or high end of the salary range for your level of experience in your line of work. If you have little or no experience and receive an offer for a salary at the low end of the range, you will realize that the offer probably is fair and reasonable. Yet, if you receive the same low-end offer but bring considerable experience to the job, you can negotiate for a higher salary that is more reasonable for someone with your background and credentials in your line of work in your region of the country.

Never say that you are unable to accept a salary below a particular figure. To keep negotiations going, simply indicate that you would have trouble accepting the first offer because it was smaller than you had expected.

Remember that you are negotiating a package and not just a starting salary. For example, benefits can offer you substantial value. If the starting salary seems low, consider negotiating for some of these possible job perks:

- The chance for an early promotion, thus higher salary within a few years
- A particular job title or special job responsibilities that would provide you with impressive chances for career growth
- Tuition credits for continued education
- Payment of relocation costs
- Paid personal leave or paid vacations
- Personal or sick days
- Overtime potential
- Flexible hours
- Health, dental, optical/eye care, disability, and life insurance

- Retirement plans, such as 401(k) and pension plans
- Profit sharing; investment or stock options
- Bonuses
- Commuting or parking cost reimbursement
- Child or elder care
- Discounts on company products and services

You might find it most comfortable to respond to an initial offer in writing, and then meet later with the potential employer for further negotiation. If possible, indicate all of your preferences and requirements at one time, instead of continually asking for new and different benefits throughout negotiations. Throughout this process, focus on what is most important to you (which might differ from what is most important to your friends) and on what you would find acceptable and comfortable.

WEB LINK ▸ FINDING SALARY INFORMATION

The following Web sites are useful resources for salary negotiations:

GENERAL ADVICE
www.collegegrad.com/neg/index.shtml
www.careertech.com/interview/negotiating.html
salarycenter.monster.com/articles/negotiate/

CALCULATING SALARIES BY PROFESSION
www.careertech.com/interview/salaries.html
www.wageweb.com
www2.homefair.com/calc/salcalc.html
www.salary.com

DEPARTMENT OF LABOR'S *OCCUPATIONAL OUTLOOK HANDBOOK*
stats.bls.gov/ocohome.htm

BUREAU OF LABOR STATISTICS
www.bls.gov/

6

Format and Visuals

Preview

This section includes entries related to the general physical appearance of a document, as discussed in **layout and design,** and entries concerning specific types of visuals, such as **drawings, graphs,** and **tables.** For an overview of creating and integrating specific types of illustrations into documents, read the entry **visuals.** Because many visuals are seen by international audiences, we have included the entry **global graphics.** See also **Web page design** (page 238) and **writing for the Web** (page 246).

drawings

The types of drawings discussed in this entry are conventional line drawings and cutaway drawings. Each type of drawing has unique advantages—the type of drawing you use should be determined by its purpose.

A conventional drawing, like that in Figure 6–1, is appropriate if your readers need a representation of an object's general appearance or an overview of a series of steps. A cutaway drawing, like the one in Figure 6–2, is used to show the internal parts of a piece of equipment and illustrate their relationship to the whole.

FIGURE 6–1. Conventional Drawing Illustrating Instructions

PULL

the pin: Some extinguishers require releasing a lock latch, pressing a puncture lever, or taking another first step.

Drawings that require a high degree of accuracy and precision generally are prepared by graphics specialists. If you need only general-interest images to illustrate newsletters and brochures or to create presentation overheads, use noncopyrighted images from clip-art libraries or such programs as PowerPoint.

Think about your need for drawings during the research and organization stages of writing, and include them in your outline. Plan your drawings from the beginning stages of your outline to ensure that they are integrated into your drafts and into the finished piece of writing. Many organizations have their own format specifications for creating drawings. In the absence of such specifications, follow the guidelines in **visuals** (page 205).

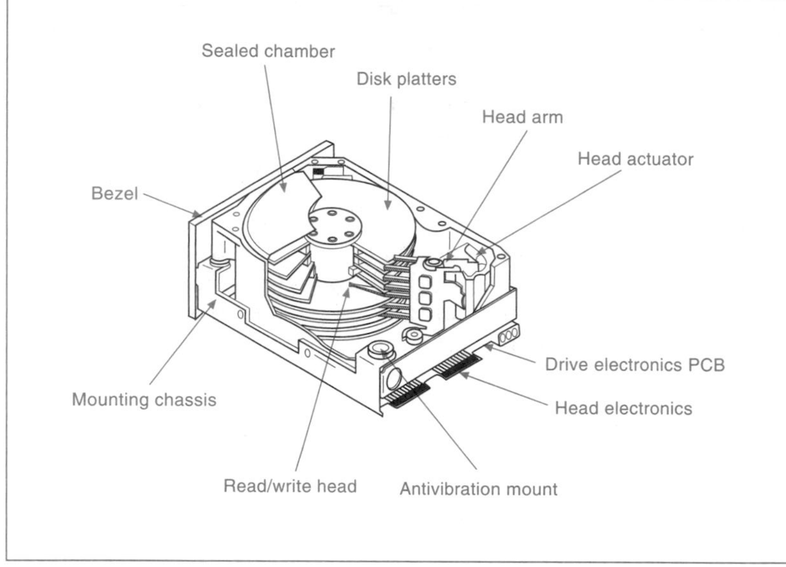

FIGURE 6–2. Cutaway Drawing of a Hard Disk Drive

flowcharts

A flowchart is a diagram of a process that involves stages, shown in sequence from beginning to end. Flowcharts can take several forms: The steps might be represented by labeled blocks, as shown in Figure 6–3; pictorial symbols, as shown in Figure 6–4; or International Organization for Standardization (ISO) symbols, as shown in Figure 6–5. (See Writer's Checklist: Creating Flowcharts on page 188.)

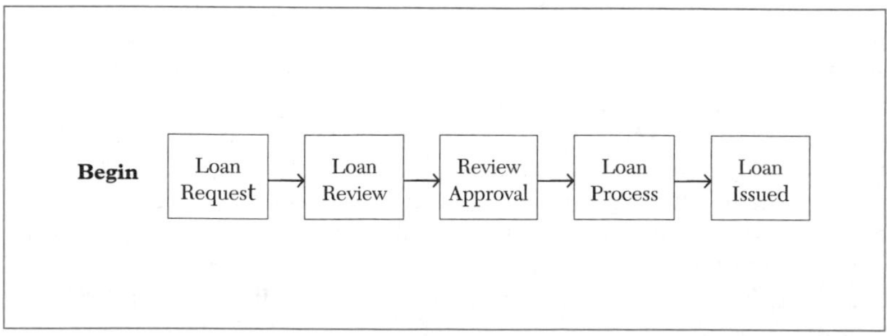

FIGURE 6–3. Flowchart Using Labeled Blocks

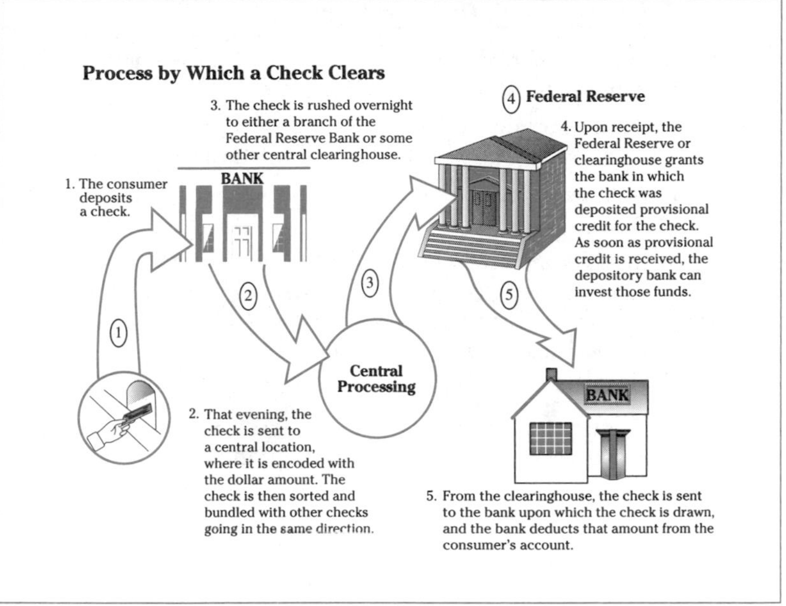

Process by Which a Check Clears
1. The consumer deposits a check.
BANK
2. That evening, the check is sent to a central location, where it is encoded with the dollar amount. The check is then sorted and bundled with other checks going in the same direction.
3. The check is rushed overnight to either a branch of the Federal Reserve Bank or some other central clearinghouse.
Central Processing
4 Federal Reserve
4. Upon receipt, the Federal Reserve or clearinghouse grants the bank in which the check was deposited provisional credit for the check. As soon as provisional credit is received, the depository bank can invest those funds.
BANK
5. From the clearinghouse, the check is sent to the bank upon which the check is drawn, and the bank deducts that amount from the consumer's account.

FIGURE 6–4. Flowchart Using Pictorial Symbols

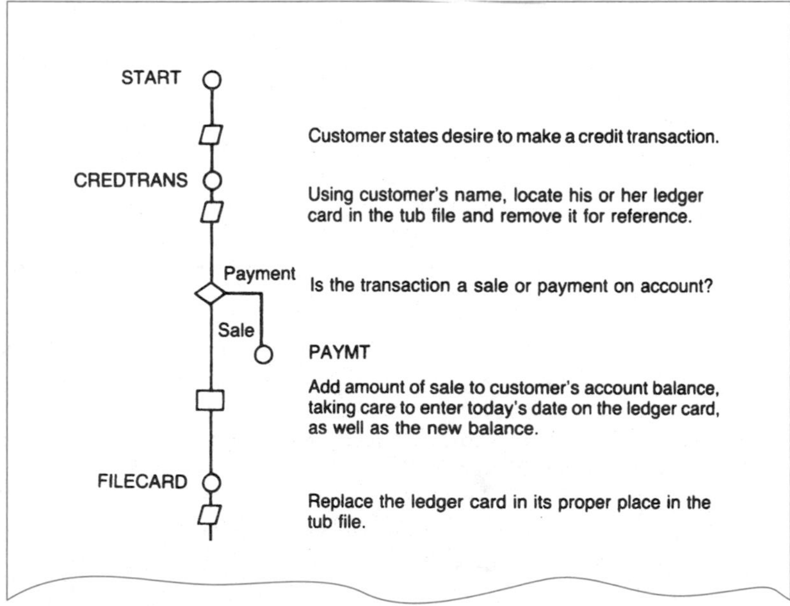

START
Customer states desire to make a credit transaction.
CREDTRANS
Using customer's name, locate his or her ledger card in the tub file and remove it for reference.
Payment
Is the transaction a sale or payment on account?
Sale
PAYMT
Add amount of sale to customer's account balance, taking care to enter today's date on the ledger card, as well as the new balance.
FILECARD
Replace the ledger card in its proper place in the tub file.

FIGURE 6–5. Flowchart Using Standardized Symbols

Writer's Checklist: Creating Flowcharts

- ☑ Label each step in the process or identify it with labeled blocks, pictorial representations, or standardized symbols.
- ☑ Follow the standard flow directions: left to right and top to bottom. When the flow is otherwise, indicate that with arrows.
- ☑ Include a key if the flowchart contains symbols your readers may not understand.
- ☑ For flowcharts that document computer programs and other information-processing procedures, use standardized symbols set forth in *Information Processing — Documentation Symbols and Conventions for Data, Program and System Flowcharts, Program Network Charts, and System Resources Charts,* ISO publication 5807-1985 (E).

For advice on integrating flowcharts into your text, see also **global graphics** (below), **graphs** (page 189), and **visuals** (page 205).

global graphics

In the global business and technological environment, graphs and visuals require the same careful attention given to other aspects of **global communication** (page 211). See also **graphs** (page 189) and **visuals** (page 205). Symbols, images, and even colors are not free from cultural associations: They depend on context, and context is culturally determined. For instance, in North America, a red cross is commonly used as a symbol for first aid or hospital. In Muslim countries, however, a cross (red or otherwise) represents Christianity, while a crescent (usually green) signifies first aid.

Careful attention to the connotations that visual elements may have for a diverse audience makes translations easier, prevents embarrassment, and earns respect for the company and its products and services. See also **presentations** (page 220).

Writer's Checklist: Communicating with Global Graphics

- ☑ Consult with someone from your intended audience's country who can recognize and explain the effect those elements will have on readers.
- ☑ Organize visual information for the intended audience according to whether they read visuals from left to right, top to bottom, or otherwise.
- ☑ Be sure that the graphics you use have no religious implications.

Writer's Checklist: Communicating with Global Graphics (continued)

- ☑ Use outlines or neutral abstractions to represent human beings. For example, use stick figures for bodies with a circle for the head. Avoid representing men and women.
- ☑ Examine how you display body positions in signs and visuals. Body positioning can carry unintended cultural meanings very different from your own.
- ☑ Try to use neutral colors in your graphics. Generally, black-and-white and gray-and-white illustrations work well. Colors can be problematic. (For example, red indicates danger in North America, but symbolizes joy in China.)
- ☑ Check your use of punctuation marks, which are as language specific as symbols.
- ☑ Create simple visuals and use consistent labels for all visual items. In most cultures, simple shapes with fewer elements are easier to read.
- ☑ Explain the meaning of icons or symbols. Include a glossary to explain technical symbols that cannot be changed, such as company logos.
- ☑ Test icons and symbols in context with members of your target audience or cultural experts.

graphs

A graph presents numerical data in visual form and offers several advantages over presenting data within the text or in **tables** (page 203). Trends, movements, distributions, comparisons, and cycles are more readily apparent in graphs than they are in tables. However, although graphs present data in a more comprehensible form than tables do, they are less precise. For that reason, graphs are often accompanied by tables that give exact data. The most common types of graphs are *line graphs, bar graphs, pie graphs,* and *picture graphs*. For additional advice, see **visuals** (page 205); for information about using presentation graphics, see **presentations** (page 220).

Line Graphs

A line graph shows the relationship between two variables or sets of numbers by plotting points in relation to two axes drawn at right angles. Line graphs that portray more than one set of variables allow for comparisons between two sets of statistics for the same period of time.

Writer's Checklist: Creating Line Graphs

☑ Indicate the zero point of the graph (the point where the two axes intersect).

☑ If the range of data shown makes it inconvenient to begin at zero, insert a break in the scale.

☑ Divide the vertical axis into equal portions, from the least amount at the bottom (or zero) to the greatest amount at the top.

☑ Divide the horizontal axis in equal units from left to right. If a label is necessary, center it directly beneath the scale.

☑ Be especially careful to proportion the vertical and horizontal scales so they give a precise presentation of the data that is free of visual distortion. To do otherwise is not only inaccurate but also potentially unethical. (See also **ethics in writing,** page 261.)

☑ When necessary, include a key or legend that lists and explains symbols, as shown in Figure 6–6.

☑ If the data comes from another source, include a source line under the graph at the lower left.

☑ Place explanatory footnotes directly below the figure caption or label.

☑ Make all lettering read horizontally if possible, although the caption or label for the vertical axis is usually positioned vertically (see Figure 6–6).

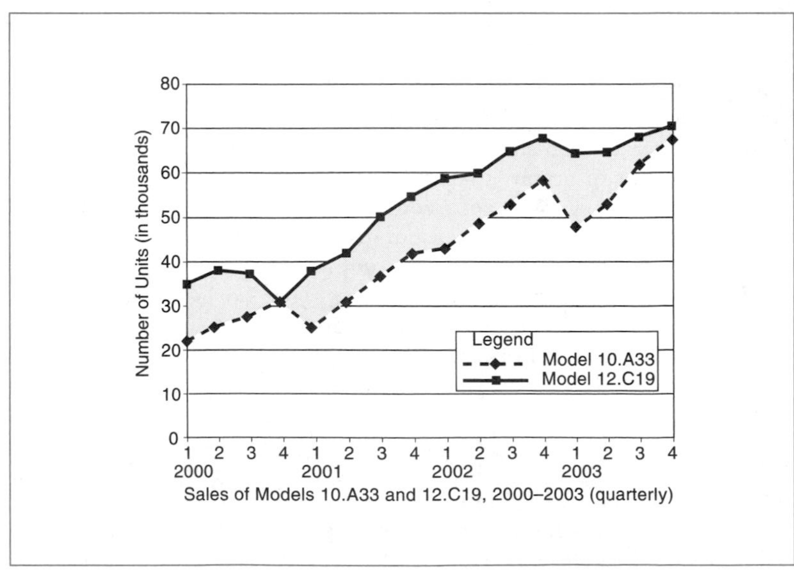

FIGURE 6–6. Double-Line Graph

Bar Graphs

Bar graphs consist of horizontal or vertical bars of equal width, scaled in length to represent some quantity. They are commonly used to show (1) quantities of the same item at different times, (2) quantities of different items at the same time, and (3) quantities of the different parts of an item that make up a whole—in this case, the segments of the bar graph must total 100 percent.

The horizontal graph in Figure 6–7 shows the quantities of different items for the same period of time.

FIGURE 6–7. Bar Graph: Quantities of Different Items during a Fixed Period

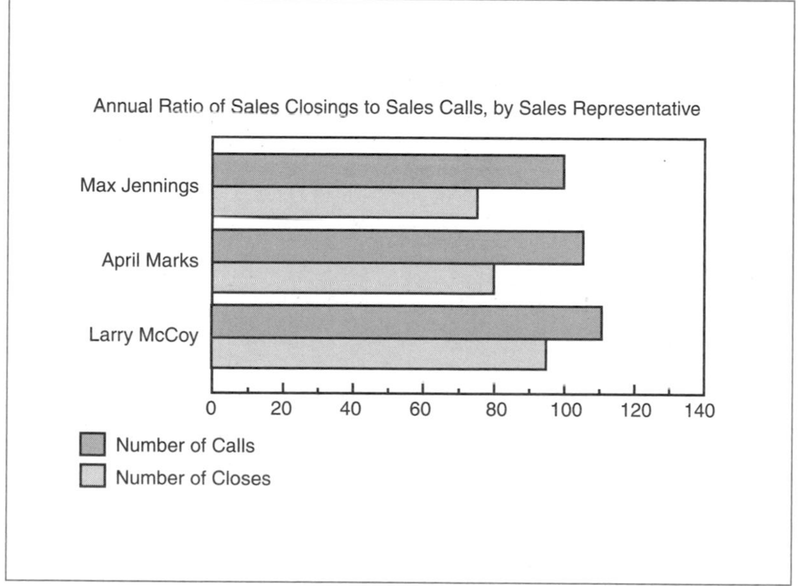

Pie Graphs

A pie graph presents data as wedge-shaped sections of a circle. Like the bar graph that shows quantities of different parts that comprise a whole, the total value of the graph (the circle) must equal 100 percent. Pie graphs, such as that shown in Figure 6–8, also provide a way of presenting information that is more immediate than a table; in fact, a table with a more detailed breakdown of the same information often accompanies a pie graph.

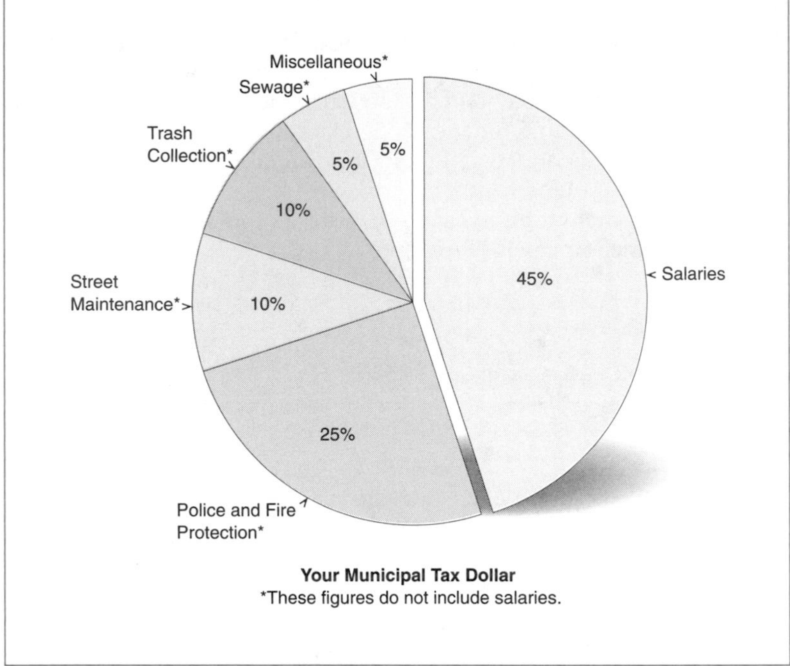

FIGURE 6–8. Pie Graph Showing Percentages of Whole

Writer's Checklist: Creating Pie Graphs

☑ When possible, begin at the 12 o'clock position and sequence the wedges clockwise, from largest to smallest.

☑ Avoid presenting too many items in a pie graph; the graph can look cluttered or the slices can be too thin to be clear.

☑ Give each wedge a distinctive pattern, shade, or texture.

☑ Label each wedge with its percentage value and keep all callouts (labels that identify the wedges) horizontal.

☑ If you want to draw attention to a particular segment of the pie graph, detach that slice, as shown in Figure 6–8.

Picture Graphs

Picture graphs are modified bar graphs that use pictorial symbols of the item portrayed. Each symbol corresponds to a specified quantity of the

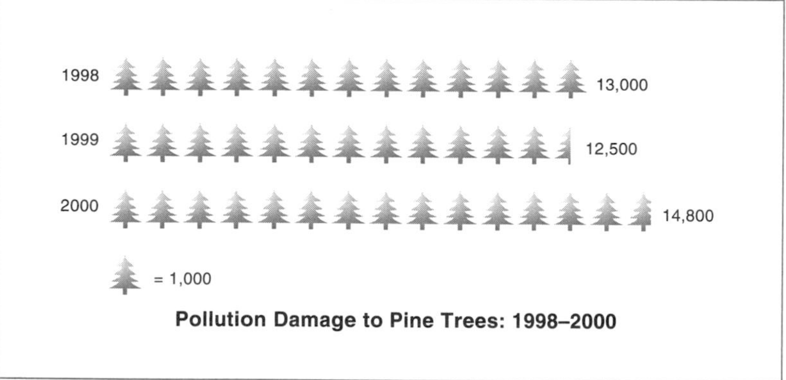

FIGURE 6–9. Picture Graph

item, as shown in Figure 6–9. They are often used to add interest to documents, such as newsletter articles, that are aimed at wide audiences.

Writer's Checklist: Creating Picture Graphs

- ☑ Make sure the symbol you choose is easily recognizable (see also **global graphics,** page 188).
- ☑ Have each symbol represent a specific number of units.
- ☑ Because it is difficult to judge relative sizes accurately, show larger quantities by increasing the number of symbols rather than by creating a larger symbol.

headers and footers

A header in a report, letter, technical manual, or other document appears at the top of each page and contains identifying information; a footer appears at the bottom of each page and contains similar information. The header often contains the topic (or topic and subtopic) dealt with in that section of the document. The footer may contain the date of the document, the page number, and sometimes the document's name and section title.

Although the information included in headers and footers varies greatly from one organization to the next, the header and footer shown in Figure 6–10 are fairly typical. For headers used in letters and memos, see **correspondence** (page 128).

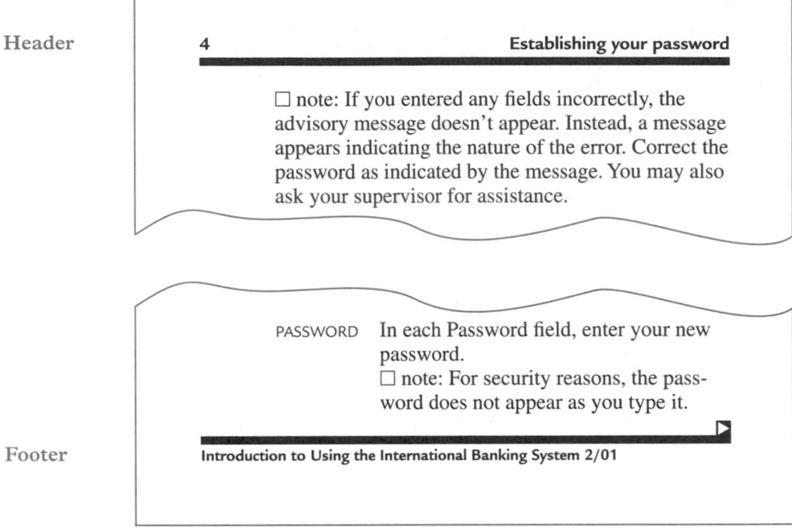

FIGURE 6–10. Header and Footer

headings

Headings (also called *heads*) are titles or subtitles within the body of a document that help readers find information, divide the material into comprehensible segments, highlight the main topics, and signal topic changes. A formal report or proposal may need several levels of headings to indicate major divisions, subdivisions, and even smaller units. However, it is better to avoid using more than three levels of headings. See also **formal reports** (page 96), **proposals** (page 78), and **layout and design** (page 196).

Headings typically represent the major topics of a document. In a short document, you can use the major divisions of your outline as headings; in a longer document, you may need to use both major and minor divisions.

General Heading Style

There is no one correct format for headings. Often a company settles on a standard format, which everyone in the company follows. Sometimes a customer for whom a report or proposal is being prepared requires a particular format. In the absence of specific guidelines, follow the system illustrated in Figure 6–11.

First-level head

DISTRIBUTION CENTER LOCATION REPORT

The committee initially considered 30 possible locations for the proposed new distribution center. Of these, 20 were eliminated almost immediately for one reason or another (unfavorable zoning regulations, inadequate transportation infrastructure, etc.). Of the remaining ten locations, the committee selected for intensive study the three that seemed most promising: Chicago, Minneapolis, and Salt Lake City. We have now visited these three cities and our observations and recommendations follow.

Second-level head

CHICAGO

Of the three cities, Chicago presently seems to the committee to offer the greatest advantages, although we wish to examine these more carefully before making a final recommendation.

Third-level head

Selected Location

Though not at the geographical center of the United States, Chicago is the demographic center to more than three-quarters of the U.S. population. It is within easy reach of our corporate headquarters in New York. And it is close to several of our most important suppliers of components and raw materials—those, for example, in Columbus, Detroit, and St. Louis. Several considerations were considered essential to the location, although some may not have had as great an impact on the selection. . . .

Fourth-level heads

Air Transportation. Chicago has two major airports (O'Hare and Midway) and is contemplating building a third. Both domestic and international air-cargo service are available. . . .

Sea Transportation. Except during the winter months when the Great Lakes are frozen, Chicago is an international seaport. . . .

Rail Transportation. Chicago is served by the following major railroads. . . .

FIGURE 6–11. Headings Used in a Document

Decimal Numbering System

The decimal numbering system uses a combination of numbers and decimal points to differentiate among levels of headings. The following outline shows the correspondence between different levels of headings and the decimal numbers used:

1. FIRST-LEVEL HEADING
   1.1 Second-Level Heading
   1.2 Second-Level Heading

1.2.1 Third-Level Heading
1.2.2 Third-Level Heading
1.2.2.1 Fourth-Level Heading
1.2.2.2 Fourth-Level Heading
1.3 Second-Level Heading
1.3.1 Third-Level Heading
1.3.2 Third-Level Heading
2. FIRST-LEVEL HEADING

Although the second-, third-, and fourth-level headings are indented in an outline or **table of contents** (page 101), they are flush with the left margins when they function as headings in the body of a report. Every heading starts on a new line, with an extra line of space above and below the heading.

Writer's Checklist: Using Headings

- ☑ Use headings to signal a new topic or, if it is a lower-level heading, a new subtopic within the larger topic.
- ☑ Avoid too many or too few headings or levels of headings; too many clutter a document and too few fail to provide recognizable structure.
- ☑ Ensure that headings at the same level are of relatively equal importance.
- ☑ Subdivide sections only as needed; not every section requires lower-level headings.
- ☑ Subdivide higher-level headings into at least two lower-level headings whenever possible.
- ☑ Make all headings at any one level follow **parallel structure** (page 269).
- ☑ Do not leave a heading as the final line of a page. If two lines of text cannot fit below a heading, start the section at the top of the next page.
- ☑ Do not allow a heading to substitute for discussion; the text should read as if the heading were not there.

layout and design

The layout and design of a document can make even the most complex information look accessible and give readers a favorable impression of the writer and the organization. To accomplish those goals, a design should help readers find information easily; offer a simple and uncluttered presentation of the topic; highlight structure, hierarchy, and order; and reinforce an organization's image.

Effective design is based on visual simplicity and harmony and can be achieved through the selection of fonts, the choice of devices to highlight information, and the arrangement of text and visual components on a page.

Typography

Typography refers to the style and arrangement of type on a printed page. A complete set of all the letters, numbers, and symbols available in one typeface (or style) is called a *font*. The letters in a typeface have a number of distinctive characteristics, as shown in Figure 6–12.

FIGURE 6–12. Primary Features of Typefaces

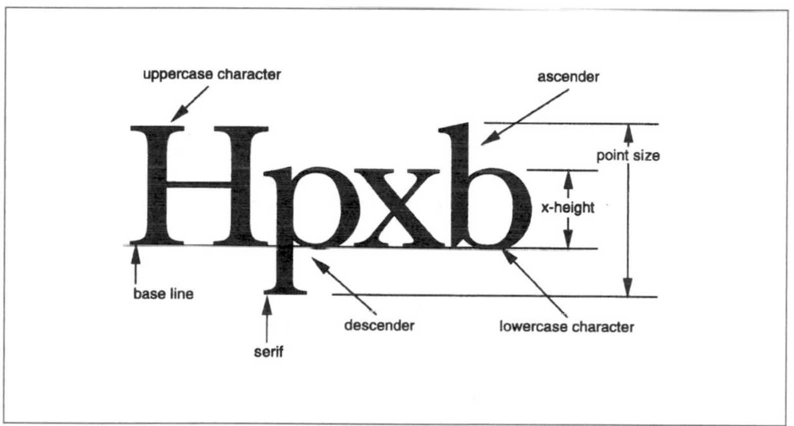

Typeface and Type Size. For most on-the-job writing, select a typeface primarily for its legibility. Avoid typefaces that may distract readers. Instead, choose popular typefaces with which readers are familiar, such as Times Roman, Garamond, or Gill Sans. Do not use more than two typefaces in the text of a document. For certain documents, such as newsletters, you may wish to create a contrast between headlines and text. To do so, use typefaces that are distinctively different. Always experiment before making final decisions. See **brochures** (page 51) and **newsletters** (page 71).

Ideal font sizes for the main text of paper documents range from 8 to 13 points; 11- and 12-point type are the most common sizes, as shown in Figure 6–13. The distance from which a document will be read should help determine type size. For example, instructions that will rest on a table at which the reader stands require a larger typeface than a document that will be read up close. Also, carefully consider your readers—some may need larger type sizes.

6 pt. This size might be used for dating a page.
8 pt. This size might be used for footnotes.
10 pt. This size might be used for figure captions.
12 pt. This size might be used for main text.
14 pt. This size might be used for headings.

FIGURE 6–13. Samples of 6- to 14-Point Type

For Web documents, preview your document on different browsers to see the effectiveness of your choice of point sizes and typefaces. Sans serif typefaces are usually the best choice for Web text. See **Web page design** (page 238) and **writing for the Web** (page 246).

Left- or Full-Justified Margins. Left-justified (ragged-right) margins are generally easier to read than full-justified margins that can produce irregular spaces between words and unwanted white space in blocks of text. However, because left-justified margins look informal, full-justified text is more appropriate for publications aimed at a broad readership that expects a more formal, polished appearance. Further, full justification is often useful with multiple-column formats because the spaces between the columns (called *alleys*) need the definition that full justification provides.

Highlighting Devices

When thoughtfully used, highlighting devices—typography; headings and captions; headers and footers; rules, icons, and color—give a document visual logic and organization. For example, rules and boxes can set off steps and illustrations from surrounding explanations. Consistency and moderation are important: Use the same technique to highlight a particular feature throughout your document and be careful not to overuse any single device.

Typographical Devices. One method of achieving emphasis through typography is to use capital letters. HOWEVER, LONG STRETCHES OF ALL UPPERCASE LETTERS ARE DIFFICULT TO READ. Use all uppercase letters only in short spans, such as in headings. Likewise, use italics sparingly because *continuous italic type reduces legibility and thus slows readers*. Of course, italics are useful if your aim is to slow readers, as in cautions and warnings. **Boldface,** used in moderation, may be the best cuing device because it is visually different yet retains the customary shapes of letters and numbers.

Headings and Captions. Headings (or heads) reveal the organization of a document and help readers decide which sections they need to read. Headings appear in many typeface variations (boldface being the most common) and often use sans serif typefaces. Never leave a heading as the final line on a page—the heading is disconnected from its text and thus ineffective. Instead, move the heading to the start of the next page. See also **headings** (page 194).

Captions are titles that highlight or describe illustrations or blocks of text. Captions often appear below or above figures and tables and in the left or right margins next to blocks of text. See also **tables** (page 203).

Headers and Footers. A header appears at the top of each page and contains identifying information; a footer appears at the bottom of each page and contains similar information. Document pages may have headers or footers or both that include the topic or subtopic of a section, identifying numbers, the date the document was written, page numbers, and the document name. Keep your headers and footers concise—too much information in them can create visual clutter. See also **headers and footers** (page 193).

Rules, Icons, and Color. Rules are vertical or horizontal lines used to divide one area of the page from another or to create boxes. They highlight elements and make information more accessible.

An icon is a pictorial representation of an idea. Commonly used icons include the small envelopes on Web pages to symbolize email links and national flags to symbolize different language versions of a document. To be effective, icons must be simple and easily recognized or defined.

Color and screening (shaded areas on page) can distinguish one part of a document from another or unify a series of documents. They can set off sections within a document, highlight examples, or emphasize warnings. In tables, screening can highlight column titles or sets of data to which you want to draw the reader's attention.

Page Design

Page design is the process of combining the various design elements on a page to make a coherent whole. The flexibility of your design is based on the capabilities of your word-processing software, how the document will be reproduced, and the budget.

Thumbnail Sketches. Before you spend time positioning actual text and visuals on a page, you may want to create a *thumbnail sketch,* in which blocks indicate the placement of elements. You can go further by roughly assembling all the thumbnail pages, showing size, shape, form, and general style of a large document. Such a mock-up, called a *dummy,* allows you to see how a finished document will look.

Columns. As you design pages, consider how columns may improve the readability of your document. A single-column format works well with larger typefaces, double spacing, and left-justified margins. For smaller typefaces and single-spaced lines, the two-column structure keeps text columns narrow enough so readers need not scan back and forth across the width of the entire page for every line.

A word on a line by itself at the end of a column is called a *widow.* A single word carried over to the top of a column or page is called an *orphan.* Avoid both widows and orphans.

White Space. White space visually frames information and breaks it into manageable chunks. For example, white space between paragraphs helps readers see the information in the paragraphs as units. Use extra white space between sections as a visual cue to signal that one section is ending and another is beginning.

Lists. Lists are an effective way to highlight words, phrases, and short sentences. Lists are particularly useful for certain types of information, such as steps in sequence, materials or parts needed, concluding points, and recommendations. See **lists** (page 201).

Illustrations. Readers notice illustrations before they notice text, and they notice larger illustrations before they notice smaller ones. Thus, the size of an illustration suggests its relative importance. For newsletter articles and publications aimed at wide audiences, consider especially the proportion of the illustration to the text. Magazine designers often use the three-fifths rule: Page layout is more dramatic and appealing when the major element (photograph, drawing, or other visual) occupies three-fifths rather than half the available space. The same principle can be used to enhance the visual appeal of a report. See **drawings** (page 185), **photographs** (page 202), and **visuals** (page 205).

Remember that clarity and usefulness take precedence over aesthetics in many business and technical documents. Illustrations can be gathered in one place (for example, at the end of a report), but placing them in the text closer to their accompanying explanations makes them more effective. Using illustrations in the text also provides visual relief. For advice on the placement of illustrations, see the Writer's Checklist: Creating and Integrating Visuals (page 206).

lists

Lists can save readers time by allowing them to see at a glance specific items, questions, or directions. Lists also help readers by breaking up complex statements and by allowing key ideas to stand out, as in the following example:

- Before we agree to hold the district meeting at the Brent Hotel, we should make sure the hotel facilities provide the following:
  - Service center with phones, faxes, Internet hookup, PCs, and copying services for the conference committee
  - Ground-floor exhibit area large enough for thirty 8-by-15-foot booths
  - Eight meeting rooms to accommodate 25 people each
  - Internet hookups, projection screens for presentations, and overhead projectors in each room
  - Ballroom and dining facilities for 250 people

  To confirm that the Brent Hotel is our best choice, we should tour the facilities during our stay in Kansas City.

Writer's Checklist: Using Lists

- ☑ List only comparable items.
- ☑ Use **parallel structure** throughout (page 269).
- ☑ Use only words, phrases, or short sentences.
- ☑ Provide context by introducing each list.
- ☑ Ensure **coherence** (page 256) by checking for adequate **transition** (page 277) before and after a list.
- ☑ Use bullets when rank or sequence is not important.
- ☑ Do not include too many items in one list.
- ☑ Do not overuse lists.

organizational charts

An organizational chart shows how the various components of an organization are related to one another. This type of visual, illustrated in Figure 6–14, is useful when you want to give your readers an overview of an organization or to display the lines of authority within it. As with all illustrations, place the organizational chart as close as possible to the text that refers to it. See **visuals** (page 205).

FIGURE 6–14. Organizational Chart

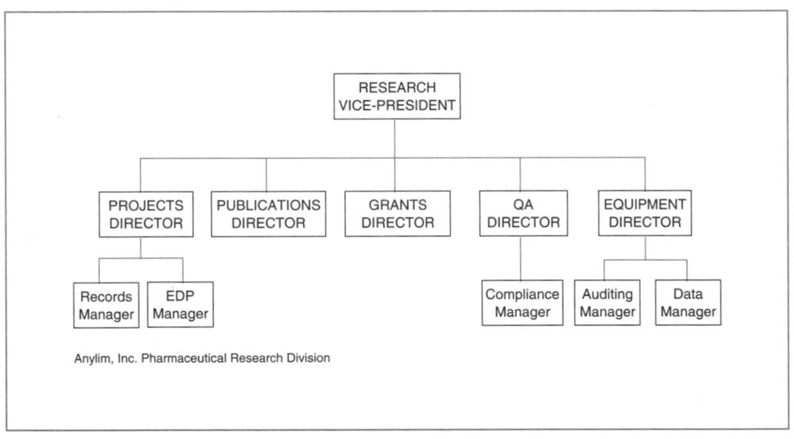

photographs

Photographs are the best way to show the surface of an object, record an event, or demonstrate the development of a phenomenon over a period of time. They are not always the best type of illustration, however. Photographs cannot depict the internal workings of a mechanism or below-the-surface details of objects or structures. Such details are better represented in **drawings** (page 185).

An effective photograph shows important details and indicates relative size of the subject by including a familiar object—such as a ruler or a person—near the subject being photographed. See Figure 6–15.

Treat photographs as you do other **visuals** (page 205). Give the photograph a figure number, callouts (labels) to identify key features in the photograph, and include a caption if needed.

FIGURE 6–15. Photo of Aircraft Door. Photo courtesy of Ken Cook Company.

tables

A table can present data, such as statistics, more concisely than text and more accurately than a graph. A table facilitates comparisons among data by organizing it into rows and columns. However, overall trends are more easily conveyed in charts and **graphs** (page 189). See also **visuals** (page 205).

Table Elements

Tables typically include the elements shown in Figure 6–16.

Table Number. Table numbers are usually Arabic and should be assigned sequentially to the tables throughout the document.

Table Title. The title, which is normally placed just above the table, should describe concisely what the table represents.

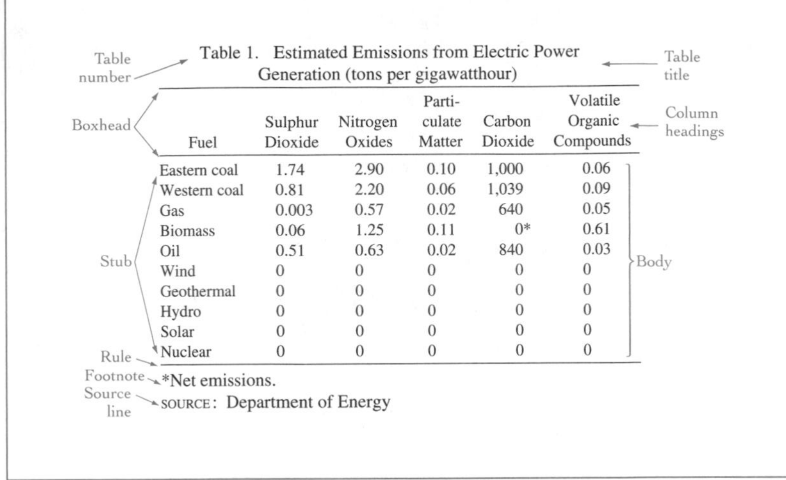

Table 1. Estimated Emissions from Electric Power Generation (tons per gigawatthour)

Fuel	Sulphur Dioxide	Nitrogen Oxides	Particulate Matter	Carbon Dioxide	Volatile Organic Compounds
Eastern coal	1.74	2.90	0.10	1,000	0.06
Western coal	0.81	2.20	0.06	1,039	0.09
Gas	0.003	0.57	0.02	640	0.05
Biomass	0.06	1.25	0.11	0*	0.61
Oil	0.51	0.63	0.02	840	0.03
Wind	0	0	0	0	0
Geothermal	0	0	0	0	0
Hydro	0	0	0	0	0
Solar	0	0	0	0	0
Nuclear	0	0	0	0	0

*Net emissions.

SOURCE: Department of Energy

FIGURE 6–16. Elements of a Typical Table

Boxhead. The boxhead contains the column headings, which should be brief but descriptive. Units of measurement, where necessary, should be either specified as part of the heading or enclosed in parentheses beneath the heading. Standard abbreviations and symbols are acceptable. Avoid vertical lettering whenever possible.

Stub. The *stub,* the left vertical column of a table, lists the items about which information is given in the body of the table.

Body. The body comprises the data below the column headings and to the right of the stub. Within the body, arrange columns so that the items to be compared appear in adjacent rows and columns. Where no information exists for a specific item, substitute a row of dots or a dash to acknowledge the gap.

Rules. Rules are the lines that separate the table into its various parts. Horizontal rules are placed below the title, below the body of the table, and between the column headings and the body of the table. Tables should be open at the sides. The columns within the table may be separated by vertical rules only if such lines aid clarity.

Footnotes. Footnotes are used for explanations of individual items in the table. Symbols (such as * and †) or lowercase letters (sometimes in parentheses) rather than numbers are ordinarily used to key table footnotes because numbers might be mistaken for numerical data or could be confused with the numbering system for text footnotes.

Source Line. The source line identifies where the data originated. When a source line is appropriate, it appears below the table. Many organizations place the source line below the footnotes. See also **copyright** (page 53) and **plagiarism** (page 73).

Continued Tables. When a table must be divided so it can be continued on another page, repeat the column headings and give the table number at the head of each new page a *continued* label (for example, "Table 3, *continued*").

Informal Tables

To list relatively few items that would be easier for the reader to grasp in tabular form, you can use an informal table, as long as you introduce it properly.

- Dear Customer:
  To order replacement parts, use the following part numbers and prices:

PART	PART NUMBER	PRICE ($)
Diverter valve	2-912	12.50
Gasket kit	2-776	0.95
Adapter	3-212	0.90

Although informal tables do not need titles or table numbers to identify them, they do require column headings that accurately describe the information listed.

visuals

Visuals can express ideas or convey information in ways that words alone cannot. They communicate by showing how things look (drawings, maps, and photographs), by representing numbers and quantities (graphs and tables), by depicting relationships (flowcharts), and by making abstract concepts and relationships concrete (organizational charts). They also highlight the most important information and emphasize key concepts succinctly and clearly, especially in documents like **brochures** (page 51) and **newsletters** (page 71). Information made concrete and concise through graphics helps your readers focus on and understand your most important points. The following entries are related to specific visuals and illustrations:

If you plan to use visuals, consider your purpose and your audience carefully. For example, you would need different illustrations for an automobile owner's manual than you would for a mechanic's diagnostic guide. Take visual requirements into account even before you begin writing—when you are planning the scope and organization of your document—by including them in your document outline. Note in your outline where each should appear, and include a simple sketch or a brief description of the visual. See also **organization** (page 27) and **scope** (page 45).

Many of the qualities of good writing—simplicity, clarity, conciseness, directness—are equally important in the creation and use of visuals. Presented with clarity and consistency, visuals can help the reader focus on key portions of your document. Be aware, though, that even the best visual only enhances or supports the text. Your writing must provide context for the visual and point out its significance. See also **layout and design** (page 196).

Writer's Checklist: Creating and Integrating Visuals

☑ Clarify why each visual is included in the text. The amount of description varies, depending on the illustration's complexity and the reader's background. Nonexperts usually require lengthier explanations than do experts.

☑ Use consistent terminology. Do not refer to something as a "proportion" in the text and as a "percentage" in the illustration.

☑ Define all abbreviations the first time they appear in the text, figure, or table. If any symbols are not self-explanatory, as in graphs, include a key that defines them.

☑ Place a visual as close as possible to the text where it is discussed, especially if an illustration is central to the discussion. No visual should precede its first text mention.

☑ If the visual is lengthy and detailed, consider placing it in an **appendix** (page 95) and refer to it in the text.

☑ Give each visual a concise title that clearly describes its content.

☑ Assign figure and table numbers, particularly if your document contains more than one illustration or table. The figure or table number precedes the title:

- Figure 1. Projected sales for 20---20--

Writer's Checklist: Creating and Integrating Visuals (continued)

☑ Refer to visuals in the text of your document by their figure or table numbers. (Note that in reports and many other documents, illustrations — drawings, maps, and photographs — are generically labeled "figures," while tables are labeled "tables.")

☑ In documents with more than five illustrations or tables, include a section titled List of Figures or List of Tables that identifies each by number, title, and page number. This list should follow the **table of contents** (page 101). See also **formal reports** (page 96).

☑ Keep visuals simple, include only information necessary to the discussion in the text and eliminate unnecessary labels, arrows, boxes, and lines.

☑ Specify the units of measurement used or include a scale of relative distances, when appropriate. Make sure relative sizes are clear or indicate distance with a scale.

☑ Position the lettering of any explanatory text or labels horizontally for readability.

☑ Allow adequate white space around and within the visual.

☑ Obtain written permission for any visuals that are copyrighted, and acknowledge borrowed material in a source or credit line below the caption for a figure and in a footnote at the bottom of a table.

☑ Acknowledge your use of any public (uncopyrighted) information, such as demographic or economic data, from federal government publications by including a credit line.

☑ When writing a trade-journal article, consult the editorial guidelines of the particular journal or recommended style manual for guidance on the preparation and format of visuals.

7

Oral Communication

Preview

Although writing is important, oral communication (especially **listening** and **presentations**) is crucial to success in the workplace. This section contains entries on these essential subjects, including an entry on conducting **meetings.** Because preparing an oral presentation is much like preparing to write, consider reviewing Tab 1, The Writing Process, noting in particular the entries on **audience/readers** (page 3), **purpose/objective** (page 41), and **organization** (page 27).

This section also covers **global communication,** a subject of increasing importance. The ability to communicate with people from other countries is essential in the global marketplace.

global communication

The prevalence of multinational corporations, international trade agreements, the emergence of Europe as a giant single market, and the increasing diversity of the U.S. workforce, and increases in immigration mean that the ability to reach audiences from varied cultural backgrounds is essential. The audiences for such communications include clients, business partners, colleagues, and current and potential employees.

Writer's Checklist: Communicating Globally

The following guidelines will help build your awareness of global and intercultural communication. However, this list cannot begin to cover the many issues important to cross-cultural communication.

☑ Consult with someone from your intended audience. Many phrases, gestures, and visual elements are so subtle that only someone who is very familiar with a given culture can explain the effect they may have on others from that culture.

☑ Acknowledge diversity within your organization. Discussing the differing cultures within your company or region will reinforce the idea that people can interpret verbal and nonverbal communications differently.

☑ Invite global and intercultural communication experts to speak to your employees. Companies in your area may have employees who could be resources for cultural discussions.

☑ Understand that the key to effective communication with global audiences is recognizing that cultural differences, despite the challenges they present, offer growth for both you and your organization.

For more information on reaching global audiences, see **international correspondence** (page 141) and **presentations** (page 220).

WEB LINK ▶ USING INTERCULTURAL RESOURCES

LIBRARY OF CONGRESS: COUNTRY STUDIES
lcweb2.loc.gov/frd/cs/cshome.html

This site presents information on the economic, social, and political institutions of over 100 countries and regions.

WWW VIRTUAL LIBRARY: INTERNATIONAL AFFAIRS RESOURCES
http://www.etown.edu/vl

This well-organized portal provides access to over 2,000 selected and annotated links.

listening

Effective listening is essential for all types of communication. It enables the listener to understand the instructions of a teacher, the goals of a manager, and the needs and wants of customers, and lays the foundation for cooperation. Productive communication occurs when both the speaker and the listener focus clearly on the content of the message and attempt to eliminate as much interference as possible.

Fallacies about Listening

Most people assume that because they can hear they know how to listen. In fact, *hearing* is passive, whereas *listening* is active. Hearing voices in a crowd or a ringing telephone requires no analysis and no active involvement. We hear such sounds without choosing to listen to them—we have no choice but to hear them. Listening, however, requires taking action, interpreting the message, and assessing its worth.

Many people believe that words have absolute meanings; however, words can have multiple meanings that are determined by the context in which they are used. Differences in meaning may be the result of differences in the speaker's and the listener's occupation, education, culture, sex, race, or other factors. The use of **idioms** (page 265) can result in misunderstanding. See also **biased language** (page 252), **English as a second language** (page 320), **jargon** (page 266), and **international correspondence** (page 141).

Active Listening

To listen actively, you should (1) make a conscious decision to listen actively, (2) define your purpose for listening, (3) take specific actions to listen more efficiently, and (4) adapt to the situation.

Step 1: Make a Conscious Decision. Make up your mind to listen actively; that is, "seek first to understand and then to be understood."

Step 2: Define Your Purpose. Knowing why you are listening can go a long way toward managing the most common listening problems: drifting attention, formulating your response while the speaker is still talking, and interrupting the speaker. To help you define your purpose for listening, ask yourself these questions:

- What kind of information do I hope to get from this exchange and how will I use it?

- What kind of message do I want to send while I am listening? (Do I want to portray understanding, determination, flexibility, competence, or patience?)
- What might interfere with listening during the interaction—boredom, daydreaming, anger, impatience? How can I keep these factors from placing a barrier between the speaker and me?

Step 3: Take Specific Actions. Becoming an active listener requires a willingness to become a responder rather than a reactor. A *responder* is a listener who slows down the communication to be certain that he or she is accurately receiving the message sent by the speaker. A *reactor* does not check the meaning of the message and simply says the first thing that comes to mind, never knowing if he or she has received an accurate version of the message. Take the following actions to help you become a responder and not a reactor.

- Make a conscious effort to be impartial when evaluating a message. For example, do not dismiss a message because you dislike the speaker or are distracted by the speaker's appearance or mannerisms.
- Slow down the communication by asking for more information or by paraphrasing the message received before you offer your thoughts. Paraphrasing lets the speaker know you are listening, gives the speaker an opportunity to clear up any misunderstanding, and keeps you focused. See also **paraphrasing** (page 34).
- Listen with empathy by putting yourself in the speaker's position. When people feel they are being listened to empathetically, they tend to respond with appreciation and cooperation, thereby improving the communication.
- To help you stay focused on what the speaker is saying, take notes while you are listening. **Note-taking** (page 26) not only communicates your attentiveness to the speaker, it also reinforces the message and helps you remember it.

Step 4: Adapt to the Situation. The requirements of active listening differ from one situation to another. For example, when you are listening to a lecture, you may be listening only for specific information. However, if you are on a team project that depends on everyone's contribution, you need to listen at the highest level so you can gather information as well as pick up on nuances the other speakers may be communicating. See also **collaborative writing** (page 4) and **presentations** (page 220).

meetings

A meeting is a face-to-face exchange among a group of people who collaborate to produce better results than any one of the participants could have produced alone. Like other communication, such as writing and presentations, a successful meeting requires planning and preparation. See also **presentations** (page 220).

Planning a Meeting

For a meeting to be successful, determine the focus of the meeting, decide who should attend, and choose the best time and place to hold the meeting. You also need to prepare an agenda for the meeting and determine who should take the minutes. See also **minutes of meetings** (page 218).

Determine the Purpose of the Meeting. The first step in planning a meeting is to focus on the desired outcome. Ask yourself the following question to help you determine the purpose of the meeting: What do I want participants to *know,* to *believe,* or to *do* or to *be able to do* as a result of attending the meeting?

Once you have focused your desired outcome, use the information to write a *purpose statement* for the meeting that answers the questions *what* and *why.*

- The purpose of this meeting is to gather ideas from the sales force [*what*] to create a successful sales campaign for our new scanner [*why*].

Decide Who Should Attend. There is really no sense in having a meeting if not enough of the key people are present. If a meeting must be held without some key participants, email those people prior to the meeting for their contributions. Of course, the meeting minutes should be distributed to everyone, including significant nonattendees.

Choose the Meeting Time. The time of day and how long the meeting lasts can influence the outcome of the meeting. Consider the following when you are planning a meeting:

- People need Monday morning to focus on the week's work after the weekend.
- People need Friday afternoon to wrap up the week and take care of tasks that must be finished before the weekend.
- Long meetings should include adequate breaks to allow participants to check their messages, make phone calls, and refresh themselves.

- A meeting held during the last 15 minutes of the day will be quick, but few people will remember what happened.

Choose the Meeting Location. Having a meeting on your own premises can give you an advantage: You feel more comfortable, which, along with your guests' newness to their surroundings, may help you get an edge. Holding the meeting on another person's premises, however, can signal cooperation. For balance, especially when people are meeting for the first time or are discussing sensitive issues, having a meeting at a neutral site may be the best solution. No one gains an advantage in off-site meetings, and attendees often feel freer to participate.

Establish the Agenda. A tool for focusing the group, the *agenda* is an outline of what the meeting will address. Never begin a meeting without an agenda, even if it is only a handwritten list of topics. Ideally, the agenda should be distributed to attendees a day or two before the meeting. For a longer meeting in which participants are required to make a presentation, try to distribute the agenda a week or more in advance.

The agenda should list the attendees, the meeting time and place, and the topics you plan to discuss. If the meeting includes presentations, list the time allotted for each speaker. Finally, indicate an approximate length for the meeting so that participants can plan the rest of their day. Figure 7–1 shows a typical agenda.

FIGURE 7–1. Meeting Agenda

Sales Meeting Agenda

Purpose:	To get input for a sales campaign for the new software
Date:	May 11, 20--
Place:	Conference Room E
Time:	9:30 A.M.–11:00 A.M.
Attendees:	New Products Advertising Manager, Equipment Sales Reps, Customer-Service Staff, and Service Managers

Topic	Presenter	Time
The Scanner	Bob Arbuckle	Presentation, 9:30–9:45
The Campaign	Maria Lopez	Presentation, 9:45–10:00
The Sales Strategy	Mary Winifred	Presentation, 10:00–10:15
Discussion	Led by Dave Crimes	Discussion, 10:15–11:00

If the agenda is distributed in advance of the meeting, it should be accompanied by a memo or email informing people of the meeting. The cover memo should include the following information:

- The purpose of the meeting
- The date and place
- The meeting start and stop times
- The names of the people invited
- Instructions on how to prepare

Figure 7–2 shows a cover memo to accompany an agenda.

FIGURE 7–2. Memo to Accompany an Agenda

Memo

TO: New Products Advertising Manager
Equipment Sales Representatives
Customer Service Staff
Service Managers
FROM: Susan McLaughlin SM
DATE: May 7, 20--
SUBJECT: Planning Meeting

Purpose of the Meeting

The purpose of this meeting is to get your ideas for the upcoming introduction and sales campaign for our new software.

Date, Time, and Location

Date: May 11, 20--
Time: 9:30 A.M.–11:00 A.M.
Place: Conference Room E (go to the ground floor, take a right off the elevator, third door on the left)

Attendees

The groups listed above

Meeting Preparation

Everyone should be prepared to offer suggestions on the following items:

- Sales features of the new software
- Techniques for selling software
- Customer profile for potential business
- FAQs—questions customers may ask
- Anticipated service needs

Assign the Minute-Taking. Delegate the minute-taking to someone other than the leader. The minute taker should record major decisions made and tasks assigned. To avoid misunderstandings, the minute taker must record each assignment, the person responsible for it, and the date on which it is due.

For a standing committee, it is best to rotate the responsibility of taking minutes. See also **minutes of meetings** (page 218) and **note-taking** (page 26).

Conducting the Meeting

Assign someone to write on a flip chart or use a computer to record information that needs to be viewed by everyone present.

During the meeting, keep to your agenda; however, allow room for differing views and foster an environment in which participants listen respectfully to one another. See also **listening** (page 212). Create a productive environment:

- Consider the feelings, thoughts, ideas, and needs of others—do not let your own agenda blind you to other points of view.
- Help other participants feel valued and respected by listening to them and responding to what they say.
- Respond positively to the comments of others as best you can.
- Consider ways of doing things that are different from your own, particularly those from other cultures. See also **global communication** (page 211).

Deal with Conflict. Despite your best efforts, conflict is inevitable. However, conflict is potentially valuable; when managed positively, it can stimulate creative thinking by challenging complacency and showing ways to achieve goals more efficiently or economically. See also **collaborative writing** (page 4).

Members of any group are likely to vary greatly in their personalities and attitudes, and you may encounter people who approach meetings differently. Consider the following tactics for the interruptive, negative, rambling, overly quiet, and territorial personality types.

- The *interruptive person* rarely lets anyone finish a sentence and intimidates the group's quieter members. Tell that person in a firm but nonhostile tone to let the others finish in the interest of getting everyone's input. By addressing the issue directly, you signal to the group the importance of putting common goals first.
- The *negative person* has difficulty accepting change and often considers a new idea or project from a negative point of view. Such negativity, if left unchecked, can demoralize the group and deflate enthusiasm for new ideas. If the negative person brings up a valid point, ask for the group's suggestions to remedy the issue being raised. If the negative person's reactions are not valid or are outside the agenda, state the necessity of staying focused on the agenda and perhaps recommend a separate meeting to address those issues.

- The *rambling person* cannot collect his or her thoughts quickly enough to verbalize them succinctly. Restate or clarify this person's ideas. Try to strike a balance between providing your own interpretation and drawing out the person's intended meaning.
- The *quiet person* may be timid or may just be deep in thought. Ask for this person's thoughts, being careful not to embarrass the person. In some cases, you can have a quiet person jot down his or her thoughts and give them to you later.
- The *territorial person* fiercely defends his or her group against real or perceived threats and may refuse to cooperate with members of other departments, companies, and so on. Point out that although such concerns may be valid, everyone is working toward the same overall goal and that goal takes precedence.

Be aware that cultural differences can influence the way people interact in a meeting. See **global communication** (page 211).

Close the Meeting. To close the meeting, review all decisions and assignments. Paraphrase each to help the group focus on what they have agreed to do and to confirm the accuracy of the minutes. This is the time to raise questions and clarify any misunderstandings. Set a date by which everyone at the meeting can expect to receive copies of the minutes. Finally, thank everyone for participating and close the meeting on a positive note.

minutes of meetings

Organizations and committees keep official records of their meetings; such records are known as *minutes.* If you attend many business meetings, you may be asked to write and distribute the minutes of a meeting. (For advice on conducting meetings, see **meetings,** page 214.)

Writer's Checklist: Preparing Minutes of Meetings

Include the following in meeting minutes:

- ☑ The name of the group or committee holding the meeting
- ☑ The topic of the meeting
- ☑ The kind of meeting (a regular meeting or a special meeting called to discuss a specific subject or problem)

Writer's Checklist: Preparing Minutes of Meetings (continued)

☑ The number of members present and, for committees or boards of ten or fewer members, their names

☑ The place, time, and date of the meeting

☑ A statement that the chair and the secretary were present or the names of any substitutes

☑ A statement that the minutes of the previous meeting were approved or revised

☑ A list of any reports that were read and approved

☑ All the main motions that were made, with statements as to whether they were carried, defeated, or tabled (vote postponed) and the names of those who made and seconded the motions (motions that were withdrawn are not mentioned)

☑ A full description of resolutions that were adopted and a simple statement of any that were rejected

☑ A record of all ballots with the number of votes cast for and against resolutions

☑ The time the meeting was adjourned (officially ended) and the place, time, and date of the next meeting

☑ The recording secretary's signature and typed name and, if desired, the signature of the chair

Because minutes are often used to settle disputes, they must be accurate, complete, and clear. When approved, minutes of meetings are official and can be used as evidence in legal proceedings.

Keep your minutes brief and to the point. Except for recording motions, which must be transcribed word for word, summarize what occurs and paraphrase discussions. To keep the minutes concise, follow a set format and use headings for each major point discussed. Be specific and use names and titles and refer to people consistently. Avoid adjectives and adverbs that suggest either good or bad qualities—minutes should be objective and impartial.

If a member of the committee is to follow up on something and report back to the committee at its next meeting, clearly state the person's name and the responsibility he or she has accepted.

An example of minutes is shown in Figure 7–3.

NORTH TAMPA MEDICAL CENTER

Minutes of the Monthly Meeting
Medical Audit Committee

DATE: July 26, 20--

PRESENT: G. Miller (Chair), C. Bloom, J. Dades, K. Gilley, D. Ingoglia (Secretary), S. Ramirez
ABSENT: D. Rowan, C. Tsien, C. Voronski, R. Fautier, R. Wolf

Dr. Gail Miller called the meeting to order at 12:45 P.M. Dr. David Ingoglia made a motion that the June 1, 20--, minutes be approved as distributed. The motion was seconded and passed.

The committee discussed and took action on the following topics.

(1) TOPIC: Meeting Time

Discussion: The most convenient time for the committee to meet.
Action taken: The committee decided to meet on the fourth Tuesday of every month, at 12:30 P.M.

FIGURE 7–3. Minutes of a Meeting

presentations

The steps required to prepare an effective presentation parallel the steps you follow to write a document. As with writing a document, you must determine your purpose and analyze your audience. You must gather the facts that will support your point of view and any actions that you propose and logically organize that information. Presentations do, however, differ from written documents in a number of important ways. They are intended for listeners, not readers. Because you are speaking, your manner of delivery, the way you organize the material, and your supporting visuals require as much attention as your content.

Determining Your Purpose

Every presentation is given for a purpose, even if it is only to share information. To determine the primary purpose of your presentation, use the following question as a guide: What do I want the audience to *know,* to *believe,* and to *do* when I have finished the presentation?

Based on the answers to that question, write a purpose statement that answers the questions *what* and *why.*

- The purpose of my presentation is to convince my company's chief information officer of the need to improve the appearance, content, and customer use of our company's Web site [*what*] so that she will be persuaded to allocate additional funds for site-development work in the next fiscal year [*why*].

You may also have secondary purposes, such as to inspire or reassure your audience, as discussed in **purpose/objective** (page 41).

Analyzing Your Audience

Once you have determined the desired end result of the presentation, you need to analyze your audience so that you can tailor your presentation to their needs. Ask yourself these questions about your audience:

- What is your audience's level of experience or knowledge about your topic?
- What is the general educational level and age of your audience?
- What is your audience's attitude toward the topic you are speaking about, and—based on that attitude—what concerns, fears, or objections might your audience have?
- Do any subgroups in the audience have different concerns or needs?
- What questions might your audience ask about this topic?

See also **audience/readers** (page 3).

Gathering Information

Once you have focused the presentation, you need to find the facts that support your point of view or the action you propose. As you gather information, keep in mind that you should give the audience only the facts necessary to accomplish your goals; too much will overwhelm them and too little will not adequately inform your listeners or support your recommendations. For detailed guidance about gathering information, see **research** (page 42), **library research** (page 20), and **Internet research** (page 10).

Structuring the Presentation

When structuring the presentation, focus on your audience. Listeners are freshest at the outset and refocus their attention as you wrap up your remarks. Take advantage of that pattern. Give your audience a brief overview of your presentation at the beginning, use the body to develop your ideas, and end with a summary of what you covered and, if appropriate, a call to action.

The Introduction. Include in the introduction an opening that focuses your audience's attention, such as in the following examples.

DEFINITION OF A PROBLEM

- You have to write an important report, but you'd like to incorporate lengthy sections of an old report into your new one. The problem is that you don't have an electronic version of the old report. You will have to rekey many pages. You groan because that seems an incredible waste of time. Have I got a solution for you!

AN ATTENTION-GETTING STATEMENT

- As many as 50 million Americans have high blood pressure.

A RHETORICAL QUESTION

- Would you be interested in a full-sized computer keyboard that is waterproof and noiseless, and can be rolled up like a rubber mat?

A PERSONAL EXPERIENCE

- As I sat at my computer one morning, deleting my eighth spam message of the day, I decided that it was time to take action to eliminate this time-waster.

AN APPROPRIATE QUOTATION

- According to researchers at the Massachusetts Institute of Technology, "Garlic and its cousin, the onion, confer major health benefits—including fighting cancer, infections, and heart disease."

For additional examples, see **introductions** (page 16).

Following your opening, use the introduction to set the stage for your audience by providing an overview of the presentation, which can include general or background information that will be needed to understand any more detailed information in the body of your presentation. It can also show how you have organized the material.

- This presentation analyzes three different scanner models for us to consider purchasing. Based on a comparison of all three, I will recommend the one I believe best meets our needs. To do so, I'll discuss the following five points:
  1. Why we need a scanner [*the problem*]
  2. The basics of scanner technology [*general information*]
  3. The criteria I used to compare the three model scanners [*comparison*]
  4. The scanner models I compared and why [*possible solutions*]
  5. The scanner I propose we buy [*proposed solution*]

The Body. In the body, present the evidence that will persuade the audience to agree with your conclusions and act on them. If there is a problem, demonstrate that it exists and offer a solution or range of possible solutions. For example, if your introduction stated that the problem is low profits, high costs, outdated technology, or high employee absenteeism, you could use the following approach.

1. Prove your point.
   - Marshal the facts and data you need.
   - Present the information using easy-to-understand visuals.
2. Offer solutions.
   - "Increase profits by lowering production costs."
   - "Cut overhead to reduce costs or abolish specific programs or product lines."
   - "Replace outdated technology or upgrade existing technology."
   - "Offer employees more flexibility in their work schedules or other incentives."
3. Anticipate questions ("How much will it cost?") and objections ("We're too busy now—when would we have time to learn the new software?") and incorporate the answers into your presentation.

The Closing. Fulfill the goals of your presentation in the closing. If your purpose is to motivate the listeners to take action, ask them to do what you want them to do; if your purpose is to get your audience to think about something, summarize what you want them to think about. Many presenters make the mistake of not actually closing—they simply quit talking, shuffle papers, and then walk away.

Because your closing is what your audience is most likely to remember, it is the time to be strong and persuasive. Consider the following possible closing.

- Based on all the data, I believe that the Worthington scanner best suits our needs. It produces 3,000 units a month more than its closest competitor and creates electronic files we can use on our Web site and on paper. The Worthington is also compatible with our current computer network and includes staff training at our site. Although the initial cost is higher than the other two models, the additional capabilities, longer life-cycle for replacement parts, and lower maintenance costs make it a better value.

  Let's allocate the funds necessary for this scanner by the 15th of this month. Then we could be up and running before the first of next month and be well prepared for next quarter's customer presentations.

That closing brings the presentation full circle and asks the audience to fulfill the purpose of the presentation—exactly what a closing should do.

Transitions. Planned transitions should appear between the introduction and the body, between points in the body, and between the body and the closing. Transitions are simply a sentence or two to let the audience know that you are moving from one topic to the next. They also prevent a choppy presentation and provide the audience with assurance that you know where you are going and how to get there.

- Before getting into the specifics of each scanner I compared, I'd like to demonstrate how scanners work in general. That information will provide you with the background you'll need to compare the differences among the scanners and their capabilities discussed in this presentation.

It is also a good idea to pause for a moment after you have delivered a transition between topics to let your listeners shift gears with you. Remember, they do not know your plan. See also **transition** (page 277).

Using Visuals

Well-planned visuals not only add interest and emphasis to your presentation they also clarify and simplify your message because they communicate clearly, quickly, and vividly. Charts, graphs, and illustrations greatly increase audience understanding and retention of information, especially for complex issues and technical information that could otherwise be misunderstood or overlooked. A bar graph, pie chart, diagram, or concise summary of key points can eliminate misunderstanding and save many words.

You can create and present the visual components of your presentation by using a variety of media—flip charts, whiteboard or chalkboard, overhead transparencies, slides, or computer presentation software.

Presentation Software. Presentation software, such as PowerPoint™, Corel Presentations™, and Freelance Graphics™, lets you create your presentation on your computer. You can develop charts and graphs with data from spreadsheet software or locate visuals on the Web, and then import those files into your presentation. This software also offers standard templates and other features that help you design effective visuals and integrated text. Enhancements include a selection of typefaces, highlighting devices, background textures and colors, and clip-art images. Avoid using too many enhancements, which may distract viewers from your message. Images can also be printed out for use as overhead transparencies or handouts.

Rehearse your presentation using your electronic slides, and practice your transitions from slide to slide. Also practice loading your presentation and anticipate any technical difficulties that might arise. Should you encounter a technical snag during the presentation, stay calm and give yourself time to solve the problem. If you cannot solve the problem, move on without the technology. As a backup, carry a printout of your electronic presentation (which you can tape onto index cards). Carry an extra copy of your presentation on diskette for backup. Figure 7–4 shows a typical computer presentation setup and PowerPoint slide; Figure 7–5, page 227, shows a pattern for a typical presentation.

FIGURE 7–4. Computer Presentation Setup

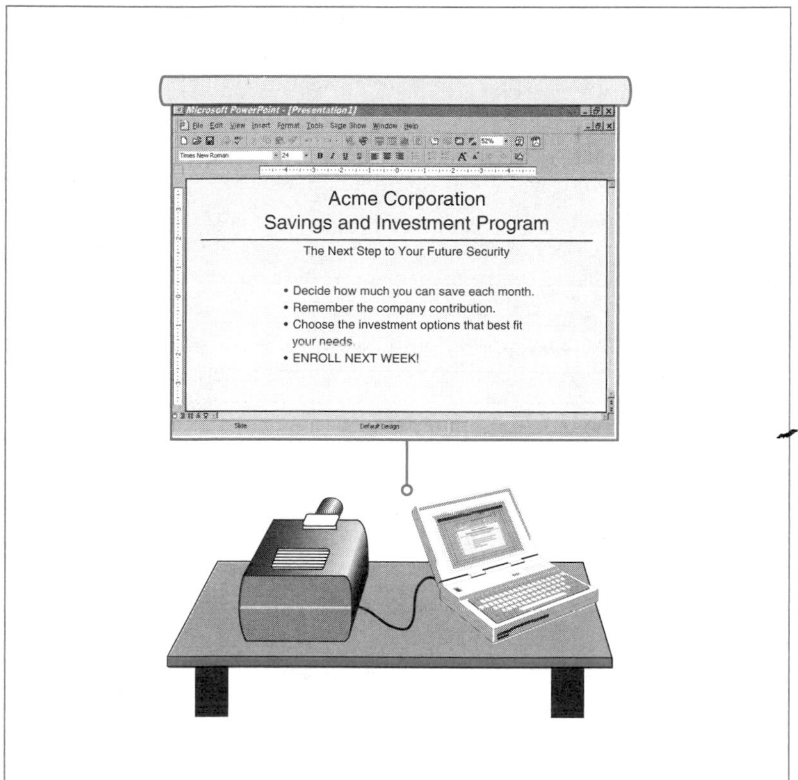

Writer's Checklist: Using Visuals in a Presentation

☑ Use text sparingly. Use bulleted or numbered lists, keeping them parallel in content and grammatical form. Use numbers if the sequence is important and bullets if it is not. (See **parallel structure,** page 269.)

☑ Limit the number of bulleted or numbered items to 5 or 6 per visual. Each visual should contain no more than 40 to 45 words. (See Figure 7–4.) Any more will clutter the visual and force you to use a smaller type size that could impair the audience's ability to read it.

☑ Make your visuals consistent in type style, size, and spacing.

Writer's Checklist: Using Visuals in a Presentation (continued)

- ☑ Use no more than 12 visuals per presentation. Any more will tax the audience's concentration.
- ☑ Use a type size visible to members of the audience in the back of the room. Type should be boldface and no smaller than 30 points. For headings, 45- or 50-point type works even better.
- ☑ Use graphs and charts to show data trends. Use only one or two illustrations per visual. Otherwise, your presentation of the data will be cluttered and confusing.
- ☑ Make the contrast between your text and the background sharp. Use light backgrounds with dark lettering and avoid textured or decorated backgrounds.
- ☑ Match your delivery of the content to your visuals. Do not put one set of words or images on the screen and talk about the previous visual or, even worse, the next one.
- ☑ Do not read the text on your visual word for word. Your audience can read the visuals; they look to you to cover the salient points in detail.

Delivering a Presentation

Once you have outlined and drafted your presentation and prepared your visuals, you are ready to practice your presentation and delivery techniques.

Practice. Familiarize yourself with the sequence of the material—major topics, notes, and visuals—in your outline. Once you feel comfortable with the content, you are ready to practice the presentation itself.

PRACTICE ON YOUR FEET AND OUT LOUD. Try to practice in the room where you will give the presentation. Practicing on-site helps you get the feel of the room: the acoustics, the lighting, the arrangement of the chairs, the position of electrical outlets and switches, and so forth. Practice out loud to make clear exactly how long your presentation will take, highlight problems such as awkward transitions, and help eliminate verbal tics, such as "um," "you know," and "like."

PRACTICE WITH YOUR VISUALS AND TEXT. Integrate your visuals into your practice sessions to help your presentation go more smoothly. Operate the equipment (computer, slide projector, or overhead projector) until you are comfortable with it. Decide if you want to use a remote

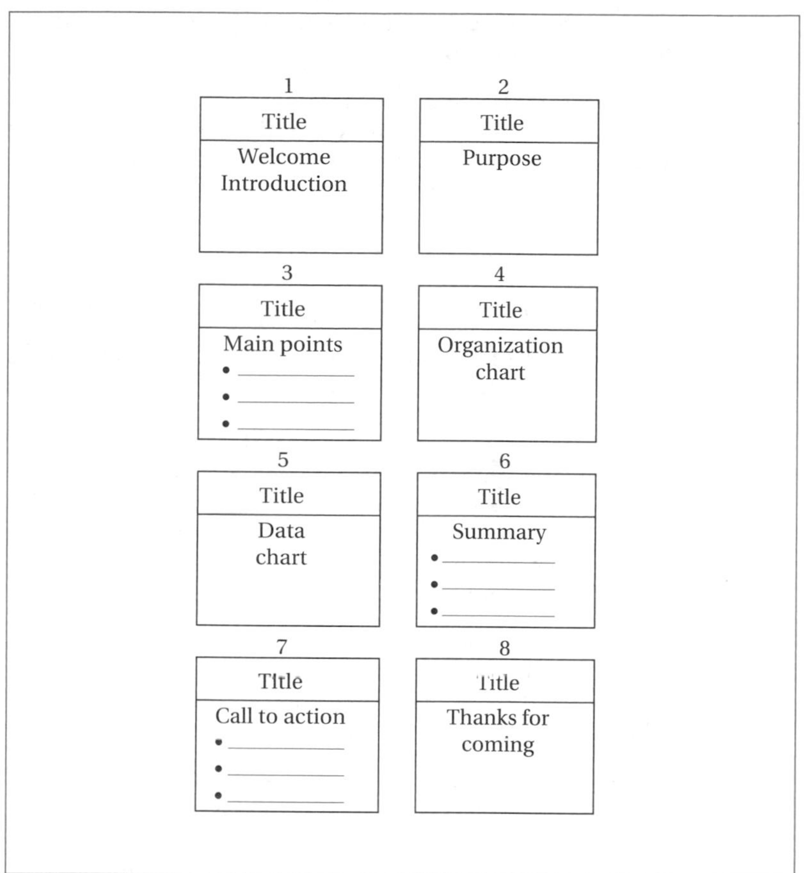

FIGURE 7–5. Pattern for a Typical Presentation

control or to have someone else advance your slides. Remember, even if things go wrong, being prepared and practiced will give you the confidence and poise to go on.

Delivery Techniques That Work. Your delivery is both audible and visual. In addition to your words and message, your nonverbal communication affects your audience. To make an impression on your listeners and keep their attention, you must be animated. Your words will have more staying power when they are delivered with physical and vocal animation. If you want listeners to share your point of view, show enthusiasm for your topic. The most common delivery techniques include making eye contact; using movement and gestures; and varying voice inflection, pace, and projection.

EYE CONTACT. The best way to establish rapport with your audience is through eye contact. In a large audience, directly address those people who seem most responsive to you in different parts of the room. Doing that helps you establish rapport with your listeners by holding their attention and gives you important visual cues that let you know how your message is being received. Are people engaged and actively listening? Or are they looking around or staring at the floor? Such cues tell you that you may need to speed up or slow down the pace of your presentation.

MOVEMENT. Animate the presentation with physical movement. Take a step or two to one side after you have been talking for a minute or so. That type of movement is most effective at transitional points in your presentation between major topics or after pauses or emphases. Too much movement, however, can be distracting, so try not to pace.

Another way to integrate movement into your presentation is to walk to the screen and point to the visual as you discuss it. Touch the screen with the pointer and then turn back to the audience before beginning to speak (remember the three *t*'s: touch, turn, and talk).

GESTURES. Gestures both animate your presentation and help communicate your message. Most people gesture naturally when they talk; nervousness, however, can inhibit gesturing during a presentation. Keep one hand free and use that hand to gesture.

VOICE. Your voice can be an effective tool in communicating your sincerity, enthusiasm, and command of your topic. Use it to your advantage to project your credibility. Vocal inflection is the rise and fall of your voice at different times, such as the way your voice naturally rises at the end of a question ("You want it *when?*"). A conversational delivery and eye contact promote the feeling among members of the audience that you are addressing them directly. Use vocal inflection to highlight differences between key and subordinate points in your presentation.

PACE. Be aware of the speed at which you deliver your presentation. If you speak too fast, your words will run together, making it difficult for your audience to follow. If you speak too slowly, your listeners will become impatient and distracted.

PROJECTION. Most speakers think they are projecting more loudly than they are. Remember that your presentation is ineffective for anyone in the audience who cannot hear you. If listeners must strain to hear you, they may give up trying to listen. Correct projection problems by practicing out loud with someone listening from the back of the room.

Presentation Anxiety. Everyone experiences nervousness before a presentation. Survey after survey reveals that for most people dread of public speaking ranks among their top five fears. Instead of letting fear inhibit you, focus on channeling your nervous energy into a helpful stimulant. The best way to master anxiety is to know your topic thoroughly—knowing what you are going to say and how you are going to say it will help you gain confidence and reduce anxiety as you become immersed in your subject.

Writer's Checklist: Delivering a Presentation

☑ Practice your presentation with visuals; practice in front of listeners, if possible.

☑ Prepare a set of notes that will trigger your memory during the presentation.

☑ Visit the location of the presentation ahead of time to familiarize yourself with the surroundings.

☑ During the presentation, make as much eye contact as possible with your audience to establish rapport and maximize opportunities for audience feedback.

☑ Animate your delivery by integrating movement, gestures, and vocal inflection into your presentation. However, keep your movements and speech patterns natural.

☑ Do not read the text on your visuals word for word; explain the salient points in detail.

☑ Speak loudly and slowly enough to be heard and understood.

For information and tips on communicating with cross-cultural audiences, see **global communication** (page 211), **global graphics** (page 188), and **international correspondence** (page 141).

8

Workplace Technology

Preview

This section presents a concise overview of the technologies that are integral to workplace writing and offers guidelines for making the most effective use of these media. See also **selecting the medium** (page 45).

The **email** entry focuses on proven techniques for managing the medium, on the evolving set of online manners (netiquette), and on the privacy and confidentiality issues that must be considered before users click the Send button.

The **Web page design** entry will help you understand how to prepare attractive and useful Web pages and sites. The entries **writing for the Web** and **Web forms design** will help you understand how to best prepare the text and interactive response forms for visitors to your site. The **Internet** entry provides a brief overview and includes the Web address of a useful glossary of Internet terms. Finally, the **word processing and writing** entry provides helpful tips for making the best use of software for preparing documents. For conducting research on the Internet, see **Internet research** (page 10).

email

Email (or *e-mail*) enables people to write and respond quickly to messages; correspondence, reports, meeting notices, questionnaires, and digital files of all kinds are routinely emailed to readers both inside and outside an organization. Email is useful for facilitating discussions and collecting opinions as well as easing the work of a collaborative writing team. See also **collaborative writing** (page 4) and **selecting the medium** (page 45).

When email replaces memos or business letters, be careful to follow the guidelines for writing style in the entries **memos** (page 143) and **correspondence** (page 128). When used for exchanging ideas rapidly, email is often more conversational. Even in a less formal exchange, you need to think carefully about accuracy and the information your readers need.

Design Considerations

Keep in mind the following design considerations when sending email:

- Break the text into brief paragraphs. No one wants to read long, dense blocks of text on a computer screen.
- Do not overwhelm your reader with lengthy passages. If your message runs much longer than a screen of text, consider sending it as an attached file along with a brief email message.
- Send tables and bulleted lists as attachments because, like many formatting features, they do not always transmit well. Check that the recipient has compatible software to view and save the attachment.
- Check before sending memory-hungry attachments (such as graphics files) that may not be accepted by your recipient's software or Internet service provider or that may download very slowly.
- Place your response to someone else's email message at the beginning (or top) of the email window. Don't make the recipient scroll down to the end of the original message to find your response.
- When quoting the message you are replying to, include only those parts relevant to your reply. To clearly indicate the difference between your response and the quoted text, mark the beginning of the quoted text with a greater-than symbol (>).
- Fill in the subject line with a concise phrase that describes the topic of your message. Recipients can then decide at a glance the importance of the message and take appropriate action. Subject lines also help your readers organize and file their incoming messages.

Some email systems do not have sophisticated typographical features or they may not be compatible with the system you are using. For that reason, avoid using boldface, italics, and a variety of fonts. Instead, use alternative highlighting devices, but be consistent. For example, capital letters or asterisks, used sparingly, can substitute for boldface, italics, and underlines as emphasis:

- Dr. Wilhoit's suggestions benefit doctors AND patients.

Intermittent underlining can replace solid underlining or italics when referring to published works in an email message:

- My report follows the format outlined in _The Business Writer's Handbook_.

Salutations, Closings, and Signature Blocks

Because email can function as a letter, memo, or personal note, finding a suitable greeting and complimentary closing can be difficult. If your employer follows a certain form, adopt that practice. Otherwise, use the following guidelines:

- When an email functions as a personal note to a friend, you can use very informal salutations and closings:

  Hi Mike, Take care, Cheers,

- When email goes outside an organization to someone with whom you have not yet corresponded, you can use the standard letter salutation and a slightly informal closing:

  Dear Professor Jucker: Best wishes,
  Dear Docuform Customer: Sincerely,

- When email functions as a memo, you may omit the salutation and closing because both your name and the name(s) of the recipient(s) appear in the "To" and "From" sections of the message. However, some email users adopt a slightly more personal greeting, especially if the distribution list is relatively small or a single individual:

  Project colleagues, Best,
  Andreas, Kathryn, [sender's first name]

Note that in some cultures, business correspondents do not use first names as quickly as they do in American correspondence. See **international correspondence** (page 141).

Because email does not provide letterhead with standard addresses and contact information, many companies and individual writers include *signature blocks* (also called *signatures*) at the bottom of their messages. Signatures, which writers can usually preprogram to appear on every email they send, supply information that company letterhead usually provides as well as links to Web sites. If your organization requires a certain format, adhere to that standard. Otherwise, use the pattern shown in Figure 8–1.

FIGURE 8–1. Signature Block

```
===============================
Daniel J. Vasquez, Publications Manager  ←  Name and Title
Medical Information Systems              ←  Department or Division
TechCom Corporation                      ←  Company Name
P.O. Box 5413   Salinas CA 93962         ←  Mailing Address
Office Phone 888-229-4511 (x 341)        ←  Phone Number
General Office Fax 888-229-1132          ←  Fax Number
www.tcc.com/                             ←  Web Address (URL)
===============================
```

Use highlighting cues, such as hyphens, equal signs, and white space to separate the signature from the message. Avoid using quotations, aphorisms, and other messages ("may the Force be with you") in professional signatures.

Review and Confidentiality

Email is a quick and easy way to communicate, but avoid the temptation to dash off a first draft and send it as is. Be careful to observe the rules of netiquette in the section that follows. As with other workplace correspondence, your message should be free of grammatical or factual errors, ambiguities, or unintended implications. It should include crucial details. Be especially careful when sending messages to superiors in your organization or to people outside the organization. Time you spend reviewing your email can save a great deal of time and embarrassment sorting out misunderstandings caused by a careless message.

Confidentiality is another issue to keep in mind when sending email. Remember, email can be intercepted by someone other than the intended recipient, and emails are never truly deleted. Most companies back up and save all company email and arc legally entitled to monitor email. Companies can also be compelled by a court of law to surrender email as evidence. Consider the content of all your messages in the light of these possibilities and carefully review your text before you click Send.

Netiquette

Because you need to maintain a high level of professionalism in workplace email, it is important to observe some rules of etiquette, or netiquette (*Internet* + *etiquette*).

- Check your incoming email regularly and respond promptly. If you receive an assignment by email that will take a few days or longer to complete, send a response saying so.
- Do not send off-color jokes, use biased language, or discuss office gossip. See also **biased language** (page 252).
- Do not send *flames,* emails that contain abusive, obscene, or derogatory language to attack someone.
- Do not send *spams,* mass-distributed emails that often promote personal projects and interests or circulate jokes and humorous stories.
- Be scrupulous about typing email addresses and otherwise ensuring that the intended recipient gets the message.
- Do not write in all-uppercase letters; it is difficult to read.
- Do not use *emoticons* (keyboard characters used to create sideways faces conveying emotions) for business and professional emails. For advice on providing typographic emphasis, review the earlier section on design considerations (page 233).
- Avoid email abbreviations used in personal email and chat rooms (*BTW* for *by the way,* for example).

Writer's Checklist: Managing Email

☑ Do not let messages pile up in your inbox.

☑ Set priorities for reading email by skimming sender names and subject lines.

☑ Copy yourself on important emails and create your own subject-line titles with care.

☑ Print and file crucial messages that are complex or that you will need for meetings.

☑ Check your inbox several times each day and try to clear your inbox by the end of the day.

☑ Create electronic folders for email, using personal names and key topics for folders.

☑ Learn the advanced features of your system so that you can use filters that organize messages as they arrive.

☑ Use the search command to find topics and individual names.

☑ Keep an up-to-date address book.

fax

Fax (facsimile transmission) is used to send documents with elements, such as handwritten corrections and notes, that must be viewed as originally created. When you have to send a drawing or diagram or a document such as a contract that contains one or more signatures, a fax is the preferred medium because it ensures authenticity.

When you send a fax, be aware that it can be intercepted by persons other than the intended recipient. If you have to fax confidential or sensitive messages, call the intended recipient first so that he or she can be waiting at the machine as you transmit your fax.

Internet

The Internet is composed of public and private computer networks that allow people around the world to communicate, find and share information, and offer commercial services. Internet services permit users to communicate with others; exchange documents, data, and software; and connect to computers in different locations. These resources include email, discussion groups, chat environments, the Web, file transfer protocol, and Telnet. Guidelines for locating and evaluating Internet sources can be found in **Internet research** (page 10).

WEB LINK ▶ CONSULTING AN INTERNET GLOSSARY

LOC INTERNET GLOSSARY

www.loc.gov/loc/guides/glossary.html

The Library of Congress offers a Web glossary that contains links to other selected glossaries.

Web forms design

Web forms are used to collect data for job applications, customer and employee surveys, and more. They are also used to initiate Web-site queries and searches.

When planning a Web form, consider the kinds of information you want to gather and arrange the fields—the places where information can be entered on the screen—in a logical order. Then draft the form on paper and circulate it for comment. After review and revision, you are ready to create the online form.

Software for designing Web forms offers various options for displaying entry fields. The objects used to create entry fields may include check boxes and radio (or option) buttons. Choose objects suited to the kind of information being requested.

Check Boxes and Radio Buttons

Use a check box to allow the user to choose one or more or all of several options, as shown in the following example:

> 9. Have you ever experienced any of the following forms of discrimination or harassment at this company?
> ❑ Racial discrimination
> ❑ Sexual harassment
> ❑ Age discrimination
> ❑ Gender discrimination
> ❑ Sexual orientation discrimination
> ❑ Other
> ❑ No

Use radio (or option) buttons to make a single choice from a group of items (❍ yes ❍ no ❍ maybe).

Text and Password Boxes

Use text boxes to type a single line of text into a form. You can specify the number of characters a user can enter, as shown here.

Name Alvin P. Doe

A password box is a security feature to control access to the form. It displays a row of asterisks when users type in their password to prevent others from reading the password as it is being typed, as shown below.

Enter Your Password *******

Text Area

Use a text-area box to type multiple lines of text into a window, as shown in this example.

Enter Your Reasons for Not Attending

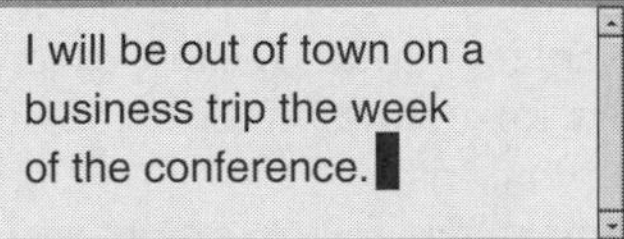

I will be out of town on a
business trip the week
of the conference.

You can control the size of the text area by setting the number of characters in each row and the length of the column.

Selection List

Use a selection list to display a window of choices. The list can be created to enable multiple choices, as shown here.

Job Function

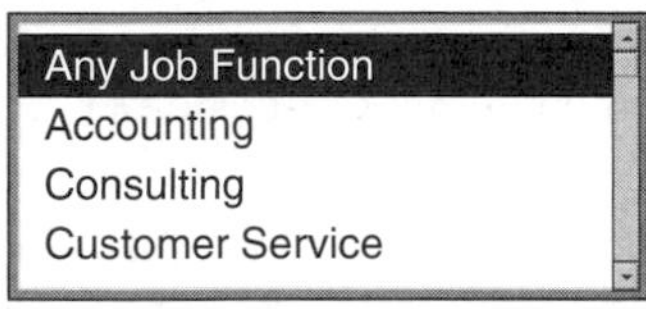

Combination Box

Use a combination box to display a drop-down menu of choices, as shown in this example.

Search for

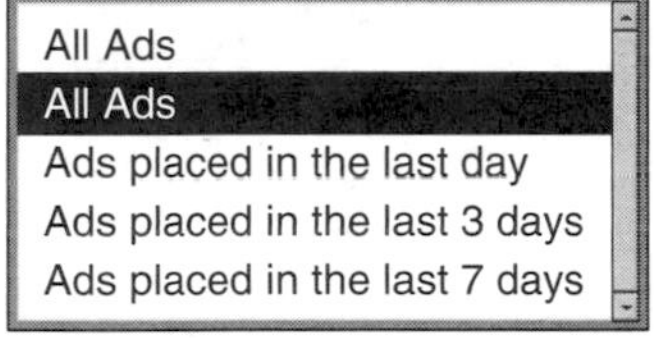

Command Buttons

Add command buttons as needed—for example, the Submit and Clear buttons at the end of a survey form could be arranged on the screen as follows.

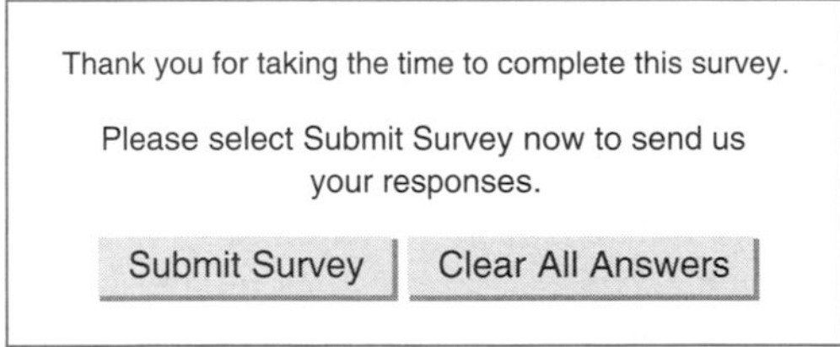

Thank you for taking the time to complete this survey.
Please select Submit Survey now to send us your responses.
Submit Survey
Clear All Answers

Web page design

You can apply many of the business writing principles covered throughout this book to designing Web pages. As you do when creating other documents, carefully consider your purpose and readers' needs as you prepare your Web pages. Most organizational sites have well-defined goals, such as reference, training, education, publicity, advocacy, or marketing. Before you begin building your site, create a clear statement of purpose that identifies your target audience.

EXTERNAL SITE The purpose of this site is to enable our customers to locate product information, place online orders, and contact our customer service department.

INTERNAL SITE The purpose of this site is to provide SNR Security Corporation employees with a single, consistent, and up-to-date resource for materials about SNR Security's Employee Benefits Package.

As the examples suggest, there are two general kinds of sites: external and internal. External sites target an audience from the entire Internet; internal sites are designed for audiences on an *intranet* (a computer network within an educational institution or company that is not accessible to audiences outside that institution or company). See also **Internet** (page 237).

Web Page Navigation and Links

Your main goal when designing a Web page is to establish a predictable environment in which users can comfortably navigate your site and easily find the information they need. This information should be logically accessible to the user in the fewest possible steps (or clicks). To design an efficient navigation plan, draft a navigation chart of your site early in the process. Figure 8–2 shows an initial navigation plan for a company Web site.

In Figure 8–2, each higher-level page (for example, Departments and Divisions) is linked to increasingly specific pages about the company's internal organization (Marketing, Accounting, Customer Relations). Human Resources, although logically a department in the company's organization, is given higher visibility on the home page because recruiting new employees is important to the company.

Hypertext links that connect to pages within and outside a site make a Web site useful. Create links to sites related to your visitors' organizational or professional needs and interests. Links to customer service and online order forms are especially useful for cultivating potential customers.

When you identify links, do not write out "Click here for more information." Instead, write the sentence as you normally would, and anchor the link on the most relevant word in the sentence, as illustrated in the following example.

- For information about employment opportunities, visit Human Resources.

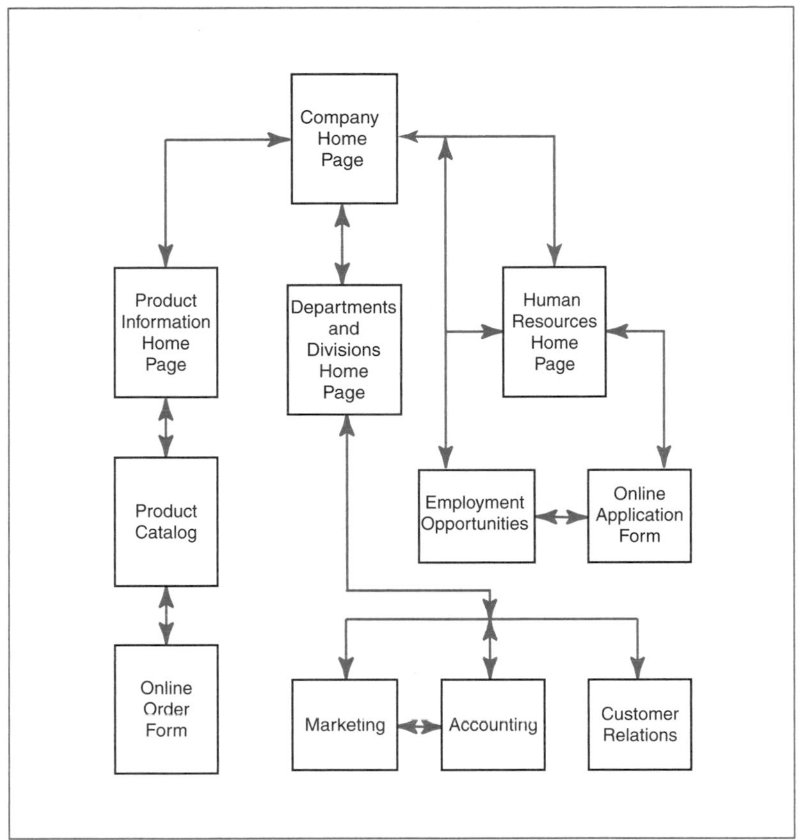

FIGURE 8–2. Navigation Plan for a Web Site

Avoid writing paragraphs that are dense with links. Instead, list links alphabetically in groups of about four to seven to make them easier for the viewer to see at a glance.

- ▶ Accounting
- ▶ Customer Relations
- ▶ Marketing
- ▶ Product Help
- ▶ Related Links

In addition to identifying links with words, you can use icons and graphics, as shown in the preceding list; they not only are easy to use but also provide the visual cues Web users expect.

Include a link that allows visitors to send you email messages; the email code can be identified with either text or a graphic. When visitors click on the link, an email dialog box opens in which they can type their message.

Because Web sites change constantly, periodically check that your links are still appropriate and working properly. Your Web pages should include the date they were created or last updated so that users can determine whether the information is current. You might also place a [new] icon next to each new or updated item to alert users to these changes.

Graphics and Typography

Your audience and purpose should determine the graphic style and theme of your Web site. Although graphic elements provide visual relief from dense text, do not overdo graphics, especially those with animation. Complex graphics and motion can clutter or slow access to your site. Avoid using multiple colors, especially bold ones. Instead, use lighter colors, especially for backgrounds. Keep in mind that large or high-resolution graphics, like color photographs, can cause long delays as they download to the user's system. Consider providing a graphics-free option for quicker access.

Writer's Checklist: Planning Web-Page Typography

Many of the guidelines on typography in **layout and design** (page 196) are applicable to Web pages; however, not all apply, so keep the following in mind:

- ☑ Limit the number of typeface colors as well as styles.
- ☑ Use typeface colors that contrast (but do not clash) with background colors.
- ☑ Use uppercase letters or boldface type sparingly.
- ☑ Use underlined text only for links.
- ☑ Separate text from graphics with generous blank space (the equivalent of white space).
- ☑ Use heading and subheading styles sparingly and consistently (see **headings,** page 194).
- ☑ Block-indent text sections that you expect viewers to read in detail.

When you have decided on fonts, spacing between paragraphs, heading sizes, and other elements, consider creating a style sheet that lists these specifications. A style sheet is especially helpful for large sites with numerous pages. In general, aim for consistency to establish a sense of unity and to provide visual cues that help visitors find information.

Page and Site Layout

Take into account the viewing capabilities of visitors to your site. Many computer monitors cannot display more than half of a typical Web page at any one time; on many screen settings, only the top four or five inches may be visible. For that reason, place important graphic elements and information in the upper half of the page. Then, use short narrative passages or lists so that viewers can scan and access the information quickly. Organize the material in a logical, predictable pattern; use general-to-specific, sequential, chronological, or other traditional methods of development. When no such pattern is appropriate, use an alphabetical or numerical sequence. See also **organization** (page 27).

Because most users do not like scrolling down long pages, many Web designers recommend that Web pages (home pages in particular) contain no more than roughly one or two screens of information. If a greater amount of information is covered, include a concise table of contents at the top of the page linked to specific sections elsewhere on the page. Viewers can select the section they want without having to scroll through the entire page. You can also provide links that return to the top of the page.

When viewers access Web pages randomly, they often have no context for where they are or who sponsors the site. Therefore, incorporate the name of your company or organization (and perhaps the logo) on each page. You can do that with page footers—sections in smaller type size that contain basic information about the origin of each page and when it was last updated—which are especially useful when they also link to other pages. Another way to orient users is to provide a set of links in graphics or words called a *tool bar* or *button bar,* as shown here.

[Home | Search | Order | What's New | About Us]

A tool bar at the top, bottom, or sides of each page serves as a table of contents and shows visitors the structure of your site. Tool bars on each page help you avoid sending users to a dead-end page (one with no link); in fact, every page should, if nothing else, link back to your home page. For advice on designing interactive forms on the Web, see **Web forms design** (page 237).

Access for People with Disabilities

Many of the advantages of Web sites include colorful graphics, animation, and streaming video and audio. However, these design elements can be barriers to people with impaired vision or hearing or those who are color blind. Use the following strategies to meet the needs of such audiences.

- Avoid frames, complex tables, animation, JavaScript, and other design elements incompatible with text-only browsers and adaptive technologies, such as voice or large-print software.
- Provide HTML versions of pages and documents whenever possible because this format is most compatible with the current generation of screen readers.
- Attach text equivalents for graphic or audio elements.
- Design for the color-blind reader by making meaning independent of color. For example, rather than asking users to "Click on the blue button for more information," label the button (Click Here) or embed a link in a sentence: "Click here for more information."

For comprehensive guidance about accessibility, visit the Web sites listed in the Web Link Box, "Improving Accessibility Online."

WEB LINK ▶ IMPROVING ACCESSIBILITY ONLINE

Numerous government and private Web sites provide help for both Web designers and those who need greater accessibility. The following sites provide guidelines, technological information, and additional links.

WORLD WIDE WEB CONSORTIUM (W3C)
www.w3.org/TR/WCAG/

DRM WEBWATCHER
www.disabilityresources.org/WEB.html

Home Pages

A home page is the point of entry for all pages in your Web site. Many organizational home pages include an image map, with links to other pages at the site. Figure 8–3 shows an image map for a federal agency, with icons that lead to content areas at the site. By clicking on a specific area, such as News & Information, viewers are linked to the relevant page or site. The image map also introduces visitors to the overall site design, identifies the purpose of the site, and provides an overview of major content areas. If you do not use an image map, at least display a small graphic banner, tool bar, or menu across the top of the home page.

Because complex home-page graphics can take a minute or longer to download, evaluate how important large graphics are to your site. Consider using relatively small ones on your home page, gradually increasing the size of the graphics for pages deeper into your site, if necessary. Users who go beyond a page or two into a site are more committed and therefore more willing to tolerate longer delays, especially if you offer them warnings that particular pages contain graphics that

FIGURE 8–3. Image Map for a Home Page
Courtesy of the Nuclear Regulatory Commission.

take awhile to download. As a final step, view your pages on a variety of browsers, operating systems, and monitors—colors, sizes, and other features can vary dramatically from one environment to another. See also **writing for the Web** (page 246).

word processing and writing

Word processing software can help your writing in many ways; determine which features will be useful to you. Be aware that working on screen may focus your attention too narrowly on sentence-level problems and cause you to lose sight of the larger problems of scope or organization. The rapid movement of the text on the screen, together with last-minute editing changes, may allow errors to creep into the text.

Writer's Checklist: Word Processing

☑ Avoid the temptation of writing first drafts on the computer *without any planning*. Plan your document carefully as described in "Five Steps to Successful Writing" (page xiii).

☑ Use the outline feature to brainstorm and organize an initial outline for your topic. As you create the outline, cut-and-paste to try alternative ways of organizing the information. See **outlining** (page 29).

☑ Use the search-and-replace command to find and delete wordy phrases such as *that is, there are, the fact that,* and *to be* and unnecessary helping verbs such as *will*. See also **conciseness/wordiness** (page 257).

☑ When writing for readers who are unfamiliar with your topic, use the search command to find technical terms, abbreviations and acronyms, and other information that may need further explanation.

☑ Use a spell checker and other specialized programs to identify and correct typographical, spelling, grammar, and word-choice errors.

☑ Do not make all of your revisions on the screen. Print a double-spaced copy of your drafts periodically for major revisions and reorganizations.

☑ Always proofread your final copy on paper because catching errors on the screen is difficult. Print an extra copy for your peers to critique before making your final revisions.

☑ Use the software for effective document design by highlighting major headings and subheadings with bold or italic type and by increasing their size relative to the regular text. Use the copy command to duplicate parallel headings throughout your document, and insert blank lines (hard returns) above and below examples and illustrations to set them off from the surrounding text.

☑ Routinely save to your hard drive and create a backup copy of your documents on separate disks or on the company network.

☑ Keep the standard version of certain documents, such as your résumé and application letters, on file so that you can revise them to meet the specific needs of each new job opportunity.

writing for the Web

This entry contains advice for how to write and organize content for the Web. For guidelines for designing Web sites, see **Web page design** (page 239). See also **Internet** (page 237).

Write for Rapid Consumption

Because users of the Web expect to get information quickly and efficiently, you need to be clear, concise, and well organized to keep the attention of your reader. Your writing style needs to be simple, straightforward, and substantive. Web users seek information: Avoid empty promotional language or business jargon that says very little about your topic.

EMPTY	The LNK Converter is the best one on the Internet! Buy one today!
SUBSTANTIVE	The LNK Converter is a powerful, cost-effective tool. It has been proven 100% effective in industry tests, and was voted the #1 Converter of the Year by *Devices Magazine*.

Note that the improved version contains hyperlinks to the sources of the evidence (industry tests and *Devices Magazine*) that support the company's claims about the product.

Use Subheads, Hyperlinks, and Keywords

Divide long documents into small sections, each containing only one or two related paragraphs. Place boldface subheads above each section to set apart a new idea or topic. Subheads should always be informative as well as interesting. You may also use boldface within the text to emphasize important pieces of information such as due dates, prices, or other essential details.

Because Web users are unlikely to read an online document from beginning to end, avoid directional cues like "as shown in the example below" or "in the graph at the top of this page." Directional phrases like these can be confusing when there is no real reference for "above" and "below" and no "top" or "bottom" of the document. Instead, use hyperlinks to connect sections of long documents.

Hyperlinks are the words or images that act as gateways to other Web pages. A hyperlinked word usually is either underlined or appears in a different color from the text so that the user's eye will be drawn to it. Although hyperlinks offer expanded information, they can be very distracting. Rather than embedding hyperlinks throughout your text, combine them into short, well-organized lists. Use these lists throughout your document to break up large blocks of text or place them at the end of the document.

Use keywords and concepts throughout your text to help users locate your site.

- The new *Alder* commemorative coin features a portrait of *Wilbur G. Alder,* the founder and president of Alder National Bank. *The*

> *coin* can be purchased online at this Web site after December 1, 20--, in honor of the 100th anniversary of the first deposit.

By using such specific words as "Alder," "Wilbur G. Alder," and "the coin," you increase the probability that search engines will point users to your site.

Writer's Checklist: Writing for the Web

Write for rapid consumption and accessibility.

- ☑ Present your information in short paragraphs.
- ☑ Use short, bulleted lists of hyperlinks to expand your information; if you have few hyperlinks, embed them in the text.
- ☑ Use informative subheads in boldface to aid skimming and to introduce new or important points.
- ☑ Avoid breaking a single article into a series of separate pages; such interruptions can irritate readers.
- ☑ Use lists, hyperlinks, and extra white space to present long documents and to break up dense passages of text.
- ☑ For documents of more than 500 words, provide a brief summary or table of contents hyperlinked to each section.
- ☑ Put keywords that describe your site in the first 50 words so that search engines will find your site (see **Internet research,** page 10).

Use a clear, straightforward style and tone.

- ☑ Avoid humor and jargon that could be easily misunderstood, especially by visitors from other cultures.
- ☑ Choose language and use a tone appropriate to the organization or product that you represent.

Check carefully for grammatical and typographical errors (see **proofreading,** page 40).

9

Style and Clarity

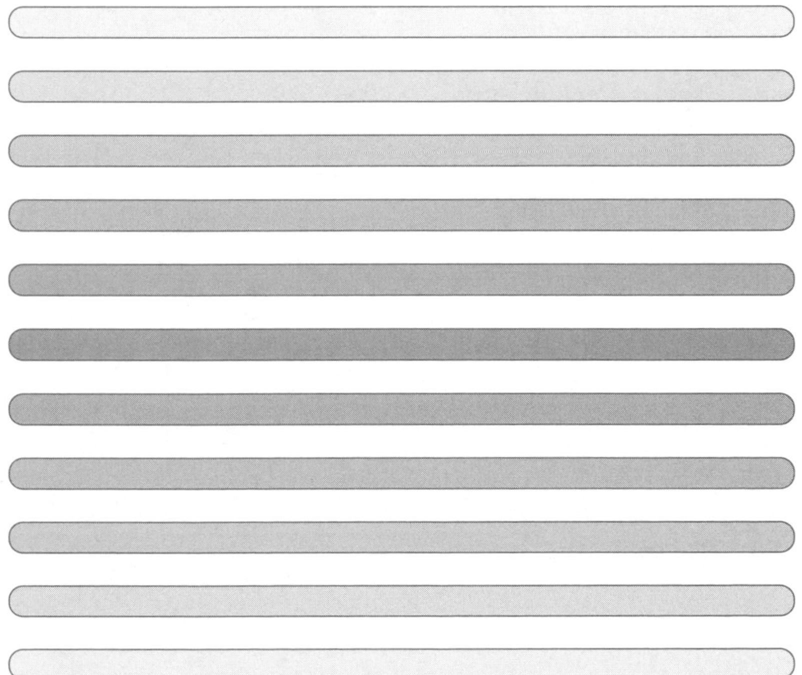

Preview

The entries in this section are intended to help you develop a style that is clear and effective—and that follows the conventions of standard English. For a number of related entries, see Tab 1, The Writing Process; Tab 10, Usage; and Tab 11, Grammar.

Some entries in this section—**awkwardness, coherence, parallel structure,** and **sentence variety**—will help you construct clear sentences and paragraphs. Other entries discuss such **word choice** issues as **abstract words/concrete words, idioms,** and **jargon.** Finally, this section covers the important subjects of **business writing style, biased language,** and **ethics in writing.**

9. Style and Clarity

absolute words

Absolute words (such as *round, unique, exact,* and *perfect*) are not logically subject to comparison, especially in business writing, where accuracy and precision are often crucial. See also **adjectives** (page 307).

- We modified our contract to more ~~exactly~~ closely reflect existing specifications.

abstract words / concrete words 

Abstract words refer to general ideas, qualities, conditions, acts, or relationships—intangible things, such as *learning, courage,* and *technology.* Concrete words identify things that can be perceived by the five senses (sight, hearing, touch, taste, and smell), such as *diploma, soldier,* and *keyboard.*

Abstract words must frequently be further defined or explained.

- The research team needs freedom to explore the problem further.

Abstract words can often be supported with concrete words, as in the following example in which the abstract idea of *transportation* is made clearer with the use of the concrete words *subway* and *buses.*

- *Transportation* was limited to the *subway* and *buses.*

See also **word choice** (page 280).

affectation

Affectation is the use of language that is more formal, technical, or showy than necessary to communicate information to the reader. Affectation is a widespread writing problem in the workplace because many people feel that affectation lends a degree of authority to their writing. In fact, affectation can alienate customers, clients, and colleagues.

Affected writing forces readers to work harder to understand the writer's meaning. It typically contains abstract, highly technical, or foreign words and is often liberally sprinkled with trendy words. **Jargon** (page 266) and **euphemisms** (page 263) can become affectation, especially if their purpose is to hide relevant facts. See **ethics in writing** (page 261).

Writers are easily lured into affectation through the use of **long variants** (page 268): words created by adding prefixes and suffixes to simpler words (*analyzation* for *analysis*). Unnecessarily formal words (such as *utilization*) and outdated words (such as *herewith*) can produce affectation. Elegant variation—attempting to avoid repeating a word within a paragraph by substituting a pretentious synonym—is also a form of affectation. Another type of affectation is gobbledygook, which is wordy, roundabout writing with many pseudolegal and pseudoscientific terms. See also **conciseness/wordiness** (page 257), **clichés** (page 255), and **nominalizations** (page 269).

awkwardness

Awkwardness has many causes, but the following guidelines will help you smooth out most awkward passages: (1) Keep your sentences as direct and simple as possible, (2) use the active **voice** (page 356) unless you have a justifiable reason to use the passive voice, and (3) eliminate excess words and phrases. See also **conciseness/wordiness** (page 257), **garbled sentences** (page 264), and **sentence construction** (page 341).

biased language

Biased language refers to words and expressions that offend because they make inappropriate assumptions or stereotypes about gender, ethnicity, physical or mental disability, age, or sexual orientation. The easiest way to avoid bias is simply not to mention differences among people unless the differences are relevant to the discussion. Keep current with accepted usage and, if you are unsure of the appropriateness of an expression or the tone of a passage, have several colleagues review the material and give you their honest assessment.

Sexist Language

Sexist language can be an outgrowth of sexism, the arbitrary stereotyping of men and women in their roles in life. Sexism, like biased language, can breed and reinforce inequality. To avoid sexism in your writing, treat men and women equally, and do not make assumptions about traditional or occupational roles. Accordingly, use nonsexist occupational descriptions in your writing.

INSTEAD OF	USE
chairman	chair, chairperson
foreman	supervisor
manpower	staff, personnel, workers
policeman/policewoman	police officer
salesman	salesperson

Use parallel terms to describe men and women.

INSTEAD OF	USE
man and wife	husband and wife
Ms. Jones and Bernard Weiss	Ms. Jones and Mr. Weiss; Mary Jones and Bernard Weiss
ladies and men	ladies and gentlemen; women and men

Sexism can creep into your writing by the unthinking use of male pronouns where a reference could apply equally to a man and a woman. One way to avoid such usage is to rewrite the sentence in the plural.

- *All employees* ~~Every employee~~ will have *their managers* ~~his manager~~ sign *their travel vouchers.* ~~his travel voucher.~~

Other possible solutions are to use *his or her* instead of *his* alone or to omit the pronoun completely if it is not essential to the meaning of the sentence.

- Everyone must submit *an* ~~his~~ expense report by Monday.

He or she can become monotonous when repeated constantly, and a pronoun cannot always be omitted without changing the meaning of a sentence. Another solution is to omit troublesome pronouns by using the imperative mood whenever possible.

- *Submit all* ~~Everyone must submit his or her~~ expense report*s* by Monday.

Other Types of Biased Language

Identifying people by racial, ethnic, or religious categories is simply not relevant in most workplace writing. Telling readers that an engineer is Native American or that a professor is African American almost never conveys useful information. It also reinforces stereotypes, implying that it is rare for a person of a certain background to have achieved such a position. It also is inappropriate stereotyping to link a profession or some characteristic to race or ethnicity: a Jewish lawyer, an African-American jazz musician, an Asian-American mathematics prodigy.

Consider how you refer to people with disabilities. If you refer to "a disabled employee," you imply that the part (*disabled*) is as significant as the whole (*employee*). Use "an employee with a disability" instead. Similarly, the preferred usage is "a person who uses a wheelchair" rather than "a wheelchair-bound person"; the latter expression inappropriately equates the wheelchair with the person.

Terms that refer to a person's age are also open to inappropriate stereotyping. Referring to older colleagues as "over the hill" and to younger colleagues as "kids" is derogatory, at the least.

In matters of sexual orientation, the preferred terms are *gay men, lesbians,* and *heterosexual* or *bisexual men* and *women*. Although *gay* can apply to men and women, the term is more often applied to men. *Lesbian* refers exclusively to women of same-sex orientation.

In most workplace writing, such issues are simply not relevant. Of course, there are contexts in which race, ethnicity, or religion should be identified. For example, if you are writing an Equal Employment Opportunity Commission report about your firm's hiring practices, the racial composition of the workforce is relevant. In such cases, you need to present the issues in ways that respect and do not demean the individuals or groups to which you refer. See also **ethics in writing** (page 261).

business writing style

Business writing has evolved from a very formal and elaborate style to one that is more personal and direct. Yet, even though business writing style is less formal today, it must adhere to the conventions of standard English with the use of conventional spelling and standard grammatical forms.

Business writing legitimately varies from the chatty, conversational style you might use in an **email** (page 233) message to a close business associate to the formal, legalistic style found in contracts. In most **memos** (page 143), email messages, and letters, a style between those two extremes generally is appropriate. Writing that is too formal can alienate readers, and an overly obvious attempt to be casual and informal may strike the reader as insincere or unprofessional.

- Dear Jane,

  Your proposal arrived today, and it looks very good.
  ~~I'm crazy about your proposal!~~
  ^

In business writing, as in all writing, know your audience.

The use of personal **pronouns** (page 336) is important in letters and memos. Do not refer to yourself in the third person by using *one* or *the writer.* It is perfectly natural and appropriate to refer to yourself as *I* and to the reader as *you.* In a report, however, you may be writing to more than one reader and may not necessarily want to refer to collective readers as *you.* Be careful as well when you use the pronoun *we* in a business letter that is written on company stationery because it commits your company to what you have written. In general, when a statement is your opinion, use *I;* when it is company policy, use *we.* See also **point of view** (page 36) and **ethics in writing** (page 261).

The best writers strive to write in a style that is so clear that their message cannot be misunderstood. To achieve a clear and effective style, use the "Five Steps to Successful Writing" (page xiii).

One way to achieve a clear style, especially during revision, is to eliminate overuse of the passive **voice** (page 356), which plagues most poor business writing. Although the passive voice is sometimes necessary, often it not only makes your writing dull but also is ambiguous, uninformative, or overly impersonal.

You can also achieve clarity with **conciseness** (page 257). Proceed cautiously here, however, because business writing should not be an endless series of short, choppy sentences. (See also **telegraphic style,** page 275, and **sentence variety,** page 272.) Don't be so concise that you become blunt or deliver too little information to be helpful to the readers. (See also **"you" viewpoint,** page 281, and **correspondence** (page 128). Finally, you can achieve clarity through the wise use of punctuation, as discussed in Tab 12, Punctuation and Mechanics. A misplaced comma or other punctuation mark can cause misunderstanding and confusion.

clichés

Clichés are expressions that have been used for so long that they are no longer fresh but come to mind easily because they are so familiar. Clichés are often wordy as well as vague and can be confusing, especially to nonnative speakers of English. Each of the following clichés is followed by a better, more direct word or phrase.

INSTEAD OF	USE
straight from the shoulder	honest, frank
last but not least	last, finally
run it up the flagpole	see what others think

Some writers use clichés in a misguided attempt to appear casual or spontaneous, just as other writers try to impress readers with trendy words (see also **affectation,** page 251). Although clichés may come to mind easily while you are writing a draft, eliminate them during revision. See also **conciseness/wordiness** (page 257) and **vague words** (page 280).

coherence

Writing is coherent when the relationships among ideas are clear to the reader. The major components of coherent writing are a logical sequence of related ideas and clear **transitions** (page 277) between these ideas. (See also **organization,** page 27.)

Presenting ideas in a logical sequence is the most important requirement in achieving coherence. The key to achieving a logical sequence is the use of a good outline (see **outlining,** page 29). An outline forces you to establish a beginning, a middle (body), and an end. That structure contributes greatly to coherence by enabling you to experiment with sequences and to lay out the most direct route to your purpose without digressing.

Thoughtful transition is also essential; without it, your writing cannot achieve the smooth flow from sentence to sentence and from paragraph to paragraph that is required for coherence.

During revision, check your draft carefully for coherence. If your writing is not coherent, you are not communicating effectively with your readers. See also **unity** (page 279).

compound words

A compound word is made from two or more words that are hyphenated, written as one word, or written as separate words that are so closely related as to constitute a single concept. If you are not certain whether a compound word should be hyphenated, check a dictionary. (See also **hyphens,** page 381.)

- courthouse, editor-in-chief, high-energy, low-level, nevertheless, online, post office, run-of-the-mill, Web site

Be careful to distinguish between compound words (*greenhouse*) and words that simply appear together but do not constitute compound words (*green house*). For plurals of compound words, generally add an *s* to the last letter (*courthouses* and *Web sites*). However, when the first word of the compound is more important to its meaning than the last, the first word takes the *s* (*editors-in-chief*). Possessives are formed by adding *'s* to the end of the compound word (the *post office's* hours; the *pipeline's* diameter). See also **possessive case** (page 332).

conciseness / wordiness

Conciseness means that extraneous words, phrases, clauses, and sentences have been removed from writing without sacrificing clarity or appropriate detail. Conciseness is not a synonym for brevity; a long report may be concise, while its abstract may be both brief and concise. Conciseness is always desirable, but brevity may or may not be desirable in a given passage, depending on the writer's objective. (See **abstracts,** page 93.) Although concise sentences are not guaranteed to be effective, wordy sentences always sacrifice some of their readability and coherence.

Causes of Wordiness

Modifiers that repeat an idea implicit or present in the word being modified contribute to wordiness by being redundant: *basic* essentials, *final* outcome, *present* status, and the reason is *because.* (See **modifiers,** page 324.) Coordinated synonyms that merely repeat each other contribute to wordiness: *each and every, basic and fundamental,* and *first and foremost.* Excess qualification—*perfectly* clear and *completely* accurate—also contributes to wordiness.

Expletives (page 263), relative pronouns, and relative adjectives, although they have legitimate purposes, often result in wordiness.

WORDY *There are* [expletive] many Web designers *who* [relative pronoun] are planning to attend the conference, *which* [relative adjective] is scheduled for May 13–15.

CONCISE Many Web designers plan to attend the conference scheduled for May 13–15.

Circumlocution (a long, indirect way of expressing things) is a leading cause of wordiness.

WORDY The payment to which a subcontractor is entitled should be made promptly so that in the event of a subsequent contractual dispute we, as general contractors, may not be held in default of our contract by virtue of nonpayment.

CONCISE Pay subcontractors promptly. Then if a contractual dispute occurs, we cannot be held in default of our contract because of nonpayment.

When conciseness is overdone, writing can become choppy and ambiguous. (See also **telegraphic style,** page 275.) Too much conciseness can produce a style that is not only too brief but also blunt. For example, if you do not understand a written request and respond by writing, "Your request was unclear" or "I don't understand your question," you risk offending your reader. Instead of attacking the writer's ability to phrase a request, ask for more information.

- I will need more information before I can answer your request. Specifically, can you give me the title and the date of the report you are looking for?

That version is a little longer than the other two responses, but it is both clear and more tactful.

Writer's Checklist: Achieving Conciseness

☑ Use **subordination** (page 274).

- The ^five-page^ financial report was carefully ^documented.^ ~~documented, and it covered five pages.~~

☑ Use simple words and phrases.

WORDY It is the policy of the company to provide Web access to enable employees to conduct the online communication necessary to discharge their responsibilities; such should not be utilized for personal communications or nonbusiness activities.

CONCISE Employee Web access should be used only for appropriate company business.

☑ Eliminate redundancy.

WORDY Postinstallation testing, which is offered to all our customers at no further cost to them whatsoever, is available with each Line Scan System One purchased from this company.

CONCISE Free postinstallation testing is offered with each Line Scan System One.

☑ Change the passive **voice** (page 356) to the active and the indicative **mood** (page 326) to the imperative. The following example does both.

WORDY Bar codes normally are used when an order is intended to be displayed on a computer, and inventory numbers normally are used when an order is to be placed with the manufacturer.

CONCISE Use bar codes to display the order on a computer, and use inventory numbers to place the order with the manufacturer.

Writer's Checklist: Achieving Conciseness (continued)

☑ Eliminate or replace wordy introductory phrases or pretentious words and phrases: *it may be said that, it appears that, in the case of, needless to say*. (See also **affectation,** page 251.)

REPLACE	WITH
in order to, with a view to	to
due to the fact that, for the reason that, owing to the fact that, the reason for	because
by means of, by using/utilizing, through the use of	by, with
at this time, at this point in time, at present, at the present	now

☑ Do not overuse intensifiers (*very, more, most, best, quite*) or adjectives and adverbs (*great, really, especially*). Instead, provide useful and specific details.

WORDY It was a *very* good meeting that was *quite* productive.

SPECIFIC Our meeting was productive. We agreed to . . .

WORDY Our Web site is *really* popular because of its *great* graphics.

SPECIFIC Our Web site attracted 5,000 visitors this week. Several clients praised the animated graphics.

connotation / denotation

The *denotation* of a word is its literal meaning, as defined in a dictionary. The *connotations* of a word are its meanings and associations beyond its literal, dictionary definitions. For example, the denotations of *Hollywood* are "a district of Los Angeles" and "the U.S. movie industry as a whole"; its connotations are "romance, glittering success, and superficiality." Use words with both the most accurate denotations and the most appropriate connotations. See also **defining terms** (page 8).

emphasis

Emphasis is the principle of stressing the most important ideas in writing, and it can be achieved in the ways outlined below.

Writer's Checklist: Achieving Emphasis

☑ Place the idea in a particular position; the first and last words of a sentence, paragraph, or document stand out in readers' minds.

Writer's Checklist: Achieving Emphasis (continued)

> Moon craters are important to understanding the earth's history because they reflect geological history.

Notice that the sentence emphasizes *moon craters* simply because the term appears at the beginning of the sentence and *geological history* because it is at the end of the sentence.

☑ Vary sentence length. A very short sentence that follows a very long sentence, or a series of long sentences, stands out in the reader's mind.

> We could continue to examine the causes of our problems and point an accusing finger at all the culprits beyond our control, but in the end it all leads to one simple conclusion. *We must cut costs.*

☑ Repeat keywords and key phrases.

> Similarly, atoms *come and go* in a molecule, but the molecule *remains;* molecules *come and go* in a cell, but the cell *remains;* cells *come and go* in a body, but the body *remains;* persons *come and go* in an organization, but the organization *remains.*
>
> —Kenneth Boulding, *Beyond Economics*

☑ Select a particular sentence type—a compound sentence, complex sentence, or simple sentence.

COMPOUND SENTENCE	The report submitted by the committee was carefully illustrated, and it covered five pages of single-spaced copy. [no special emphasis because the sentence contains two coordinate independent clauses]
COMPLEX SENTENCE	The committee's report, which was carefully illustrated, covered five pages of single-spaced copy. [emphasizes the size of the report]
SIMPLE SENTENCE	The carefully illustrated report submitted by the committee covered five pages of single-spaced copy. [emphasizes that the report was carefully illustrated]

☑ Use a climactic order of ideas or facts within a sentence, listing them in a sequence from least important to most important.

> Over subsequent weeks the Human Resources Department worked diligently, management showed tact and patience, and the employees demonstrated remarkable support for the policy changes.

☑ Set an item apart with a long dash, also called an *em dash*. ("The job will be done—after we are under contract.")

☑ Use intensifiers (*most, very, really*), but, because this technique is so easily abused, use it cautiously. ("The final proposal is *much* more persuasive than the first.")

Writer's Checklist: Achieving Emphasis (continued)

☑ Use mechanical devices, such as *italics,* **bold type,** underlining, and CAPITAL LETTERS, but use them sparingly. (Email messages that overuse capital letters are referred to as "shouting.") See also **email** (page 233).

☑ Use direct statement (*most important, foremost*), as well as direct address.

> *Most important* of all, keep in mind that everything you do affects the company's bottom line.
>
> *Andreas,* I believe we should rethink our plans.

See also **subordination** (page 274) and active **voice** (page 356).

ethics in writing

Ethics refers to the choices we make that affect others for good or ill. Ethical issues are inherent in writing and speaking because what we write and say can influence others. Further, how we express ideas affects our readers' perceptions of us and our company's ethical stance. Obviously, no book can describe how to act ethically in every situation, but here are some typical ethical lapses to watch for and address during revision.*

- Avoid language that attempts to evade responsibility. Some writers use the passive **voice** (page 356) because they hope to avoid responsibility or obscure an issue.

  > It has been decided. [*Who has decided?*]
  >
  > Several oversights were discovered. [*What were the oversights?*]

- Avoid deceptive language. Do not use words with more than one meaning, especially as a means to circumvent the truth. Consider the company document that stated, "A nominal charge will be assessed for using our facilities." When clients objected that the charge was actually very high, the writer pointed out that the word *nominal* means "the named amount" as well as "very small." In that situation, clients had a strong case in charging that the company was attempting to be deceptive. Various **abstract words** (page 251), technical and legal **jargon** (page 266), and **euphemisms** (page 263) are unethical when they are used to mislead

*Adapted from Brenda R. Sims, "Linking Ethics and Language in the Technical Communication Classroom," *Technical Communication Quarterly* 2.3 (Summer 1993): 285–99.

readers or to hide a serious or dangerous situation, even though technical or legal experts could interpret them as accurate. See also **word choice** (page 280).

- Do not de-emphasize or suppress important information. Not including information that a reader would want to have, such as potential safety hazards or hidden costs for which a customer might be responsible, is unethical. Such omissions may also be illegal. (See also **copyright,** page 53, and **plagiarism,** page 73.) Use **layout and design** (page 196) features like typeface size, bullets, lists, and footnotes to highlight—not hide—information that is important to readers.
- Do not emphasize misleading or incorrect information. Avoid the temptation to highlight a feature or service that readers would find attractive but that is available only with some product models or at extra cost. (See also **logic errors,** page 266, and **positive writing,** page 271.) Readers could justifiably object that you have given them a false impression to sell a product or service, especially if you also de-emphasize the extra cost or other special conditions.
- Treat others fairly and respectfully. Avoid language that is biased, racist, sexist, or that perpetuates stereotypes. (See also **biased language,** page 252.)

Writer's Checklist: Writing Ethically

- ☑ *Is the document honest and truthful?* Scrutinize findings and conclusions carefully. Make sure that the data support them.
- ☑ *Am I acting in my employer's best interest? my client's or the public's best interest? my own best long-term interest?* Have someone outside your company review and comment on what you have said.
- ☑ *What if everybody acted or communicated in this way?* If you were the intended audience, would the message be acceptable and respectful?
- ☑ *Am I willing to take responsibility, publicly and privately, for what the document says?* Will you stand behind what you have written? To your employer? To your family and friends?
- ☑ *Does the document violate anyone's rights?* Have people from different backgrounds review your writing.
- ☑ *Am I ethically consistent in my writing?* Apply consistently the principles outlined here and those you have assimilated throughout your life to meet this standard.

euphemisms

A *euphemism* is an inoffensive substitute for a word or phrase that could be distasteful, offensive, or too blunt: *passed away* for *died; previously owned* or *preowned* for *used.* Used judiciously, a euphemism can help you avoid embarrassing or offending someone. Used carelessly, however, a euphemism can hide the facts of a situation (*incident* or *event* for *accident*) or be a form of **affectation** (page 251). See also **ethics in writing** (page 261).

expletives 

An *expletive* is a word that fills the position of another word, phrase, or clause. *It* and *there* are common expletives.

- *It* is certain that he will be promoted.

In the example, the expletive *it* occupies the position of subject in place of the real subject, *that he will be promoted.* Expletives are sometimes necessary to avoid **awkwardness** (page 252), but they are commonly overused, and most sentences can be better stated without them.

- ~~There were many~~ *Many* orders *were* lost because of a software error.

In addition to its usage as a grammatical term, the word *expletive* means an exclamation or oath, especially one that is profane.

figures of speech

A *figure of speech* is an imaginative expression that often compares two things that are basically not alike but have at least one thing in common. For example, if a device is cone-shaped and has an opening at the top, you might say that it looks like a volcano.

Figures of speech can clarify the unfamiliar by relating a new concept to one with which readers are familiar. In that respect, figures of speech help establish understanding between the specialist and the nonspecialist. Figures of speech can also help translate the abstract into the concrete; in the process of doing so, figures of speech also make writing more colorful and graphic. (See also **abstract words/concrete**

words, page 251.) A figure of speech must make sense, however, to achieve the desired effect.

ILLOGICAL Without the fuel of tax incentives, our economic engine would operate less efficiently. [It would not operate at all without fuel.]

Figures of speech also must be consistent to be effective.

- We must get our research program *back on track,* and we are counting on you to ~~carry the ball.~~ do it.

A figure of speech should not overshadow the point the writer is trying to make. In addition, it is better to use no figure of speech at all than to use a trite one. A surprise that comes "like a bolt out of the blue" seems stale and not much of a surprise. See also **clichés** (page 255).

garbled sentences

A *garbled sentence* is one that is so tangled with structural and grammatical problems that it cannot be repaired. Garbled sentences often result from an attempt to squeeze too many ideas into one sentence.

- My job objectives are accomplished by my having a diversified background which enables me to operate effectively and efficiently, consisting of a degree in computer science, along with twelve years of experience, including three years in Staff Engineering-Packaging sets a foundation for a strong background in areas of analyzing problems and assessing economical and reasonable solutions.

Do not try to patch such a sentence; rather, analyze the ideas it contains, list them in a logical sequence, and then construct one or more entirely new sentences.

An analysis of the preceding example yields the following five ideas:

- My job requires that I analyze problems to find economical and workable solutions.
- My diversified background helps me accomplish my job.
- I have a computer-science degree.
- I have twelve years of job experience.
- Three of these years have been in Staff Engineering-Packaging.

Using those five ideas — together with **parallel structure** (page 269), **sentence variety** (page 272), **subordination** (page 274), and **transition** (page 277) — the writer might have described the job as follows:

- My job requires that I analyze problems to find economical and workable solutions. Both my training and my experience help me achieve this goal. Specifically, I have a computer-science degree and twelve years of job experience, three of which have been in the Staff Engineering-Packaging Department.

See also **sentence construction** (page 341).

idioms 

An *idiom* is a group of words that has a special meaning apart from its literal meaning. Someone who "runs for office" in the United States, for example, need not be an athlete. The same candidate would "stand for office" in the United Kingdom. Because such expressions are specific to a culture, nonnative speakers must memorize them.

Idioms often provide helpful shortcuts. In fact, they can make writing more natural and vigorous. Avoid them, however, if your writing is to be translated into another language or read in other English-speaking countries.

Idiom also refers to the practice of using certain **prepositions** (page 334) following some adjectives (*similar to*), nouns (*need for*), and verbs (*approve of*). Because there is no sure system to explain such usages, the best advice is to check a dictionary. The Web Link box below also suggests some useful resources. See also **international correspondence** (page 141) and **English as a second language** (page 320).

WEB LINK ▸ USING PREPOSITIONAL IDIOMS

ARIZONA STATE UNIVERSITY WRITING CENTER
www.asu.edu/duas/wcenter/prepositions.html

This online writing center offers handouts on prepositions to use with common verbs and adjectives.

PURDUE UNIVERSITY ONLINE WRITING LAB (OWL)
owl.english.purdue.edu/handouts/esl/eslphrasal.html

This site provides a list of idiomatic phrases and provides clear definitions of the phrases.

intensifiers

Intensifiers are adverbs that emphasize degree, such as *very, quite, rather, such,* and *too.* Although they serve a legitimate and necessary function, they are often overused. Too many intensifiers weaken your writing. Eliminate intensifiers that do not make a definite contribution or replace them with specific details.

- The team was ~~quite~~ happy to ~~receive the very good news~~ learn that it had been awarded a ~~rather substantial monetary~~ $5000 prize for its design.

Some words (such as *perfect, impossible,* and *final*) do not logically permit intensification because, by definition, they do not allow degrees of comparison. Although usage often ignores that logical restriction, to ignore it is, strictly speaking, to defy the basic meanings of such words. See Tab 10, Usage. See also **absolute words** (page 251) and **conciseness** (page 257).

jargon

Jargon is a highly specialized slang that is unique to an occupational or professional group. Jargon is at first understood only by insiders; later, it may become known more widely. For example, human resources professionals adopted the term *headhunting* to describe the recruitment of executive personnel. If all your readers are members of a particular occupational group, jargon may provide an efficient means of communicating. However, if you have any doubt that your entire reading audience is part of such a group, avoid using jargon. See also **affectation** (page 251).

logic errors

In persuasive writing, logic is essential to convincing readers that your conclusions are valid. (See also **persuasion,** page 35.) Errors in logic can undermine the point you are trying to communicate and your credibility.

Lack of Reason

When a statement is contrary to the reader's common sense, that statement is not reasonable. If, for example, you stated "Los Angeles is a small town," your reader might immediately question your logic. If, however, you stated "Although Los Angeles is a large sprawling city, it is composed of many areas that are more like small towns," your reader could probably accept the statement as reasonable.

Sweeping Generalizations

Sweeping generalizations are statements that are too large or all-inclusive to be supportable; they generally enlarge an observation about a small group to refer to an entire population.

- Management is never concerned about employees.

That statement ignores any possibility that some companies show great concern for employee welfare. Using such generalizations weakens your credibility.

Non Sequiturs

A *non sequitur* is a statement that does not logically follow a previous statement.

- I arrived at work early today, so the weather is calm.

Common sense tells us that arriving early for work is unrelated to the weather; thus, the second part of the sentence does not follow logically from the first. In your own writing, be careful that all points stand logically connected.

False Analogies

A *false analogy* (also called *post hoc, ergo propter hoc*) refers to the logical fallacy that because one event happened after another event, the first somehow caused the second. (I didn't bring my umbrella today. No wonder it is now raining.) In on-the-job writing, such an error in reasoning can happen when the writer hastily concludes that two events are related without examining the logical connection between them.

Biased or Suppressed Evidence

A conclusion reached as a result of self-serving data, questionable sources, suppressed evidence, or incomplete facts is both illogical and unethical. Suppose you are preparing a report on the acceptance of a new policy among employees. If you distribute questionnaires only to those who think the policy is effective, the resulting evidence will be biased. If you purposely ignore employees who do not believe the policy is effective, you will be suppressing evidence. Intentionally ignoring relevant data that might not support your position not only produces inaccurate results, but, perhaps more importantly, it is unethical. See also **ethics in writing** (page 261).

Fact versus Opinion

Distinguish between fact and opinion. Facts include verifiable data or statements, whereas opinions are personal conclusions that may or may not be based on facts. For example, it is verifiable that distilled water boils at 100 degrees centigrade; that it tastes better than tap water is an opinion. Distinguish the facts from your opinions in your writing so that your readers can draw their own conclusions.

Loaded Arguments

When you include an opinion in a statement and then reach conclusions that are based on that statement, you are loading the argument. Consider the following opening for a memo:

- I have several suggestions to improve the poorly written policy manual. First, we should change . . .

By opening with the assumption that the manual is poorly written, the writer has loaded the statement to get readers to accept his or her arguments and conclusions. Do not load arguments in your writing; conclusions reached with loaded statements are weak and can produce negative reactions in readers who detect the loading.

WEB LINK ▶ UNDERSTANDING AN ARGUMENT

IDENTIFYING THE ARGUMENT OF AN ESSAY
commhum.mccneb.edu/argument/summary.htm

This tutorial provides practice for recognizing the logical components of an argument and thinking critically. It is part of a course offered by Dr. Frank Edler at the Metropolitan Community College in Omaha, Nebraska.

long variants

A *long variant* is an inflated version of a simpler word and should be avoided. Guard against adding prefixes or suffixes to plain words—a practice that creates long variants. The following is a list of words and their inflated counterparts.

SIMPLE	INFLATED
use	utilization (see **utilize,** page 301)
priority	prioritization
orient	orientate
finish	finalize

See also **affectation** (page 251) and **word choice** (page 280).

nominalizations

A nominalization is a weak verb (*make, do, conduct, perform*) combined with a noun, when the verb form of the noun would communicate the same idea more effectively and concisely.

- The quality assurance team will ~~perform an evaluation of~~ *evaluate* the new software.

If you use nominalizations just to make your writing sound more formal, the result will be **affectation** (page 251). You may occasionally have a legitimate use for a nominalization. For example, you might use a nominalization to slow down the pace of your writing. See also **business writing style** (page 254) and **conciseness/wordiness** (page 257).

parallel structure

Parallel sentence structure requires that sentence elements that are alike in function be alike in construction as well. Parallel structure achieves an economy of words, clarifies meaning, expresses the equality of its ideas, and achieves **emphasis** (page 259). The technique assists readers because it allows them to anticipate the meaning of a sentence element on the basis of its parallel construction.

Parallel structure can be achieved with words, phrases, or clauses.

- If you want to earn a satisfactory grade in the training program, you must be *punctual, courteous,* and *conscientious.* [parallel words]
- If you want to earn a satisfactory grade in the training program, you must recognize the importance *of punctuality, of courtesy,* and *of conscientiousness.* [parallel phrases]
- If you want to earn a satisfactory grade in the training program, *you must arrive punctually, you must behave courteously,* and *you must study conscientiously.* [parallel clauses]

Correlative conjunctions (*either . . . or, neither . . . nor, not only . . . but also*) should always use parallel structure. (See **conjunctions,** page 318.) Both parts of the pairs should be followed immediately by the same grammatical form: two similar words, two similar phrases, or two similar clauses.

- Viruses carry either *DNA* or *RNA,* never both. [parallel words]
- Clearly, neither *serological tests* nor *virus isolation studies* alone would have been adequate. [parallel phrases]

- Either *we must increase our production efficiency* or *we must decrease our production goals.* [parallel clauses]

To make a parallel construction clear and effective, it is often best to repeat an article, a pronoun, a helping verb, a preposition, a subordinating conjunction, or the mark of an infinitive (*to*). (The Babylonians had *a* rudimentary geometry and *a* rudimentary astronomy.)

Parallel structure is especially important in creating your outline, your table of contents, and your headings, because it lets your readers know the relative value of each item in your table of contents and each head in the body of your document. (See also **outlining,** page 29.)

Faulty Parallelism

Faulty parallelism results when joined elements are intended to serve equal grammatical functions but do not have equal grammatical form. To avoid faulty parallelism, make certain that each element in a series is similar in form and structure to all others in the same series. In work-related writing, **lists** (page 201) often cause problems with parallel structure. When you use a list that consists of phrases or clauses, each phrase or clause in the list should begin with the same part of speech.

PARALLEL — The following recommendations were made regarding the Cost Containment Committee's position statement:

1. *Stress* that this statement is for all departments.
2. *Start* the statement with, "If the company continues to grow, the following steps must be taken."
3. *Emphasize* that it applies both to department managers and to staff.
4. *Replace* such strong words as *obligation, owe,* and *must* with words that are less harsh.

Faulty parallelism sometimes occurs because a writer tries to compare items that are not comparable.

NOT PARALLEL — The company offers special university training to help nonexempt employees move into professional careers like human resources, accounting, *customer representatives,* and *sales trainees.* [Notice that occupations—*human resources* and *accounting*—are being compared to people—*customer representatives* and *sales trainees.*]

PARALLEL — The company offers special university training to help nonexempt employees move into professional careers like *human resources, accounting, customer service,* and *sales.*

9. Style and Clarity

positive writing

Consider the way that you present positive information. Because of the complexity of some topics, writers may inadvertently use negative terms to describe something positive.

NEGATIVE	If the error does not involve data transmission, the scan function will not be used.
POSITIVE	The scan function is used only if the error involves data transmission.

Negative facts or conclusions should be stated negatively; stating a negative fact or conclusion positively is deceptive because it can mislead the reader. (See also **ethics in writing,** page 261.)

DECEPTIVE	In the first quarter of this year, employee exposure to airborne lead was within 10 percent of acceptable state health standards.
ACCURATE	In the first quarter of this year, employee exposure to airborne lead was 10 percent above acceptable state health standards.

Even if what you are saying is negative, do not use more negative words than necessary.

NEGATIVE	We are withholding your shipment until we receive your payment.
POSITIVE	We will forward your shipment as soon as we receive your payment.

repetition

The deliberate use of repetition to build a sustained effect or to emphasize a feeling or idea can be a powerful device. (See also **emphasis,** page 259.)

- Similarly, atoms *come and go* in a molecule, but the molecule *remains;* molecules *come and go* in a cell, but the cell *remains;* cells *come and go* in a body, but the body *remains;* persons *come and go* in an organization, but the organization *remains.*

  —Kenneth Boulding, *Beyond Economics*

Repeating keywords from a previous sentence or paragraph can also be used effectively to achieve **transition** (page 277).

- For many years, *oil* has been a major industrial energy source. However, *oil* supplies are limited, and other sources of energy must be developed.

Be consistent in the word or phrase you use to refer to something. In business writing, it is generally better to repeat a word (so there will be no question in the reader's mind that you mean the same thing) than to use synonyms to avoid repetition.

SYNONYMS	Several recent *analyses* support our conclusion. These *studies* cast doubt on the feasibility of long-range forecasting. The *reports,* however, are strictly theoretical.
CONSISTENT TERMS	Several recent theoretical *studies* support our conclusion. These *studies* cast doubt on the feasibility of long-range forecasting. They are, however, strictly theoretical.

Purposeless repetition, however, makes a sentence awkward and hides its key ideas.

- She said that the customer ^ *canceled the order.* ~~said that the order was to be canceled.~~

See also **conciseness/wordiness** (page 257).

sentence variety

Sentences can vary in length, structure, and complexity. As you revise, make sure your sentences have not become tiresomely alike.

Sentence Length

Because a series of sentences of the same length is monotonous, varying sentence length makes writing less tedious to the reader. For example, avoid stringing together a number of short independent clauses. Either connect them with subordinating connectives, thereby making some dependent clauses, or make some clauses into separate sentences. (See also **subordination,** page 274.)

STRING	The river is 60 miles long, and it averages 50 yards in width, and its depth averages 8 feet.
IMPROVED	The river, which is 60 miles long and averages 50 yards in width, has an average depth of 8 feet.
IMPROVED	The river is 60 miles long. It averages 50 yards in width and 8 feet in depth.

You can often effectively combine short sentences by converting verbs into adjectives.

- The *failed* digital shift indicator ~~failed. It~~ was pulled from the market.

Although too many short sentences make your writing sound choppy and immature, a short sentence can be effective following a long one.

- During the past two decades, many changes have occurred in American life—the extent, durability, and significance of which no one has yet measured. *No one can.*

In general, short sentences are good for emphatic, memorable statements. Long sentences are good for detailed explanations and support. Nothing is inherently wrong with a long sentence, or even with a complicated one, as long as its meaning is clear and direct. Sentence length becomes an element of style when varied for emphasis or contrast; a conspicuously short or long sentence can be used to good effect.

Word Order

When a series of sentences all begin in exactly the same way (usually with an article and a noun) the result is likely to be monotonous. You can make your sentences more interesting by occasionally starting with a modifying word, phrase, or clause. However, overuse of this technique itself can be monotonous, so use it in moderation.

- *To salvage the project,* she presented alternatives when existing policies failed to produce results. [modifying phrase]

Inverted sentence order can be an effective way to achieve variety, but do not overdo it.

EFFECTIVE	Never have sales been so good.
AWKWARD	Then occurred the event that gained us the contract.

For variety, you can alter normal sentence order by inserting a phrase or clause.

- Titanium fills the gap, *both in weight and in strength,* between aluminum and steel.

The technique of inserting a phrase or clause is good for emphasis, providing detail, breaking monotony, and regulating pace.

Loose and Periodic Sentences

A loose sentence makes its major point at the beginning and then adds subordinate phrases and clauses that develop or modify the point. A loose sentence could end at one or more points before it actually does end, as the periods in brackets illustrate in the following example.

- It went up[.], a great ball of fire about a mile in diameter[.], an elemental force freed from its bonds[.] after being chained for billions of years.

A periodic sentence delays its main idea until the end by presenting modifiers or subordinate ideas first, thus holding the readers' interest until the end.

- During the last century, the attitude of the American citizen toward technology underwent a profound change.

Experiment with shifts from loose sentences to periodic sentences in your own writing, especially during revision. Avoid the singsong monotony of a long series of loose sentences, particularly a series containing coordinate clauses joined by **conjunctions** (page 318). Subordinating some thoughts to others makes your sentences more interesting. (See also **sentence construction,** page 341.)

subordination

Writers use subordination to show, by the structure of a sentence, the appropriate relationship between ideas of unequal importance by subordinating the less important ideas to the more important ideas.

- Pacific Enterprises now employs 500 people. It was founded just three years ago. [The two ideas are equally important.]
- Pacific Enterprises, *which now employs 500 people,* was founded just three years ago. [The number of employees is subordinated.]
- Pacific Enterprises, *which was founded just three years ago,* now employs 500 people. [The founding date is subordinated.]

Effective subordination can be used to achieve sentence variety, conciseness, and emphasis. For example, consider the following sentences.

DEPENDENT CLAUSE	The regional manager's report, *which covered five pages,* was carefully illustrated.
PHRASE	The regional manager's report, *covering five pages,* was carefully illustrated.
SINGLE MODIFIER	The regional manager's *five-page report* was carefully illustrated.

Use a coordinating conjunction (*and, but, for, or, so, yet*) to concede that an opposite or balancing fact is true; however, a subordinating conjunction (*although, since, while*) can often make the point more smoothly. (*Although* their bank has a lower interest rate on loans, ours provides a wider range of essential services.) The relationship between a conditional statement and a statement of consequences is clearer if the condition is expressed as a subordinate clause. (*Because* the bill was incorrect, the customer was angry.)

Subordinating conjunctions (*because, if, while, when, though*) achieve subordination effectively. (An increase in local sales is unlikely *because* the local population has declined.)

Relative pronouns (*who, whom, which, that*) can be used effectively to combine related ideas that would be less smooth as independent clauses or sentences. (The generator, which is the most common source of electric current, uses mechanical energy to produce electricity.)

Avoid overlapping subordinate constructions that depend on the preceding construction. Overlapping can make the relationship between a relative pronoun and its antecedent less clear.

OVERLAPPING Shock, *which* often accompanies severe injuries and infections, is a failure of the circulation, *which* is marked by a fall in blood pressure *that* initially affects the skin (*which* explains pallor) and later the vital organs such as the kidneys and brain.

CLEAR Shock often accompanies severe injuries and infections. It is a failure of the circulation, initially to the skin (this explains pallor) and later to the vital organs such as the kidneys and the brain.

telegraphic style 

Telegraphic style condenses writing by omitting articles, pronouns, conjunctions, and transitional expressions. Although conciseness is important, especially in instructions, writers sometimes try to achieve conciseness by omitting necessary words. (See also **conciseness/wordiness,** page 257.) Telegraphic style forces readers to supply the missing words mentally, thus creating the potential for misunderstandings. Compare the following two passages and notice how much easier the revised version reads (the added words are italicized).

TELEGRAPHIC Per 1/21 memo, 12 copies of instruction sheet and questionnaire enclosed. Report can be complete as soon as above materials received. March filling quickly so let's set date. Please advise.

CLEAR	*As I promised in my* 1/21 memo, enclosed *are* 12 copies of *the* instruction sheet and *the* questionnaire. *We can* complete *the* report as soon as *we* receive *the questionnaires. Our* March *calendar is* filling quickly, so *we should* set *a meeting* date *soon.* Please *give me a possible date when you return the questionnaire.*

Telegraphic style can also produce ambiguity, as the following example demonstrates.

AMBIGUOUS	The director wants report written by New York office. [Does the director want a report that the New York office *wrote in the past,* or does the director want the New York office *to write a report in the future?*]
CLEAR	The director wants the report *that was* written by the New York office.
CLEAR	The director wants the report *to be* written by the New York office.

Although you may save yourself work by writing telegraphically, your readers will have to work that much harder to decipher your meaning. See also **transition** (page 277).

tone

Tone is the writer's attitude toward the subject and his or her readers. In workplace writing, tone may range widely—depending on the purpose, situation, context, audience, and even the medium of a communication. For example, in an email message to be read only by an associate who is also a friend, your tone might be casual.

- Your proposal to Smith and Kline is super. We'll just need to hammer out the schedule. If we get the contract, I owe you lunch!

In a memo to your manager or superior, however, your tone might be more formal and respectful.

- I think your proposal to Smith and Kline is excellent. I have marked a couple of places where I'm concerned that we are committing ourselves to a schedule that we might not be able to keep. If I can help in any other way, please let me know.

In a message that serves as a report to numerous readers, the tone would be professional, without casual language that could be misinterpreted.

- The Smith and Kline proposal appears complete and thorough, based on our department's evaluation. Several small revisions, however, would ensure that the company is not committing itself to an unrealistic schedule. These are marked on the copy of the report being circulated.

The choice of words, the introduction, the opening, and even the title contribute to the overall tone of your document. For instance, a title such as "Ecological Consequences of Diminishing Water Resources in California" clearly sets a different tone from "What Happens When We've Pumped California Dry?" The first title would be appropriate for a report; the second title would be appropriate for a newsletter or popular magazine article. Make sure that your tone is suited to your purpose and your readers. See also **correspondence** (page 128), **email** (page 233), and **titles** (page 86).

transition

Transition is the means of achieving a smooth flow of ideas from sentence to sentence, paragraph to paragraph, and subject to subject. Transition is a two-way indicator of what has been said and what will be said; it provides a means of linking ideas to clarify the relationship between them. You can achieve transition with a word, a phrase, a sentence, or even a paragraph.

Transition can be obvious.

- *Having considered* the benefits of a new facility, *we turn* to the question of adequate staffing.

Transition can be subtle.

- *Even if* this facility can be built at a reasonable cost, there *still remains* the problem of adequate staffing.

Either way, you now have your readers' attention fastened on the problem of adequate staffing, exactly what you set out to do.

Certain words and phrases are inherently transitional. Consider the following terms and their functions:

FUNCTION	TERMS
Result	therefore, as a result, consequently, thus, hence
Example	for example, for instance, specifically, as an illustration
Comparison	similarly, likewise

FUNCTION	TERMS
Contrast	but, yet, still, however, nevertheless, on the other hand
Addition	moreover, furthermore, also, too, besides, in addition
Time	now, later, meanwhile, since then, after that, before that time
Sequence	first, second, third, then, next, finally

Within a paragraph, such transitional expressions clarify and smooth the movement from idea to idea. Conversely, the lack of transitional devices can make for disjointed reading.

Transition between Sentences

You can achieve effective transition between sentences by repeating keywords or ideas from preceding sentences and by using pronouns that refer to antecedents in previous sentences. Consider the following short paragraph, which uses both of those means.

- Representative of many American university towns is Middletown. *This midwestern town,* formerly a *sleepy farming community,* is today the home of a large and bustling *academic community.* Attracting students from all over the Midwest, *this university town* has grown very rapidly in the last ten years.

Enumeration is another device for achieving transition.

- The recommendation rests on *two conditions. First,* the department staff must be expanded to handle the increased workload. *Second,* sufficient time must be provided for the training of the new staff.

Transition between Paragraphs

The means discussed so far for achieving transition between sentences can also be effective for achieving transition between paragraphs. For paragraphs, however, longer transitional elements are often required. One technique is to use an opening sentence that summarizes the preceding paragraph and then moves on to a new paragraph.

- One property of material considered for manufacturing processes is hardness. Hardness is the internal resistance of the material to the forcing apart or closing together of its molecules. Another property is ductility, the characteristic of material that permits it to be drawn into a wire. The smaller the diameter of the wire into which the material can be drawn, the greater the ductility. Material also may possess malleability, the property that makes it capable of being rolled or hammered into thin sheets of various shapes. Engineers, in selecting materials to employ in manufacturing, must consider these properties before deciding on the most desirable for use in production.

The requirements of hardness, ductility, and malleability account for the high cost of such materials. . . .

Another technique is to ask a question at the end of one paragraph and answer it at the beginning of the next.

- New technology has always been feared because it has at times displaced some jobs. However, it invariably creates many more jobs than it eliminates. Historically, the vast number of people employed in the automobile industry as compared with the number of people that had been employed in the harness-and-carriage-making business is a classic example. Almost always, the jobs eliminated by technological advances have been menial, unskilled jobs, and workers who have been displaced have been forced to increase their skills, which resulted in better and higher-paying jobs for them. *In view of these facts, is new technology really bad?*

  Certainly technology has given us an unparalleled access to information and created many new roles for employees. . . .

A purely transitional paragraph may be inserted to aid readability.

- The problem of poor management was a key factor that has caused the weak performance of the company.

  Two other setbacks to the company's fortunes that year also marked the company's decline: the loss of many skilled workers through the early retirement program and the intensification of the devastating rate of employee turnover.

  The early retirement program caused the failure . . .

If you provide logical organization and you have prepared an outline, your transitional needs will easily be satisfied and your writing will have unity and coherence. During revision, look for places where transition is missing, and add it. Look for places where it is weak, and strengthen it. See also **paragraphs** (page 31), **organization** (page 27), **unity** (page 279), and **coherence** (page 256).

unity

Unity is singleness of purpose and treatment, the cohesive element that holds a document together; it means that everything in the document is essentially about one idea.

To achieve unity, the writer must select one topic and then treat it with singleness of purpose, without digressing into unrelated or loosely related paths. The logical sequence provided by a good outline is essential to achieving unity. An outline enables you to lay out the most direct route from introduction to conclusion. After completing your outline, check it to see that each part relates to your subject.

Effective transition is also a prime contributor to unity. Be certain that your transitional terms make clear the relationship of each part to what precedes it. See **transition,** page 277; see also **coherence** (page 256) and **outlining** (page 29).

vague words

A *vague word* is one that is imprecise in the context in which it is used. Some words encompass such a broad range of meanings that there is no focus for their definition. Words such as *real, nice, important, good, bad, contact, thing,* and *fine* are often called "omnibus words" because they can mean everything to everybody. In speech, we sometimes use words that are imprecise, but our vocal inflections and the context of our conversation make their meanings clear. Because you cannot rely on vocal inflections when you are writing, avoid using vague words. Be concrete and specific. (See also **abstract words/concrete words,** page 251.)

VAGUE It was a *good* meeting. [Why was it good?]

SPECIFIC The meeting resolved three questions: pay scales, fringe benefits, and workloads.

word choice

Mark Twain once said, "The difference between the right word and almost the right word is the difference between 'lightning' and 'lightning bug.'" The most important goal in choosing the right word in business writing is the preciseness implied by Twain's comment. Vague words and abstract words defeat preciseness because they do not convey the writer's meaning directly and clearly.

VAGUE It was a *meaningful* meeting.

PRECISE The meeting helped both sides understand each other's positions.

In the first sentence, *meaningful* ironically conveys no meaning at all. See how the revised sentence says specifically what made the meeting "meaningful." Although abstract words may at times be appropriate to your topic, using them unnecessarily will make your writing dry and lifeless.

Being aware of the connotations and denotations of words will help you anticipate the reader's reaction to the words you choose. (See also **connotation/denotation,** page 259.) Understanding antonyms (*fresh/stale*) and synonyms (*notorious/infamous*) will increase your ability to choose the proper word. Make other usage decisions carefully, especially in technical contexts, such as **average/median** (page 288). For such usages, see Tab 10, Usage.

Although many of the entries throughout this book will help you improve your word choices and avoid problems, the following entries should be particularly helpful:

abstract words/concrete words	page 251
affectation	page 251
biased language	page 252
clichés	page 255
conciseness/wordiness	page 257
connotation/denotation	page 259
euphemisms	page 263
idioms	page 265
jargon	page 266
vague words	page 280

A key to choosing the correct and precise word is to keep current in your reading and to be aware of new words in your profession and in the language. In your quest for the right word, remember that there is no substitute for a good dictionary. See **English as a second language** (page 320).

"you" viewpoint

The *"you" viewpoint* is a writing technique that places your readers' interest and perspective foremost. It is based on the principle that your readers are naturally more concerned about their own needs than they are about those of the writer or organization. The "you" viewpoint often, but not always, means using the words *you* and *your* rather than *we, our, I,* and *mine.* Consider the following sentence that focuses on the needs of the writer rather than on those of the reader.

- *We must receive* your receipt with the merchandise before *we can process* your refund.

Even though the sentence uses *your* twice, the words in italics suggest that the point of view centers on the writer's need to receive the receipt in order to process the refund. Using the "you" viewpoint means seeing a situation from the reader's perspective and, when appropriate, writing to reflect that perspective. Consider the following revision, written with the "you" viewpoint.

- So you can receive your refund promptly, please enclose the sales receipt with the returned merchandise.

Because the benefit to the reader is stressed, the writer is more likely to accomplish the purpose of getting the reader to act. See also **correspondence** (page 128), **persuasion** (page 35), and **tone** (page 276).

10

Usage

Preview

Usage describes the choices we make among the various words and constructions available in our language. The line between standard and nonstandard English, or between formal and informal English, is determined by these choices. (See Tab 9, Style and Clarity.) Your choices in any writing situation should be guided by appropriateness: Is the word or expression appropriate to your audience and subject? When it is, you are practicing good usage.

The entries in this section are designed to help you sort out the appropriate from the inappropriate. Just look up the word or term in question here or in the index. A good dictionary is also an invaluable aid in helping you select the right word.

10. Usage

a / an

See **articles** (page 314).

a lot / alot

A lot is often incorrectly written as one word (*alot*). Write the phrase as two words: *a lot*. It is, however, an informal phrase that normally should not be used in business writing. Use *many* or *numerous* instead or give a specific number or amount.

- The peer review group had *numerous* ~~a lot of~~ objections.

above

Avoid using *above* to refer to a preceding passage unless the reference is very clear. The same is true of *aforesaid, aforementioned, the former,* and *the latter,* which are vague and make your writing difficult to follow. To refer to something previously mentioned, repeat the noun or pronoun, or construct your paragraph so that your reference is obvious.

- Please fill out and submit *your travel voucher* ~~the above~~ by March 1.

accept / except

Accept is a verb meaning "consent to," "agree to take," or "admit willingly." (I *accept* the responsibility that goes with the appointment.) *Except* is normally used as a preposition meaning "other than" or "excluding." (We agreed on everything *except* the schedule.)

affect / effect

Affect is a verb that means "influence." (The public utility commission's decisions *affect* all state utilities.) *Effect* can function either as a noun that means "result" (The change had a good *effect*.) or as a verb that means "to bring about." (Only the commissioner can *effect* such a change.) However, *effect* as a verb is formal; other words, such as *made* or *produce,* are usually preferable.

all right / alright

All right means "all correct," as in "The answers were all right." In formal writing, it should not be used to mean "good" or "acceptable." It is always written as two words, with no hyphen; *alright* is nonstandard.

also

Also is an adverb that means "additionally."

- Two 5,000-gallon tanks have been constructed on site. Several 2,500-gallon tanks are *also* available, if needed.

Also should not be used as a connective in the sense of "and."

- He brought the reports, the letters, *and* ~~also~~ the section supervisor's recommendations.

Avoid opening sentences with *also.* It is a weak transitional word that suggests an afterthought rather than planned writing.

- *In addition,* ~~Also,~~ he brought statistical data to support his proposal.
- *He also* ~~Also, he~~ brought statistical data to support his proposal.

amount / number

Amount is used with things that are thought of in bulk and that cannot be counted (mass nouns), as in "the *amount* of electricity." *Number* is used with things that can be counted as individual items (count nouns), as in "the *number* of employees." See also **nouns** (page 328).

and / or

And/or means that either both circumstances are possible or only one of two circumstances is possible. This term is awkward and confusing because it makes the reader stop to puzzle over your distinction.

AWKWARD Use A *and/or* B.

IMPROVED Use A or B or both.

as / since / because

As and *since* are commonly used to mean "because." To express cause, *because* is the strongest and most specific connective; *because* is unequivocal in stating a causal relationship. (*Because* she did not have an MBA, she was not offered the job.)

Since is a weak substitute for *because* as a connective to express cause. However, *since* is an appropriate connective when the emphasis is on circumstance, condition, or time rather than on cause and effect. (*Since* it went public, the company has earned a profit every year.)

As is the least definite connective to indicate cause; its use for that purpose is best avoided. See also **subordination** (page 274).

as such

The phrase *as such* is seldom useful and should be omitted.

as well as

Do not use *as well as* with *both.* The two expressions have similar meanings; use one or the other.

augment / supplement

Augment means to increase or magnify in size, degree, or effect. (Many employees *augment* their incomes by freelancing.) *Supplement* means to add something to make up for a deficiency. (The physician told him to *supplement* his diet with vitamins.)

average / median

The *average* is determined by adding two or more quantities and dividing the sum by the number of items totaled. For example, if one report is 10 pages, another is 30 pages, and a third is 20 pages, their *average* length is 20 pages. It is incorrect to say that "each report averages 20 pages" because each report is a specific length.

- *The three reports average* ~~Each report averages~~ 20 pages.

A *median* is the middle number in a sequence of numbers. For example, the *median* of the series 1, 3, 4, 7, 8, is 4.

bad / badly 

Bad is the adjective form that follows such linking verbs as *feel* and *look*. (We don't want our department to look *bad* at the meeting.) *Badly* is an adverb. (The test model performed *badly* during the trial run.) To say "I feel *badly*" would mean, literally, that your sense of touch is impaired. See also **good/well** (page 293).

between / among

Between is normally used to relate two items or persons. (Preferred stock offers a buyer a middle ground *between* bonds and common stock.) *Among* is used to relate more than two. (The subcontracting was distributed *among* the three firms.)

bi- / semi-

When used with periods of time, *bi-* means "two" or "every two." *Bimonthly* means "once in two months"; *biweekly* means "once in two weeks." When used with periods of time, *semi-* means "half of" or "occurring twice within a period of time." *Semimonthly* means "twice a month"; *semiweekly* means "twice a week." Both *bi-* and *semi-* normally are joined with the following element without a space or a hyphen.

can / may 

In writing, *can* refers to capability and *may* refers to possibility or permission.

- I *can* have the project finished by the end of the year. [capability]
- I *may* be in Boston on Thursday. [possibility]
- *May* I proceed with the project? [permission]

chair / chairperson

The words *chair, chairperson, chairman,* and *chairwoman* are used to refer to a presiding officer. The titles *chair* and *chairperson,* however, are better choices because they avoid any sexual bias that might be implied by the other titles. See also **biased language** (page 252).

compose / comprise

Compose means "create" or "make up the whole." The parts *compose* the whole. (The 13 offices *compose* the division; or, the division is *composed* of 13 offices.) *Comprise* means "include," "contain," or "consist of." The whole *comprises* the parts. (The division *comprises* 13 offices.)

criteria / criterion

Criterion means "an established standard for judging or testing." *Criteria* and *criterions* are both acceptable plural forms of *criterion,* but *criteria* is generally preferred.

data / datum

In much informal writing, *data* is considered a collective singular noun. In formal scientific and scholarly writing, however, *data* is generally used as a plural, with *datum* as the singular form. Base your decision on whether your readers should consider the data as a single collection or as a group of individual facts. Whatever you decide, be sure that your pronouns and verbs agree in number with the selected usage. See also **agreement** (page 313).

different from / different than

In formal writing, the preposition *from* is used with *different.* (The Quantum PC is *different from* the Macintosh computer.) *Different than* is acceptable when it is followed by a clause. (The job cost was *different than* we had estimated it.)

each

When *each* is used as a subject, it takes a singular verb or pronoun. (*Each* of the reports *is* to be submitted ten weeks after *it* is assigned.) When *each* occurs after a plural subject with which it is in apposition, it takes a plural verb or pronoun. (The reports *each have* white embossed titles on *their* covers.) See also **agreement,** page 313.

e.g. / i.e.

The abbreviation *e.g.* stands for the Latin *exempli gratia,* meaning "for example"; *i.e.* stands for the Latin *id est,* meaning "that is." Because the English expressions (*for example* and *that is*) serve the same purpose, there is no need to use the Latin expressions or abbreviations except to save space in notes and illustrations.

If you must use *i.e.* or *e.g.,* punctuate them as follows. If *i.e.* or *e.g.* connects two independent clauses, a semicolon should precede it and a comma should follow it. If *i.e.* or *e.g.* connects a noun and an appositive, a comma should precede it and follow it. (We were a fairly heterogeneous group, *i.e.,* managers, engineers, and sales representatives.)

etc.

Etc. is an abbreviation for the Latin *et cetera,* meaning "and others" or "and so forth"; therefore, *etc.* should not be used with *and.* (He brought pencils, pads, erasers, a calculator, etc.) Do not use *etc.* at the end of a list or series introduced by the phrase *such as* or *for example*—those phrases already indicate items of the same category that are not named.

explicit / implicit

An *explicit* statement is one expressed directly, with precision and clarity. An *implicit* meaning is one that is not directly expressed.

- His directions to the Wausau facility were *explicit,* and we found it with no trouble.
- Although the CEO did not mention the company's financial condition, the danger of overconfidence was *implicit* in her speech.

fact

Expressions containing the word *fact* ("due to the *fact* that," "except for the *fact* that," "as a matter of *fact*," or "because of the *fact* that") are often wordy substitutes for more accurate terms.

- ~~Due to the fact that~~ *Because* the sales force has a high turnover rate, sales have declined.

Do not use the word *fact* to refer to matters of judgment or opinion.

- ~~It is a fact that~~ *In my opinion,* sales are poor in the Midwest because of insuffficent market research.

The word *fact* is, of course, valid when facts are what is meant.

- Our tests uncovered numerous *facts* to support your conclusion.

See also **conciseness/wordiness** (page 257) and **logic errors** (page 266).

few / a few

In certain contexts, *few* carries more negative overtones than does the phrase *a few*.

POSITIVE	There are *a few* good points in your report.
NEGATIVE	There are *few* good points in your report.

fewer / less

Fewer refers to items that can be counted (count nouns). (*Fewer* employees took the offer than we expected.) *Less* refers to mass quantities or amounts (mass nouns). (The crop yield decreased this year because we had *less* rain than necessary for an optimum yield.) See also **nouns** (page 328).

first / firstly

Firstly is an unnecessary attempt to add the *-ly* suffix to an adjective to form an adverb. Avoid *firstly* in favor of *first*. *First* is an adverb in its own right and sounds less stiff than *firstly*. The same is true of other ordinal numbers. See also **numbers** (page 384).

former / latter

Former and *latter* should be used to refer to only two items in a sentence or paragraph.

- The president and his aide emerged from the conference, the *former* looking nervous and the *latter* looking glum.

Because these terms make the reader look to previous material to identify the reference, they complicate reading and are best avoided.

good / well

Good is an adjective, and *well* is an adverb.

ADJECTIVE	Janet presented a *good* plan.
ADVERB	The plan was presented *well*.

Well also can be used as an adjective to describe someone's health.

ADJECTIVE	He is not a *well* man.

See also **bad/badly** (page 289).

he / she

The use of either *he* or *she* to refer to both sexes excludes half of the population. To avoid this problem, you could use the phrases *he or she* and *his or her.*

- Whoever is appointed will find *his or her* task difficult.

However, *he or she* and *his or her* are clumsy when used repeatedly, and the *s/he* construction is awkward. One solution is to reword the sentence to use a plural pronoun; if you do, change the noun to which the pronoun refers to its plural form.

- ~~The administrator~~ *Administrators* cannot do ~~his or her job~~ *their jobs* until ~~he or she understands~~ *they understand* the concept.

In other cases, you may be able to avoid using a pronoun altogether.

- Whoever is appointed will find ~~his or her~~ *the* task difficult.

See also **biased language** (page 252).

imply / infer

If you *imply* something, you hint or suggest it. (Her email *implied* that the project would be delayed.) If you *infer* something, you reach a conclusion on the basis of evidence. (The manager *inferred* from the email that the project would be delayed.)

in / into 

In means "inside of"; *into* implies movement from the outside to the inside. (The equipment was *in* the test chamber, so she sent her lab assistant *into* the chamber to get it.)

irregardless / regardless

Irregardless is nonstandard English because it expresses a double negative. The prefix *ir-* renders the base word negative, but *regardless* is already negative, meaning "unmindful." Always use *regardless* or *irrespective*.

its / it's

Its is the possessive case form of *it; it's* is a contraction of *it is.* (*It's* important that the sales department meet *its* quota.) Although pronouns normally form the possessive by the addition of an apostrophe and an *s,* the contraction of *it is* (*it's*) already uses that device. Therefore, the possessive form of the pronoun *it* is formed by adding only the *s.*

kind of / sort of

In writing, *kind of* and *sort of* should be used only to refer to a class or type of things. (They used a special *kind of* metal in the process.) Do not use *kind of* or *sort of* to mean "rather," "somewhat," or "somehow."

lay / lie

Lay is a transitive verb (a verb that requires a direct object to complete its meaning) that means "place" or "put."

- We will *lay* the foundation of the building one section at a time.

The past tense form of *lay* is *laid.*

- We *laid* the first section of the foundation on the 27th of June.

The perfect tense form of *lay* is also *laid.*

- Since June, we *have laid* all but two sections of the foundation.

Lay is frequently confused with *lie,* which is an intransitive verb (a verb that does not require an object to complete its meaning) that means "recline" or "remain."

- Injured employees should *lie* down and remain still until the doctor arrives.

The past tense form of *lie* is *lay.* (This form causes the confusion between *lie* and *lay.*)

- The injured employee *lay* still for approximately five minutes.

The perfect tense form of *lie* is *lain.*

- The injured employee *had lain* still for approximately five minutes before the doctor arrived.

See also **verbs** (page 351).

like / as

To avoid confusion between *like* and *as,* remember that *like* is a preposition and *as* (or *as if*) is a conjunction. Use *like* with a noun or pronoun that is not followed by a verb.

- The new supervisor behaves *like* a novice.

Use *as* before clauses (which contain verbs).

- He responded *as* we expected he would.
- It seemed *as if* the presentation would never end.

Like may be used in elliptical constructions that omit the verb.

- She adapted to the new system *like* a duck to water.

See also **figures of speech** (page 263).

media / medium

Media is the plural of *medium* and should always be used with a plural verb.

- Many communication *media* are available today.
- The Internet is a multifaceted *medium.*

Ms. / Miss / Mrs.

Ms. is widely used in business and public life to address or refer to a woman, especially if her marital status is either unknown or irrelevant to the context. More traditionally, *Miss* is used to refer to an unmarried woman, and *Mrs.* is used to refer to a married woman. Some women may indicate a preference for *Ms., Miss,* or *Mrs.,* which you should honor. If a woman has an academic or professional title, use the appropriate form of address (*Doctor, Professor, Captain*) instead of *Ms., Miss,* or *Mrs.*

nature

Nature, when used to mean "kind" or "sort," is vague. Avoid this usage in your writing. Say exactly what you mean.

- The ~~nature of~~ *exclusionary clause in* the contract caused the problem.

OK / okay 

The expression *okay* (also spelled *OK*) is common in informal writing but should be avoided in more formal documents, such as reports.

- Mr. Sturgess ~~gave his okay to~~ *approved* the project.

on / onto / upon 

On is normally used as a preposition meaning "attached to" or "located at." (Install the phone *on* the wall.) *Onto* implies movement to a position on or movement up and on. (The commuters surged *onto* the platform.)

Similarly, *on* stresses a position of rest (A book lay *on* the table.), and *upon* emphasizes movement (She put a book *upon* the table.).

only

In writing, the word *only* should be placed immediately before the word or phrase it modifies.

- We ~~only~~ lack *only* financial backing.

Incorrect placement of *only* can change the meaning of a sentence.

- *Only* he said that he was tired.
  [He alone said that he was tired.]
- He *only* said that he was tired.
  [He actually was not tired, although he said he was.]
- He said *only* that he was tired.
  [He said nothing except that he was tired.]
- He said that he was *only* tired.
  [He said that he was nothing except tired.]

oral / verbal

Oral refers to what is spoken. (He offered an *oral* argument to the court.) Although it is sometimes used synonymously with *oral, verbal* literally means "in words" and can refer to what is spoken or written. To avoid possible confusion, do not use *verbal* if you can use *written* or *oral.* When you must refer to something both written and spoken, use both *written* and *oral* (rather than *verbal*) to make your meaning clear.

- He demanded either a *written* or an *oral* agreement before he would continue the project.

per

When *per* is used to mean "for each," "by means of," "through," or "on account of," it is appropriate (*per* annum, *per* capita, *per* diem, *per* head). When used to mean "according to" (*per* your request, *per* your order), the expression is jargon and should be avoided. Equally incorrect is the phrase *as per.*

percent / percentage

Percent is normally used instead of the symbol %, except in tables, where space is at a premium. (Only 25 *percent* of the members attended the meeting.) *Percentage,* which is never used with numbers, indicates a general size. (Only a small *percentage* of the managers attended the meeting.)

phenomenon / phenomena

A *phenomenon* is an observable thing, fact, or occurrence. Its plural form is *phenomena.*

- The natural *phenomenon* of earth tremors is a problem we must anticipate on the west coast.
- The *phenomena* associated with the onset of the disease are not fully understood.

reason is because

The redundant phrase *the reason is because* is a colloquial expression that should be avoided in writing. In that phrase, the word *because* (which only repeats the notion of cause) should be replaced by *that.* You could also delete *the reason is* and use only *because.*

shall / will 

Although traditionally *shall* was used to express the future tense with *I* and *we, will* is now generally accepted with all persons. *Shall* is commonly used today only in questions requesting an opinion or a preference rather than a prediction (compare "*Shall* we go?" to "*Will* we go?") and in statements expressing determination ("I *shall* return.").

that 

Include *that* in a sentence if it is necessary for the reader's understanding.

- Some designers fail to recognize sufficiently ^*that* the human beings who operate the equipment constitute an important safety system.

Avoid the unnecessary repetition of *that.*

INCORRECT	You will note *that,* as you assume greater responsibility, *that* your benefits will increase accordingly.
CORRECT	You will note *that* your benefits will increase as you assume greater responsibility.

See also **conciseness/wordiness** (page 257).

that / which / who

That and *which* refer to animals and things; *who* refers to people.

- Companies *that* fund basic research must not expect immediate results.
- The jet stream, *which* is approximately 8 miles above the earth, blows at an average of 64 miles per hour.
- Diane Stoltzfus, *who* is retiring tomorrow, has worked for the company for 20 years.

The word *that* is often overused. However, do not eliminate it if doing so would cause ambiguity or problems with pace. See also **that** (page 299).

Use *which,* not *that,* with nonrestrictive clauses (clauses that do not change the meaning of the basic sentence).

NONRESTRICTIVE	After John left the facility, *which* is one of the best in the region, he came directly to my office.
RESTRICTIVE	Companies *that* diversify usually succeed.

See also **restrictive and nonrestrictive elements** (page 343).

there / their / they're

There is an expletive (a word that fills the position of another word, phrase, or clause) or an adverb.

EXPLETIVE	*There* were more than 1,500 people at the conference.
ADVERB	More than 1,500 people were *there.*

Their is the possessive form of *they.* (Our employees are expected to keep *their* records current.) *They're* is a contraction of *they are.* (If *they're* right, we should change the design.) See also **contractions** (page 378).

to / too / two 

To, too, and *two* are confused only because they sound alike. *To* is used as a preposition or to mark an infinitive.

- Send the report *to* the district manager. [preposition]
- I do not wish *to* go! [mark of the infinitive]

Too is an adverb meaning "excessively" or "also."

- The price was *too* high. [excessively]
- I, *too,* thought it was high. [also]

Two is a number.

- Only *two* buildings have been built this fiscal year.

utilize

Do not use *utilize* as a long variant of *use,* which is the general word for "employ for some purpose." *Use* will almost always be clearer and less pretentious. (See **affectation,** page 251.)

via

Via is Latin for "by way of." (The package was shipped to Los Angeles *via* Chicago.) The term should be used only in routing instructions.

- Her project was funded ~~via~~ *as the result of* the recent legislation.

where / that

Do not substitute *where* for *that* to anticipate an idea or fact to follow.

- I read in the newsletter ~~where~~ *that* computer chips will be used in the new process.

whether or not

When *whether or not* is used to indicate a choice between alternatives, omit *or not;* it is redundant, because *whether* communicates the notion of a choice.

- The project director asked whether ~~or not~~ the request for proposals had been issued.

while

While, meaning "during an interval of time," is sometimes substituted for connectives like *and, but, although,* and *whereas.* Used as a connective in that way, *while* often causes ambiguity.

- Ian Evans is sales manager, ~~while~~ *and* Joan Thomas is in charge of research.

Do not use *while* to mean *although* or *whereas.*

- ~~While~~ *Although* Ryan Patterson wants the job of production manager, he has not yet applied for it.

Restrict *while* to its meaning of "during the time that."

- I'll have to catch up on my reading *while* I am on vacation.

who / whom 

Writers are often unsure whether to use *who* or *whom. Who* is the subjective case form, whereas *whom* is the objective case form. When in doubt about which form to use, substitute a personal pronoun to see which one fits. If *he, she,* or *they* fits, use *who.*

- *Who* is the sales representative for our area?
  [You would say, "*She* is the sales representative for our area."]

If *him*, *her*, or *them* fits, use *whom*.

- It depends on *whom?*
  [You would say, "It depends on *them*."]

whose / of which

Normally, *whose* is used with persons, and *of which* is used with inanimate objects.

- The man *whose* car had been towed away was angry.
- The mantel clock, the parts *of which* work perfectly, is over 100 years old.

If *of which* causes a sentence to sound awkward, *whose* may be used with inanimate objects. (There are added fields, for example, *whose* totals should never be zero.)

your / you're

Your is a personal pronoun denoting possession; *you're* is the contraction of *you are*. (If *you're* going to the conference in Seattle, be sure to pack *your* umbrella.)

11

Grammar

Preview

Grammar is the systematic description of the way words work together to form a coherent language; in this sense, it explains the structure of a language. *Parts of speech* is a term used to describe the class of words to which a particular word belongs, according to its function in a sentence. If a word's function is to name something, for example, it is a **noun** or **pronoun.** If a word's function is to make an assertion about something, it is a **verb.** If its function is to describe or modify something, the word is an **adjective** or an **adverb.** If its function is to join one element of the sentence to another, it is a **conjunction** or a **preposition.** The entries in this section are intended to help you understand grammar and parts of speech in order to diagnose and correct problems that may occur in your writing.

However, to be an effective writer, you also need to know the conventions of usage that help writers select the appropriate word or expression as well as the principles of effective business writing style. Therefore, you may wish to consult Tab 9, Style and Clarity; Tab 10, Usage; and Tab 12, Punctuation and Mechanics.

WEB LINK ▶ GETTING HELP WITH GRAMMAR

THE PURDUE UNIVERSITY ONLINE WRITING LAB (OWL)
owl.english.purdue.edu/handouts/grammar/index.html

The Purdue OWL, a quality resource for student writers and instructors, includes a "Grammar, Spelling, and Punctuation" page with clear explanations and examples.

adjectives 

An *adjective* is any word that modifies a noun or pronoun. An adjective makes the meaning of a noun or a pronoun more specific by highlighting one of its qualities (descriptive adjective) or by imposing boundaries on it (limiting adjective).

- a *hot* iron [descriptive]
- *his three* phone lines [limiting]

Limiting Adjectives

Limiting adjectives include these categories:

- Articles (*a, an, the*)
- Demonstrative adjectives (*this, that, these, those*)
- Possessive adjectives (*my, your, his, her, its, our, their*)
- Numeral adjectives (*two, first*)
- Indefinite adjectives (*all, none, some, any*)

Articles. Articles are adjectives because they modify words or phrases by either limiting them or making them more precise. (See also

a/an, page 286, **articles,** page 314, and **English as a second language,** page 320.)

Demonstrative Adjectives. A demonstrative adjective points to the thing it modifies, specifying the object's position in space or time. *This* and *these* specify a closer position; *that* and *those* specify a more remote position.

- *This* report received today is more current than *that* report received earlier.
- *These* sales figures reported today are better than *those* figures reported last week.

Demonstrative adjectives often cause problems when they modify the nouns *kind, type,* and *sort.* Demonstrative adjectives used with those nouns should agree with them in number.

- *this* kind / *these* kinds; *that* type / *those* types

Confusion often develops when the preposition *of* is added (*this kind of, these kinds of*) and the object of the preposition does not conform in number to the demonstrative adjective and its noun. (See also **prepositions,** page 334.)

- *This kind* of human resources ~~policies~~ *policy* is standard.
- *These kinds* of human resources ~~policy is~~ *policies are* standard.

Using demonstrative adjectives with words like *kind, type,* and *sort* can also easily lead to vagueness. It is better to be more specific. See also **kind of/sort of** (page 295).

Possessive Adjectives. Because possessive adjectives (*my, your, his, her, its, our, their*) directly modify nouns, they function as adjectives, even though they are pronoun forms. (*My* ideas conflicted with *her* plans for the project.)

Numeral Adjectives. Numeral adjectives identify quantity, degree, or place in a sequence. They always modify count nouns. Numeral adjectives are divided into two subclasses: cardinal and ordinal. A *cardinal adjective* expresses an exact quantity (*one* pencil, *two* computers); an *ordinal adjective* expresses degree or sequence (*first* quarter, *second* edition).

In most writing, an ordinal adjective should be spelled out if it is a single word (*tenth*) and written in figures if it is more than one word

(*312th*). Ordinal numbers can also function as adverbs (John arrived *first.*). See also **first/firstly** (page 293) and **numbers** (page 384).

Indefinite Adjectives. Indefinite adjectives do not designate anything specific about the nouns they modify (*some* CD-ROMs, *all* designers). The articles *a* and *an* are included among the indefinite adjectives (*a* minute, *an* hour).

Comparison of Adjectives

Most adjectives in the positive form show the comparative form with the suffix *er* for two items and the superlative form with the suffix *est* for three or more items.

- The first report is *long*. [positive form]
- The second report is *longer*. [comparative form]
- The third report is *longest*. [superlative form]

Many two-syllable adjectives and most three-syllable adjectives are preceded by the word *more* or *most* to form the comparative or the superlative.

- The new library is *more* impressive than the old one. It is the *most* impressive in the county.

A few adjectives have irregular forms of comparison (*much, more, most; little, less, least*).

Some adjectives (*round, unique, exact, accurate*) are not logically subject to comparison. See also **absolute words** (page 251).

Placement of Adjectives

When limiting and descriptive adjectives appear together, the limiting adjectives precede the descriptive adjectives, with the articles usually in the first position.

- *The ten red* cars were parked in a row.
  [article (*The*), limiting adjective (*ten*), descriptive adjective (*red*)]

Within a sentence, adjectives may appear before the nouns they modify (the attributive position) or after the nouns they modify (the predicative position).

- *The small* jobs are given priority. [attributive position]
- The exposure is *brief*. [predicative position]

TIPS FOR USING ADJECTIVES

Unlike in many other languages, adjectives in English have only one form. Do not add *s* or *es* to an adjective to make it plural.

- the *long* trip
- the *long* trips

Capitalize adjectives of origin (city, state, nation, continent).

- the *Venetian* canals
- the *Texan* hat
- the *French* government
- the *African* deserts

In English, verbs of feeling (for example, *bore, interest, surprise*) have two adjectival forms: the present participle (*ing*) and the past participle (*ed*). Use the present participle to describe what causes the feeling. Use the past participle to describe the person who experiences the feeling.

- We heard the *surprising* election results.
  [The *election results* cause the feeling.]
- Only the losing candidate was *surprised* by the election results.
  [The *candidate* experienced the feeling of surprise.]

Adjectives follow nouns in English in only two cases: when the adjective functions as a subjective complement, as in

- That project is not *finished.*

and when an adjective phrase or clause modifies the noun, as in

- The project *that was suspended temporarily* . . .

In all other cases, adjectives are placed before the noun.

When there are multiple adjectives, it is often difficult to know the right order. The guidelines illustrated in the following example would apply in most circumstances, but there are exceptions. (Normally do not use a phrase with so many stacked **modifiers,** page 324.) (See also **articles,** page 314.)

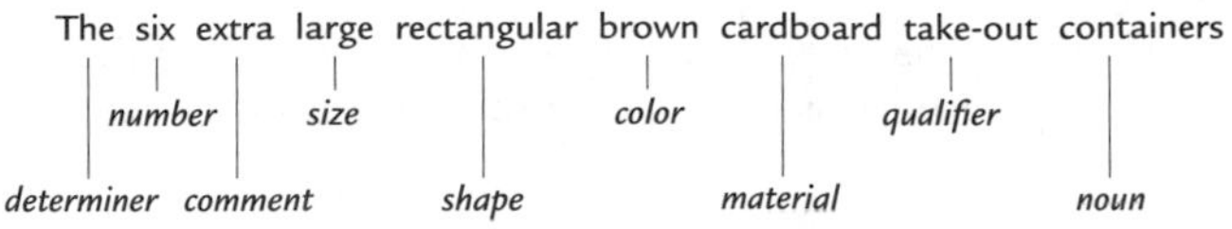

Use of Adjectives

Because of the need for precise description, it is often necessary to use nouns as adjectives.

- The *focus group's* conclusions resulted in the redesign of the product.

When adjectives modifying the same noun can be reversed and still make sense or when they can be separated by *and* or *or,* they should be separated by commas.

- The company is seeking a *young, energetic, creative* management team.

Notice that there is no comma after *creative*. Never use a comma between a final adjective and the noun it modifies. When an adjective modifies a phrase, no comma is required.

- We need an *accessible Web page design.*
  [*Accessible* modifies the phrase *Web page design*.]

See also **modifiers** (page 324).

adverbs

An adverb modifies the action or condition expressed by a **verb** (page 352).

- The wrecking ball hit the side of the building *hard.*
  [The adverb tells *how* the wrecking ball hit the building.]

An adverb also can modify an **adjective** (page 307), another **adverb** (page 311), or a **clause** (page 316).

- The brochure design used *extremely* bright colors.
  [*Extremely* modifies the adjective *bright.*]
- The redesigned brake pad lasted *much* longer.
  [*Much* modifies the adverb *longer.*]
- *Surprisingly,* the machine failed.
  [*Surprisingly* modifies the clause *the machine failed.*]

An adverb answers one of the following questions:

Where? (adverb of place)

- Move the display *forward* slightly.

When? (adverb of time)

- Replace the thermostat *immediately.*

How? (adverb of manner)

- Add the solvent *cautiously.*

How much? (adverb of degree)

- The *nearly* completed report was deleted from his disk.

Types of Adverbs

An adverb may be a common, a conjunctive, an interrogative, or a numeric **modifier** (page 324). Typical common adverbs are *almost, seldom, down, also, now, ever,* and *always.* (I *rarely* work on weekends.)

A *conjunctive adverb* modifies the clause that it introduces; it operates as a conjunction because it joins two independent clauses. The most common conjunctive adverbs are *however, nevertheless, moreover, therefore, further, then, consequently, besides, accordingly, also,* and *thus.* (I rarely work on weekends; *however,* this weekend will be an exception.) In this example, note that a semicolon precedes and a comma follows *however.* The conjunctive adverb (*however*) introduces the independent clause (*this weekend will be an exception*) and indicates its relationship to the preceding independent clause (*I rarely work on weekends*). See also **semicolons** (page 392).

Interrogative adverbs ask questions. Common interrogative adverbs are *where, when, why,* and *how.* (*How* many hours did you work last week?)

Numeric adverbs tell how often. Typical numeric adverbs are *once* and *twice.* (I have worked overtime *twice* this week.)

Comparison of Adverbs

With most one-syllable adverbs, the suffix *er* is added to show comparison with one other item, and the suffix *est* is added to show comparison with two or more items.

- This copier is *fast.* [positive form]
- This copier is *faster* than the old one. [comparative form]
- This copier is the *fastest* of the three tested. [superlative form]

Most adverbs with two or more syllables end in *ly,* and most adverbs ending in *ly* are compared by inserting the comparative *more* or *less* or the superlative *most* or *least* in front of them.

- She moved *more quickly* than any other company's sales representative.
- *Most surprisingly,* the engine failed during the final test phase.

A few irregular adverbs require a change in form to indicate comparison (*well, better, best; badly, worse, worst; far, farther, farthest*).

- The training program functions *well.*
- Our training program functions *better* than most others in the industry.
- Many consider our training program the *best* known in the industry.

Placement of Adverbs

An adverb usually should be placed in front of the verb it modifies.

- The pilot *meticulously* performed the preflight check.

An adverb may, however, follow the verb (or the verb and its object) that it modifies.

- The gauge dipped *suddenly.*
- They repaired my computer *quickly.*

An adverb may be placed between a helping verb and a main verb.

- In this temperature range, the pressure will *quickly* drop.

Adverbs such as *only, nearly, almost, just,* and *hardly* should be placed immediately before the words they limit. See also **only** (page 297) and **modifiers** (page 324).

agreement 

In grammar, *agreement* means the correspondence in form between different elements of a sentence to indicate number, person, gender, and case.

A subject and its verb must agree in number.

- The *design is* acceptable.
  [The singular subject, *design,* requires the singular verb, *is.*]
- The new *products are* going into production soon.
  [The plural subject, *products,* requires the plural verb, *are.*]

A subject and its verb must agree in person.

- *I am* the designer.
  [The first-person singular subject, *I,* requires the first-person singular verb, *am.*]

- *They are* the designers.
  [The third-person plural subject, *they,* requires the third-person plural verb, *are.*]

(See also **verbs,** page 352.)

A pronoun and its antecedent must agree in person, number, gender, and case.

- The *employees* report that *they* are more efficient in the new facility.
  [The third-person plural subject, *employees,* requires the third-person plural pronoun, *they.*]

- *Kaye McGuire* will meet with the staff on Friday, when *she* will assign duties.
  [The feminine pronoun *she* is in the subjective case because it agrees with its antecedent, *Kaye McGuire,* which is the subject of the sentence.]

See also **pronouns** (page 336).

articles

Articles (*a, an, the*) function as adjectives because they modify the items they designate by either limiting them or making them more precise. The two kinds of articles are indefinite and definite. (See also **a/an,** page 286, and **English as a second language,** page 320.)

The indefinite articles, *a* and *an,* denote an unspecified item.

- *A* package was delivered yesterday.
  [This is not a specific package but an unspecified package.]

The choice between *a* and *an* depends on the sound rather than on the letter following the article. Use *a* before words beginning with a consonant sound (*a* person, *a* happy person, *a* historic event). Use *an* before words beginning with a vowel sound (*an* uncle, *an* hour). With abbreviations, use *a* before initial letters having a consonant sound (*a* DNR order). Use *an* before initial letters having a vowel sound (*an* SLN report).

- The project manager felt that it was *a* unique situation.
  [The *u* in *unique* is the consonant sound of *y,* as in *you.*]

The definite article, *the,* denotes a particular item.

- *The* package was delivered yesterday.
  [This is not just any package but *the* specific package.]

Do not omit all articles from your writing. Including articles costs nothing; eliminating them makes reading more difficult. (See also **tele-**

graphic style, page 275.) However, do not overdo it. An article can be superfluous.

- I'll meet you in *a* half *an* hour
  [Choose one article and eliminate the other.]

Do not capitalize articles in titles except when they are the first word. (See also **capital letters,** page 368.)

- *The Economist* reviewed *Winning the Talent Wars.*

TIPS FOR USING ARTICLES

Whether to use a definite or an indefinite article is determined by what you can safely assume about your audience's knowledge. In each of these sentences, you can safely assume that the reader can clearly identify the noun. Therefore, use a definite article.

- *The* sun rises in the east. [The Earth has only one *sun.*]
- Did you know that yesterday was *the* coldest day of the year so far? [The modified noun refers to *yesterday.*]
- *The* man who left his briefcase in the conference room was in a hurry. [The relative phrase *who left his briefcase in the conference room* restricts and, therefore, identifies the meaning of *man.*]

In the following sentence, however, you cannot assume that the reader can clearly identify the noun.

- *A* package is on the way.
  [It is impossible to identify specifically what package is meant.]

A more important question for some nonnative speakers of English is when *not* to use articles. These generalizations will help. Do not use articles with:

singular proper nouns

- Utah, Main Street, Harvard University, Mount Hood

plural nonspecific countable nouns (when making generalizations)

- Helicopters are the new choice of transportation for the rich and famous.

singular uncountable nouns

- She loves chocolate.

plural countable nouns used as complements

- Those women are physicians.

clauses 

A *clause* is a group of words that contains a subject and a predicate and that functions as a sentence or as part of a sentence. (See **sentence construction,** page 341.) Every subject-predicate word group in a sentence is a clause, and every sentence must contain at least one independent clause; otherwise, it is a sentence fragment. (See also **sentence fragments,** page 347.)

A clause that could stand alone as a simple sentence is an *independent clause.* (*The scaffolding fell* when the rope broke.) A clause that could not stand alone if the rest of the sentence were deleted is a *dependent clause.* (I was at the St. Louis branch *when the decision was made.*)

Dependent (or *subordinate*) clauses are useful in making the relationship between thoughts clearer and more succinct than if the ideas were presented in a series of simple sentences or compound sentences.

FRAGMENTED	The recycling facility is located between Millville and Darrtown. Both villages use it. [two thoughts of approximately equal importance]
SUBORDINATED	The recycling facility, *which is located between Millville and Darrtown,* is used by both villages. [one thought subordinated to the other]

Subordinate clauses are especially effective for expressing thoughts that describe or explain another statement. Too much subordination, however, can be confusing.

- He selected instructors whose classes *were* ~~had a slant that was~~ specifically directed *to accounting students.* ~~toward students who intended to go into accounting.~~

A clause can be connected with the rest of its sentence by a coordinating conjunction, a subordinating conjunction, a relative pronoun, or a conjunctive adverb.

- It was 500 miles to the facility, *so* we made arrangements to fly. [coordinating conjunction]
- Mission control will have to be alert *because* at launch the space laboratory will contain a highly flammable fuel. [subordinating conjunction]
- It was Robert M. Fano *who* designed and developed the earliest multiple-access computer system at MIT. [relative pronoun]

- It was dark when we arrived; *nevertheless,* we began the tour of the facility. [conjunctive adverb]

See also **adverbs** (page 311), **conjunctions** (page 318), and **pronouns** (page 336).

complements 

A *complement* is a word, phrase, or clause used in the predicate of a sentence to complete the meaning of the sentence.

- Pilots fly *airplanes.* [word]
- To live is *to risk death.* [phrase]
- John knew *that he would be late.* [clause]

Four kinds of complements are generally recognized: direct object, indirect object, objective complement, and subjective complement.

A *direct object* is a noun or noun equivalent that receives the action of a transitive verb; it answers the question "What?" or "Whom?" after the verb.

- I designed *a Web page.* [noun]
- I like *to work.* [verbal]
- I like *it.* [pronoun]
- I like *what I saw.* [noun clause]

An *indirect object* is a noun or noun equivalent that occurs with a direct object after certain kinds of transitive verbs such as *give, wish, cause,* and *tell.* It answers the question "To whom or what?" or "For whom or what?"

- We should buy *the Milwaukee office* a color copier. [*Color copier* is the direct object.]

An *objective complement* completes the meaning of a sentence by revealing something about the object of its transitive verb. An objective complement may be either a noun or an adjective.

- They call him *a genius.* [noun phrase]
- We painted the building *white.* [adjective]

A *subjective complement,* which follows a linking verb rather than a transitive verb, describes the subject. A subjective complement may be either a noun or an adjective.

- Her sister is *a consultant.* [noun phrase]
- His brother is *ill.* [adjective]

See also **sentence construction** (page 341) and **verbs** (page 352).

conjunctions

A conjunction connects words, phrases, or clauses and can also indicate the relationship between the elements it connects.

A *coordinating conjunction* joins two sentence elements that have identical functions. The coordinating conjunctions are *and, but, or, for, nor, yet,* and *so.*

- Nature *and* technology are only two conditions that affect petroleum operations around the world. [joins two nouns]
- To hear *and* to listen are two different things. [joins two phrases]
- I would like to include the survey, *but* that would make the report too long. [joins two clauses]

Correlative conjunctions are used in pairs. The correlative conjunctions are *either . . . or, neither . . . nor, not only . . . but also, both . . . and,* and *whether . . . or.*

- The auditor will arrive *either* on Wednesday *or* on Thursday.

A *subordinating conjunction* connects sentence elements of different weights, normally independent and dependent clauses. The most frequently used subordinating conjunctions are *so, although, after, because, if, where, than, since, as, unless, before, that, though, when,* and *whereas.*

- I left the office *after* finishing the report.

A *conjunctive adverb* has the force of a conjunction because it joins two independent clauses. The most common conjunctive adverbs are *however, moreover, therefore, further, then, consequently, besides, accordingly, also,* and *thus.*

- The engine performed well in the laboratory; *however,* it failed under road conditions.

Coordinating conjunctions in the titles of books, articles, plays, and movies should not be capitalized unless they are the first or last word in the title.

- *Personal and Professional Web Site Development* is in our library.

Occasionally, a conjunction may begin a sentence; in fact, conjunctions can be strong transitional words and at times can provide emphasis.

- I realize that the project is more difficult than expected and that you have encountered personnel problems. *But* we must meet our deadline.

See also **transition** (page 277).

dangling modifiers

Phrases that do not clearly and logically refer to the correct noun or pronoun are called *dangling modifiers.* Dangling modifiers usually appear at the beginning of a sentence as an introductory phrase.

DANGLING *While eating lunch in the cafeteria,* my computer crashed.
[*Who* was eating lunch in the cafeteria?]

CORRECT While *I* was eating lunch in the cafeteria, my computer crashed.

Dangling modifiers can appear at the end of the sentence as well.

DANGLING The program gains efficiency *by eliminating the superfluous instructions.*
[*Who* eliminates the superfluous instructions?]

CORRECT The program gains efficiency *when you* eliminate the superfluous instructions.

To test whether a phrase is a dangling modifier, turn it into a clause with a subject and a verb. If the expanded phrase and the independent clause do not have the same subject, the phrase is dangling.

DANGLING After finishing the research, the proposal was easy to write.
[The implied subject of the phrase is *I,* but the subject of the independent clause is *the proposal.*]

CORRECT After finishing the research, *I found that* the proposal was easy to write.
[Now the subject of the independent clause agrees with the implied subject of the introductory phrase.]

CORRECT After *I* finished the research, the proposal was easy to write.
[Here the phrase is a dependent clause with an explicit subject.]

English as a second language

Learning to write well in a second language takes a great deal of effort and practice. The most effective way to improve your command of written English is to read widely beyond the reports and professional articles your job requires. Read magazine and newspaper articles, novels, biographies, short stories, and any other writing that interests you. In addition, listen carefully to native speakers on television, on radio, and in person.

Count and Mass Nouns

Count nouns refer to things that can be counted (*tables, pencils, projects, reports*). *Mass nouns* identify things that cannot be counted (*electricity, water, air, loyalty, information*). This distinction can be confusing with words like *electricity* and *water.* Although we can count watt hours of electricity and bottles of water, counting becomes inappropriate when we use the words *electricity* and *water* in a general sense, as in "Water is an essential resource."

The distinction between whether something can or cannot be counted determines the form of the noun to use (singular or plural), the kind of article that precedes it (*a, an, the,* or no article), and the kind of limiting adjective it requires (*fewer* or *less, much* or *many,* and so on). (See also **fewer/less,** page 292.)

Articles

This discussion of articles applies only to common nouns (not to proper nouns, such as the names of people) because count and mass nouns are always common nouns.

The general rule is that every count noun must be preceded by an article (*a, an,* or *the*), a demonstrative adjective (*this, that, these, those*), a possessive adjective (*my, your, her, his, its, their*), or some expression of quantity (such as *one, two, several, many, a few, a lot of, some,* or *no*). The article, adjective, or expression of quantity appears either directly in front of the noun or in front of the whole noun phrase.

- Beth read *a* report last week. [article]
- *Those* reports Beth read were long. [demonstrative adjective]
- *Their* report was long. [possessive adjective]
- *Some* reports Beth read were long. [indefinite adjective]

The articles *a* and *an* are used with count nouns that refer to one item of the whole class of like items.

- Matthew has *a* pen. [Matthew could have *any* pen.]

The article *the* is used with nouns that refer to a specific item that both the reader and the writer can identify.

- Matthew has *the* pen. [Matthew has a *specific* pen that is known to both the reader and the writer.]
- Matthew needs *the* space for his work. [Matthew needs a *specific* space that is known to both the reader and the writer.]

When making generalizations with count nouns, writers can either use *a* or *an* with a singular count noun or use no article with a plural count noun. Consider the following generalization using an article.

- An egg is a good source of protein. [*any egg, all eggs, eggs in general*]

However, the following generalization uses a plural count noun with no article.

- Eggs are good sources of protein. [*any egg, all eggs, eggs in general*]

When you are making a generalization with a mass noun, do not use an article in front of the mass noun.

- Sugar is bad for your teeth.

(See also the discussion of articles in the entry **adjectives,** page 307.)

Gerunds and Infinitives

Nonnative writers of English are often puzzled by which form of a *verbal* (a verb used as another part of speech) to use when it functions as the direct object of a **verb** (page 352). No consistent rule exists for distinguishing between the use of an infinitive and a gerund (a noun formed from an *ing* verb) as the object of a verb. Sometimes a verb takes an infinitive as its object, sometimes it takes a gerund, and sometimes it takes either an infinitive or a gerund. At times, even the base form of the verb is used.

- He enjoys *working.* [gerund as a complement]
- She promised *to fulfill* her part of the contract. [infinitive as a complement]
- The president had the manager *assign* her staff to another project. [basic verb form as a complement]

To make such distinctions accurately, rely on what you hear native speakers use or what you read. You might also consult a reference book for ESL students.

Adjective Clauses

Because of the variety of ways adjective clauses are constructed in different languages, they can be particularly troublesome for nonnative writers of English. The following guidelines will help you form adjective clauses correctly.

Place an adjective clause directly after the noun it modifies.

- *who is standing across the room*
The tall woman ^ is a vice-president of the company ~~who is standing across the room~~.

The adjective clause *who is standing across the room* modifies *woman,* not *company,* and thus comes directly after *woman.*

Avoid using a relative pronoun with another pronoun in an adjective clause.

- The man who ~~he~~ sits at that desk is my boss.

Present Perfect Verb Tense

As a general rule, use the present perfect tense to refer to events completed in the past that have some implication for the present. When a specific time is mentioned, however, use the simple past.

PRESENT PERFECT	I *have written* the letter and I am waiting for an answer. [No specific time is mentioned, but the action, *have written,* affects the present.]
SIMPLE PAST	I *wrote* the letter yesterday. [The time when the action took place is specified, and the action, *wrote,* has no relation to the present.]

Use the present perfect tense to describe actions that occurred in the past and have some bearing on the present.

- She *has revised* that report three times. [She might revise it again.]

Use the present perfect with a *since* or *for* phrase to describe actions that began in the past and continue in the present.

- This company *has been* in business *for* seventeen years.
- This company *has been* in business *since* 1985.

Present Progressive Verb Tense

The present progressive tense is especially difficult for those whose native language does not use this tense. The present progressive tense is used to describe some action or condition that is ongoing (or in progress) in the present and may continue into the future.

- I *am searching* for an error in the document.
  [The search is occurring now and may continue.]

In contrast, the simple present tense more often relates to habitual actions.

- I *search* for errors in my documents.
  [I regularly search for errors, but I am not necessarily searching now.]

ESL Entries

Throughout this book, entries of particular relevance to speakers of English as a second language are marked with an ESL symbol (ESL). The following entries also include ESL Tips boxes with useful information for nonnative speakers.

adjectives	Using Adjectives
articles	Using Articles
Five Steps to Successful Writing (page xiii)	Considering Audiences
meetings	Participating in Meetings
mood	Determining Mood
numbers	Punctuating Numbers
pronouns	Using Possessive Pronouns
quotations marks	Using Quotations Marks and Punctuation
sentence construction	Understanding the Subject of a Sentence
	Understanding the Requirements of a Sentence
tense	Using the Progressive Form
there/their/they're	Omitting a Relative Pronoun
verbs	Avoiding Shifts in Voice, Mood, or Tense

mixed constructions

A *mixed construction* is a sentence in which the elements do not sensibly fit together. The problem may be a grammar error, a logic error, or both, as in the following example.

MIXED I have a degree in accounting along with 12 years of experience sets a foundation for a strong background in analyzing problems and assessing solutions.

The writer begins with an independent clause (*I have a degree in accounting*), then follows with a phrase (*along with 12 years of experience*), and then adds a predicate (*sets a foundation . . .*) as though the independent clause had instead been a subject in need of a predicate. Consider the following revision, which puts the elements together in a grammatical and logical complex sentence.

CORRECT I have a degree in accounting and 12 years of experience, which provide me with a strong background in analyzing problems and assessing solutions.

See also **sentence construction** (page 341).

modifiers

Modifiers are words, phrases, or clauses that expand, limit, or make more precise the meaning of other elements in a sentence. Although we can create sentences without modifiers, we often need the detail and clarification they provide.

WITHOUT MODIFIERS Production decreased.

WITH MODIFIERS *Automobile* production decreased *rapidly*.

Most modifiers function as adjectives or adverbs. The adjectives in the following example impose boundaries on the words they modify.

- *ten* automobiles; *this* printer; *an* animal; *loud* machinery

An adverb modifies an adjective, another adverb, a verb, or an entire clause.

- Under test conditions, the brake pad showed *much* less wear than it did under actual conditions. [The adjective *less* is modified.]
- The brake pad wear was *very* much less than under actual conditions. [The adverb *much* is modified.]
- The wrecking ball hit the wall of the building *hard*. [The verb *hit* is modified.]

- *Surprisingly,* the machine failed even after all the durability and performance tests it had passed.
  [The main clause *the machine failed* is modified.]

Adverbs are intensifiers when they increase the impact of adjectives (*very* fine, *too* high) or adverbs (*rather* quickly, *very* slowly). Be cautious using intensifiers; their overuse can lead to exaggeration and hence to inaccuracies.

Stacked (Jammed) Modifiers

Stacked modifiers are strings of modifiers preceding nouns that make writing unclear or difficult to read.

- Your *staffing-level authorization reassessment* plan should result in a major improvement.

The noun *plan* is preceded by three long modifiers, a string that slows the reader down and makes the sentence awkward. Stacked modifiers are often the result of an overuse of **jargon** (page 266) or **vague words** (page 280). See how breaking up the stacked modifiers makes the example easier to read.

- Your plan for reassessing the staffing-level authorizations should result in a major improvement.

Misplaced Modifiers

A modifier is misplaced when it modifies the wrong word or phrase. A misplaced modifier can cause ambiguity.

- We *almost* lost all of the parts.
  [The parts were *almost* lost but were not.]
- We lost *almost* all of the parts. [Most of the parts were in fact lost.]

To avoid ambiguity, place modifiers as close as possible to the words they are intended to modify. Likewise, place phrases near the words they modify. Note the two meanings possible when the phrase is shifted in the following sentences:

- The equipment *without the accessories* sold the best.
  [Different types of equipment were available, some with and some without accessories.]
- The equipment sold the best *without the accessories*.
  [One type of equipment was available, and the accessories were optional.]

Place clauses as close as possible to the words they modify.

REMOTE We sent the brochure to four local firms *that had four-color art.*

CLOSE We sent the brochure *that had four-color art* to four local firms.

Squinting Modifiers

A modifier squints when it can be interpreted as modifying either of two sentence elements simultaneously, thereby confusing readers about which is intended.

- We agreed *on the next day* to make the adjustments. [Did they agree *to make the adjustments on the next day*? Or *on the next day,* did they agree to make the adjustments?]

A squinting modifier can sometimes be corrected simply by changing its position, but often it is better to rewrite the sentence:

- We agreed that *on the next day* we would make the adjustments. [The adjustments were to be made on the next day.]
- *On the next day,* we agreed that we would make the adjustments. [The agreement was made on the next day.]

See also **dangling modifiers** (page 319).

mood

The grammatical term *mood* refers to the verb functions that indicate whether the verb is intended to make a statement or ask a question, give a command, or express a hypothetical possibility.

The *indicative mood* states a fact, gives an opinion, or asks a question.

- The setting *is* correct.
- *Is* the setting correct?

The *imperative mood* expresses a command, suggestion, request, or entreaty. In the imperative mood, the implied subject *you* is not expressed.

- *Install* the system today.

The *subjunctive mood* expresses something that is contrary to fact, conditional, hypothetical, or purely imaginative; it can also express a wish, a doubt, or a possibility. In the subjunctive mood, *were* is used instead of *was* in clauses that speculate about the present or future, and the base form (*be*) is used following certain verbs, such as *propose, request,* or *insist.*

- If we *were* to close the sale today, we would meet our monthly quota.
- The senior partner insisted that she [I, you, we, they] *be* in charge of the project.

The most common use of the subjunctive mood is to express clearly that the writer considers a condition to be contrary to fact. If the condition is not considered to be contrary to fact, use the indicative mood.

SUBJUNCTIVE	If I *were* president of the firm, I would change several hiring policies.
INDICATIVE	Although I *am* president of the firm, I don't feel that I control every aspect of its policies.

TIPS FOR DETERMINING MOOD

In written and especially in spoken English, there is an increasing tendency to use the indicative mood where the subjunctive traditionally has been used. Note the differences between traditional and contemporary usage in the following examples.

Traditional use of the subjunctive mood

- I wish he *were* here now.
- If I *were* going to the conference, I would room with him.
- I requested that she *show* up on time.

Contemporary (informal) use of the indicative mood

- I wish he *was* here now.
- If I *was* going to the conference, I would room with him.
- I requested that she *shows* up on time.

You may wish to master both the subjunctive and indicative moods and be able to move freely between the two usages. However, in formal business writing, it is best to use the more traditional subjunctive mood.

nouns

A *noun* names a person, place, thing, concept, action, or quality.

Types of Nouns

The two basic types of nouns are proper nouns and common nouns. *Proper nouns,* which are capitalized, name specific people, places, and things (Abraham Lincoln, New York, U.S. Army, Nobel Prize). (See also **capital letters,** page 368.)

Common nouns, which are not capitalized unless they begin sentences, name general classes or categories of persons, places, things, concepts, actions, and qualities (human, city, organization, award). Common nouns include all other types of nouns except proper nouns.

Other types of nouns are collective nouns, abstract nouns, concrete nouns, count nouns, and mass nouns. *Collective nouns* are common nouns that indicate a group or collection. They are plural in meaning but singular in form (audience, jury, brigade, staff, committee). (See the subsection Collective Nouns, page 329, for advice on using singular or plural forms with collective nouns.)

Abstract nouns are common nouns that refer to things that cannot be discerned by the five senses (love, loyalty, pride, valor, peace, devotion).

Concrete nouns are common nouns used to identify those things that can be discerned by the five senses (house, paper, keyboard, glue, nail, grease).

Count nouns are concrete nouns that identify things that can be separated into countable units (desks, chisels, envelopes, engines, pencils).

Mass nouns are concrete nouns that identify things that are a mass rather than individual units and that cannot be easily separated into countable units (electricity, water, sand, wood, air, oil, wheat, cement).

Noun Usage

Nouns function as subjects of verbs, direct and indirect objects of verbs and prepositions, subjective and objective complements, or appositives.

- The *metal* bent as *pressure* was applied to it. [subjects]
- The bricklayer cemented the *blocks* efficiently. [direct object of a verb]
- The company awarded our *department* a plaque for safety. [indirect object of a verb]

- The event occurred within the *year.* [object of a preposition]
- A dynamo is a *generator.* [subjective complement]
- We elected the sales manager *chairperson.* [objective complement]
- George Thomas, the *treasurer,* gave his report last. [appositive]

Words normally used as nouns can also be used as adjectives and adverbs.

- It is *company* policy. [adjective]
- He went *home.* [adverb]

Collective Nouns

When a collective noun refers to a group as a whole, it takes a singular verb and pronoun.

- The staff *was* divided on the issue and could not reach *its* decision until May 15.

When a collective noun refers to individuals within a group, it takes a plural verb and pronoun.

- The staff *returned* to *their* offices after the conference.

A better way to emphasize the individuals on the staff would be to use the phrase *members of the staff.*

- The members of the staff *returned* to *their* offices after the conference.

Treat organization names and titles as singular.

- The LRM Corporation *has* grown 30 percent in the last three years; *it* will move to a new facility in January.

Some collective nouns regularly take singular verbs (*crowd*); others do not (*people*).

- The crowd *was* growing impatient.
- Many people *were* able to watch the space shuttle land safely.

Forming Plurals

Most nouns form the plural by adding *s.* (*Dolphins* are capable of communication.) Nouns ending in *ch, s, sh, x,* and *z* form the plural by adding *es* (search/searches, glass/glasses, wish/wishes, six/sixes, buzz/buzzes).

Nouns that end in a consonant plus *y* form the plural by changing the *y* to *ies* (delivery/deliveries). Some nouns ending in *o* add *es* to form the plural, but others add only *s* (tomato/tomatoes, dynamo/dynamos). Some nouns ending in *f* or *fe* add *s* to form the plural; others change the *f* or *fe* to *ves* (cliff/cliffs, fife/fifes, hoof/hooves, knife/knives). Some nouns require an internal change to form the plural (woman/women, man/men, mouse/mice, goose/geese). Some nouns do not change in the plural form (many *fish,* several *deer,* fifty *sheep*). Hyphenated and open compound nouns form the plural in the main word (sons-in-law, high schools, editors-in-chief). Compound nouns written as one word add *s* to the end. (Use seven *tablespoonfuls* of ground coffee.) If you are unsure of the proper usage, check a dictionary. See **possessive case** (page 332) for a discussion of how nouns form the possessive case.

objects

The three kinds of objects are direct objects, indirect objects, and objects of prepositions. All objects are nouns or noun equivalents: pronouns, verbals, and noun phrases and clauses. See also **nouns** (page 328), **pronouns** (page 336), and **verbs** (page 352).

A *direct object* answers the question "What?" or "Whom?" about a verb and its subject.

- Sheila designed a new *circuit.* [Sheila designed *what?*]
- Bill telephoned the *client.* [Bill telephoned *whom?*]

An *indirect object* is a noun or noun equivalent that occurs with a direct object after certain kinds of transitive verbs, such as *give, wish, cause,* and *tell.* The indirect object answers the question "To whom or what?" or "For whom or what?" The indirect object always precedes the direct object.

- We sent the *general manager* a full report.
  [*Report* is the direct object; the indirect object, *general manager,* answers the question, "We sent a full report *to whom?*"]

The *object of a preposition* is a noun or pronoun that is introduced by a preposition, forming a prepositional phrase.

- At the *meeting,* the district managers approved the contract.
  [*Meeting* is the object and *at the meeting* is the prepositional phrase.]

See also **complements** (page 317).

person

Person refers to the form of a personal pronoun that indicates whether the pronoun represents the speaker, the person spoken to, or the person or thing spoken about. A pronoun representing the speaker is in the *first* person. (*I* could not find the answer in the manual.) A pronoun that represents the person or people spoken to is in the *second* person. (*You* are going to be a good manager.) A pronoun that represents the person or people spoken about is in the *third* person. (*They* received the news quietly.) The following list shows first-, second-, and third-person pronouns.

PERSON	SINGULAR	PLURAL
First	I, me, my, mine	we, us, our, ours
Second	you, your, yours	you, your, yours
Third	he, him, his, she her, hers, it, its	they, them, their, theirs

See also **pronouns** (page 336).

phrases

Phrases are groups of words within sentences that are based on nouns, nonfinite verb forms, or verb combinations without subjects. (See also **clauses,** page 316.)

- She encouraged her staff *by her calm confidence.* [phrase]

A phrase may function as an adjective, an adverb, a noun, or a verb.

- The subjects *on the agenda* were all discussed. [adjective]
- We discussed the project *with great enthusiasm.* [adverb]
- *Working hard* is her way of life. [noun]
- The chief engineer *should have been notified.* [verb]

Even though phrases function as adjectives, adverbs, nouns, or verbs, they are normally named for the kind of word around which they are constructed—preposition, participle, infinitive, gerund, verb, or noun. A phrase that begins with a preposition is a prepositional phrase, a phrase that begins with a participle is a participial phrase, and so on. See also **prepositions** (page 334) and **verbs** (page 352).

possessive case

A noun or pronoun is in the possessive case when it represents a person, place, or thing that possesses something. Possession is generally expressed with an apostrophe and an *s* (the *report's* title), with a prepositional phrase using *of* (the title *of the report*), or with the possessive form of a pronoun (*our* report).

General Guidelines

Singular nouns usually show the possessive case with *'s*, and plural nouns that end in *s* show the possessive case with only an apostrophe.

SINGULAR	PLURAL
a *manager's* office	the *managers'* reports
an *employee's* job satisfaction	the *employees'* paychecks
the *company's* stock value	the *companies'* joint project

Singular nouns that end in *s* generally form the possessive with *'s* or (when the word that follows begins with an *s* or *sh* sound) with only an apostrophe.

- the *witness's* testimony
- the *witness'* statement [*s* sound follows *witness*]

However, singular nouns of one syllable that end with *s* form the possessive by adding *'s*.

- the *bus's* schedule

Plural forms of such nouns use only the apostrophe to show the possessive.

- the *witnesses'* reports
- The *busses'* schedules

Plural nouns that do not end in *s* show the possessive with *'s*.

- *children's* clothing, *women's* resources, *men's* room

Proper nouns and ancient names (*Moses, Ramses, Xerxes*) that end in consecutive *s* or *z* sounds, form the possessive by adding only an apostrophe.

- Jesús Castillo was assigned to the new Global Systems Division. *Jesús'* responsibilities will include expanding our European operations.

Apostrophes are not used in some cases for possessive nouns that function as adjectives (*taxpayers* meeting, *carpenters* union, *consumers* group). See also **adjectives** (page 307).

Compound Nouns

Compound words form the possessive with *'s* following the final letter.

- the *vice-president's* proposal, the *pipeline's* diameter, the *editor-in-chief's* desk

Plurals of some compound expressions are often best expressed with a prepositional phrase (presentations *of the editors-in-chief*).

Coordinate Nouns

Coordinate nouns show joint possession with *'s* following the last noun.

- *Michelson and Morely's* famous experiment on the velocity of light was completed in 1887.

Coordinate nouns show individual possession with *'s* following each noun.

- The difference between *Barker's* and *Washburne's* test results was statistically insignificant.

Possessive Pronouns

The possessive form of a pronoun (*my, its, whose, his, her, our, your,* and *their*) is also used to show possession and does not require an apostrophe.

- Even good systems have *their* flaws.

Only the possessive form of a pronoun should be used with a gerund (a noun formed from an *ing* verb).

- The safety officer insisted on *our* wearing protective clothing. [*Wearing* is the gerund.]

Possessive pronouns are also used to replace nouns.

- The responsibility was *theirs.*

Indefinite Pronouns

Some indefinite pronouns (*all, any, each, few, most, none,* and *some*) form the possessive case with the preposition *of.*

- Both desks were stored in the warehouse, but water ruined the surface *of each.*

Other indefinite pronouns (*everyone, someone, anyone,* and *no one*), however, use an *'s.*

- *Everyone's* contribution is welcome.

See also **apostrophes** (page 367), **its/it's** (page 295), **prepositions** (page 334), **pronouns** (page 336), and **verbs** (page 352).

prepositions

A *preposition* is a word that links a noun or pronoun (its object) to another sentence element by expressing such relationships as direction (*to, into, across, toward*), location (*at, in, on, under, over, beside, among, by, between, through*), time (*before, after, during, until, since*), or figurative location (*for, against, with*). Together, the preposition, its object, and the object's modifiers form a prepositional phrase that acts as a modifier.

- Answer customers' questions *in a courteous manner.*
  [The prepositional phrase *in a courteous manner* modifies the verb *answer.*]

Preposition Functions

The object of a preposition (the word or phrase following it) is always in the objective case. When the object is a compound noun, both nouns should be in the objective case. For example, the phrase "between you and *me*" is frequently and incorrectly written as "between you and *I.*" *Me* is the objective form of the pronoun, and *I* is the subjective form.

Many words that function as prepositions also function as adverbs. If the word takes an object and functions as a connective, it is a preposition; if it has no object and functions as a modifier, it is an adverb.

PREPOSITIONS	The manager sat *behind* the desk *in* her office.
ADVERBS	The customer lagged *behind;* then he came *in* and sat down.

Certain verbs, adverbs, and adjectives are used with certain prepositions, such as "interested *in,*" "aware *of,*" "equated *with,*" "adhere *to,*" "capable *of,*" "object *to,*" and "infer *from.*" A more detailed list of such usages appears in the entry **idioms** (page 265).

Prepositions at the End of a Sentence

A preposition at the end of a sentence can be an indication that the sentence is awkwardly constructed.

She was at the
- ~~The~~ branch office ~~is where she was at~~.

However, if a preposition falls naturally at the end of a sentence, leave it there.

- I don't remember which file name I saved it *under*.

Prepositions in Titles

When a preposition appears in a title, it is capitalized only if it is the first word in the title or if it has four letters or more.

- The article "New Concerns About Distance Education" was reviewed recently in the newspaper column "In My Opinion."

(See also **capital letters,** page 368.)

Preposition Errors

Do not use redundant prepositions, such as "off *of*," "in back *of*," "inside *of*," and "at *about*." (See also **conciseness/wordiness,** page 257).

EXACT	The client arrived at ~~about~~ four o'clock.
APPROXIMATE	The client arrived ~~at~~ about four o'clock.

Avoid unnecessarily adding the preposition *up* to verbs.

to
- Call ~~up and~~ see if he is in his office.

Do not omit necessary prepositions.

to
- He was oblivious and not distracted by the view from his office window.

pronoun reference 

A pronoun should refer clearly to a specific antecedent. Avoid vague and uncertain references.

, which was a big one,
- We got the account after we wrote the proposal. ~~It was a big one.~~

For the sake of coherence, place pronouns as close as possible to their antecedents. (See also **coherence,** page 256.)

, *praised for its architectural design, is*

- The office building ^ next to City Hall ~~was praised for its architectural design~~.

Avoid general and hidden references. A general (or broad) reference or one that has no real antecedent is a problem that often occurs when the word *this* is used by itself.

experience

- He deals with personnel problems in his work. This ^ helps him in his personal life.

A hidden reference is one that has only an implied antecedent.

- A high-lipid, low-carbohydrate diet is "ketogenic" because it favors
the *of ketone bodies*
~~their~~ ^ formation ^ .

Do not repeat an antecedent in parentheses following the pronoun. If you feel you must identify the pronoun's antecedent in that way, you need to rewrite the sentence.

AWKWARD	The senior partner first met Bob Evans when he (Evans) was a trainee.
IMPROVED	Bob Evans was a trainee when the senior partner first met him.

For advice on avoiding pronoun reference problems with gender, see **biased language** (page 252).

pronouns

A *pronoun* is a word that is used as a substitute for a noun (the noun for which a pronoun substitutes is called the *antecedent*). Using pronouns in place of nouns relieves the monotony of repeating the same noun over and over. (See also **pronoun reference,** page 335.)

Personal pronouns refer to the person or people speaking (*I, me, my, mine; we, us, our, ours*); the person or people spoken to (*you, your, yours*); or the person, people, or thing(s) spoken of (*he, him, his; she, her, hers; it, its*; *they, them, their, theirs*). (See also **person,** page 331, and **point of view,** page 36.)

- If *their* figures are correct, *ours* must be in error.

Demonstrative pronouns (*this, these, that, those*) indicate or point out the thing being referred to.

- *This* is my desk.

- *These* are my coworkers.
- *That* will be a difficult job.
- *Those* are incorrect figures.

Relative pronouns (*who, whom, which, that*) perform a dual function: (1) They take the place of nouns, and (2) they connect and establish the relationship between a dependent **clause** (page 316) and its main clause.

- The department manager decided *who* would be hired.

Interrogative pronouns (*who, whom, what, which*) are used only to ask questions.

- *What* is the trouble?

Indefinite pronouns (such as *all, another, any, anyone, anything, both, each, either, everybody, few, many, most, much, neither, nobody, none, several, some,* and *such*) specify a class or group of persons or things rather than a particular person or thing.

- Not *everyone* liked the new procedures; *some* even refused to follow them.

A *reflexive pronoun,* which always ends with the suffix *self* or *selves,* indicates that the subject of the sentence acts upon itself. (See also **sentence construction,** page 341.)

- The electrician accidentally shocked *herself.*

The reflexive pronouns are *myself, yourself, himself, herself, itself, oneself, ourselves, yourselves,* and *themselves. Myself* is not a substitute for *I* or *me* as a personal pronoun.

- Victor and ~~myself~~ I completed the report on time.
- The assignment was given to Ingrid and ~~myself~~ me.

Intensive pronouns are identical in form to the reflexive pronouns, but they perform a different function: to emphasize their antecedents.

- I *myself* asked the same question.

Reciprocal pronouns (*one another* and *each other*) indicate the relationship of one item to another. *Each other* is commonly used when referring to two persons or things and *one another* when referring to more than two.

- Salih and Kara work well with *each other.*
- The crew members work well with *one another.*

Case

Pronouns have forms to show the subjective, objective, and possessive cases.

SINGULAR	SUBJECTIVE	OBJECTIVE	POSSESSIVE
First person	I	me	my, mine
Second person	you	you	your, yours
Third person	he, she, it	him, her, it	his, her, hers, its

PLURAL	SUBJECTIVE	OBJECTIVE	POSSESSIVE
First person	we	us	our, ours
Second person	you	you	your, yours
Third person	they	them	their, theirs

A pronoun that is used as the subject of a clause or sentence is in the subjective case (*I, we, he, she, it, you, they, who*). The subjective case is also used when the pronoun follows a linking verb.

- *She* is my boss.
- My boss is *she.*

A pronoun that is used as the object of a verb or preposition is in the objective case (*me, us, him, her, it, you, them, whom*).

- Ms. Davis hired Tom and *me.* [object of verb]
- Between you and *me,* she's wrong. [object of preposition]

A pronoun that is used to express ownership is in the possessive case (*my, mine, our, ours, his, hers, its, your, yours, their, theirs, whose*).

- He took *his* notes with him on the business trip.
- We took *our* notes with us on the business trip.

A pronoun appositive takes the case of its antecedents.

- Two systems analysts, Joe and *I,* were selected to represent the company.
  [*Joe and I* is in apposition to the subject, *systems analysts,* and must therefore be in the subjective case.]
- The systems analysts selected two members—Joe and *me.*
  [*Joe and me* is in apposition to *two members,* which is the object of the verb, *selected,* and therefore must be in the objective case.]

If you have difficulty determining the case of a compound pronoun, try using the pronoun singly.

- In his letter, Eldon mentioned *him* and *me*.
  In his letter, Eldon mentioned *him*.
  In his letter, Eldon mentioned *me*.
- *They* and *we* must discuss the terms of the merger.
  They must discuss the terms of the merger.
  We must discuss the terms of the merger.

When a pronoun modifies a noun, try it without the noun to determine its case.

- [*We/Us?*] pilots fly our own planes.
  We fly our own planes.
  [You would not write, "*Us* fly our own planes."]
- He addressed his remarks directly to [*we/us?*] technicians.
  He addressed his remarks directly to *us*.
  [You would not write, "He addressed his remarks directly to *we*."]

Gender

A pronoun must agree in gender with its antecedent. A problem sometimes occurs because the masculine pronoun has traditionally been used to refer to both sexes. To avoid the sexual bias implied in such usage, use *he or she* or the plural form of the pronoun, *they*.

- ~~Each~~ *All* may stay or go as ~~he chooses.~~ *they choose.*

If you use the plural form of the pronoun, be sure to change the indefinite pronoun *each* to its plural form, *all*. (See also **biased language,** page 252.)

Number

Number is a frequent problem with only a few indefinite pronouns (*each, either, neither,* and those ending with *body* or *one,* such as *anybody, anyone, everybody, everyone, nobody, no one, somebody, someone*) that are normally singular and so require singular verbs and are referred to by singular pronouns.

- As *each member arrives* for the meeting, please hand *him or her* a copy of the confidential report. *Everyone* must return the copy before *he or she* leaves. *Everybody* on the committee *understands* that *neither* of our major competitors *is* aware of the new process we have developed.

TIPS FOR USING POSSESSIVE PRONOUNS

In many languages, possessive pronouns agree in number and gender with the nouns they modify. In English, however, possessive pronouns agree in number and gender with their antecedents. Check your writing carefully for agreement between a possessive pronoun and the word, phrase, or clause that it refers to.

- The *woman* brought *her* brother a cup of soup.
- *Robert* sent *his* mother flowers on Mother's Day.

Person

Third-person personal pronouns usually have antecedents.

- Gina presented the report to the members of the board of directors. *She* [Gina] first summarized *it* [the report] for *them* [the directors] and then asked for questions.

First- and second-person personal pronouns do not normally require antecedents.

- *I* like my job.
- *You* were there at the time.
- *We* all worked hard on the project.

restrictive and nonrestrictive elements

Modifying phrases and clauses may be either restrictive or nonrestrictive. A nonrestrictive phrase or clause provides additional information about what it modifies, but it does not restrict the meaning of what it modifies. The nonrestrictive phrase or clause can be removed without changing the essential meaning of the sentence. It is, in effect, a parenthetical element that is set off by commas to show its loose relationship with the rest of the sentence.

- The annual report, *which was distributed yesterday,* shows that sales increased 20 percent last year. [nonrestrictive]

A restrictive phrase or clause limits, or restricts, the meaning of what it modifies. If it were removed, the essential meaning of the sentence would be changed. Because a restrictive phrase or clause is essential to the meaning of the sentence, it is never set off by commas.

- All employees *wishing to donate blood* may take Thursday afternoon off. [restrictive]

It is important for writers to distinguish between nonrestrictive and restrictive elements. The same sentence can take on two entirely different meanings, depending on whether a modifying element is set off by commas (because it is nonrestrictive) or not (because it is restrictive). A slip by the writer can not only mislead readers but also embarrass the writer.

MISLEADING	He gave a poor performance evaluation to the staff members who protested to the Human Resources Director. [suggests he gave the poor evaluation because the staff members had protested]
ACCURATE	He gave a poor performance evaluation to the staff members, who protested to the Human Resources Director. [suggests that the staff members protested because of the poor evaluations]

Use *which* to introduce nonrestrictive clauses and *that* to introduce restrictive clauses.

- After John left the restaurant, *which* is one of the finest in New York, he came directly to my office. [nonrestrictive]
- Companies *that* diversify usually succeed. [restrictive]

sentence construction 

A sentence is the most fundamental and versatile tool available to the writer. Sentences generally flow from a subject to a verb to any objects, complements, or modifiers, but they can be ordered in a variety of ways to achieve **emphasis** (page 259). When shifting word order for emphasis, however, be aware that word order can make a great difference in the meaning of a sentence.

- He was *only* the accountant.
- He was the *only* accountant.

Subjects

The most basic components of sentences are subjects and predicates. The *subject* of a sentence is a noun or pronoun (and its modifiers) about which the predicate of the sentence makes a statement. Although a subject may appear anywhere in a sentence, it most often appears at the beginning.

- *To increase sales* is our goal.

Grammatically, a subject must agree with its verb in number.

- These *departments have* much in common.
- This *department has* several functions.

The subject is the actor in active-voice sentences.

- The *Web master* reported a record number of hits in November.

TIPS FOR UNDERSTANDING THE SUBJECT OF A SENTENCE

In English, every sentence, except commands, must have an explicit subject.

- *Ozzie* worked fast. ^ *He established* ~~Established~~ the parameters for the project.

In commands, the subject *you* is understood and is used only for emphasis.

- (*You*) Show up at the airport at 6:30 tomorrow morning.
- *You* do your homework, young man. [parent to child]

If you move the subject from its normal position (subject-verb-object), English often requires you to replace the subject with an expletive (*there, it*). In this construction, the verb agrees with the subject that follows it.

- *There are* two files on the desk. [The subject is *files.*]
- *It is* presumptuous for me to speak for Jim.
  [The subject is *to speak for Jim.*]

Time, distance, weather, temperature, and environmental expressions use *it* as their subject.

- *It* is ten o'clock.
- *It* is ten miles down the road.
- *It* never snows in Florida.
- *It* is very hot in Jorge's office.

A compound subject has two or more substantives as the subject of one verb.

- *The president* and *the treasurer* agreed to begin the audit.

Predicates

The *predicate* is the part of a sentence that contains the main verb and any other words used to complete the thought of the sentence (the verb's modifiers and complements). The principal part of the predicate is the verb, just as a noun (or noun substitute) is the principal part of the subject. The *simple predicate* is the verb (or verb phrase) alone. The *complete predicate* is the verb and its modifiers and complements.

- Bill *piloted the airplane.*

A *compound predicate* consists of two or more verbs with the same subject. It is an important device for conciseness in writing.

- The company *tried* but *did not succeed* in that field.

A *predicate nominative* is a noun construction that follows a linking verb and renames the subject.

NOUN	She is my *attorney.*
NOUN CLAUSE	His excuse was *that he had been sick.*

Sentence Types

Sentences may be classified according to *structure* (simple, compound, complex, compound-complex); *intention* (declarative, interrogative, imperative, exclamatory); and *stylistic use* (loose, periodic, minor).

Structure. A *simple sentence* consists of one independent clause. At its most basic, the simple sentence contains only a subject and a predicate.

- Profits [subject] rose [predicate].
- The storm [subject] finally ended [predicate].

A *compound sentence* consists of two or more independent clauses connected by a comma and a coordinating conjunction, by a semicolon, or by a semicolon and a conjunctive adverb.

- Drilling is the only way to collect samples of the layers of sediment below the ocean floor, *but* it is not the only way to gather information about these strata. [comma and coordinating conjunction]
- There is little similarity between the chemical composition of sea water and that of river water*;* the various elements are present in entirely different proportions. [semicolon]

- It was 500 miles to the site; *therefore,* we made arrangements to fly. [semicolon and conjunctive adverb]

A *complex sentence* contains one independent clause and at least one dependent clause that expresses a subordinate idea.

- The generator will shut off automatically [independent clause] if the temperature rises above a specified point [dependent clause].

A *compound-complex* sentence consists of two or more independent clauses plus at least one dependent clause.

- Productivity is central to controlling inflation [independent clause]; when productivity rises [dependent clause], employers can raise wages without raising prices [independent clause].

Intention. A *declarative sentence* conveys information or makes a factual statement. (The motor powers the conveyor belt.) An *interrogative sentence* asks a direct question. (Does the conveyor belt run constantly?) An *imperative sentence* issues a command. (Restart in MS-DOS mode.) An *exclamatory sentence* is an emphatic expression of feeling, fact, or opinion. It is a declarative sentence that is stated with great feeling. (The files were deleted!)

Stylistic Use. A *loose sentence* makes its major point at the beginning and then adds subordinate phrases and clauses that develop or modify that major point. A loose sentence might seem to end at one or more points before it actually does end, as the periods in brackets illustrate in the following sentence.

- It went up [.], a great ball of fire about a mile in diameter [.], changing colors as it kept shooting upward [.], an elemental force freed from its bonds [.] after being chained for billions of years.

A *periodic sentence* delays its main ideas until the end by presenting subordinate ideas or modifiers first.

- During the last century, the attitude of the American citizen toward automation underwent a profound change.

A *minor sentence* is an incomplete sentence. It makes sense in its context because the missing element is clearly implied by the preceding sentence.

- In view of these facts, is the service contract really useful? *Or economical?*

Constructing Effective Sentences

The subject-verb-object pattern is effective because it is most familiar to readers. In "The company dismissed Joe," we know the subject and the object by their positions relative to the verb. The knowledge that the usual sentence order is subject-verb-object helps readers interpret what they read.

An *inverted sentence* places the elements in other than normal order.

- A better job I never had. [direct object-subject-verb]
- More optimistic I have never been.
  [subjective complement-subject-linking verb]
- A poor image we presented. [complement-subject-verb]

Use uncomplicated sentences to state complex ideas. If readers have to cope with a complicated sentence in addition to a complex idea, they are likely to become confused. Just as simpler sentences make complex ideas more digestible, a complex sentence construction makes a series of simple ideas more smooth and less choppy.

Avoid loading sentences with a number of thoughts carelessly tacked together. Such sentences are monotonous and hard to read because all ideas seem to be of equal importance. Rather, distinguish the relative importance of sentence elements with **subordination** (page 274).

LOADED	We started the program three years ago, there were only three members on the staff, and each member was responsible for a separate state, but it was not an efficient operation.
IMPROVED	When we started the program three years ago, there were only three members on the staff, each having responsibility for a separate state; however, that arrangement was not efficient.

Express coordinate or equivalent ideas in similar form. The very construction of the sentence helps the reader grasp the similarity of its components, as illustrated in **parallel structure** (page 269). See also **garbled sentences** (page 264).

Other Entries about Sentences and Their Elements

The following list directs you to other entries that relate to constructing sentences.

 **TIPS FOR UNDERSTANDING THE REQUIREMENTS OF A SENTENCE**

- A sentence must start with a capital letter.
- A sentence must end with a period, a question mark, or an exclamation point.
- A sentence must have a subject.
- A sentence must have a verb.
- A sentence must conform to subject-verb-object word order (or inverted word order for questions or emphasis).
- A sentence must express an idea that can stand on its own (called the main or independent clause).

sentence faults 

A number of problems can create sentence faults, including faulty subordination, clauses with no subjects, rambling sentences, and omitted verbs.

Faulty subordination occurs (1) when a grammatically subordinate element actually contains the main idea of the sentence or (2) when a subordinate element is so long or detailed that it obscures the main idea. Both of the following sentences are logical, depending on what the writer intends as the main idea and as the subordinate element.

- Although the new filing system saves money, many of the staff are unhappy with it.
  [If the main point is that *many of the staff are unhappy,* this sentence is correct.]
- The new filing system saves money, although many of the staff are unhappy with it.
  [If the writer's main point is that *the new filing system saves money,* this sentence is correct.]

In the following example, the subordinate element overwhelms the main point.

FAULTY Because the noise level in the assembly area on a typical shift is as loud as a smoke detector's alarm ten feet away, employees often develop hearing problems.

IMPROVED Because the noise level in the assembly area is so high, employees often develop hearing problems. In fact, the noise level on a typical shift is as loud as a smoke detector's alarm ten feet away.

Writers sometimes inappropriately assume a subject that is not stated in a clause—thus the clause has no subject.

CONFUSING	Your application program can request to end the session after the next command. [request *who* or *what* to end the session?]
CLEAR	Your application program can request *the host program* to end the session after the next command.

Rambling sentences contain more information than the reader can comfortably absorb. The obvious remedy for a rambling sentence is to divide it into two or more sentences. When you do that, put the main message of the rambling sentence into the first of the revised sentences.

RAMBLING	The payment to which a subcontractor is entitled should be made promptly in order that in the event of a subsequent contractual dispute we, as general contractors, may not be held in default of our contract by virtue of nonpayment.
DIRECT	Pay subcontractors promptly. Then if a contractual dispute occurs, we cannot be held in default of our contract because of nonpayment.

Do not omit a required verb.

written
- I never have ^ and probably never will write the annual report.

The assertion that a sentence's predicate makes about its subject must be logical. "Mr. Wilson's *job* is a sales representative" is not logical, but "*Mr. Wilson* is a sales representative" is. "Jim's *height* is six feet tall" is not logical, but "*Jim* is six feet tall" is. See also **sentence fragments** below.

sentence fragments 

A *sentence fragment* is an incomplete grammatical unit that is punctuated as a sentence.

SENTENCE	He quit his job.
FRAGMENT	And quit his job.

A sentence fragment lacks either a subject or a verb or is a subordinate clause or phrase. Sentence fragments are often introduced by relative pronouns (*who, which, that*) or subordinating conjunctions (such as *although, because, if, when,* and *while*).

- The new manager instituted several new procedures ~~. Although~~ *, although* she didn't train her staff first.

A sentence must contain a finite verb; verbals do not function as verbs. The following examples are sentence fragments because their verbals (*providing, to work, waiting*) cannot function as finite verbs.

FRAGMENTS	*Providing* all employees with disability insurance.
	To work a 40-hour week.
SENTENCES	The company *must provide* all employees with disability insurance.
	All employees *are expected* to work a 40-hour week.

Explanatory phrases beginning with *such as, for example,* and similar terms often lead writers to create sentence fragments.

- The staff wants additional benefits ~~. For example,~~ *, such as* the use of company cars.

A hopelessly snarled fragment simply has to be rewritten. To rewrite such a fragment, pull the main points out of the fragment, list them in the proper sequence, and then rewrite the sentence (see **garbled sentences,** page 264). See also **sentence construction** (page 341) and **sentence faults** (page 346).

spelling

The use of a computer spellchecker helps enormously with spelling problems; however, it will not catch all mistakes. It cannot detect a spelling error if the error results in a valid word; for example, if you mean *to* but inadvertently type *too,* the spellchecker will not detect the error. So, you still must check your document carefully. (See also **proofreading,** page 40.)

Writer's Checklist: Catching Spelling Errors

- ☑ If you are unsure about the spelling of a word, do not rely on guesswork—consult a dictionary. When you look up a word, focus on both its spelling and its meaning.
- ☑ After you have looked in the dictionary for the spelling of the word, write the word from memory several times. Otherwise, you lose the chance of retaining it for future use.

Writer's Checklist: Catching Spelling Errors (continued)

- ☑ Keep a list of frequently used words that you commonly misspell, and work regularly at whittling it down.
- ☑ Proofread all your writing for misspellings.

tense

Tense is the grammatical term for verb forms that indicate time distinctions. There are six tenses in English: past, past perfect, present, present perfect, future, and future perfect. Each tense also has a corresponding progressive form.

TENSE	BASIC FORM	PROGRESSIVE FORM
Past	I began	I was beginning
Past perfect	I had begun	I had been beginning
Present	I begin	I am beginning
Present perfect	I have begun	I have been beginning
Future	I will begin	I will be beginning
Future perfect	I will have begun	I will have been beginning

Perfect tenses allow you to express a prior action or condition that continues in a present, past, or future time.

PRESENT PERFECT	*I have begun* to write the annual report and will continue for the rest of the month.
PAST PERFECT	*I had begun* to read the manual when the lights went out.
FUTURE PERFECT	*I will have begun* this project by the time funds are allocated.

Progressive tenses allow you to describe some ongoing action or condition in the present, past, or future.

PRESENT PROGRESSIVE	*I am beginning* to be concerned that we will not meet the deadline.
PAST PROGRESSIVE	*I was beginning* to think we would not finish by the deadline.
FUTURE PROGRESSIVE	*I will be requesting* a leave of absence when this project is finished.

Past Tense

The simple past tense indicates that an action took place in its entirety in the past. The past tense is usually formed by adding *d* or *ed* to the root form of the verb. (We *closed* the office early yesterday.)

Past Perfect Tense

The past perfect tense (sometimes called *pluperfect*) indicates that one past event preceded another. It is formed by combining the helping verb *had* with the past participle form of the main verb. (He *had finished* by the time I arrived.)

Present Tense

The simple present tense represents action occurring in the present, without any indication of time duration. (I *use* a cell phone.) A general truth is always expressed in the present tense. (He learned that the saying "time *heals* all wounds" is true.) The present tense can be used to present actions or conditions that have no time restrictions. (Water *boils* at 212 degrees Fahrenheit.) The present tense can be used to indicate habitual action. (I *pass* the paint shop on the way to my department every day.) The present tense can be used as a "historical present" to make things that occurred in the past more vivid.

- "FDA Approves New Cancer Drug"
  [news headline: *approves* is in the present tense]

Present Perfect Tense

The present perfect tense describes something from the recent past that has a bearing on the present—a period of time before the present but after the simple past. The present perfect tense is formed by combining a form of the helping verb *have* with the past participle form of the main verb. (We *have finished* the draft and can now revise it.)

Future Tense

The simple future tense indicates a time that will occur after the present. It uses the helping verb *will* (or *shall*) plus the main verb. (I *will finish* the job tomorrow.) Do not use the future tense needlessly; doing so merely adds complexity.

- This system ~~will be~~ *is* explained on page 3.

- When you press this button, the feeder ~~will move~~ *moves* the paper into position.

 **TIPS FOR USING THE PROGRESSIVE FORM**

The progressive form of the verb is composed of two features: a form of the helping verb *be* and the *ing* form of the base verb.

PRESENT PROGRESSIVE	I *am rewriting* the memo.
PAST PROGRESSIVE	I *was rewriting* the memo for several days.
FUTURE PROGRESSIVE	I *will be rewriting* that memo forever.

The present progressive is used in three ways:

1. To refer to an action that is in progress at the moment of speaking or writing
   - The parliamentarian *is taking* the meeting minutes.
2. To highlight that a state or action is not permanent
   - The office temp *is helping* us for a few weeks.
3. To express future plans
   - The summer intern *is leaving* to return to school this Friday.

The past progressive is used to refer to a continuing action or condition in the past, usually with specified limits.

- I *was failing* calculus until I got a tutor.

The future progressive is used to refer to a continuous action or condition in the future.

- We *will be monitoring* his condition all night.

Verbs that express mental activity (*believe, know, see,* and so on) are generally not used in the progressive.

- I ~~am believing~~ *believe* the defendant's testimony.

Future Perfect Tense

The future perfect tense indicates action that will have been completed at a future time. It is formed by linking the helping verbs *will have* to the past participle form of the main verb. (She *will have driven* the test car 40 miles by the time she returns.)

Shift in Tense

Be consistent in your use of tense. The only legitimate shift in tense records a real change in time. Illogical shifts in tense will only confuse your readers.

- Before he *installed* the printed circuit board, the technician ~~cleans~~ cleaned the contacts.

verbs

A *verb* is a word or group of words that describes an action (The copier *jammed* at the beginning of the job.), states the way in which something or someone is affected by an action (He *was disappointed* that the proposal was rejected.), or affirms a state of existence (She *is* a district manager now.).

Types of Verbs

Verbs are either transitive or intransitive. A *transitive verb* requires a direct object to complete its meaning.

- They *laid* the foundation on October 24.
  [*Foundation* is the direct object of the transitive verb *laid.*]
- Rosalie Anderson *wrote* the treasurer a letter.
  [*Letter* is the direct object of the transitive verb *wrote.*]

An *intransitive verb* does not require an object to complete its meaning. It makes a full assertion about the subject without assistance (although it may have modifiers).

- The engine *ran.* / The engine *ran* smoothly and quietly.

A *linking verb* is an intransitive verb that links a complement to the subject. When the complement is a noun or a pronoun, it refers to the same person or thing as the noun or pronoun that is the subject.

- The carpet *is* stained.
  [*Is* is a linking verb; *stained* is an adjective modifying *carpet.*]

Some intransitive verbs, such as *be, become, seem,* and *appear,* are almost always linking verbs. A number of others, such as *look, sound, taste, smell,* and *feel,* can function as either linking verbs or simple intransitive verbs. If you are unsure about whether one of those verbs is a linking verb, try substituting *seem;* if the sentence still makes sense, the verb is probably a linking verb.

- Their antennae *feel* delicate. [*Seem* can be substituted for *feel*—thus *feel* is a linking verb.]
- Their antennae *feel* delicately for their prey. [*Seem* cannot be substituted for *feel*; in this case, *feel* is a simple intransitive verb.]

Forms of Verbs

Verbs are described as being either *finite* or *nonfinite.*

Finite Verbs. A finite verb is the main verb of a clause or sentence. It makes an assertion about its subject and often serves as the only verb in its clause or sentence. (The telephone *rang* and the receptionist *answered* it.) A *helping verb* (sometimes called an *auxiliary verb*) is used in a verb phrase to help indicate mood, tense, and voice. (The phone *had* rung.) Phrases that function as helping verbs are often made up of combinations with the sign of the infinitive, *to* (for example, *am going to, is about to, has to,* and *ought to*).

The helping verb always precedes the main verb, although other words may intervene. (Machines *will* never completely *replace* people.)

Nonfinite Verbs. Nonfinite verbs are *verbals*—verb forms that function as nouns, adjectives, or adverbs.

A *gerund* is a noun that is derived from the *ing* form of a verb. (*Seeing* is *believing.*) An *infinitive,* which uses the root form of a verb (usually preceded by *to*), can function as a noun, an adverb, or an adjective.

- He hates *to complain.* [noun, direct object of *hates*]
  The valve closes *to stop* the flow. [adverb, modifies *closes*]
  This is the proposal *to consider.* [adjective, modifies *proposal*]

A *participle* is a verb form that can function as an adjective.

- The *rejected* proposal was ours.
  [*Rejected* is a verb form that is used as an adjective modifying *proposal.*]

Properties of Verbs

Verbs must (1) agree in person with personal pronouns functioning as subjects, (2) agree in tense and number with their subjects, and (3) be in the appropriate voice.

Person is the term for the form of a personal pronoun that indicates whether the pronoun refers to the speaker, the person spoken to, or the person (or thing) spoken about. Verbs change their forms to agree in person with their subjects.

- I *see* [first person] a yellow tint, but she *sees* [third person] a yellow-green hue.

Tense refers to verb forms that indicate time distinctions. There are six tenses: present, past, future, present perfect, past perfect, and future perfect. (See **tense,** page 349.)

Number refers to the two forms of a verb that indicate whether the subject of a verb is singular (The copier *was* repaired.) or plural (The copiers *were* repaired.).

Most verbs show the singular of the third person, present tense, indicative mood by adding *s* or *es* (he *stands,* she *works,* it *goes*). To indicate the plural form, the verb *to be* normally changes from singular (I *am* ready) to plural (we *are* ready).

Voice refers to the two forms of a verb that indicate whether the subject of the verb acts or receives the action. The verb is in the *active*

TIPS FOR AVOIDING SHIFTS IN VOICE, MOOD, OR TENSE

To achieve clarity in your writing, it is important to maintain consistency and avoid shifts. A shift occurs when there is an abrupt change in voice, mood, or tense. Pay special attention when you edit your writing to check for the following types of shifts.

Voice

- The captain permits his crew to go ashore, but *he does not permit* ~~they are not~~ *them* ~~permitted~~ to go downtown.

  [The entire sentence is now in the active voice.]

Mood

- Reboot your computer~~,~~ and ~~you should~~ empty the cache, too.

  [The entire sentence is now in the imperative mood.]

Tense

- I was working quickly, and suddenly a box *fell* ~~falls~~ off the conveyor belt and *broke* ~~breaks~~ my foot.

  [The entire sentence is now in the past tense.]

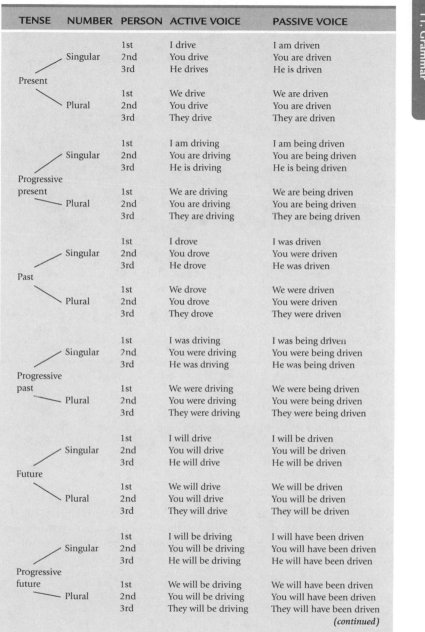

TENSE	NUMBER	PERSON	ACTIVE VOICE	PASSIVE VOICE
Present	Singular	1st	I drive	I am driven
		2nd	You drive	You are driven
		3rd	He drives	He is driven
	Plural	1st	We drive	We are driven
		2nd	You drive	You are driven
		3rd	They drive	They are driven
Progressive present	Singular	1st	I am driving	I am being driven
		2nd	You are driving	You are being driven
		3rd	He is driving	He is being driven
	Plural	1st	We are driving	We are being driven
		2nd	You are driving	You are being driven
		3rd	They are driving	They are being driven
Past	Singular	1st	I drove	I was driven
		2nd	You drove	You were driven
		3rd	He drove	He was driven
	Plural	1st	We drove	We were driven
		2nd	You drove	You were driven
		3rd	They drove	They were driven
Progressive past	Singular	1st	I was driving	I was being driven
		2nd	You were driving	You were being driven
		3rd	He was driving	He was being driven
	Plural	1st	We were driving	We were being driven
		2nd	You were driving	You were being driven
		3rd	They were driving	They were being driven
Future	Singular	1st	I will drive	I will be driven
		2nd	You will drive	You will be driven
		3rd	He will drive	He will be driven
	Plural	1st	We will drive	We will be driven
		2nd	You will drive	You will be driven
		3rd	They will drive	They will be driven
Progressive future	Singular	1st	I will be driving	I will have been driven
		2nd	You will be driving	You will have been driven
		3rd	He will be driving	He will have been driven
	Plural	1st	We will be driving	We will have been driven
		2nd	You will be driving	You will have been driven
		3rd	They will be driving	They will have been driven

(continued)

FIGURE 11–1. Verb Chart

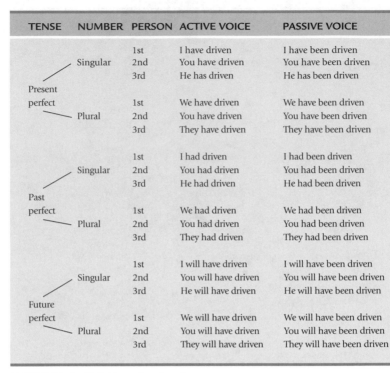

TENSE	NUMBER	PERSON	ACTIVE VOICE	PASSIVE VOICE
Present perfect	Singular	1st	I have driven	I have been driven
		2nd	You have driven	You have been driven
		3rd	He has driven	He has been driven
	Plural	1st	We have driven	We have been driven
		2nd	You have driven	You have been driven
		3rd	They have driven	They have been driven
Past perfect	Singular	1st	I had driven	I had been driven
		2nd	You had driven	You had been driven
		3rd	He had driven	He had been driven
	Plural	1st	We had driven	We had been driven
		2nd	You had driven	You had been driven
		3rd	They had driven	They had been driven
Future perfect	Singular	1st	I will have driven	I will have been driven
		2nd	You will have driven	You will have been driven
		3rd	He will have driven	He will have been driven
	Plural	1st	We will have driven	We will have been driven
		2nd	You will have driven	You will have been driven
		3rd	They will have driven	They will have been driven

FIGURE 11–1. Verb Chart *(continued)*

voice if the subject of the verb acts (The bacteria *grow.*); the verb is in the *passive voice* if it receives the action (The bacteria *are grown* in a petri dish.). See also **voice** below.

Conjugation of Verbs

The conjugation of a verb arranges all forms of the verb so that the differences caused by the changing of the tense, number, person, and voice are readily apparent. Figure 11–1 shows the conjugation of the verb *drive.*

voice

In grammar, *voice* indicates the relation of the subject to the action of the verb. When the verb is in the *active voice,* the subject acts; when it is in the *passive voice,* the subject is acted upon.

ACTIVE David Cohen *wrote* the newsletter article.
[The subject, *David Cohen,* performs the action; the verb *wrote* describes the action.]

PASSIVE The newsletter article *was written* by David Cohen.
[The subject, *the newsletter article,* is acted upon; the verb *was written* describes the action.]

The two sentences say the same thing, but each has a different emphasis: the first emphasizes *David Cohen;* the second emphasizes *the newsletter article*. In business writing, it is often important to emphasize who or what performs an action. Further, the passive-voice version is indirect because it places the performer of the action behind the verb instead of in front of it. Because the active voice is generally more direct, concise, and easier for readers to understand, use the active voice unless the passive voice is more appropriate, as described on page 358.

Using the Active Voice

Improving Clarity. The active voice improves clarity and avoids confusion, especially in instructions and procedures. (See also **policies and procedures,** page 73.)

PASSIVE Sections B and C *should be marked* for revision.
[Are they already marked?]

ACTIVE *Note* sections B and C for revision.
[The performer of the action, *you,* is understood: (You) *Note* the sections.]

Active voice can also help avoid **dangling modifiers** (page 319).

PASSIVE Hurrying to complete the work, the cables *were connected* improperly.
[*Who* was hurrying?]

ACTIVE Hurrying to complete the work, the technician *connected* the cables improperly.
[Here, *hurrying to complete the work* properly modifies the performer of the action: *the technician.*]

Highlighting Subjects. One difficulty with passive sentences is that they can bury the performer of the action in expletives and prepositional phrases.

PASSIVE It *was reported by* the agency that the new model is defective.

ACTIVE The agency *reported* that the new model is defective.

Sometimes writers using the passive voice fail to name the performer—information that might be missed.

PASSIVE The problem *was discovered* yesterday.

ACTIVE The Maintenance Department *discovered* the problem yesterday.

Be careful not to use the passive voice to hide information from the reader, evade responsibility, or obscure an issue. (See also **ethics in writing,** page 261.)

- Several mistakes were made. [*Who* made the mistakes?]
- It has been decided. [*Who* has decided?]

Avoiding Wordiness. The active voice helps avoid wordiness because it eliminates the need for an additional helping verb as well as an extra preposition to identify the performer of the action.

PASSIVE Changes in policy *are resented by* employees.

ACTIVE Employees *resent* changes in policy.

The active-voice version takes one verb (*resent*); the passive-voice version takes two verbs (*are resented*) and an extra preposition (*by*). See also **conciseness/wordiness** (page 257).

Using the Passive Voice

There are instances when the passive voice is effective or even necessary. Indeed, for reasons of tact and diplomacy, you might need to use the passive voice to avoid identifying the performer of the action.

ACTIVE Your sales force did not meet the quota last month.

PASSIVE The quota was not met last month.

When the performer of the action is either unknown or unimportant, use the passive voice. (The copper mine *was discovered* in 1929.) When the performer of the action is less important than the receiver of that action, the passive voice is sometimes more appropriate. (Ann Bryant *was presented* with an award by the president.) When you are explaining an operation in which the reader is not actively involved or when you are explaining a process or a procedure, the passive voice may be more appropriate. In the following example, anyone—it really does not matter who—could be the performer of the action.

- Area strip mining *is used* in regions of flat-to-gently rolling terrain, like that found in the Midwest. Depending on applicable reclamation laws, the topsoil *may be removed* from the area to be *mined, stored,* and later *reapplied* as surface material during reclamation of the mined land. After the removal of the topsoil, a trench *is cut* through the overburden to expose the upper surface of the coal to be mined. The overburden from the first cut *is placed* on the unmined land adjacent to the cut. After the first cut *has been completed,* the coal *is removed.*

Do not, however, simply assume that any such explanation should be in the passive voice. Ask yourself, "Would it be of any advantage to the reader to know the performer of the action?" If the answer is yes, use the active voice, as in the following example.

- In the operation of an internal combustion engine, an explosion in the combustion chamber *forces* the pistons down in the cylinders. The movement of the pistons in the cylinders *turns* the crankshaft.

12

Punctuation and Mechanics

Preview

Understanding punctuation and mechanics is essential to you as a writer because it enables you to communicate clearly and precisely. Punctuation is a system of symbols that helps readers understand the structural relationship within a sentence. The use of punctuation is determined by grammatical convention and a writer's intention.

Marks of punctuation may link, separate, enclose, indicate omissions, terminate, and classify. This section provides detailed information on each of the thirteen marks of punctuation as well as entries on **abbreviations, capital letters, comma splice, contractions, dates, ellipses, italics,** and **numbers.**

abbreviations

Abbreviations are shortened versions of words or combinations of the first letters of words, such as Avenue/Ave., Corporation/Corp., and hypertext markup language/HTML. Abbreviations that are formed by combining the first letter or letters of several words are called *acronyms*. Acronyms are pronounced as words and are written without periods, such as *l*ocal *a*rea *n*etwork/LAN, *d*isk *o*perating *s*ystem/DOS, and *s*elf-*c*ontained *u*nderwater *b*reathing *a*pparatus/scuba. Abbreviations that are formed by combining the initial letter of each word in a multiword term are called *initialisms*. Initialisms are pronounced as separate letters: *f*or *y*our *i*nformation/FYI and *p*ost *m*eridiem/P.M.

Abbreviations, if used appropriately, can be convenient for both the reader and the writer. Like symbols, they can be important space savers in business writing because it is often necessary to provide the maximum amount of information in a limited amount of space.

Using Abbreviations

In business, industry, and government, specialists and people working together on particular projects often use abbreviations, particularly acronyms and initialisms. Within a group of specialists, shortened forms will be easily understood—outside of the group, however, they might be incomprehensible. In fact, abbreviations can be easily overused, either as an affectation or in a misguided attempt to make writing concise, especially in email (see also **email,** page 233). Remember that memos or reports addressed to specific people may be read by other people; you must consider those secondary readers as well. A good rule to follow: When in doubt, spell it out.

Writer's Checklist: Using Abbreviations

- ☑ Except for commonly used abbreviations (U.S., A.M.), spell out a term to be abbreviated the first time it is used, followed by the abbreviation in parentheses. Thereafter, the abbreviation may be used alone.
- ☑ In a long document, repeat the full term in parentheses after the abbreviation at regular intervals so readers do not have to search back to the first time the acronym or initialism was used to find its meaning.

  Remember that the CAR (Capital Appropriations Request) controls the corporate spending.
- ☑ Do not add an additional period at the end of a sentence that ends with an abbreviation. (The official name of the company is DataBase, Inc.)

Writer's Checklist: Using Abbreviations (continued)

- ☑ For abbreviations specific to your profession, use a style guide provided by your professional organization or company. (A listing of style guides appears at the end of **documenting sources**, page 54.)
- ☑ Do not make up your own abbreviations; they will confuse your readers.
- ☑ Write acronyms in capital letters without periods. The only exceptions are acronyms that have become accepted as common nouns, which are written in lowercase letters, such as *laser* (*l*ight *a*mplification by *s*timulated *e*mission of *r*adiation).
- ☑ Initialisms may be written in either uppercase or lowercase. Generally, use periods for lowercase initialisms but not for uppercase ones, such as EDP/e.d.p., EOM/e.o.m., OD/o.d. Two exceptions are geographic names (U.S., U.K., E.U.) and academic degrees (B.A., M.B.A., Ph.D.).
- ☑ Form the plural of an acronym or initialism by adding a lowercase *s*. Do not use an apostrophe (CARs, CRTs).

Forming Abbreviations

Measurements. The following list contains some common abbreviations used with units of measurement. Notice that, except for abbreviations that form words (fig./fig or in./in), abbreviations of measurements do not require periods.

cal, calorie
cm, centimeter
doz or dz, dozen
F, Fahrenheit
fig., figure (illustration)
ft, foot (or feet)
gal., gallon
hr, hour
in., inch
km, kilometer
lb, pound
min, minute
oz, ounce
ppm, parts per million
qt, quart
sec, second or secant
yd, yard
yr, year

Abbreviations of units of measure are identical in the singular and plural: 1 *cm* and 15 *cm* (not 15 *cms*).

Personal Names and Titles. Personal names generally should not be abbreviated: Thomas (*not* Thos.) and William (*not* Wm.). An academic, civil, religious, or military title should be spelled out and in lowercase when it does not precede a name. (The *captain* wanted to check the orders.) When they precede names, some titles are customarily abbreviated (Dr. Smith, Mr. Mills, Ms. Katz). (See also **Ms./Miss/Mrs.,** page 296.)

An abbreviation of a title may follow the name; however, be certain that it does not duplicate a title before the name (Angeline Martinez, Ph.D. *or* Dr. Angeline Martinez). When addressing correspondence and including names in other documents, you normally should spell out titles (The Honorable Mary J. Holt; Professor Charles Matlin). (See also **correspondence,** page 128.) The following is a list of common abbreviations for personal and professional titles.

Atty.	Attorney
Dr.	Doctor (used for anyone with a doctorate)
Drs.	Plural of Dr.
Ed.D.	Doctor of Education
Hon.	Honorable (used with various political and judicial titles)
Jr.	Junior (used when a father with the same name is living)
M.A.	Master of Arts
M.B.A.	Master of Business Administration
M.D.	Doctor of Medicine
Messrs.	Plural of Mr.
Mr.	Mister (spelled out only in the most formal contexts)
Mrs.	Married woman
Ms.	Female equivalent of Mr.
M.S.	Master of Science
Ph.D.	Doctor of Philosophy (for many disciplines)
Rev.	Reverend
Sr.	Senior (used when a son with the same name is living)

Common Scholarly Abbreviations. The following is a partial list of abbreviations commonly used in reference books and for documenting sources in research papers and reports. Latin abbreviations generally should be avoided in all but formal scholarly work.

anon.	anonymous
assn.	association
bibliog.	bibliography, bibliographer, bibliographic, bibliographical
c., ca.	*circa,* "about" (used with approximate dates: c. 1756)
cf.	*confer,* "compare"
ch., chs.	chapter, chapters
cit.	citation, cited
diss.	dissertation

ed., eds.	edited by, editor(s), edition(s)
e.g.	*exempli gratia,* "for example" (see **e.g./i.e.,** page 291)
enl.	enlarged (as in "rev. and enl. ed.")
esp.	especially
et al.	*et alii,* "and others"
etc.	*et cetera,* "and so forth" (see **etc.,** page 291)
f., ff.	and the following page(s) or line(s)
fwd.	foreword, foreword by
GPO	Government Printing Office, Washington, D.C.
i.e.	*id est,* "that is" (see **e.g./i.e.,** page 291)
l., ll.	line, lines
ms, mss	manuscript, manuscripts
n., nn.	note, notes (used immediately after page number: 56n., 56n.3, 56nn.3–5)
N.B.	*nota bene,* "take notice, mark well"
n.d.	no date (of publication)
n.p.	no place (of publication); no publisher
n. pag.	no pagination
p., pp.	page, pages
pref.	preface, preface by
proc.	proceedings
pseud.	pseudonym
pub (publ.)	published by, publisher, publication
rev.	revised by, revised, revision; review, reviewed by (spell out "review" where "rev." might be ambiguous)
rpt.	reprinted by, reprint
sec., secs.	section, sections
supp.	supplement
trans.	translated by, translator, translation
UP	University Press (used in MLA style of **documenting sources,** page 54, as in Oxford UP)
viz.	*videlicet,* "namely"
vol., vols.	volume, volumes
vs., v.	*versus,* "against" (v. preferred in titles of legal cases)

WEB LINK ▶ USING POSTAL ABBREVIATIONS

THE U.S. POSTAL SERVICE (USPS) ABBREVIATIONS
usps.gov/ncsc/lookups/usps_abbreviations.html

The USPS provides the official postal abbreviations for the names of states, streets, and other geographical areas.

apostrophes

An apostrophe (') is used to show possession and to indicate the omission of letters.

To Show Possession

An apostrophe is used with an *s* to form the possessive case of some nouns (the *report's* title). See also **possessive case,** page 332.

To Form Plurals

The trend for indicating the plural forms of words mentioned as words, of numbers used as nouns, and of abbreviations shown as single or multiple letters is currently to add only *s* rather than using *'s*.

When a word (or letter) mentioned as a word is italicized, it is current usage to add *s* in roman type. (There were five *and*s in his first sentence.) Rather than using italics, you may place a word in quotation marks. If you choose this option, use an apostrophe and *s*. (There were five "and's" in his first sentence.) To indicate the plural of a number, add *s* (7s; the late 1990s). If the letter and the *s* form a word, you may want to consider using an apostrophe to avoid confusion (*A*'s). Use *s* to pluralize an abbreviation that is in all capital letters or that ends with a capital letter (IOUs). However, if the abbreviated term contains periods, some writers use an apostrophe to prevent confusion. (They will be asked for their I.D.'s) Whatever practice you follow, be consistent.

To Indicate Omission

An apostrophe is used to mark the omission of letters or **numbers** (page 384) in a **contraction** (page 378) or a date (can't, I'm, I'll; the class of '99).

brackets

The primary use of brackets ([ ]) is to enclose a word or words inserted by the writer or an editor into a quotation.

- The text stated, "Hypertext systems can be categorized as either modest [not modifiable] or robust [modifiable]."

Brackets are used to set off a parenthetical item within parentheses.

- We should be sure to give Emanuel Foose (and his brother Emilio [1812–1882]) credit for his role in founding the institute.

Brackets are also used in academic writing to insert the Latin word *sic,* which indicates that the writer has quoted material exactly as it appears in the original, even though it contains an obvious error.

- Dr. Smith wrote that "the earth does not revolve around the son [*sic*] at a constant rate."

If you are following MLA style in your writing, use brackets around ellipsis dots to show that some words have been omitted from the original source. See also **documenting sources** (page 54) and **ellipses** (page 380).

- "The vast majority of the Internet's inhabitants are [. . .] between the ages of eighteen and thirty-four" (5).

capital letters

The use of capital, or uppercase, letters is determined by custom. Capital letters are used to call attention to certain words, such as proper nouns and the first word of a sentence. Exercise care in using capital letters because they can affect the meaning of words (march/March, china/China, turkey/Turkey). The proper use of capital letters can help eliminate ambiguity.

Proper Nouns

Proper nouns name specific persons, places, things, concepts, or qualities and are capitalized (Physics 101, Microsoft, Jennifer Wilde, Argentina).

Common Nouns

Common nouns name general classes or categories of people, places, things, concepts, or qualities rather than specific ones and are not capitalized (a physics class, a company, a person, a country).

First Words

The first letter of the first word in a sentence is always capitalized. (Of all the plans you mentioned, the first one seems the best.) The first word after a colon may be capitalized if the statement following is a complete sentence or if it is a formal resolution or question. (Today's meeting will deal with only one issue: What is the firm's role in environmental protection?) If a subordinate element follows the colon or if the thought is closely related, use a lowercase letter following the colon. (We had to keep working for one reason: the approaching deadline.) The first word of a complete sentence in quotation marks is capitalized. (Dr. Vesely stated, "Decisions should not be made until all the relevant information is assembled.") The first word in the salutation and complimentary close of a letter is capitalized. (See also **correspondence,** page 128.)

- Dear Mr. Smith:
- Sincerely yours,

Specific Groups

Capitalize the names of ethnic groups, religions, and nationalities (Native American, Italian, Jewish). Do not capitalize the names of social and economic groups (middle class, working class, unemployed).

Specific Places

Capitalize the names of all political divisions (Ward Six, Chicago, Cook County, Ontario, Canada). Capitalize the names of geographical divisions (Europe, Asia, North America, the Middle East). The words *north, south, east,* and *west* are capitalized when they refer to sections of the country. They are not capitalized when they refer to directions. (I may travel *north* when I relocate, but my family will remain in the *South.*)

Specific Institutions, Events, and Concepts

Capitalize the names of institutions, organizations, and associations (Department of Housing and Urban Development). An organization usually capitalizes the names of its internal divisions and departments (Faculty, Board of Directors, Human Resources). Types of organizations are not capitalized unless they are part of an official name (a business writers' association; the American Association of Business Writers). Capitalize historical events (the Great Depression). Capitalize words that designate holidays, specific periods of time, months, or days of the week (Labor Day, the Renaissance, January, Monday, Ramadan, Easter, Passover). Do not capitalize seasons of the year (spring, autumn, winter, summer).

Capitalize the scientific names of classes, families, and orders but not the names of species or English derivatives of scientific names (Mammalia, Carnivora/mammal, carnivorous).

Titles of Works

Capitalize the initial letters of the first and last words of the title of a book, article, play, or film, as well as all major words in the title. Do not capitalize articles (*a, an, the*), coordinating conjunctions (*and* and *but*), or short prepositions (*at, in, on, of*) unless they begin or end the title (*The Lives of a Cell*). Capitalize prepositions that contain more than four letters (*between, because, until, after*). The same rules apply to the subject line of a memo or an email.

Personal, Professional, and Job Titles

Titles preceding proper names are capitalized (Ms. March, Professor Galbraith). Appositives following proper names normally are not capitalized (Chuck Schumer, *senator* from New York; but *Senator* Schumer). However, the word *President* usually is capitalized when it refers to the chief executive of a national government.

Job titles used with personal names are capitalized. (Ho-shik Kim, *Division Manager,* will meet with us on Wednesday.) Job titles used without personal names are not capitalized. (The *division manager* will meet with us on Wednesday.) Use capital letters to designate family relationships only when they occur before a name or substitute for a name (my uncle; Uncle Fred).

Abbreviations

Capitalize abbreviations if the words they stand for would be capitalized, such as UCLA (University of California at Los Angeles).

Letters

Capitalize letters that serve as names or indicate shapes (X-ray, vitamin B, T-square, U-turn, I-beam).

colons

The colon (:) is a mark of introduction that alerts readers to the close connection between the first statement and what follows.

A colon is used to connect a list or series to a word, clause, or phrase that identifies or renames another expression (thus, in apposition).

- Two topics will be discussed: the new accounting system and the new bookkeeping procedures.

Do not, however, place a colon between a verb and its objects.

- Three fluids that clean pipettes are~~:~~ water, alcohol, and acetone.

One common exception is made when a verb is followed by a stacked **list** (page 201).

- Corporations that manufacture computers include:

Apple	Compaq	Micron
IBM	Dell	Gateway

Do not use a colon between a preposition and its object.

- I would like to be transferred to~~:~~ Tucson, Boston, or Miami.

A colon is used to link one statement to another statement that develops, explains, amplifies, or illustrates the first.

- Any organization is confronted with two separate, though related, information problems: It must maintain an effective internal communication system and an effective external communication system.

A colon is used to link an appositive phrase to its related statement if more emphasis is needed and if the phrase comes at the end of the sentence.

- There is only one thing that will satisfy Mr. Sturgess: our finished report.

Colons are used to link numbers that signify different nouns.

- Matthew *14:1* [chapter 14, verse 1]
- *9:30* A.M. [9 hours, 30 minutes]

In proportions, colons indicate ratios (7:3 = 14:x). A colon follows the salutation in business **correspondence** (page 128), even when the salutation refers to a person by first name.

- Dear Ms. Jeffers:

A colon always goes outside quotation marks.

- This was the real meaning of his "suggestion": the division must show a profit by the end of the year.

comma splice 

A *comma splice* is a grammatical error in which two independent clauses are joined by only a comma. (See also **commas,** page 372.)

INCORRECT It was 500 miles to the facility, we arranged to fly.

A comma splice can be corrected in several ways.

Substitute a **semicolon** (page 392), a semicolon and a conjunctive **adverb** (page 311), or a coordinating **conjunction** (page 318).

- It was 500 miles to the facility*;* we arranged to fly.
- It was 500 miles to the facility; *therefore,* we arranged to fly.
- It was 500 miles to the facility, so we arranged to fly.

Create two sentences.

- It was 500 miles to the facility. *We* arranged to fly.

Subordinate one clause to the other.

- *Because* it was 500 miles to the facility, we arranged to fly.

commas

Like all punctuation, the comma (,) helps readers understand the writer's meaning and prevents ambiguity. Notice how the comma helps make the meaning clear in the second example:

AMBIGUOUS To be successful managers with MBAs must continue to learn.

CLEAR To be successful, managers with MBAs must continue to learn.
[The comma makes clear where the main part of the sentence begins.]

Do not follow the old myth that you should insert a comma wherever you would pause if you were speaking. Although you would pause wherever you encounter a comma, you should not insert a comma wherever you might pause. As the previous example illustrates, effective use of commas depends on an understanding of **sentence construction** (page 341).

Linking Independent Clauses

Use a comma before a coordinating conjunction (*and, but, or, nor,* and sometimes *so, yet,* and *for*) that links independent clauses.

- The new systems are in place, *but* they are not functioning.

However, if two independent clauses are short and closely related—and there is no danger of confusing the reader—the comma may be omitted. Both of the following examples are correct.

- The cable snapped and the power failed.
- The cable snapped, and the power failed.

Enclosing Elements

Commas are used to enclose nonrestrictive clauses and phrases and parenthetical elements. For other means of punctuating parenthetical elements, see **dashes,** page 378, and **parentheses,** page 386. See also **restrictive and nonrestrictive elements,** page 340.

- Our new factory, *which began operations last month,* should add 25 percent to total output. [nonrestrictive clause]
- The accountant, *working quickly and efficiently,* finished early. [nonrestrictive phrase]
- We can, *of course,* expect their lawyer to call us. [parenthetical element]

Yes and *no* are set off by commas in such uses as the following:

- I agree with you, *yes.*
- *No,* I do not think we can finish as soon as we would like.

A direct address should be enclosed in commas.

- You will note, *Mark,* that the procedure complies with the company policy.

A phrase in apposition (which identifies another expression) is enclosed in commas.

- Our company, *Blaylok Precision Company,* did well this year.

Interrupting parenthetical and transitional words or phrases are usually set off with commas.

- The report, *however,* was incorrect.

Commas are omitted when the word or phrase does not interrupt the continuity of thought.

- I *therefore* suggest that we begin construction.

Introducing Elements

Clauses and Phrases. It is generally a good idea to put a comma after an introductory clause or phrase. Identifying where the introductory element ends helps indicate where the main part of the sentence begins.

Always place a comma after a long introductory clause.

- *Because we have not yet contained the disease,* we recommend the vaccine.

A long modifying phrase that precedes the main clause should always be followed by a comma.

- *During the field-performance tests at our Colorado proving ground,* the new engine failed to meet our expectations.

When an introductory phrase is short and closely related to the main clause, the comma may be omitted.

- *In two seconds* a temperature of 20 degrees Fahrenheit is created in the test tube.

A comma should always follow an introductory absolute phrase.

- *The tests completed,* we organized the data for the final report.

Words and Quotations. Certain types of introductory words are followed by a comma. One such is a proper noun used in direct address.

- *Nancy,* enclosed is the article you asked me to review.

An introductory interjection (such as *oh, well, why, indeed, yes,* and *no*) is followed by a comma.

- *Yes,* I will make sure your request is approved.

A transitional word or phrase like *moreover* or *furthermore* is usually followed by a comma to connect the following thought with the preceding clause or sentence.

- *In addition,* we can expect a better world market as a result of this move.

When adverbs closely modify the verb or the entire sentence, they should not be followed by a comma.

- *Perhaps* we can still solve the environmental problem.

Use a comma to separate a direct quotation from its introduction.

- Morton and Lucia White said, "People live in cities but dream of the countryside."

Do not use a comma when giving an indirect quotation. (See also **quotation marks,** page 390.)

- Morton and Lucia White said that people dream of the countryside, even though they live in cities.

Separating Items in a Series

Although the comma before the last item in a series is sometimes omitted, it is generally clearer to include it.

- Random House, Bantam, Doubleday, and Dell were individual publishing companies.

Phrases and clauses in coordinate series, like words, are punctuated with commas.

- Plants absorb noxious gases, act as receptors of dirt particles, and cleanse the air of other impurities.

When adjectives modifying the same noun can be reversed and make sense, or when they can be separated by *and* or *or,* they should be separated by commas.

- The drawing was of a *modern, sleek, swept-wing* airplane.

When an adjective modifies a phrase, no comma is required.

- She was investigating the *damaged inventory-control system.* [The adjective *damaged* modifies the phrase *inventory-control system.*]

Never separate a final adjective from its noun.

- He is a conscientious, honest, reliable,/ worker.

Clarifying and Contrasting

Use a comma to separate two contrasting thoughts or ideas.

- The project was finished on time, but not within the budget.

Use a comma after an independent clause that is only loosely related to the dependent clause that follows it.

- I should be able to finish the plan by July, even though I lost time because of illness.

Showing Omissions

A comma sometimes replaces a verb in certain elliptical constructions.

- Some were punctual; *others, late.* [The comma replaces *were.*]

It is better, however, to avoid such constructions in workplace writing.

Using with Other Punctuation

Conjunctive adverbs (*however, nevertheless, consequently, for example, on the other hand*) that join independent clauses are preceded by a **semicolon** (page 392) and followed by a comma. Such adverbs function both as modifiers and as connectives.

- Your idea is good; *however,* your format is poor.

Use a semicolon to separate phrases or clauses in a series when one or more of the phrases or clauses contain commas.

- Our new products include amitriptyline, which has sold very well; dipyridamole, which has not sold well; and cholestyramine, which was just released.

When an introductory phrase or clause ends with a **parenthesis** (page 386), the comma separating the introductory phrase or clause from the rest of the sentence always appears outside the parenthesis.

- Although we left late (at 7:30 P.M.), we arrived in time for the keynote address.

Commas always go inside **quotation marks** (page 390).

- The operator placed the discharge bypass switch at "normal," which triggered a second discharge.

Except with **abbreviations** (page 363), a comma should not be used with a **period** (page 387), **question mark** (page 389), **exclamation mark** (page 381), or **dash** (page 378).

- "Have you finished the project?," I asked.

Using with Numbers and Names

Commas are conventionally used to separate distinct items. Use commas between the elements of an address written on the same line (but not between the state and the zip code).

- Kristen James, 4119 Mill Road, Dayton, Ohio 45401

A date can be written with or without a comma following the year if the date is in the month-day-year format.

- October 26, 20--, was the date the project began.
- October 26, 20-- was the date the project began.

If the date is in the day-month-year format, as is typical in **international correspondence** (page 141), do not set off the date with commas.

- The project began on 26 October 20--.

Use commas to separate the elements of Arabic numbers.

- 1,528,200 feet

However, because many countries use the comma as the decimal marker, use spaces or periods rather than commas in international documents.

- 1 528 200 meters
- 1.528.200 meters

A comma may be substituted for the colon in the salutation of a personal letter. Do not, however, use a comma in a business letter, even if you use the person's first name.

- Dear Marie, [personal letter]
- Dear Marie: [business letter]

Use commas to separate the elements of geographical names.

- Toronto, Ontario, Canada

Use a comma to separate names that are reversed or that are followed by an abbreviation.

- Smith, Alvin
- Jane Rogers, Ph.D.

Use commas to separate certain elements of bibliography, footnote, and reference entries. (See also **bibliographies,** page 51, and **documenting sources,** page 54.)

- Hall, Walter P., ed. *Handbook of Communication Methods.* New York: Stoddard Press, 1999. [bibliography entry]

Avoiding Unnecessary Commas

A number of common writing errors involve placing commas where they do not belong. As stated earlier, such errors often occur because writers assume that a pause in a sentence should be indicated by a comma. Be careful not to place a comma between a subject and verb or between a verb and its object.

- The conditions at the test site in the Arctic, made accurate readings difficult.
- She has often said, that one company's failure is another's opportunity.

Do not use a comma between the elements of a compound subject or a compound predicate consisting of only two elements.

- The director of the design department,/ and the supervisor of the quality-control section were opposed to the new schedules.
- The design director listed five major objections,/ and asked that the new schedule be reconsidered.

Placing a comma after a coordinating conjunction such as *and* or *but* is a common error.

- The chairperson formally adjourned the meeting, *but,/* the members of the committee continued to argue.

Do not place a comma before the first item or after the last item of a series.

- The new products we are considering include,/ calculators, scanners, and cameras.
- It was a fast, simple, inexpensive,/ process.

Do not use a comma to separate a prepositional phrase from the rest of the sentence unnecessarily.

- We discussed the final report,/ on the new project.

contractions 

A *contraction* is a shortened spelling of a word or phrase with an apostrophe substituting for the missing letter or letters (cannot/can't; will not/won't; have not/haven't; it is/it's). Contractions are often used in speech but should rarely be used in reports, formal letters, and most business writing. See also **business writing style** (page 254).

dashes 

The dash (—) can perform all the duties of punctuation: linking, separating, and enclosing. It is an emphatic mark that is easily overused. Use the dash cautiously for **emphasis** (page 259). A dash can emphasize a sharp turn in thought.

- The project will end January 15—unless the company provides additional funds.

A dash can indicate an emphatic pause.

- The job will be done—after we are under contract.

Sometimes, to emphasize contrast, a dash is used with *but*.

- We may have produced work more quickly—but the result was not as good.

A dash can be used before a final summarizing statement or before repetition that has the effect of an afterthought.

- It was hot near the ovens—steaming hot.

Such a statement may also complete the meaning of the clause preceding the dash.

- We try to speak as we write—or so we believe.

A dash can be used to set off an explanatory or appositive series.

- Three of the applicants—John Evans, Rosalita Fontiana, and Kyong-Shik Choi—seem well qualified for the job.

Dashes set off parenthetical elements more sharply and emphatically than **commas** (page 372). Unlike dashes, **parentheses** (page 386) tend to reduce the importance of what they enclose. Compare the following sentences:

- Only one person—the president—can authorize such activity.
- Only one person, the president, can authorize such activity.
- Only one person (the president) can authorize such activity.

dates 

In the United States, dates are generally indicated by the month, day, and year, with a comma separating the figures.

- October 26, 20--

The day-month-year system used in other parts of the world and by the U.S. military does not require commas.

- 26 October 20--

Use the strictly numerical form for dates (10/26/--) sparingly and never in business letters or formal documents, because the date is not always immediately clear. In fact, the numerical form may be confusing in **international correspondence** (page 141). Writing out the name of the month makes the entire date immediately clear to all readers.

Centuries

Confusion often occurs because the spelled-out numbers of centuries do not correspond to the numeral designations.

- The twentieth century is the 1900s (1900–1999).

When the century is written as a noun, do not use a hyphen.

- The sixteenth century produced great literature.

When the century is written as an adjective, however, use a hyphen.

- Twenty-first-century communication relies on technology.

ellipses

When you omit words in quoted material, use a series of three spaced periods, called *ellipsis dots,* to indicate the omission. (See also **quotations,** page 83.) Do not use ellipsis dots for any purpose other than to indicate omission.

WITHOUT OMISSION	"Promotional material is sometimes charged for, particularly in high-volume distribution to schools, although prices for these publications are much lower than the cost of developing them."
WITH OMISSION	"Promotional material is sometimes charged for . . . although prices for these publications are much lower than the cost of developing them."

If you are following MLA style in your writing, use **brackets** (page 367) around the ellipsis dots to show that words have been omitted from the original source.

- "The vast majority of the Internet's inhabitants are middle class [. . .] between the ages of eighteen and thirty-four" (5).

When the beginning of the sentence is omitted, begin the quotation with a lowercase letter and without ellipsis dots.

WITHOUT OMISSION	"When the programmer has determined a system of runs, he or she must create a flowchart to provide a picture of the data flow through the system."
WITH OMISSION	The letter states that the programmer "must create a flowchart to provide a picture of the data flow through the system."

When the omission comes at the end of a sentence and the quotation continues following the omission, use four dots. The first dot is the period that ends the sentence, and the other dots indicate the omission. (See also **sentence construction,** page 341.)

WITHOUT OMISSION	"In all departments except ours, researchers control research funds after the funds have been reviewed and approved by the board of directors. In addition, researchers control their own editorial and printing funds."
WITH OMISSION	"In all departments except ours, researchers control research funds. . . . In addition, researchers control their own editorial and printing funds."

Use a full line of dots across the page to indicate the omission of one or more paragraphs.

exclamation marks

The exclamation mark (!) indicates strong feeling. The most common use of an exclamation mark is after a word, phrase, clause, or sentence to indicate urgency, elation, or surprise.

- Hurry! Great! Wow!

In business writing, the exclamation mark is often used in cautions and warnings.

- Notice! Stop! Danger!

An exclamation mark can be used after a whole sentence or an element of a sentence.

- The subject of this meeting—please note it well!—is our budget deficit.

When used with quotation marks, the exclamation mark goes outside, unless what is quoted is an exclamation.

- The manager yelled, "Get in here!" Then Ben, according to Ray, "jumped like a kangaroo"!

hyphens

The hyphen (-) serves both to link and to separate words. The hyphen's most common linking function is to join compound words (able-bodied; self-contained; self-esteem). A hyphen is used to form compound numbers from twenty-one through ninety-nine and fractions when they are written out (forty-one; three-quarters).

Hyphens Used with Modifiers

Two- and three-word **modifiers** (page 324) that express a single thought are hyphenated when they precede a **noun** (page 328). (It was a *well-written* report.) However, a modifying phrase is not hyphenated when it follows the noun it modifies. (The report was *well written.*) If each of the words can modify the noun without the aid of the other modifying word or words, do not use a hyphen (a *new laser* printer). If the first word is an **adverb** (page 311) ending in *ly*, do not use a hyphen (a *newly* minted coin). A hyphen is always used as part of a letter or number modifier (9-inch; A-frame). In a series of unit modifiers that all have the same term following the hyphen, the term following the hyphen need not be repeated throughout the series; for greater smoothness and brevity, use the term only at the end of the series. (The third-, fourth-, and fifth-floor rooms were recently painted.)

Hyphens Used with Prefixes and Suffixes

A hyphen is used with a prefix when the root word is a proper noun (pre-Columbian; anti-American; post-Newtonian). A hyphen may be used when the prefix ends and the root word begins with the same vowel (re-elect; re-enter; anti-inflammatory). A hyphen is used when *ex* means "former" (ex-president; ex-spouse). A hyphen may be used to emphasize a prefix. (She was anti-everything.) The suffix *elect* is hyphenated (president-elect).

Hyphens and Clarity

The presence or absence of a hyphen can alter the meaning of a sentence.

AMBIGUOUS We need a biological waste management system.

That sentence could mean one of two things: (1) We need a system to manage "biological waste," or (2) We need a "biological" system to manage waste.

CLEAR We need a biological-waste management system.

CLEAR We need a biological waste-management system.

To avoid confusion, some words and modifiers should always be hyphenated. *Re-cover* does not mean the same thing as *recover*, for example; the same is true of *re-sent* and *resent*, *re-form* and *reform*, *re-sign* and *resign.*

italics

Italics is a style of type used to denote **emphasis** (page 259) and to distinguish foreign expressions, book titles, and certain other elements. Italic typeface is signaled by underlining, for example, in manuscript submitted for publication or where italic font is not available (see also **email,** page 233). *This sentence is printed in italics.* You may need to italicize words that require special emphasis in a sentence. (Contrary to projections, sales have *not* improved.) Do not overuse italics for emphasis, however. (This will hurt *you* more than *me.*)

Foreign Words and Phrases

Foreign words and phrases that have not been assimilated into the English language are italicized (*sine qua non, coup de grâce, in res, in camera*). Foreign words that have been fully assimilated into the language, however, need not be italicized. A word may be considered assimilated if it appears in most standard dictionaries and is familiar to most readers (cliché, etiquette, vis-à-vis, de facto, siesta).

Titles

Italicize the titles of books, periodicals, newspapers, movies, television programs, and paintings.

- The *New York Times* is one of the nation's oldest newspapers.

Abbreviations of such titles are italicized if their spelled-out forms would be italicized.

- The *NYT* is one of the nation's oldest newspapers.

Titles of chapters, articles, and reports are placed in **quotation marks** (page 390), not italicized.

- "Clarity and Conciseness: The Writer's Tightrope" was an article in the *New York Times.*

Titles of holy books and legislative documents are not italicized.

- The Bible and the Magna Carta changed the history of Western civilization.

Titles of long poems and musical works are italicized, but titles of short poems, musical works, and songs are enclosed in quotation marks.

LONG POEM	Milton's *Paradise Lost*
LONG MUSICAL WORK	Handel's *Messiah*

SHORT POEM	T. S. Eliot's "The Love Song of J. Alfred Prufrock"
SONG	Elton John's "Candle in the Wind"

Words, Letters, and Figures

Words, letters, and figures discussed as such are italicized.

- The word *inflammable* is often misinterpreted.
- I need a new keyboard because the *s* and *6* keys on my old one do not function.

Subheads

Subheads in a report are sometimes italicized.

- *Training Writers.* We are certainly leading the way in developing first-line managers who not only are professionally competent but . . .

See also **headings** (page 194) and **layout and design** (page 196).

numbers

The standards for using numbers vary; however, unless you are following an organizational or professional style guide, observe the following guidelines.

Numerals or Words

Write numbers from zero to ten as words and numbers above ten as numerals. Spell out approximate numbers.

- We've had *over a thousand* requests this month.

In most writing, do not spell out ordinal numbers, which express degree or sequence (42nd), unless they are single words (tenth, sixteenth). When several numbers appear in the same sentence or paragraph, write them the same way, regardless of other rules and guidelines.

- The company owned *150* trucks, employed *271* people, and rented *7* warehouses.

Spell out numbers that begin a sentence, even if they would otherwise be written as figures.

- *One hundred and fifty* people attended the meeting.

If spelling out such a number seems awkward, rewrite the sentence so that the number does not appear at the beginning.

- The meeting was attended by *150* people.

Plurals

The plural of a written number is formed by adding *s* or *es* or by dropping *y* and adding *ies,* depending on the last letter, just as the plural of any other noun is formed (elevens, sixes, twenties). The plural of a numeral may be written either with *s* alone or with *'s* (20s or 20's).

Measurements

Express units of measurement as numerals (3 miles, 45 cubic feet, 9 meters, 27 cubic centimeters, 4 picas). When numbers run together in the same phrase, write one as a numeral and the other as a word.

- The order was for ~~12~~ *twelve* 6-inch pipes.

Generally give percentages as numerals and write out the word *percent,* except when the number is in a table. (Approximately *85 percent* of the land has been sold.)

Fractions

Express fractions as numerals when they are written with whole numbers (27½ inches, 4¼ miles). Spell out fractions when they are expressed without a whole number (one-fourth, seven-eighths). Always write numbers with decimals as numerals (5.21 meters).

Time

Express hours and minutes as numerals when *A.M.* or *P.M.* follows (11:30 A.M., 7:30 P.M.). Spell out time that is not followed by *A.M.* or *P.M.* (four o'clock, eleven o'clock).

Dates

The year and the day of the month should be written as numerals. Dates are usually written in a month-day-year sequence, in which the year may or may not be followed by a comma. (*August 26, 20--,* is the payoff date for the loan.) Use the strictly numerical form for dates (8/26/--) in informal writing only. See also **dates** (page 379).

TIPS FOR PUNCTUATING NUMBERS

Some rules for punctuating numbers in English are summarized as follows.

Use a comma to separate numbers with four or more digits into groups of three, starting from the right (*5,289,112,001* atoms).

Do not use a comma in years, house numbers, zip codes, and page numbers.

- June *1995*
- *92401* East Alameda Drive
- The zip code is *91601*.
- Page *1204*

Use a period to represent the decimal point (*4.2* percent; *$3,742,097.43*).

See also **global graphics** (page 188).

Addresses

Spell out numbered streets from one to ten unless space is at a premium (East Tenth Street). Write building numbers as numerals. The only exception is the building number *one* (4862 East Monument Street; One East Monument Street). Write highway numbers as numerals (U.S. 70, Ohio 271, I-94).

Documents

In manuscripts, page numbers are written as numerals, but chapter and volume numbers may appear as numerals or words (Page 37; Chapter 2 or Chapter Two; Volume 1 or Volume One). Express figure and table numbers as numerals (Figure 4 and Table 3). Do not follow a word representing a number with a numeral in parentheses that represents the same number. Doing so is redundant.

- Send five ~~(5)~~ copies of the report.

parentheses

Parentheses are used to enclose explanatory or digressive words, phrases, or sentences. The material in parentheses often clarifies a sentence or passage without altering its meaning. Parenthetical information may not be essential to a sentence—in fact, parentheses deemphasize the enclosed material—but it may be interesting or helpful to some readers. Parenthetical material applies to the word or phrase immediately preceding it.

- She severely bruised her shin (or *tibia*) in the accident.

Parenthetical material does not affect the punctuation of a sentence. If a parenthesis appears at the end of a sentence, the ending punctuation should appear after the parenthesis. A comma following a parenthetical word, phrase, or clause also appears outside the closing parenthesis.

- She severely bruised her shin (or tibia), and he tore the cartilage in his knee (or meniscus).

However, when a complete sentence within parentheses stands independently, the ending punctuation goes inside the final parenthesis.

- Most of our regional managers report increases of 15 to 30 percent. (The only important exceptions are the Denver and Houston offices.)

Parentheses also are used to enclose numerals or letters that indicate sequence.

- The following sections deal with (1) preparation, (2) research, (3) organization, (4) writing, and (5) revision.

Use **brackets** (page 367) to set off a parenthetical item that is already within parentheses.

- We should be sure to give Emanuel Foose (and his brother Emilio [1812–1882]) credit for his part in founding the institute.

See also **documenting sources** (page 54) and **numbers** (page 384).

periods

A period usually indicates the end of a declarative or imperative sentence. Periods also link when used as leaders (for example, in a table of contents) and indicate omissions when used as **ellipses** (page 380). Periods may also end questions that are actually polite requests and questions to which an affirmative response is assumed. (Will you please send me the financial statement.) See also **sentence construction,** page 341.

Periods in Quotations

Use a comma, not a period, after a declarative sentence that is quoted in the context of another sentence.

- "There is every chance of success," she stated.

A period is conventionally placed inside **quotation marks** (page 390). (See also **quotations,** page 83.)

- He stated clearly, "My vote is yes."

Periods with Parentheses

If a sentence ends with a parenthesis, the period should follow the parenthesis.

- The institute was founded by Harry Denman (1902–1972).

If a whole sentence (beginning with an initial capital letter) is enclosed in parentheses, the period (or other end mark) should be placed inside the final parenthesis.

- The project director listed the problems her staff faced. (This was the third time she had complained to the board.)

Other Uses of Periods

Use periods after initials in names (Wilma T. Grant, J. P. Morgan). Use periods as decimal points with **numbers** (page 384) (109.2 degrees, $540.26, 6.9 percent). Use periods to indicate **abbreviations** (page 363) (Ms., Dr., Inc.). When a sentence ends with an abbreviation that ends with a period, do not add another period. (Please meet me at 3:30 P.M.) Use periods following the numerals in a numbered list.

- 1. Enter your name.
  2. Enter your address.
  3. Enter your telephone number.

Period Faults

The incorrect use of a period is sometimes referred to as a *period fault.* When a period is inserted prematurely, the result is a **sentence fragment** (page 347).

FRAGMENT	After a long day at the office during which we finished the quarterly report. We left hurriedly for home.
SENTENCE	After a long day at the office, during which we finished the quarterly report, we left hurriedly for home.

When two independent clauses are joined without any punctuation, the result is a *fused,* or *run-on,* sentence. Adding a period between the clauses is one way to correct a fused sentence.

FUSED Bill was late for ten days in a row Ms. Sturgess had to fire him.

CORRECT Bill was late for ten days in a row. Ms. Sturgess had to fire him.

Other options are to add a comma and a coordinating conjunction (*and, but, for, or, nor, yet*) between the clauses, to add a **semicolon** (page 392), or to add a semicolon with a conjunctive adverb (such as *therefore* or *however*).

question marks 

The question mark (?) has several uses. Use a question mark to end a sentence that is a direct question. (Where did you put the tax report?)

Never use a question mark to end a sentence that is an indirect question.

- He asked me whether sales had increased this year?

Use a question mark to end a statement that has an interrogative meaning (a statement that is declarative in form but asks a question). (The tax report is finished?)

Use a question mark to end an interrogative clause within a declarative sentence.

- It was not until July (or was it August?) that we submitted the report.

When a directive is phrased as a question, a question mark is usually not used. However, a request (to a customer or a superior, for instance) almost always requires a question mark.

- Will you make sure that the system is operational by August 15. [directive]
- Will you email me if your entire shipment does not arrive by June 10? [request]

Question marks may follow a series of separate items within an interrogative sentence.

- Do you remember the date of the contract? Its terms? Whether you signed it?

Retain the question mark in a title that is being cited, even though the sentence in which it appears has not ended. (*Should Engineers Be Writers?* is the title of her book.)

When used with quotations, the placement of the question mark is important. When the writer is asking a question, the question mark belongs outside the quotation marks. (Did she say, "I don't think the project should continue"?) If the quotation itself is a question, the question mark goes inside the quotation marks. (She asked, "When will we go?") If both cases apply—the writer is asking a question and the quotation itself is a question—use a single question mark inside the quotation marks. (Did she ask, "Will you go in my place?")

quotation marks

Quotation marks (" ") are used to enclose a direct quotation of spoken or written words. Quotation marks have other special uses, but they should not be used for **emphasis** (page 259).

Enclose in quotation marks anything that is quoted word for word (a direct quotation) from speech or written material. (She said clearly, "I want the progress report by three o'clock.") Do not enclose indirect quotations—usually introduced by the word *that*—in quotation marks. Indirect quotations are paraphrases of a speaker's words or ideas. (See also **paraphrasing,** page 34.) (She said that she wanted the progress report by three o'clock.)

When you use quotation marks to indicate that you are quoting, do not make any changes in the quoted material unless you clearly indicate what you have done. For further information on using and incorporating quoted material, see **quotations** (page 83).

Use single quotation marks to enclose a quotation that appears within a quotation.

- John said, "Jane told me that she was going to 'stay with the project if it takes all year.' "

Use quotation marks to set off special words or terms only to point out that the term is used in context for a unique or special purpose (that is, in the sense of the term *so-called*).

- What chain of events caused the sinking of the "unsinkable" *Titanic* on its maiden voyage?

Slang, colloquial expressions, and attempts at humor, although infrequent in workplace writing, should seldom be set off by quotation marks.

shakedown cruise.

- Our first six months amounted to a ~~“shakedown cruise.”~~

Use quotation marks to enclose titles of reports, short stories, articles, essays, single episodes of radio and television programs, short musical works, paintings, and other artworks.

- Did you see the article “No-Fault Insurance and Your Motorcycle” in last Sunday’s *Journal?*

Do not use quotation marks for titles of books and periodicals, which should appear in italics. Some titles, by convention, are not set off by quotation marks, underlining, or italics, although they are capitalized.

- Professional Writing [college course title], the Bible, the Constitution, Lincoln’s Gettysburg Address, the Lands’ End Catalog

Commas and periods always go inside closing quotation marks.

- “Reading *Computer World* gives me the insider’s view,” he says, adding, “it’s like a conversation with the top experts.”

Semicolons and colons always go outside closing quotation marks.

- He said, “I will pay the full amount”; this statement surprised us.

TIPS FOR USING QUOTATION MARKS AND PUNCTUATION

When making choices about using quotation marks with other punctuation, keep the following examples in mind.

Correct use of a comma with quotation marks

- “as a last resort,” (*not* “as a last resort”,)

Correct use of a period with quotation marks

- “to the bitter end.” (*not* “to the bitter end”.)

Correct use of a semicolon or colon with quotation marks

- “there is no doubt”; (*not* “there is no doubt;”)

All other punctuation follows the logic of the context: If the punctuation is a part of the material quoted, it goes inside the quotation marks; if the punctuation is not part of the material quoted, it goes outside the quotation marks.

semicolons 

The semicolon (;) links independent clauses or other sentence elements of equal weight and grammatical rank, especially a series of phrases containing commas. The semicolon indicates a greater pause between clauses than a comma, but not as great a pause as a period.

When the independent clauses of a compound sentence are not joined by a comma and a conjunction, they are linked by a semicolon. (No one applied for the position; the job was too difficult.) Make sure, however, that such clauses balance or contrast with each other. The relationship between the two statements should be so clear that further explanation is not necessary.

- The new Web site was very successful; every division reported increased online sales.

Do not use a semicolon between a dependent clause and its main clause. Remember that elements joined by semicolons must be of equal grammatical rank or weight.

- No one applied for the *position,* ~~position;~~ even though it was heavily advertised.

With Strong Connectives

In complicated sentences, a semicolon may be used before transitional words or phrases (*that is, for example, namely*) that introduce examples or further explanation.

- The study group was aware of her position on the issue; that is, federal funds should not be used for the housing project.

(See also **transition,** page 277.)

A semicolon should also be used before conjunctive adverbs (such as *therefore, moreover, consequently, furthermore, indeed, in fact, however*) that connect independent clauses.

- The test results are not complete*; therefore,* I cannot make a recommendation.

The semicolon in the example shows that *therefore* belongs to the second clause.

For Clarity in Long Sentences

Use a semicolon between two independent clauses connected by a coordinating conjunction (*and, but, for, or, nor, yet*) if the clauses are long and contain other punctuation.

- In most cases, these individuals are executives, bankers, lawyers; *but* they do not, as the press seems to believe, simply push the button of their economic power to affect local politics.

A semicolon may also be used if any items in a series contain commas.

- Among those present were John Howard, president of the Omega Company; Carol Delgado, president of Environex; and Larry Stanley, president of Stanley Papers.

Do not use semicolons to enclose a parenthetical element that contains commas. Use **parentheses** (page 386) or **dashes** (page 378) for that purpose.

- All affected job classifications (receptionists, secretaries, transcriptionists, and clerks) will be upgraded this month.

Do not use a semicolon as a mark of anticipation or enumeration. Use a **colon** (page 370) for that purpose.

- Three decontamination methods are under *consideration:* ~~consideration;~~ a zeolite-resin system, an evaporation system, and a filtration system.

The semicolon always appears outside closing **quotation marks** (page 390).

- The attorney said, “You must be accurate”; her client replied, “I will.”

slashes

The slash (/) performs punctuating duties by separating and showing omission. The slash is called a variety of names, including *slant line, diagonal, virgule, bar, solidus,* and *shilling.*

The slash is often used to separate parts of addresses in continuous writing.

- The return address on the envelope was Ms. Rose Howard/ Kleinlindener Str. 62/Giessen/D-35394/Germany.

The slash can indicate alternative items.

- David’s telephone number is 549-2278/2335.

The slash often indicates omitted words and letters.

- miles/hour for “miles per hour”

- w/o for "without"

In fractions, the slash separates the numerator from the denominator.

- 2/3 [2 of 3 parts], 3/4 [3 of 4 parts], 27/32 [27 of 32 parts]

The slash also separates items in the URL (Uniform Resource Locator) address for sites on the World Wide Web.

- www.bedfordstmartins.com/

In informal writing, the slash separates day from month and month from year in **dates** (page 379).

- 12/29/--

Do not use this form for **international correspondence** (page 141), because the order of the items varies.

Index

Complete Contents

PROOFREADERS' MARKS

Mark in margin	Instructions	Mark on manuscript	Corrected type
ℓ	Delete	the ~~lawyer's~~ Bible	the Bible
lawyer's	Insert	the bible	the lawyer's bible
(stet)	Let stand	the ~~lawyer's~~ bible	the lawyer's bible
(cap)	Capitalize	the bible	the Bible
(lc)	Make lowercase	the Law	the law
(ital)	Italicize	the lawyer's bible	the *lawyer's* bible
(tr)	Transpose	the bible lawyer's	the lawyer's bible
	Close space	the Bi ble	the Bible
(sp)	Spell out	(2) bibles	two bibles
#	Insert space	theBible	the Bible
¶	Start paragraph	¶ The lawyer's . . .	The lawyer's . . .
(run in)	No paragraph	. . . marks. Below is a . . .	. . . marks. Below is a . . .
(sc)	Set in small capitals	the bible	the BIBLE
(rom)	Set in roman type	the *bible*	the bible
(bf)	Set in boldface	the bible	the **bible**
(lf)	Set in lightface	the **bible**	the bible
⊙	Insert period	The lawyers have their own bible	The lawyers have their own bible.
	Insert comma	However we cannot . . .	However, we cannot . . .
	Insert hyphens	half and half	half-and-half
	Insert colon	We need the following	We need the following:
	Insert semicolon	Use the law don't . . .	Use the law; don't . . .
	Insert apostrophe	Johns law book	John's law book
	Insert quotation marks	The law is law.	The "law" is law.
(/)/	Insert parentheses	John's law book	John's (law) book
[/]/	Insert brackets	(John Martin 1920–1962 went . . .)	(John Martin [1920–1962] went . . .)
1/N	Insert en dash	1920 1962	1920–1962
1/M	Insert em dash	Our goal victory	Our goal—victory
	Insert superior type	3 = 9	$3^2 = 9$
	Insert inferior type	HSO_4	H_2SO_4